JIM GOAD'S
GIGANTIC
BOOK OF
SEX

An Oversized, Jaunty, and Highly Colorful
Compendium Containing Over 100 Articles
and Essays Comprising an Insightful
and Informative Treatise on This Most
Personal of Human Bodily Functions

Published by FERAL HOUSE, Los Angeles, CA • www.feralhouse.com

S0-BSO-700

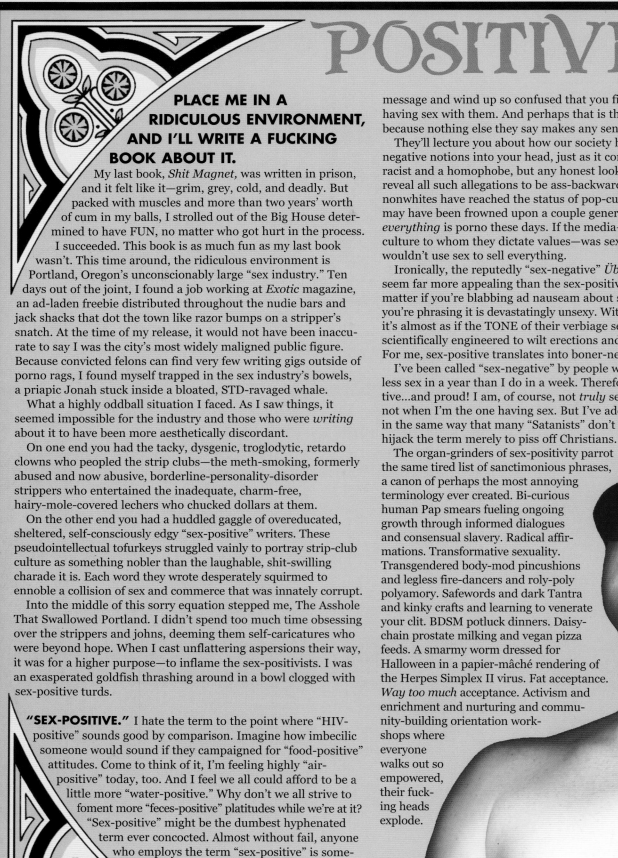

POSITIVELY

PLACE ME IN A RIDICULOUS ENVIRONMENT, AND I'LL WRITE A FUCKING BOOK ABOUT IT.

My last book, *Shit Magnet,* was written in prison, and it felt like it—grim, grey, cold, and deadly. But packed with muscles and more than two years' worth of cum in my balls, I strolled out of the Big House determined to have FUN, no matter who got hurt in the process. I succeeded. This book is as much fun as my last book wasn't. This time around, the ridiculous environment is Portland, Oregon's unconscionably large "sex industry." Ten days out of the joint, I found a job working at *Exotic* magazine, an ad-laden freebie distributed throughout the nudie bars and jack shacks that dot the town like razor bumps on a stripper's snatch. At the time of my release, it would not have been inaccurate to say I was the city's most widely maligned public figure. Because convicted felons can find very few writing gigs outside of porno rags, I found myself trapped in the sex industry's bowels, a priapic Jonah stuck inside a bloated, STD-ravaged whale.

What a highly oddball situation I faced. As I saw things, it seemed impossible for the industry and those who were *writing* about it to have been more aesthetically discordant.

On one end you had the tacky, dysgenic, troglodytic, retardo clowns who peopled the strip clubs—the meth-smoking, formerly abused and now abusive, borderline-personality-disorder strippers who entertained the inadequate, charm-free, hairy-mole-covered lechers who chucked dollars at them.

On the other end you had a huddled gaggle of overeducated, sheltered, self-consciously edgy "sex-positive" writers. These pseudointellectual tofurkeys struggled vainly to portray strip-club culture as something nobler than the laughable, shit-swilling charade it is. Each word they wrote desperately squirmed to ennoble a collision of sex and commerce that was innately corrupt.

Into the middle of this sorry equation stepped me, The Asshole That Swallowed Portland. I didn't spend too much time obsessing over the strippers and johns, deeming them self-caricatures who were beyond hope. When I cast unflattering aspersions their way, it was for a higher purpose—to inflame the sex-positivists. I was an exasperated goldfish thrashing around in a bowl clogged with sex-positive turds.

"SEX-POSITIVE." I hate the term to the point where "HIV-positive" sounds good by comparison. Imagine how imbecilic someone would sound if they campaigned for "food-positive" attitudes. Come to think of it, I'm feeling highly "air-positive" today, too. And I feel we all could afford to be a little more "water-positive." Why don't we all strive to foment more "feces-positive" platitudes while we're at it? "Sex-positive" might be the dumbest hyphenated term ever concocted. Almost without fail, anyone who employs the term "sex-positive" is someone with whom I would positively *not* want to have sex.

Surveying the sad specimens of sex-positivity, it's almost as if they prattle about sex in the hopes that you'll mistake the messenger for the message and wind up so confused that you finally consent to having sex with them. And perhaps that is their true agenda, because nothing else they say makes any sense.

They'll lecture you about how our society hammers sex-negative notions into your head, just as it conditions you to be a racist and a homophobe, but any honest look at our media would reveal all such allegations to be ass-backwards. Homos and nonwhites have reached the status of pop-culture saints. And sex may have been frowned upon a couple generations ago, but *everything* is porno these days. If the media—and the general culture to whom they dictate values—was sex-negative, they wouldn't use sex to sell everything.

Ironically, the reputedly "sex-negative" *Überkultur* makes sex seem far more appealing than the sex-positivists do. It doesn't matter if you're blabbing ad nauseam about sex when the WAY you're phrasing it is devastatingly unsexy. With the sex-positivists, it's almost as if the TONE of their verbiage sends out sonic waves scientifically engineered to wilt erections and wither vaginas. For me, sex-positive translates into boner-negative.

I've been called "sex-negative" by people whom I'd reckon have less sex in a year than I do in a week. Therefore, I am sex-negative...and proud! I am, of course, not *truly* sex-negative, at least not when I'm the one having sex. But I've adopted "sex-negative" in the same way that many "Satanists" don't believe in Satan but hijack the term merely to piss off Christians.

The organ-grinders of sex-positivity parrot the same tired list of sanctimonious phrases, a canon of perhaps the most annoying terminology ever created. Bi-curious human Pap smears fueling ongoing growth through informed dialogues and consensual slavery. Radical affirmations. Transformative sexuality. Transgendered body-mod pincushions and legless fire-dancers and roly-poly polyamory. Safewords and dark Tantra and kinky crafts and learning to venerate your clit. BDSM potluck dinners. Daisy-chain prostate milking and vegan pizza feeds. A smarmy worm dressed for Halloween in a papier-mâché rendering of the Herpes Simplex II virus. Fat acceptance. *Way too much* acceptance. Activism and enrichment and nurturing and community-building orientation workshops where everyone walks out so empowered, their fucking heads explode.

SEX-NEGATIVE

Most of the cloying, astringent, rankly pharisaical lizard dung that passes itself off as "sex writing" these days manages to infuse the subject with a piety often eclipsing that of the Christian censors against whom they're ostensibly rebelling. Their words generate more bullshit than a bull farm. Their prose is shot through with such penis-shriveling, vagina-drying holiness, they might as well be talking about aboriginal class struggle or hard abdominal masses. One would be hard-pressed to find a group of people at once sillier and who takes themselves more seriously.

They declare themselves "experts" in many cases for no other reason than the fact that they've declared themselves experts. These self-appointed "professionals" and "activists" aren't helping to accomplish anything except to make themselves feel important. Has any of their "literature" freed even ONE person from Puritanism's rusty shackles? Methinks not, ye salty buckaroos, methinks not. In most cases, they sound more like cult members than professionals, anyway. No matter what their formal training, they're unnecessary middlemen—brokers who charge a fee, and that fee is your natural-born enjoyment of sex. They're like college professors who try to explain the mechanics of a joke rather than actually being funny themselves.

The bulk of them, naturally, come from protected backgrounds—the cream of repressed society—yet they think it's daring to write about sex a good 50 years after it ceased being legally dangerous to do so. They are invariably rich white people who think they have insight about race and class. They also think they understand sex, although rich white Americans are possibly less adept at the sex act than anyone else on Earth. Many of them survive on donations and grants, while the rest of us actually work for a living. Portland's a place where no one starves, no one is poor, and yet everyone still manages to feel oppressed. What is it about having a trust fund that makes you think you're Third World?

THE QUINTESSENTIAL EXAMPLE of what I'm driving at here regarding the inescapably nausea-inducing properties of sex-positivity is an e-mailed invitation I once saw from a Blue Ribbon-winning sex writer who calls herself Darklady, whom I savage repeatedly in this book and whom I'll gore one last time merely for sport. The invitation was for one of the "naughty" and "depraved" group-grope parties she's always throwing in Portland. It made a point of stressing that the event would be "wheelchair-accessible."

WHEELCHAIR-ACCESSIBLE!!!

Now, I wouldn't mind watching the wheelchair-bound having sex due to some sick curiosity on my part—or merely for a laugh—but the invitation's unavoidable implication was that it's both POSITIVE and SEXY for these gimps to toss themselves onto the naked pink hog-pile. That one invitation encapsulates everything that's wrong with sex-positivity. When you're too tolerant, it's only proof that you have no taste. What person with the tiniest scrap of discernment would think sex is good no matter who's doing it?

Sex is not always positive. It carries potential danger, both physically and emotionally. A huge part of the FUN is that it's risky. Safe sex? Count me out.

SO HERE YOU HAVE MY *GIGANTIC BOOK OF SEX,* a proper antidote to sex-positive writing. It is a vaccine intended to slay a viral meme which has flourished unhindered for far too long. This book is a fist-puppet shoved up the asses of sex-positive writers everywhere. Behold, I bestow unto you a bold new era of sex-negativity. This book is a giant squeegee wiping clean the muddled bullshit which has prevented us from looking clearly not only at pornography itself, but also its practitioners and consumers. I understand why the sex industry exists, but I insist we finally be HONEST about it.

I've split the book into four highly arbitrary sections—FAKE, REAL, PERSONAL, and OPINION—but these are not rigid classifications. For example, "Queefer Madness" is part factual and part personal, but in an act of typically mercurial whimsy, I placed it in the REAL section. "Cash4Gash" and "Women Stink" are filled with facts, but since they're also packed with my sermonizing, I filed them under OPINION. As a general rule, anything in the FAKE section is not to be taken at face value, while any fact stated outside of that section should be presumed to be true, at least to the best of my knowledge. And yet even that rule isn't ironclad—although "How Your Mouth Can Help You Keep a Man" is in the FAKE section and was not meant to be taken literally, the sidebar of "Fellatio Fun Facts" is on the fo'-real-a tip.

The FAKE section is by far my favorite part of the book, as it's the clearest manifestation of my inability to take the subject matter seriously. While compiling it, I found that it's nearly impossible for the jokes to be too obvious. The *Exotic* office received dozens of calls asking for the directions to Stinky's and café BEEF-CAKE nightclubs. A concerned mother once grilled me about the "Adult Films Made by Children" piece. And just the other day, someone said they were planning an Australian vacation and wanted to know more about Sharkee's, where every stripper is a victim of shark bites. In the end, if you can't tell the difference between what's real and what's fake in here, it's useless trying to explain it to you.

GET ON YOUR KNEES AND SHARE MY SEX LIFE WITH ME. Although I've been obsessed with sex for as long as I can remember—in grade school, kids referred to me as a "sex dictionary," and I remember tearing out photos from my brother's *Playboys* at age eight—I didn't learn to enjoy sex until my mid-thirties. I've been making up for lost time ever since.

When people ask me what I do all day, the answer is always the same: "I feel sexy." Before you scoff, please note that I did not always feel sexy. But now that I do, I will never let you forget it. I quite enjoy this extended midlife crisis of mine, this prolonged state of satyriasis.

A lot of my pent-up post-prison tension has been relieved through my penis. I'd say that I hope you have as much fun reading this book as I did writing it, but I don't see how that's possible. Nor do I care, really. In the end, my penis is the only one that matters.

Photo by Shaun Partridge

FAKE

REAL

CONT

PERSONAL

OPINION

ENTS

HOME BREAST-IMPLANT KITS

"THESE GODDAMNED HOME KITS are putting a lot of plastic surgeons out of business," gripes **Thane Rothschild,** a licensed dermatologist from Lake Oswego, as we sit in his parked car and stare at passersby through binoculars. Rothschild, a towering seven-foot-one Colossus with a prominent nose and almost no chin, says that 50 percent of his business used to be breast-implant surgeries, but the home breast-implant market has cut into that share to where only one in ten of his operations now features breast implants. "There's other stuff to pick up the slack," he tells me, removing a Desert Eagle handgun from his glove compartment, "like penis enlargement and vaginal episiotomy and rectal dilation and scrotal electrolysis and hemorrhoidal cauterization. It keeps me busy, you know?"

"Uh-huh," I assented. "Are you gonna put the gun away now?"

"If it makes you nervous, sure," he tells me.

"Thanks," comes my reply.

"IT'S BARBARIC, IT'S PATRIARCHAL, IT'S SICK, it's foul, it's abominable, and it's degrading to *all* women, including my recently deceased mother, who died of breast cancer," says **Myrtle Tushner,** founder of WAHBIK (Women Against Home Breast-Implant Kits), an organization which describes itself as "a grassroots guerrilla street-theater troupe fighting the Powers That Be in defense of all women," but which in reality is composed of rich, sheltered, white, suburban women such as Tushner who already hold a disproportionate amount of wealth and power in this country and who should really enjoy the remaining benefits they have before the precious "underclass" they champion rises up and eats them alive.

Like all fanatics, Tushner is a master of emotional propaganda and frequently resorts to manipulative breast-implant horror stories in order to pluck her listener's heartstrings and win them to her side. As I sit in Tushner's office, surrounded by nauseating full-color posters of home breast-implant surgeries gone wrong, she tells of cheap, useless anesthetics and carcinogenic glues. She tells of Peruvian implants that explode inside the woman's body under the merest pressure, immediately poisoning her to death. She tells of forcible home breast-implant surgeries performed in Somalia by street gangs armed only with kitchen knives and two tennis balls.

After a half-hour or so of battering me with such tales, she pauses. "Doesn't this all make you *sick*?" she asks me.

"Yes, it does," I retort. "That's why I don't understand how you're able to subject yourself to this sort of material day after day."

"Hmm," she says, sitting back with a befuddled expression. "Maybe it means that *I'm* sick, too."

IT WAS AN INVENTION AS REVOLUTIONARY as the home computer, one that promised a porn star's body for every dumpy housewife in Peoria—the "Home Breast-Implant Kit" exploded into the national consciousness two years ago, providing endless material for comedians, millions in profits for manufacturers, and bigger, better boobies for countless grateful women.

All women desire nicer, more robust breasts—and all men like to look at them—but until the advent of the home breast-implant kit, the cost of plastic surgery put such breasts out of reach for all but the richest of women. Whereas the old cosmetic breast-implant surgery cost anywhere from a few thousand to tens of thousands, most home breast-implant kits retail for under 400 dollars... with some as low as 40 dollars! These days, all a gal needs is a few hundred bucks, a sink or bathtub, a steady hand, a strong stomach, and a tolerance for certain anesthetics and painkillers, and she's able to give herself the sort of breasts that she and her suitors always wanted. It's a revolution in human sexuality!

Recent advances in anesthesia, as well as the development of the "home stitch gun," a handheld device which is like a miniature sewing machine that enables someone to give themselves surgical stitches, made the home breast-implant kit possible. At home, and for pennies on the dollar compared to what she used to spend, a woman is now able to anesthetize her breast area, make a surgical incision, insert a medical-grade saline bag, stitch herself up, apply the proper antibiotics, anesthetics, and bandages, and be walking around town with a spectacular new pair of McGuffeys within a week or two after the healing begins.

WHAT ARE THEY?

HOW MUCH DO THEY COST?

ARE THEY SAFE?

"WE GIVE THEM BETTER TITS FOR A LOW PRICE, and *still* they complain," **Sal Bugberg** shrugs as we play *Super Mario Bros.* in a NW Portland arcade near Bugberg's million-dollar home. Bugberg has sold an estimated 100,000 units of his **10-Minute RACK ATTACK!!!** home breast-enhancement kit, widely regarded as the cheapest and most dangerous kit on the market. Bugberg's many critics say that he has built a fortune on the savage mutilation of gullible females, most of them working-class or poor. He currently faces over two dozen lawsuits in ten states from permanently maimed and terminally ill victims of his RACK ATTACK!!! Still, Bugberg acts as if he's done nothing wrong and instead says his detractors "are acting like assholes because finally they have to deal with a real professional like me."

"I try to do people a favor, and this is the thanks I get," Bugberg sighs, expelling a breath cloud that smells like salami and mothballs. "These bitches were born with shitty tits, then they use my product, and suddenly they have some self-esteem and they start looking for someone to blame besides themselves, and it falls on me. I sell a nice, solid product. A *safe* product. I'm not to blame if a lot of bitches are crazy."

"But Sal," I counter, firmly placing my thumb and forefinger on pressure points in his shoulder like they taught me in Wing Chun class, "women are *dying* because of your product. They're getting mutilated for *life*. They're getting *cancer*. You promise them beauty, and they wind up *deformed* or *dead*."

"Oh, really?" Bugberg responds, assuming the "Praying Mantis" Kung Fu position and making snakelike hissing noises as if to warn me that he's ready to defend himself against an attack. "Huh. Must *suck* to be dead. That's too bad. I got my *own* problems."

JANIS PRINGLER DISPUTES SAL BUGBERG'S CLAIM that his product is safe. A small, bitter woman with sharp features, thin ankles, and naturally tiny breasts as pointy as two cheese wedges, Pringler was initially delighted to receive a 10-Minute RACK ATTACK!!! kit for Christmas last year.

"By New Year's Eve, I had the new tits on," Pringler tells me as we enjoy a plate of cream puffs and ladyfingers at a local homosexual bakery. "I looked a lot better. All the men wanted to fuck me. I felt great. I had new tits and a new attitude."

But by St. Patrick's Day, those "new tits" had fallen off, along with her *old* ones, leading to severe blood loss and nearly causing her death. What's worse, much of the tissue that remains in her chest area has been diagnosed as cancerous.

"I wanted bigger tits," she says, wiping some confectioner's sugar from her chin, "and all I got was big tumors."

I nervously bite into a ladyfinger, trying to avoid the sadness in her eyes.

"Like all American women, I was excited about the home breast-implant kits when they first came out," Pringler volunteers as we daintily chew our pastries and try to ignore the hostile glares of the surrounding crowd of spoiled homosexuals. But to Pringler, her initial excitement soon curdled into heartache, physical pain, and $30,000 in hospital bills for remedial surgery.

"I wish I had my old tits," Pringler says, looking off into the distance. "I wish I had my old tits. I don't want justice, I want VENGEANCE!" Pringler suddenly blurts out, eyeing me up and down as if I was a potential foe. "I want them to feel a *hundred* times the pain I felt. I want to torture them and take pleasure in their suffering. I want to teach them that what they did to me was wrong. Even when I finally go to heaven, I still won't have the original tits that God gave me, and to me that's *wrong*."

WE ALL WANT BETTER TITS for our women. That's not the problem. But the question is—at what cost to their health and dignity? Are we *killing* our women just because we want to see them with bigger, better, rounder, more succulent tits? Are we *slaughtering* them because we're taking the money we would have spent on legitimate plastic surgery and spending that money on hookers and drugs? Do we sacrifice our souls...and the lives of our girlfriends...in order to have a nice set of *maracas* to squeeze every night? These are serious questions, comrade.

Nice tits shouldn't have to come at the expense of human life. But either way, they sure are nice.

RATING THE "TIT KITS"
Reviewing the Three Top-Selling Home Breast-Implant Kits on the Market

PRODUCT: HOMEMADE HOOTERS!

SUMMARY:
With sales of over a quarter-million units (meaning over a half-million fake breasts), **Homemade Hooters** has every right to call itself "America's Favorite Do-it-Yourself Breast-Implant Kit!" It first broke on the market two years ago, a full year before any other home breast-implant kit became available, and it still controls over 50 percent of the self-performed mammarian-enhancement market.

PROS:
It comes with three saline bags instead of two, which is a godsend for the nervous novices out there who invariably botch either one breast or the other and then "have to buy a whole 'nother kit just to get another bag." It contains a small tube of industrial-strength anesthetic to lessen the pain during the self-operation as well as during the healing process. The scalpels and the instruction manual are the finest we've seen.

CONS:
The price (**$299⁹⁹**) makes it difficult to afford for the average working woman who wants a bigger set of breasts. **Homemade Hooters!** is a fun, safe product, but it is also the most *classist* of the home breast-implant kits.

PRODUCT: TITS...IN A JIFFY!

SUMMARY:
The newest and most innovative home breast-implant kit currently available, **Tits...in a Jiffy!** is the first product of its kind which can be customized to fit a woman's body type and ethnicity. The aspiring self-performed breast-implant recipient merely fills out a questionnaire on **TitsinaJiffy.com**, pays **$249⁹⁹** in e-cash, and within three working days, they will receive a FedExed home breast-implant kit uniquely tailored to their individual needs.

PROS:
The **Tits...in a Jiffy!** people host a toll-free hotline whereby the self-surgeon can talk to a home-breast-implant expert who will guide them through those first crucial incisions.

CONS:
The chick on the **Tits...in a Jiffy!** box looks like a lesbian.

PRODUCT: 10-minute RACK ATTACK!!!

SUMMARY:
The most notorious kit of all. The source of most of the physical disfigurement and class-action lawsuits in the home breast-implant kit industry. In fact, it wouldn't be proper to call these breast implants—shockingly, the kit consists of a hard-plastic simulated set of breasts which are permanently glued OUTSIDE the woman's real breasts and can never be removed without severe tissue trauma.

PROS:
That plastic set of tits is a really *nice-looking* set of plastic tits. The home "surgery," which consists of gluing the plastic rack onto one's chest, takes even less time than the ten minutes advertised in the product's name. And at **$39⁹⁹**, it's by far the cheapest of the home breast-implant kits we've surveyed.

CONS:
The glue leaks into the woman's real breasts, causing cancer and death.

the sad, strange world of
ADULT FILMS MADE BY CHILDREN

The film I'm watching certainly isn't going to win any Academy Awards. The camera work is shoddy, the lighting is dismal, the pacing is clumsy, and the plotline nonexistent. There are no credits, and the only "label" on the video is a tattered strip of masking tape onto which is scrawled *TICKLE MI CULO* in thick black crayon. The action is straight hetero porn: just two dimly perceived brown adult bodies humping sweatily on what appears to be the dirt floor of a jungle shack. The woman performs fellatio briefly on her partner, but he does not reciprocate with cunnilingus. The couple's screams and exclamations are uttered in Spanish. Immediately after the male money-shoots all over his friend's olive-hued face, the screen goes blank.

The only thing that distinguishes this film from the seeming millions of other pornographic features made yearly is that it was scripted, directed, and filmed by a four-year-old boy. Although the video is barely 18 minutes long, bootlegged copies of it are reportedly selling for over 100 dollars on the Internet. And there are reportedly *thousands* more videos just like it—adult films starring adult actors using adult genitals—but filmed by youngsters imprisoned in "porn camps" hidden deep within Brazil's rain forests.

"This is the most difficult criminal case I've ever had to investigate," says Alberto Luis Sanchez Villareal, a police detective in São Paulo, Brazil. A portly, greasy, rumpled little man with sour breath and a twinkle in his eye, Villareal has been assigned the daunting task of dismantling a lucrative underground film industry in which homeless children are kidnapped on Brazil's city streets, shipped up the Amazon, and forced to create pornographic films "from scratch" under dreary conditions. "The main misconception I'm fighting, from both a criminal standpoint and a public-relations standpoint," Villareal says, "is that this is kiddie porn. Truly, I wish that it *was* kiddie porn, because it'd be much easier to bring these bastards to justice. But children are involved in every phase of film production, EXCEPT they're not involved in the sex scenes as participants. So it's not really kiddie porn—it's BY-kiddie porn."

Brazil's by-kiddie porn industry involves millions of dollars, thousands of films, and hundreds of children in a Pyramid of Oppression atop which sit the fat-cat entrepreneurs who exploit human suffering for profit. Up in the porn camps, armed guards patrol self-contained jungle villages devoted to producing erotic adult feature films. Slaving away in sweltering, *Apocalypse Now*-style jungle-river compounds, children are herded together and taught the art of film making in a most inauspicious setting. Kids as young as three years old are shouting "Cut!" and "That's a wrap!" with the finesse of seasoned Hollywood professionals. An entire film is typically scripted, rehearsed, shot, and transferred to video in the course of a morning, leaving the whole afternoon for the children to do the village's menial labor.

"What makes this phenomenon almost impossible to eliminate," Villareal continues, interrupting my train of thought, "is that they're operating under the jungle's protective cover. These 'film sets' are merely temporary campgrounds. If they hear that the *federales* are coming, they can just break camp and go further up the river. It's hard to keep chasing them. The logistics are wrong."

"The logistics are wrong?"

"What are you—*deaf*?"

Villareal says it'll be difficult to prosecute the films' producers on child-pornography charges because it's a stretch to argue that the children are being used sexually.

"It's a legal quandary. We can nail them on child-slavery charges, but it'd be hard to make a kiddie-porn beef stick."

"A kiddie-porn beefstick?"

"Huh?"

"What's a kiddie-porn beefstick?"

"No, no—I meant it'd be hard to make kiddie-porn *charges* stick."

"Oh."

"All right?"

"Yeah, OK, I guess."

Since things got tense, I left.

brazilian police chase a sinister sex ring into the jungle

"THERE'S SO MUCH INJUSTICE in the world already," says Linda Mulgrew-Christy, chairperson of children's-rights organization Save the Damn Children, "so when you hear about something like these by-kiddie porn films, well, that's the straw that breaks the camel's back. That's when you realize it's time to get involved on all three levels—personal, community, and spiritual." Mulgrew-Christy's organization boasts that it's devoted to "fighting child abuse with the ferocity of a child abuser."

"It's inconceivable that in this day and age, something like these by-kiddie porn films could happen," she says, leaning back in a really nice vinyl comfy chair. "We need to stop it, and we need to stop it now."

"I agree. How do you propose to do that?"

She leans back and her eyes assume a faraway glaze. "Oh—well...hmm...I really hadn't considered *that.*"

Instead of answering my question, she pops in a CD featuring a female folk singer

Scenes from Brazilian underground porno films that feature adults but were scripted and directed by children. L-R: Money shot in Mas Leche, Mi Mama...blurry humping scene in Amazon, Tu Es Mi Corazon...penis approaches ass in Tickle Mi Culo...urinating vagina in Panocha a Pestosa.

decrying the horrors of child abuse in a manner that some would consider unnecessarily graphic. "When a child has no innocence, what does it have?" Mulgrew-Christy asks me, her piercing eyes fixed on an imaginary dot on my forehead.

"Its body?" I offer.

"You took the words right out of my mouth," she says, winking.

I ask her why she got involved in helping to protect children from sexual and financial exploitation. "As long as one child somewhere is unhappy," she says, "I'm unhappy."

"I would think you'd be unhappy a lot."

"Exactly," she says.

display an emotional complexity almost unknown in *mainstream* cinema, much less pornography. His use of the jungle's natural lighting is almost heartbreaking in its evocative power. It's fair to call him the Hitchcock of By-Kiddie Porn."

Bernstein's website also features a page devoted to a strange subgenre of the by-kiddie porn movement: anal slapstick comedies such as *Tickle Mi Culo* and *Chupa Mi Verga*. "The kids just love everything poop-related," Bernstein says, smiling. "They just love a good ass joke. They're very playful with anal themes. And they're making their presence known in the ass-porn marketplace. Children have already cornered the market on scat, and they're making inroads on anal."

of them into a bamboo hut. It doesn't really take much to teach them to push the RECORD button on a camera. All things considered, the overhead is preferable when using children. The kids help the bottom line. Do the math, Einstein—kids are simply more cost-effective. It's not a moral issue—it's a financial issue."

"But it IS a moral issue," I insist.

He stares at me with cold slits of eyes. "Do you know I could have you killed right now?"

I feel stymied by the heat. Intimidated by his armed guards. Scared of encountering cheetahs and leopards in the underbrush. Worried about giant mosquitos and what diseases they might carry. Terrified of finding a tarantula in my sleeping bag.

"Children are involved in every phase of film production, EXCEPT they're not involved in the sex scenes as participants. So it's not really kiddie porn—it's BY-kiddie porn."

"CHILDREN BRING AN ENERGY and magic to pornography that adults simply don't have," says Ray Lee Bernstein, webmaster of ByKiddiePorn.com, a site devoted to the by-kiddie porn phenomenon. "They bring a fresh, bright vision to adult cinema. These kids are writing amazingly well-paced scripts. Since kids tend to be short, they come up with some interesting camera angles. It's refreshing to see how much talent was laying dormant amid homeless street waifs from São Paulo." Bernstein is a former film critic for the *Missoula Messenger* who was forced to leave that paper under dark whispers of scandal. He is one among a growing number of critics who find artistic merit in the by-kiddie films. He mentions the canon of the legendary "Mario," a six-year-old Brazilian boy whose films such as *Amazon, Tu Es Mi Corazon* and *Mas Leche, Mi Mama* have received critical acclaim from such unlikely sources as *The New York Times, Variety,* and *PDXS.* "Mario deserves the appellation of *auteur*," Bernstein says. "His films

MY RIVER GUIDE JULIO steers me up the evil demon Amazon which spares no man. Our boat skims beneath the banana trees. We're up in the lair of the angry mosquito. Up in the land of muddy water and hot, still air. The land of wild, scary jungle cats with big teeth. Poisonous snakes, too.

By greasing a few palms and calling in a few favors, I was able to arrange a meeting with Augusto Hector Del Fuego, the so-called "Pimp Daddy of By-Kiddie Porn." Del Fuego has allegedly made over 30 million dollars by overseeing a web of by-kiddie-porn camps in the Brazilian outback. For all his power, though, I am unimpressed when I finally meet him in a small, poorly ventilated shack along the Amazon. He is a fat man. A charmless man. A man who emits a sharp, foul odor.

"The kids are so much cheaper to use," Del Fuego explains. "For starters, they're little. They don't eat as much as an adult, and you can fit more

So I refuse to answer his question and ask Julio to get the boat ready.

I quietly leave Del Fuego's haunts, happy to be alive. Happy to be headed back to the city. Happy I'm not a small Brazilian child.

THE UNIVERSE SCREAMS out about this injustice. We need to save the children. We need to save the children. WE NEED TO SAVE THE CHILDREN. How many times do I need to say it? If we can save one child—just one little fuzzy canary of a child—it'll all be worth it.

The events of 9/11/01 brought us all a little closer together. It even brought us closer to the Amazon rain forest, where children suffer unimaginable indignities while filming pornographic features. We all need to keep our kids safe and ignorant about sex for as long as we can. There's plenty we can do. You can do something. I can do something. We can all do something. Together, we can *do* something.

If we can stop one more by-kiddie porn film from being made, one day we can look down at our OWN kids with confidence and say, "Nobody will ever kidnap YOU and take you up to the Amazon jungle where you'll be forced to make porno films starring adult actors. No-sirree, Bob!"

Photos at bottom, from page left: Group of child porn-film makers after a grueling jungle photo shoot; children relax after a long day of filming; "Mario," widely considered to be "the Hitchcock of By-Kiddie Porn"; the Santiago Brothers, also known as "The Wayans Brothers of Brazilian Ass Films."

Sexually Transmitted Diseases, a.k.a. STDs, are an unfortunate factor in every sex worker's life. We all like to pretend that life within the industry is nothing but glamor, fast cash, and reduced cover prices at Sinferno, but the sobering truth is that our clients sometimes leave us with more than blown wads and $100 bills...they sometimes litter our crotches with a veritable flea circus of beasties invisible to the naked eye.

The Devil never rests, and neither do STDs. Just when we thought we had a handle on HIV, Hep-C, and the clap, along comes a bold New Wave of intimately transferred maladies such as Scrotal Mice, Genital Leprosy, and Ass Moss. As a token of our concern for the well-being of sex workers everywhere, I present this overview of the latest, hottest venereal diseases.

As sex workers, we need to educate ourselves about this frightening New Wave of microscopic critters that threatens our health and livelihood. We need to hold workshops. We need to build communities. We need government subsidies for needle-exchange and free-condom programs. We need federal grants to film educational videos and to produce "virally aware" pornography. We need to do everything within our power to ensure that we never, ever have to get a real job.

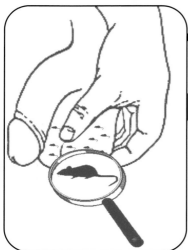

"NUT RATS"

DISEASE: Human Scrotal Micro-Rodent Infestation (HSM-RI)

SLANG TERMS: "Scrote Mice"… "Nut Rats"

DESCRIPTION: The male testes become overrun with actual tiny Rhodesian Micro-Mice, each about the size of a picnic ant. The scrotum becomes itchy and reddened. The vermin are passed between partners during genital contact. Although the mini-mice afflict both genders, they tend to prefer nesting in male genitals because they allegedly taste better.

TREATMENT: There is no cure for scrotal mice; you just have to learn to feed and care for them.

DISEASE: Genital Leprosy

SLANG TERMS: "Leper Dick"… "Purple Penis Eater"

DESCRIPTION: Over the past two decades, a mutant strain of *Mycobacterium leprae* has been identified, one which zeroes in on human "naughty bits" and ignores the rest of the body. In male Genital Leprosy, the penis develops purple, mushy blotches as if it were an overripe banana. In time, the organ falls off the body, leading to shattered relationships and heartache. In females, the disease gnaws all the way up the vaginal walls until the uterus dislodges and plops to the ground, often at the worst possible moment.

"LEPER DICK"

TREATMENT: Until a cure is found, I recommend relocating all those diagnosed with Genital Leprosy to Genital Leper Colonies, where they will huddle together and suffer the condemnation, fear, ridicule, and good-natured ribbing of mainstream society.

THEY'RE CONTAGIOUS!
THEY'RE REVOLTING!
THEY'RE THE...
NEW WAVE

DISEASE: Sapphic Mammarian Acne Syndrome ("SMAS")

SLANG TERMS: "Tit Zits"… "Boobie Pimples" … "Dyke Bumps" … "Pizza Tits"

DESCRIPTION: Government-funded dermatologists working covertly within the lesbian underground have recently discovered an epidemic of "lesbian acne" that only afflicts lesbians, and only their chest area. Sapphic Mammarian Acne Syndrome is similar to classic acne in that it is more of a cosmetic nuisance than a full-bore health problem, more unsightly than painful. It is spread when

"PIZZA TITS"

lesbians engage in breast-on-breast contact (i.e., "rubbin' boobs") as part of Lesbian Foreplay. Since the "Lesbian Code" forbids lesbians from talking to non-lesbian reporters, police, and health workers, it has been difficult for us Normal People out here in the Real World to study this disease and search for a cure. Because of the Lesbian Wall of Silence, the disease has spread unchecked throughout the girl-on-girl community. Experts estimate that roughly 85% of lesbians now suffer to some degree with the everyday shame of "Pizza Tits." Although science has yet to isolate the culpable microbe, its prevalence within the lesbian community is thought to be due to their countless unhygienic practices.

TREATMENT: There is no known cure for lesbianism.

DISEASE: Opportunistic Sphincteral Mold-Spore Infestation ("OSM-SI")

SLANG TERMS: "Butt Mold"… "Ass Moss" … "Anal Mildew"

DESCRIPTION: This sexually transmitted mold spore, *Hemorrhalis Rectillus,* is a close cousin of the bright-green moss which clings to the tall trees in the Pacific Northwest's coastal forests. The mold thrives on the rich bacterial flora and fauna which call the human rectum their home. During anal sex, microscopic spores are rubbed loose from the host penis onto the recipient's rectal walls and sphincteral rim. Within a week or so, a rich green blanket lines the victim's rectum and grows outward from his or her anus. Because of the mossy obstruction, defecation becomes extremely painful. The mold is thought to have been initially spread among male coastal loggers during rainy winters away from their families.

"ASS MOSS"

TREATMENT: Most home-and-garden centers are now aware of the ass-moss problem and sell a product called MOSS LOSS that kills the spore which causes Opportunistic Sphincteral Mold-Spore Infestation. (Due to the embarrassment and social ostracism that invariably accompany an ass-moss diagnosis, most stores discreetly sell MOSS LOSS behind the counter.) It comes in a spray bottle. Just squirt it on your anus three times a day for a week, and your butt-mold problem disappears! It also works wonders on dandelion and ragweed!

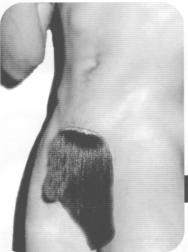

DISEASE: Involuntary Pubic Hair Conditioning Virus ("IPHCV")

SLANG TERMS: "Relaxed Pubes"… "Pubo-Sheen" … "Salon Crotch"

DESCRIPTION: This virus is transmitted almost exclusively via saliva from the mouths of hair stylists, both male and female, when performing oral sex

"SALON CROTCH"

upon their partners and/or customers. The virus attaches itself to pubic follicles and, feeding on proteins contained therein, excretes a viscous waste fluid that has an emollient effect similar to the priciest hair conditioners purchased in salons from Paris to Milan. Almost overnight, pubic hair straightens out and grows long 'n' lustrous as if it were flowing from atop a supermodel's head—sassy, shiny, bouncy, and tangle-free!

TREATMENT: Treatment?!? Are you kidding? People would KILL for a mane of pubes like that!

# of S.T.D.s

MESSIEST MASTURBATOR

Over a span of 16 years ending with his death from a heart attack in 1982, **Herb Maalox** of Cleveland, OH, digitally pleasured himself to climax 6,322 times without once cleaning up his mess.

LARGEST GENITAL WART

Until it was removed by government physicians in 2001, **Plangence Trafalgar** of Nottingham, England, carried an HPV cluster between her legs described as "bigger than the Hope Diamond."

BIGGEST DIFFERENTIAL IN TESTICLE SIZE

Mervyn Sleet of Cairns, Australia, had one testicle weighing 24.5 grams, while the other weighed only three grams—a difference of more than 800%!

LARGEST ARTIFICIAL PENIS

In 1953, **Edd Bullhorn** of Safford, AZ, cemented a nine-foot stretch of rubber tubing onto his penis and walked around town one hot summer evening, bragging about it. Due to health concerns, both the penis and the rubber tube were later removed.

MOST ITEMS LIFTED WITH ERECT PENIS

Flaco Kornbluth, a Sephardic magician/prestidigitator/somnambulist from the Ukraine, would routinely wow audiences by using his penis to lift a large bale of hay on which slept a baby burro.

LARGEST ITEM MOVED WITH PENIS

Canadian underwater daredevil **R. Michael Meteor** once swam from Vancouver to Victoria Island toting a boat with six adult passengers using only his penis and a length of nautical rope.

LONGEST PUBIC HAIR

In protest against British imperialism, Hindu shaman **Pardu Cukta** once grew a testicular hair which was said to reach all the way from his yoga mat across Chutney Street in Calcutta and down 32 steps into the River Ganges.

MOST ATTRACTIVE SEX OFFENDER

It is generally agreed that **Orson Corsica** of Ghent, Belgium—a man who raped over three dozen rural Belgian women and a handful of Dutch tourists—was the most charismatic, physically striking, and all-around "gobble-icious" sexual predator ever to sexually prey upon people.

FEWEST AVERAGE THRUSTS BEFORE EJACULATION

Tod Croppy, an itinerant snow shovel man from Anaconda, MT, engaged in 1,289 acts of coitus during his lifetime while making only 2,216 total thrusts—an average of only 1.7 thrusts before ejaculating!

LARGEST VAGINA

Acting on a drunken dare, **Kongtiq'a Veldon** of Gary, IN, once inserted a Samsung VCR/DVD player entirely within her womb.

BEST MEMORY REGARDING ONE-NIGHT STANDS

In 1988, Dutch onion farmer **Skink Matson** of Shartlesville, PA, was able to recall the first names of 23 women with whom he'd had one-night stands, shattering a previous record of 21 held since the early 1920s by an Irishman named **Corbin Primate**.

WORLDWIDE SEXUAL ACHIEVEMENT HALL OF FAME

HONORING ORDINARY PEOPLE AND THEIR EXTRAORDINARY SEXUAL FEATS

SMALLEST ARTIFICIAL BREASTS

After five straight sleepless nights of meth-smoking, **Bitsi Winnemucca** of Dover, DE, used a kitchen knife to surgically implant two cherry stones wrapped in cellophane under her nipples.

WEAKEST ORGASM

In 1973, **Leotha Gurnwipe** of Caracas, Venezuela, thinks she had an orgasm during intercourse with her husband. It's possible that she didn't—but she thinks that she might have.

QUICKEST MARITAL LOSS OF INTEREST

After **Panda Rickets** of Alexandria, Egypt, married her husband Mark in 1944, she claims she lost the desire to have sex with him "almost immediately."

YOUNGEST SEX PREDATOR

For reasons which are unprintable, a Brazilian infant identified only as **Chico** had to be separated from other infants at the hospital nursery.

MOST MEANINGFUL SEXUAL RELATIONSHIP BETWEEN MASTER AND SLAVE

Alabama slave-driver **Lord Ashleigh St. John** and his female slave **Kitty** carried on a physically intimate relationship throughout the 1840s, and neither one of them had a complaint.

LONGEST SUSTAINED HUMAN/ANIMAL RELATIONSHIP

For all but a few weeks during the entire span of his 14 years on the planet, a Mongolian sheep named **Ali** was anally penetrated by his owner, **Elver Taipan**.

MOST EPIC WET DREAM

In 1993, **Jeremiah Thunderbreast** of Mexicali, Mexico, had a dream lasting over 45 minutes that ended in a nocturnal emission. The dream spanned dozens of women and four continents. From start to finish, the soundtrack to *Loverboy's Greatest Hits* played within Thunderbreast's head.

DEADLIEST HANDJOB

A Russian prostitute named **Eurasia Minsk** once yanked on a client's penis so vigorously that the organ was removed entirely from its socket.

MOST EXCUSES FOR IMPOTENCE

During 470 bouts of impotence during his life, **Charno Bloodwort** of Batsto, NJ, came up with 273 unique excuses for why he couldn't get it up, including "I was upset about global hunger" and "I like you too much to think of you as a sexual object."

GENITAL COSMETIC SURGERY

Let's face it: Genitals are important. Genitals are the rickshaws that carry life into the world. You only live once, and you only get one set of genitals. There's no second chance for a second set. So doesn't it make sense to give yourself the best set of genitals money can buy?

One's appearance "down there" is crucial in these hectic, hurried "modern times." It seems that everywhere you turn these days, someone is getting genital plastic surgery. Genital cosmetic surgery—it's all the rage! And, truth be told, it's undeniable that everyone would do better with at least a little of it. Everybody's lap could do with a li'l nip/tuck. There is no set of genitals on Earth so eye-catching that it couldn't do with a little improvement. The question is: How much and which kind of genital cosmetic surgery is right for *you*?

And what about the genitals of your loved ones? Wouldn't you prefer that it had been an attractive and presentable pair of genitals which ushered you into this life? Don't you think it would help your children's self-esteem if they could be confident that their parents had genitals that were a sight for sore eyes? It's a controversial topic, and one that deserves to be discussed among consenting adults.

It may be blasphemous—although entirely accurate—to suggest that God made human beings beautiful everywhere except their genitals. Quite frankly, genitals in their natural state are ugly. The penis is droopy, ancient, and dinosauric—a glum swamp reptile. The vagina, at worst, can look like pink brains blasted out by a shotgun. God made human beings, but it took man to make their genitals attractive. Maybe that is the ultimate purpose of human beings on earth—making genitals more beautiful. Beautifying genitals. Carefully sculpting the raw work which God had started.

Men, do you feel the red-cheeked embarrassment that comes from knowing you aren't "up to snuff" with the other boys in the locker room? Ladies, do you remember the shame of the first time you undressed in front of that "special guy" and it took a while for your vagina to unfold?

When you look in the mirror, do you wish your genitals were more attractive? Are you afraid of what "they" might say? Do you avoid public activities and sporting events in which your genitals might be exposed? Do you shy away from public restrooms because others might see your genitals there? Do you feel that your penis is too tiny or your vagina too flappy? Do you think that other people must feel that your genitals are unattractive? Do you compare your genitals to those of others and routinely conclude that yours are less beautiful? Is it difficult to enjoy sex because you're constantly worried that your partner might find your genitals to be homely? Have your aesthetically unappealing sex organs caused "distancing" from your romantic partner? Are you obsessed with guilt feelings revolving around your ugly private parts? Would you change your genitals if given the opportunity? Would this enhance your self-image and bolster your genital self-esteem?

For centuries, men and women suffered with uncomely sex organs, and there wasn't a darn thing they could do about it. But

how much... and what kind... is right for YOU?

there is no longer any acceptable or appropriate excuse for unsightly genitalia. Modern technology has put a handsome penis within the reach of most working men. And ladies, recent medical advances can turn that wizened scrubwoman between your legs into a dainty tree nymph. I can't even imagine the surgically enhanced penises and vaginas of a generation or two in the future. I silently and resolutely envy them. Deciding which sort of genital surgery—and how much of it—is right for you can be an arduous, thankless task.

ALLOPLASTY PATIENT (BEFORE)

The most important decision you'll make about your genital cosmetic surgery is also the most basic: It all depends on whether you have a penis or a vagina. Here at the *Perkiomen Valley Consortium for Genital Beauty,* we boast two pleasant, high-tech, space-age clinics specializing in pubic cosmetic surgery: one for men *(ManPlus)* and one for women *(VenusTrim).*

MEN: "Phalloplasty"

For males, it's a simple equation: BIGGER = MORE ATTRACTIVE. Fellas, why would you want the biggest muscles and the biggest paycheck and the biggest, fastest car...without having the biggest penis to go along with it? Women may say that "size isn't important" when there are sensitive men around whose feelings they don't want to hurt, but when they get amongst themselves and start talking, trust me—size IS important. It's the ONLY important thing to them.

Our expert genital surgeons specialize in both LENGTH ENHANCEMENT and GIRTH INCREASE. A small, whiny minority of critics (as well as Federal Law) insist that we remind you of the risks involved: partial necrosis; asymmetry; urinary fistula and/or incontinence; swelling, bruising, and blinding pain; bacterial infection and so-called "flesh-eating viruses"; altered or complete loss of sensation; jagged scarring; impotence; and severe, permanent disfigurement. The post-op recovery period may be filled with uncontrolled bleeding, blinding pain, dirty bedpans, and two-pound weights attached to the penis for months to ensure adequate size increase. Pessimists may tell you that there are drawbacks, and they may be right *technically,* but never in spirit. They don't realize that you must *want* your penis to get better for miracles to happen. You must remember that life itself is the biggest risk of all.

WOMEN: "Labiaplasty"

Women want "designer vaginas" for all sorts of reasons: because childbirth blew their vadge lips to smithereens; because large labia can make tight clothing and rough sex uncomfortable; and because they don't want to gross out their partners or, by extension, society itself.

COSMETIC LABIAPLASTY is the modern solution for ugly vaginas everywhere. Under local anesthesia while wide awake, patients will watch our surgeons trim their "deli-sized roast-beef sandwich" down to "a slice of cheese encased tightly within flat pita bread." After several weeks of vaginal ice packs and excessive bleeding, the sutures dissolve and self-esteem is restored. Your vagina will be more youthful, sassy, and aesthetically pleasing. A woman's highest treasure—her vagina—is again ready to be presented to an approving world.

LET US HELP YOU

At the *Perkiomen Valley Consortium for Genital Beauty,* we offer several options, flexible payment plans, and free consultations regarding which method would be best for your first experience with genital cosmetic surgery. Payments are gauged according to a sliding scale based on income, insurance, and liquid assets. Our rates average thousands of dollars less than the competition. But we're not just some cut-rate "clip shack" out to make a buck. We're a sensible, affordable, *tasteful* genital-surgery outpatient clinic. Our prices are reasonable but not disreputable.

Our "crack team" of surgeons will wreak a perceptible difference in your genital appearance, as illustrated in the BEFORE and AFTER photos on this page. One's genitals are one's identity. Don't you want a pretty identity? Don't get "between the sheets" 'til you go "under the knife." Enhance your genital self-esteem. Get up on the hospital table and start walking on the road to recovery.

In order to heal, we must, of course, first have surgery. Once a month, we offer a round-table support group for post-op genital-surgery patients in which we all hold hands and sing our theme song:

Courage to cut/Courage to heal/Courage to trust/ Courage to feel.

We can help you, but you have to *accept* our help. We can take your frightened mouse of a penis and turn it into a proud field elephant. We can take a vagina that's a sagging purple platypus and turn it into a neat, trim paper cut. The technology is available. We own the machines and know how to use the tools. We can give you better genitals. You just need to give us—and yourself!—a chance.

For more information about the *Perkiomen Valley Consortium for Genital Beauty* and its "VenusTrim/ ManPlus Clinics for Genital Rejuvenating Surgery," visit www.jimgoad.net.

PHALLOPLASTY PATIENT (AFTER)

what every man should know about

CUNNILINGUS

a sane, sensible guide to the
erotic art of pleasuring
a woman's vagina
with your mouth

bored and unsatisfied even after the most vigorous round of penile-vaginal rutting. And unsatisfied women, as we a know from the tabloids and divorce statistics, are wont to run into the arms and mouths of eager, husky lesbians, living on alimony payments while her ex-husband and squealing offspring are left to fend for themselves.

Women, since they own vaginas and are generally mor sensuous than men anyway, are innately better at orally pleasuring women than any man could ever aspire to be. Man's only hope—and it's a flimsy, desperate, inevitably *doomed* hope at that—is that he can follow a rigorous program of sensitivity training and oral calisthenics that ultimately give him the Mouth of a Lesbian.

A man who can eat a vagina with the aplomb of a Hoov vacuum sucking waste particles from a carpet will find th he is "Joe Popular" and a "hit with the ladies." His social calendar will suddenly fill up months in advance as the neighborhood women line up around the block in order t strap their gams around his gums.

"CUNNILINGUS," QUITE SIMPLY, is the act of usin your mouth to orally pleasure a woman's private parts, hopefully until she achieves the proper release. It has bee shrouded in superstition and cloaked in taboo since civilization first emerged from the monkey-laden plains of th lower Kalahari. Due to pervasive cultural ignorance and rampant patriarchal bigotry, as well as huge measures of healthy natural instinct, it has historically been deemed degrading, disgusting, and inherently effeminizing to all males who perform it. And while the stark, shameful trut remains that it is almost exclusively the domain of tragica under-endowed she-men who can't satisfy a woman a other way it behoov us to not rub your inadequacies in your face, at least not within th sanctimonious confines of a purportedly informational instructional manual such as this one pretends to be. As sad as it is that you're reading this in the vain hope that you'll ultimately be able to charm even *one* woman, it'd b much sadder for you to soberly apprehend your eternal sexual worthlessness and wind up on a commuter train wielding a machine gun. So on with the fantasy games!

Modern man lives in a modern world filled with modern conveniences and modern problems. One of modern man's most problematic modern problems is the fact that modernization has also swept over the female of the species, who is no longer content to languish in the background blindly supporting her husband while he receives all the trophies and all the oral sex.

Modern woman demands that modern man provide her with robust, satisfying orgasms, the sort that Mother Nature, in her arbitrarily cruel design, has generally denied her through the blunt routine of traditional sexual intercourse. Since a woman's Pleasure Trigger resides due *north* of her vagina rather than *inside* of it, many if not most women are left

"There she is, spread before you—a moist, nourishing buffet of saucy spices and tantalizing flavo A delightful, sensuous feast of vaginal morsels an tasty fluids. An exotic fondue of gooey treats and intoxicating odors. So dive in like you're on Deat Row and this is your last meal."

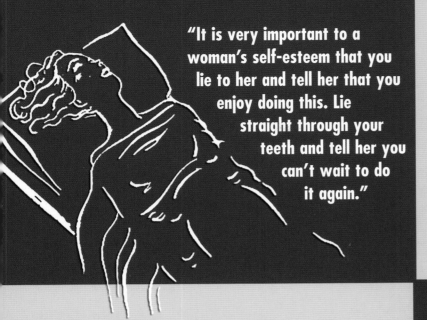

"It is very important to a woman's self-esteem that you lie to her and tell her that you enjoy doing this. Lie straight through your teeth and tell her you can't wait to do it again."

Although communication is said to be the most important part of a successful sexual relationship, it is paramount that you do not disclose your overweening fears regarding your fundamental inadequacy. Your insecurities, although entirely justified, must remain as dark and mysterious to her as her vaginal mysteries remain obscure and shut-off to you. As you kneel there, hunched-over and buried face-deep in her sex, it is crucial that you maintain the charade and continue to lie both to yourself and to her. In the off chance that you've mastered enough finesse to orally escort her to Heaven's Gate and she forcibly grabs your ears and plants your face suffocatingly inside her Meadow of Hairy Wetness while shrieking like a mongoose in estrus, take bitter comfort in the knowledge that her pleasure and the future of your relationship depend solely on the truth never, ever rising to the surface.

YOUR LOVER'S VAGINA is a secret perfumed garden, a dank, musty cave, a deep, briny ocean containing all of life's mysteries within its mucus-lathered walls. There she is, spread before you—a moist, nourishing buffet of saucy spices and tantalizing flavors. A delightful, sensuous feast of vaginal morsels and tasty fluids. An exotic fondue of gooey treats and intoxicating odors. So dive in like you're on Death Row and this is your last meal.

Although there is scant pleasure in craning your neck and lapping away like a mechanical robot dog, there is nothing to be gained by admitting this fact. Although women are strong, bold, noble Moon Daughters, even the fairest flower in the bunch is beset with a tangled complex of gnawing insecurities and "body-image" issues which it is always wiser to humor and patronize than to directly confront.

Therefore, the most crucial skill of any would-be successful cunnilinguist is to ACT AS IF YOU LIKE DOING IT. It is very important to a woman's self-esteem that you lie to her and tell her that you enjoy doing this. Lie straight through your teeth and tell her you can't wait to do it again. In certain delicate life situations, it is almost always better to lie. This is one of those situations.

Before proceeding to "Eat at the Y," you should take certain precautions to set the proper erotic mood. Demand documented proof that she is not HIV-positive nor afflicted with Hep-C, gonorrhea, and/or syphilis. Under harsh overhead lights, scrutinize her pubis to ensure that it boasts neither pus-oozing herpes sores nor a lunar landscape of crusty genital warts. If cleanliness is a concern, require her to vigorously scrub her rancid nether regions with warm water, industrial-grade solvents, and a loofah sponge. Once you've forced her to jump through an impersonal series of hoops regarding her microbial and olfactory acceptability, you both should be relaxed and confident enough to engage in oral-genital intimacy.

Speak to her gently and softly, realizing that women are much more complex (neurotic) than men and require much more time and understanding (laborious effort) in order to attain physical ecstasy. Tell her she's the prettiest plum to fall from the whole darn plum tree and that you're the luckiest fella on Earth to be sitting there with your head crammed between her thighs, making your jaw sore all in the name of her pleasure, which obviously takes precedence over your extended discomfort. Kiss her softly and slowly up and down her body, whispering into her waxy ear that you'd much rather be doing this than jamming your bone straight up her ass, popping your load in under a minute, and falling away snoring. Inform her that you've expended hundreds of hours scrutinizing clinical diagrams of Vagina Parts and invested years poring over dusty guidebooks featuring step-by-step instructions on How to Please a Woman. Nothing lubes a girl's loins faster than a lonely, mortifyingly self-conscious shlub who approaches the sex act as if it were a Community College degree in Accounting. Women crave the attentive ministrations of men entirely unaware that good sex occurs in almost mathematically inverse proportion to how hard you consciously struggle to make it good.

Helpful Suggestions for Orally Pleasuring a Woman's Privates:

1) Playfully flick your tongue around her clitoris as if you were a mischievous hummingbird teasing a horny flower bulb.

2) From memory, write the Declaration of Independence on her inner thigh using only the tip of your tongue.

3) Light some sensuous candles, preferably scented ones, to "enhance the mood." Favorite flavors include: Warm Vanilla Cookie, Key Lime Pie, and Pumpkin Surprise.

4) Lick sideways, then up, then down, then in criss-cross patterns, then in a "Figure 8," then slowly and softly grasp her vaginal lips with your teeth, continuing to lick up and down in a vertical motion, then run the entire length of your tongue up and down on her clitoris while bobbing your head as if nodding "yes," then expel a small amount of spittle directly onto her clitoris from your mouth, smearing it onto her vulva using rapid tongue motions, then make eye contact with her as you passionately lap at her outer labia, then stiffen your tongue and probe into her vaginal canal as if you were an eel seeking an underwater cave, then nuzzle her pubic hair with your nose while you make a "buzzing" sound a half-inch over her clitoris with your mouth. Women LOVE when you do this.

Before we go any further, I need to make it uncomfortably clear that NONE of the fellatio tips I'm sharing with you are gleaned from any personal experience with having penises in my mouth. These observations are STRICTLY the result of having women stick *my* penis in *their* mouths and sometimes sharing their "tricks of the trade" with me during the tenderly playful "afterglow" phase. In a world that honors respectfulness, this sort of thing shouldn't need explaining, but our world is rapidly filling up with Smart Alecs and know-it-alls who think I won't hunt them down and bop them in the nose for making a few off-color remarks about my sexual orientation. I'm as heterosexual as a T-bone steak, and the blind red rage with which I react toward any aspersions cast upon my well-adjusted maleness should, by itself, stand as proof that I am not, under any circumstances, nor any reasonable definition of the term, a homosexual.

HOW YOUR MOUTH
CAN HELP YOU KEEP A MAN

THE ROLE OF FELLATIO IN ACHIEVING AND MAINTAINING HUMAN INTIMACY

YOU WANT TO KEEP YOUR MAN, DON'T YOU? Keeping a man is a woman's fundamental project in life. No self-respecting lady wants to grow old alone, a crabby, unwanted spinster cursing the fact that love and beauty have passed over her like the Angel of Death sailing straight over a blood-splattered doorway.

In today's fast-paced workaday world, with women expected to perform increasingly extreme sexual acts merely to keep their man from wandering, it becomes difficult to master the latest methods of pleasing your man even while frantically employing every hole that God gave you.

Above all else, you don't want to be alone, and that's where your mouth can help. The mouth that God gave you was never solely intended for whistling Dixie and nibbling on Lean Cuisine microwave dinners. That mouth is a wet, warm, wondrously supple instrument designed to bring you and your man closer together under the giant floppy umbrella of intimacy.

Intimacy means sharing, and sharing means caring, and caring means sex, and sex means really good blowjobs on demand. And nothing—not a tight vagina, not a pretty face, not a multi-million-dollar trust fund, and *definitely* not "conversational skills" or a "good personality"—will keep your man better than really good blowjobs on demand. With your dick in his mouth, it's not like he's going anywhere.

If you master the attitudes and techniques I'm about to share, you can sleep soundly at night without worrying whether he's out getting a "beej" from some slut he met on the public transit system. I must warn you that the learning curve will not be easy. There will be casualties, just as there always are in wartime. But, just as in war, there will be glory—great, noble glory. Your mouth will become his Disneyland—the happiest place on Earth—and his penis would be a fool to vacation anywhere else.

1. Respect Your Man—Put it in Your Mouth

Of all the known methods which human beings use to express love and respect for one another, there exists no better way to show your man you care about him than to put his penis in your mouth. When you get down on your knees and fill your piehole with his manliness, you are saying, "I honor you. I am taking a very special part of your body into my mouth. I am taking your body into my body in a way that is far more intimate and deliberate than the base, rote ministrations of barnyard sexual intercourse. Even mosquitoes, those nasty jungle pests, routinely indulge in sexual intercourse, but a mosquito has not yet been born which can perform fellatio. And even chimpanzees will occasionally lick another chimp's monkey vagina, but only Homo sapiens is known to perform fellatio. Because fellatio, even though it sounds like the name of a two-bit Italian opera clown, is a gift only shared among the highest known vertebrates. This is more than a physical act—it is a spiritual celebration. It's a celebration of the body—*your* body, exemplified in your penis." Believe it or not, you are actually saying all of this when you put his penis in your mouth, but he probably can't hear you because, you know, you have his penis in your mouth.

2. Don't Be so Hung-Up on "Cleanliness"

It's hard to believe that in this so-called "enlightened" day and age, there exists a certain type of female throwback who finds the noble act of lovingly slurping her man's sexual organ to be "dirty" or "disgusting." Granted, there are some men who have hygiene problems and have yet to discover the glories of gel-based body soap, but they are a tiny minority. You need to remember that if you are rejecting the taste or stench of a man's private region, you are rejecting his core, his soul, his vaporous essence. Teach yourself to love, embrace, and ultimately *savor* his various tastes and smells. It must also be noted that every sexual act is a potentially biohazardous disaster. Sucking a man's penis, combined with the *de rigueur* act of ingesting his semen, is "risky business" in this day and age of HIV, crab lice, and genital leprosy. So put your mind at ease—ask your man whether he has any STDs, and trust his answer unquestioningly.

3. Do Not Blow on It
It's not a flute—it's a dick. Etymologists are unsure why it's called a "blowjob" when it's actually a "suckjob," but they all agree that blowing on his penis makes you seem a wee bit retarded. Suck, don't blow. He's not a blow-up doll, he's a *man with feelings,* and if you try blowing air into his urethra, you put him at danger of embolisms, "the bends," and other serious medical consequences. What's worse, your sloppy technique will put you at risk of losing him to a more skilled fellatrix.

4. Don't Bite it, Either
It's not a kielbasa—it's a dick. You're not a lady beaver lazily gnawing on a wood stump—you're a female human being offering oral homage to his Scepter of Life. It is part of your womanly duty to master the technique of wrapping your lips over your choppers to protect his beautiful sausage skin from any nicks, cuts, or scrapes that your careless teeth might inflict.

5. Pout
How warm, confident, and complete you feel with it in your mouth. It is an adult woman's pacifier. And how sad it makes you when your hungry maw lacks its comforting girth. How empty and alone your mouth feels without his penis inside. It is nearly impossible to overstress the importance of hovering near his penis, looking up at him innocently, and *pouting* about the fact that you don't get to suck it as much as you'd like. Pouting is perhaps the most important part of fellatio.

6. Do More Than Just Suck It

Lick it. Kiss it. Nuzzle it. Talk to it. Run your lips up and down the shaft like you're prying meat from a stubborn spare rib. Flick your tongue on his

oft-neglected corona, meatus, and frenulum. Engage in mild scrotal worship. Orally stimulate his perineum and anus in ways that don't force him to question his sexuality.

7. Swallow
Imagine how hurt, offended, and dejected you'd feel if your man, while paying oral attention to your nasty bits, was to suddenly go "P-tooey!" and spit out your so-called "precious" vaginal fluids in disgust. You wouldn't like it, would you? You'd cry, wouldn't you? Of *course* you would—you cry about *everything*. Yet there are still women who act as if they have a *choice* in whether to spit or swallow. It's *très* simple—to spit is to reject him. To swallow his thick, creamy New England Clam Chowder is to *accept* him. It is the ultimate sign of love and respect for a man when you allow him to spray his man-sauce *in* you and *on* you however he pleases. Besides, his semen is low in calories while plumb burstin' with vitamins, minerals, and protein. So don't be hollow—swallow. Don't be shallow—swallow.

8. Tell Him How Much You Enjoyed Doing It
It's a verified medical fact that all women find fellatio intensely pleasurable. There is not a woman alive who can control her vagina from vigorously lubricating while she has a man's penis inside her mouth. Some women are even able to achieve orgasm while blowing her beloved. Any woman who claims she doesn't enjoy doing it is simply one who has a deep-seated hatred of men and is desperately fearful of commitment and allowing herself to be swooningly swept up in her man's overpowering biceps. She enjoys fellatio, all right—she simply doesn't enjoy what enjoying it *implies*. But you are not like these shrieking she-beasts, are you? No—you are a *normal* woman who is secure enough to admit to herself that there is nothing on God's Green Earth more fun that bobbing up and down on Big Daddy's knob. But don't be selfish, honey—*share* that information with him. He needs to know it, lest he go a-roamin'. He might go a-roamin' anyway, but at least you did your best.

FELLATIO FUN FACTS
WEIRD, WACKY, AND WILD CASES OF COCKSUCKING THROUGHOUT HISTORY AND ACROSS THE GLOBE

- Fellatio has been depicted in ancient artwork dating back to prehistoric cave paintings.

- According to Egyptian myth, the goddess Iris "blew" life into a clay penis by sucking on it.

- Cleopatra was once said to have blown dozens of soldiers in a single night. Other famous noblewomen allegedly adept at fellatio were Russia's Catherine the Great and America's own Nancy Reagan.

- Ancient Greeks referred to fellatio as "playing the flute."

- The Kama Sutra (circa 100 A.D.) features an entire chapter of fellatio techniques, including "The Butterfly Lick" and "Sucking the Mango Fruit."

- Declaring fellatio to be "the worst of all evils," Theodore the Archibishop of Canterbury in 670 A.D. prescribed a lengthier punishment for sucking a cock than for murdering someone.

- A Japanese woman named Kaho claims that she's able to tell a man's fortune by sucking his penis. "It depends, I suppose, on what the member feels like when I first put it in my mouth, what shape it takes when it gets hard, the color and what it tastes like when (the client's) finished," says Kaho, who claims to have "told" over 1,000 such "fortunes" in a single year. "I take all these things into account, then read the fortune."

- Fellatio is nearly unheard of in Eskimo culture. Fuck, they don't even use their mouths to *kiss*.

- According to one estimate, fellatio is still illegal in more than a dozen states.

"The mouth that God gave you was never solely intended for whistling Dixie and nibbling on Lean Cuisine microwave dinners."

Penis Sizes of World Religious Figures

according to the women who loved them

NAME: JESUS

RELIGION: CHRISTIANITY

ESTIMATED PENIS SIZE: 5.5" LONG X 1.5" WIDE

COMMENTS: "He was kinda cute, but he was totally clammy in bed...It took a while for him to get it up, and when he did, he shot it in about three seconds... He paid more attention to his apostles than he did to me. A nice guy, but I think he might be gay."

NAME: KRISHNA

RELIGION: HINDUISM

ESTIMATED PENIS SIZE: 7" LONG X 1.5" WIDE

COMMENTS: "The blue cock took a little getting used to...He smelled like curry, which was a turn-off... I looked inside his asshole and saw the universe."

NAME: MOSES

RELIGION: JUDAISM

ESTIMATED PENIS SIZE: 5.75" LONG X 2.5" WIDE

COMMENTS: "He was always commanding me to do stuff...I like men with facial hair, so I thought the beard was totally hot...He told me I have a 'burning bush,' which is the dumbest pick-up line I ever heard."

...unding a major world religion can be difficult. But it has its perks, chief among them the groupies. ...en rock musicians can't moisten the ladies' laps like someone who promises to plow them with the ol' God Rod. ...t prophets tend to be arrogant and self-absorbed, and when they've finished using the bodies of their ...ling female supplicants, they toss them in the garbage like a half-eaten tray of fish 'n' chips.

...t now the God Groupies are having their revenge. A website called **messiahs-exes.com** is run by and ...dicated to the women who've been used and then cast aside by prophets of the Lord. Through lively ...at-room discussions and catty message boards, these women detail their sexual encounters with famous ...orld religious figures. Their comments are often shocking, frequently graphic, and always honest.

Judging from the site's thousands of postings, these men of God were busy li'l bumblebees with the ladies, up there with bedroom champs such as Wilt Chamberlain and Gene Simmons. By pooling together their comments, we've **estimated** each religious leader's **penis size**. We've also provided **three** representative **comments** about each prophet's lovemaking technique.

NAME: **BUDDHA**

RELIGION: **BUDDHISM**

ESTIMATED PENIS SIZE: **4" LONG x 1" WIDE**

COMMENTS: "Dude was hung like a grain of rice...
He sat there without moving and wanted me to do all the work...
No wonder his religion is all about killing one's desires,
because that's exactly the effect he had on me!"

NAME: **MUHAMMAD**

RELIGION: **ISLAM**

ESTIMATED PENIS SIZE: **10" LONG x 3" WIDE**

COMMENTS: "He made me believe in One True God,
the one dangling between his legs...He was a bit of
a player. I didn't allow myself to trust him...Big dick, but
I still didn't get off. It was all about his pleasure, not mine.
When I started moaning, he told me to cover my face
and be quiet."

VIRGIN MARY'S FACE APPEARS IN WET SPOT!

HUNDREDS OF BELIEVERS SILENTLY HUDDLE outside the Midniter Motel in Troutdale, Oregon. They endure cold rain and high winds, hoping for the Blessed Virgin Mary to appear above the motel again. About 300 of them—mostly women, mostly Hispanic—have been flocking to the motel from all over the Northwest since the Virgin Mary's face appeared on a bedsheet wet spot after a couple's one-night stand here more than a month ago.

A short, squat, brownish woman stands near the motel's front office, leading the group in a recitation of the rosary. Suddenly she stops, gasps, twitches, rolls her eyes in the back of her head, and announces, "The Virgin Mother is among us!"

THE SHROUD OF TROUTDALE: Virgin Mary's face appears in wet spot after couple had sex at the Midniter Motel in Troutdale, Oregon.

The crowd stops, gasps, twitches, and rolls their eyes in the back of their heads, too.

A blue-whale-sized Blessed Virgin Mary hovers above the motel, bathed in celestial light. She seems taller and more attractive than she appears in pictures. She scans the crowd and begins speaking:

Because of your fornicating ways, your lustful attachment to hot, steaming, heterosexual intercourse, I will crush you under my feet and allow the serpent to drag you into hell with his tail. God will abandon mankind and send down bucketfuls of hot molten lead upon their sinful heads. He will strike you with his iron rod and make you drink from the chalice of His wrath. The sinners will cry for mercy, but God will laugh and continue punishing them. God will take great delight in punishing them. He will keep going and going until He's satisfied. Terrible scourges and grave events will befall the Earth. Frogs will rain from heaven. The genitals of the faithless will shrivel up and fall off.

Everyone's cell phones will stop working.

The Giant Blessed Mother vanishes as soon as she finishes speaking.

"Whoa, that was some *heavy* shit," mutters a man near the back of the crowd.

"WE MUST HAVE FUCKED FOUR OR FIVE TIMES THAT NIGHT," says Gresham resident Steve Plodgett of the one-night stand which has inspired awe, fascination, and a renewal of faith throughout the Catholic world. Plodgett says he met his sex partner for the now-legendary one-night stand, Hillsboro native Mary Ellen Mumford, at a Gresham karaoke bar. "She seemed a little shy," Plodgett says, "so I asked her if she'd help me do a duet of 'Islands in the Stream.' After we did the song, we started drinking and talking, and before you knew it, we were at The Midniter, knockin' the boots. I guess we left a little bit of a mess behind." Plodgett and Mumford have hired an agent to negotiate the film rights to their story and are still dating one another. "I figure that when the Virgin Mary put her face in our wet spot, she was trying to tell us we should be together," Plodgett speculates.

"Frogs will rain from heaven. The genitals of the faithless will shrivel up and fall off. Everyone's cell phones will stop working."

MIRACLE COUPLE: Steve Plodgett and Mary Ellen Mumford's one-night stand has turned into the most celebrated Marian apparition of the 21st century.

THE BLESSED MOTHER hovers over the Midniter Motel in Troutdale, Oregon, in protest of all the adultery that transpires there.

THE COUPLE'S HOLY WET SPOT

was discovered by Maria Conchita Acuña Sandoval, a maid at The Midniter, which is a popular motel for one-night stands in the Gresham/Troutdale area. Sandoval, a mother of 12 children, immediately notified the motel's desk clerk, who called local news agencies and the Catholic Diocese of Portland. A lab test of the wet spot revealed the moisture to be composed of semen and vaginal fluids, and a photo of the stained bedsheet clearly reveals the Blessed Virgin Mother's face. Crowds began forming while the stain was still wet and have kept a steady vigil outside Room 104, where the miraculous bodily fluid apparition occurred. Seemingly overnight, "Our Lady of the Holy Wet Spot" T-shirts and key chains were being sold outside The Midniter. The motel's owners are currently charging a five-dollar admission to enter Room 104 and view the Shroud of Troutdale. They plan to change their motel to a "religious amusement park" with Virgin Mary-themed games, rides, and "Catholic-family-oriented entertainment."

"THE VIRGIN MARY CURED ME OF HERPES,"

claims an erotic dancer who goes by the name of Swastika, "and I know this other stripper who doesn't get those little pink razor bumps when she shaves her snatch anymore, and she attributes the miracle to Our Lady of the Holy Wet Spot." Standing outside Room 104 and fiddling with a shiny black set of over-sized rosary beads, Swastika has a pedigree familiar to the Portland sex-industry worker: unhappy childhood, hot body, and bad decisions. "I've had a hard life," she says philosophically. "There are some nights where I pretty much fall asleep at the rack because nobody's tipping. I've had boyfriends try to break up with me and stuff, so I know what pain is like. I've felt *tons* of guilt. I've done some *bad* things. I've hurt a *lot* of people. But when I think of the Blessed Mother's face appearing in that wet spot, suddenly I don't feel so dirty anymore. I close my eyes real hard and think of Mother Mary, and I feel *clean.* It's awesome!"

Swastika claims that Virgin Mary-worship is becoming popular among Portland's stripper community. She says she recently attended an all-girl party which included a clothes swap, a recitation of the rosary, and lesbian group sex.

"The Blessed Mother is emerging as an icon for all the dancers I know," Swastika beams. "Even though she's a virgin and we aren't, she's cool about it. When her face appeared in that wet spot, it's like she was telling us it's *OK* to have lots and lots of sex with anonymous people." In the Blessed Mother, Swastika sees a New Age pro-sex feminist rather than the submissive homebody which has been the Virgin's image for 2,000 years now. "I work in an industry dominated by men. I live in a *universe* dominated by a patriarchal father-son combo and a sex-neutral white dove. The Virgin Mary comes along saying, 'Girls kick ass!,' and suddenly I feel like I *belong* to something. Don't be surprised if you see a lot of tattooed strippers up in heaven, and don't be shocked if the Blessed Mother throws some girls-only parties up there, too."

THE VIRGIN MARY DECLINED TO SPEAK

with *Exotic* for this article, although she said she would have spoken with *The T&A Times* if they were still around. She also refused a $10,000,000 offer to appear naked in *Penthouse.* Through her press agent in Tel Aviv, she delivered the following statement:

I understand that being a media figure tends to open up one's private life for public speculation, but the media have caused my family and me untold mental distress regarding the Shroud of Troutdale. Once and for all: Yes, that's my face. And yes, I have a "special man" in my life. But the cruel allegations that I'm no longer a virgin and have been spotted in London night clubs disco-dancing with Guy Ritchie are forming the basis of a libel lawsuit which I can and will pursue. No one has the right to get upset if I choose to have a little fun these days. It's been a long time coming. Times change. People change. No big woop.

VIRGINS KICK ASS: Artist's rendering of a sex-positive "alternative" Virgin Mary, complete with nose piercings and tribal facial tattoos.

PRIEST TURNS CONFESSION BOOTH into "erotic lingerie modeling booth for boys"...

The boy spins his skinny body lazily around the brass pole which juts phallically up through the cramped wooden booth. He is clad only in underwear, his creamy ten-year-old skin a pale canvas freckled with red splotches of light that bounce off the mirrored disco ball. The priest crouches in the dark on the other side of a small grated window, straining to see the boy's every move. Although the pumping anal-piston sound of British Trance music rumbles inside the small wooden booth, it is barely audible throughout the rest of the church.

After the requisite three songs are finished, the red light goes off and the priest declares that all the boy's sins are forgiven. The boy gathers his clothes and leaves. The priest waits a minute, then does the same.

The priest's name is **Father Brad Chomenstein**, and he's been shepherding the flock at the Saint Scrotus School for Boys in Tillamook since 1984. It was only recently, claims the tall, shifty, baldheaded Chomenstein, that God presented him with a "vision" that inspired him to construct his first-of-its-kind "erotic lingerie modeling confession booth for boys," which resembles a standard "jack shack" except for the fact that it's in a church and is intended to be used exclusively by pre-pubescent males. "The Lord knows it gets lonely for me

TOP LEFT: The controversial "erotic lingerie modeling booth for boys," a traditional Catholic confessional which Father Brad Chomenstein has refitted with red lights, a brass pole, a disco ball, a paper-towel rack, a framed photo of a boy in underwear, and a state-of-the-art stereo system.

LEFT: Father Ignatius Rectalopagus, a Catholic scholar who says Father Chomenstein's booth violates no church or biblical laws.

BELOW: Father Chomenstein and "Li'l" Davey Geary, who confesses his sins at least twice a week in Chomenstein's booth.

...and there's nothing the cops can do about it!

out here on the coast teaching at an all-boy school, so he entered my bedroom one warm summer night with some surprisingly bawdy, yet *tasteful*, ideas for what eventually became my erotic modeling confessional booth for boys," Chomenstein tells me as we walk barefoot in a field of daffodils near his church. "The Lord said, 'Brad, my son, thou hast been living a chaste life devoid of carnal pleasures. Thou knowest that the body is the Temple of the Holy Ghost, so why dost thou not erect a shrine so that thou mayest pay tribute to the supple little Temples of the youngest lambs within mine flock?'"

"You mean God *really* talks like that," I ask him, "with the King James Bible shit like 'thou mayest' and 'why dost thou not'?"

"Yeah," Chomenstein says. "It's awesome!"

"I'VE BEEN DANCING FOR FATHER CHOMENSTEIN for almost a year now," says "Li'l" Davey Geary, a student at Saint Scrotus who Chomenstein claims is his "absolute favorite confession-booth boy." Chomenstein describes Geary as "a so-so student with a wonderful smile and a grace not unlike that of a salamander." Geary views his role as erotic confessional-booth dancer much more pragmatically: "The way I see it, I'd rather dance to three songs in my underwear than say a dozen Hail Marys. It's easier, and I walk out of that booth with my sins cleansed. Sometimes he even lets me play my own music in the booth," claims Geary, adding that his favorite music artists are P. Diddy and Kid Rock.

"THERE'S NOTHING WRONG with an erotic lingerie-modeling booth for boys," insists Father Ignatius Rectalopagus, a professional Catholic scholar and Chief Rector of the rectory at Saint Prostatus Church in McMinnville. "The Holy Bible, as well as apostolic tradition, is explicit on this matter—there is ABSOLUTELY NO prohibition on underwear-clad boys dancing for the pleasure of priests in the confessional. This practice is forbidden NOWHERE in Holy Scripture or papal decrees."

"Yes," I challenge him, "but neither does the Bible *explicitly* forbid people to download pictures of naked boys from the Internet."

"You're *right*, sir," Rectalopagus says, his beard-fringed, vulva-like lips pursed into a smile. "The Lord allows us some mighty big loopholes, doesn't He?"

"I'D LOVE TO NAIL HIM on sex charges," says Portland police officer Frank Rhino, "but technically, Father Chomenstein's not doing anything illegal. The boys don't get totally naked. He's not touching them. There's no force involved or threats made—the boys can leave the booth any time they want. Plus, there's the legal matter of priest-client confidentiality. Since we're not permitted into the church to do surveillance and witness the act as it's happening, we'd have trouble convicting him even if he *were* committing crimes. Young boys are notoriously unreliable witnesses. I mean, they lie about *me* all the time!"

"I'D LIKE TO CRUSH CHOMENSTEIN'S BALLS under a pile-driver," says Tex "Itchy" Geary, father of "Li'l" Davey Geary, the boy who is currently Chomenstein's favorite sin-confessor/erotic dancer. "I'd like to take a pair of tweezers and pluck every hair from Chomenstein's body one at a time and watch him scream in pain while I laugh. I'd like to shove a red-hot iron rod up his ass and videotape it, then make him watch the videotape. I'd like to slowly make cut marks all over his body with a straight razor and then pour a bucket of rubbing alcohol on him while I recited the 23rd Psalm. I'd like to cut off his dick and balls, make him eat them, wait until he shits them out, and make him eat the shit that's composed of the dick and balls he ate, and THEN eat THAT shit when it comes through again. I'd like to force him to watch kiddie porn and then smash his genitals with a mallet every time he starts to get excited, and then make him lick up the blood that splurts out of his little dick every time I hit him with the mallet. A 'modeling booth for boys'—what kind of a SICK MIND would think of such a thing?"

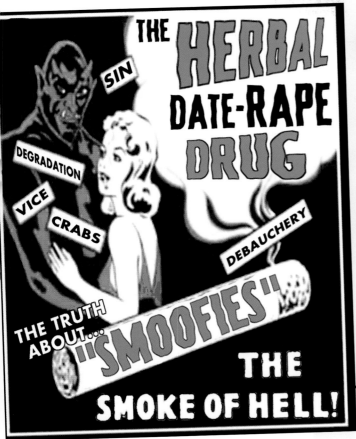

THE HERBAL DATE-RAPE DRUG

SIN

DEGRADATION

VICE

CRABS

DEBAUCHERY

THE TRUTH ABOUT... "SMOOFIES"

THE SMOKE OF HELL!

ABOVE: Pictures of an herb called *rohydra*, known as "the herbal date-rape drug." Rohydra is the herbal analogue to rohypnol, a pill which gained fame as "the date-rape drug." Sex offenders and other thrill-seekers will often mix some rohydra into a cigarette or joint of marijuana, which is given to their intended prey, who are rendered unconscious within one minute of smoking a "smoofie."

WHAT IS THIS "HERBAL DATE-RAPE DRUG" I KEEP HEARING ABOUT, DOCTOR?

I'm glad you asked. The "herbal date-rape drug" refers to a simple herb named *rohydra,* which grows naturally throughout the Northwest. Just as ephedra is an herb which forms the organic basis of methamphetamines (i.e., "speed" or "crank"), pharmacists use the herb rohydra to derive a compound called *rohypnol,* which in pill form is called "the date-rape drug." In short, the *herbal* date-rape drug rohydra is merely the natural source for the *pharmaceutical* date-rape drug rohypnol. Only it's herbal.

WHAT IS A "SMOOFIE"?

"Smoofie" is street slang used by certain elements of the criminal underworld who traffic in the illicit sale of rohydra, a.k.a. "the herbal date-rape drug." The word "smoofie" refers to a cigarette or marijuana joint which has been "laced" with rohydra. Those of the criminal ilk often refer to the pill form of the date-rape drug rohypnol as a "roofie." By melding the words "smokeable" and "roofie," we arrive at the term "smoofie."

HOW DOES A "SMOOFIE" DIFFER FROM A "ROOFIE"?

A "roofie," as I just stated and which you would have *known* had you been paying *attention,* is the PILL form of the date-rape drug. Roofies are typically dissolved into the victim's drink when she isn't looking. A "smoofie," on the other hand, is *smoked.* You *smoke* a smoofie. It is often slipped surreptitiously into a tobacco cigarette or a marijuana joint and then unknowingly *inhaled* by the victim.

HOW CAN I TELL IF SOMEONE HAS SLIPPED ME A "SMOOFIE"?

It's hard to tell, and that's why this drug is so dangerous. Rohydra is tasteless and odorless. A tiny pinch of rohydra rolled into a joint of dank skunk bud is enough to knock Shaquille O'Neal on his ass for six hours.

IF THAT'S THE CASE, HOW DO I PROTECT MYSELF FROM SMOKING A "SMOOFIE"?

My simple advice would be, "Roll your own." Roll your own joints and smoke your own cigarettes. That's the easiest anti-smoofie step you could take.

WHAT IF I ROLL MY OWN, BUT MY DEALER LACED MY 40-SACK WITH ROHYDRA BECAUSE HE'S BEEN ITCHIN' TO GET IN MY PANTS?

I hadn't considered that. Really, I mean it—that's a *really* good question.

ARE THERE ANY DANGEROUS SIDE-EFFECTS THAT RESULT FROM SMOKING A "SMOOFIE"?

Apart from getting raped, no. Rohydra actually provides a strong, pleasant buzz with little in the way of reported hangovers or adverse health effects. Smoked in high quantities, it induces ecstatic hallucinations and epic dreams in the user. It's not addictive, and it's impossible to overdose. The main drawback is that the shit is so good, it flattens you on your back pretty much instantly after you exhale the smoke, rendering it easier for people to rape you and stuff like that, which, as I pointed out earlier, is wrong.

HOW DO WE EDUCATE PEOPLE ABOUT THE DANGERS OF "SMOOFIES"?

I've started an ad campaign whose slogan is "Don't Be Goofy—Don't Smoke a Smoofie!" We've been hitting a lot of local high schools with a life-sized costumed character called the Smoofasaurus, who lectures these teenaged kids, who are at their most impressionable, tender, and firm-bodied age, about the perils of smoofie-smoking.

HOW MANY RAPES HAVE OCCURRED FROM SMOOFIE-SMOKING?

The estimates range anywhere from a few dozen to over 100,000,000. We've just discovered the smoofie, so the data isn't as precise as we'd like it to be. It's too early to tell how many forced sexual penetrations this drug has enabled. It's hard to get my finger firmly placed on exactly how many smoofie-rapes there have been. But I want to make it clear that even one smoofie-rape is too many.

A MEDICAL EXCLUSIVE
Answers by Dr. Shlomo Nachas

WHERE CAN I BUY A "SMOOFIE"?

I don't think that's an appropriate question.

Because of **the herbal date-rape drug,** women are cautioned from accepting cigarettes or joints from strange men. What seems like an innocent smoke might be a **"smoofie,"** and it might lead to trouble.

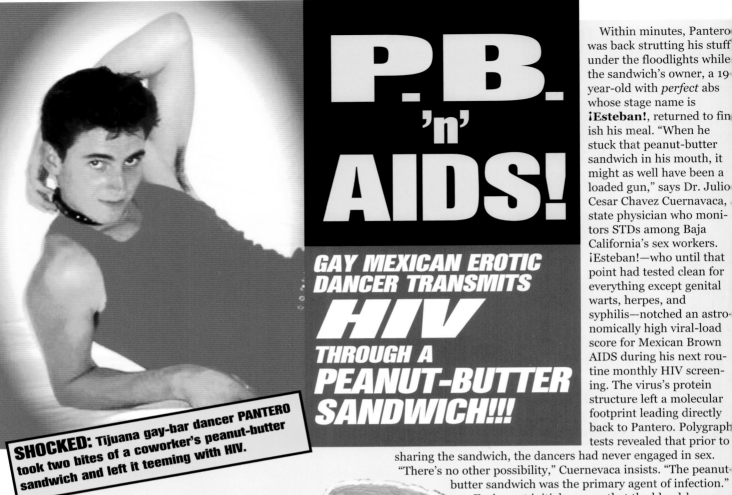

P.B. 'n' AIDS!

GAY MEXICAN EROTIC DANCER TRANSMITS *HIV* THROUGH A PEANUT-BUTTER SANDWICH!!!

SHOCKED: Tijuana gay-bar dancer PANTERO took two bites of a coworker's peanut-butter sandwich and left it teeming with HIV.

Peanut butter is a popular sandwich spread rarely associated with life-threatening STDs.

Maricon's is the name of a gay strip club housed in a small Quonset hut with a thatched roof on the dusty outskirts of Tijuana. Out here among the bumpy sand dunes and rusted vehicles that scar the landscape, bronze-skinned young naked gay males have been dancing to the delight of pasty American and German sex-industry tourists for over three decades. Maricon's is renowned for featuring the world's first (and longest-running) all-male donkey show.

One of Maricon's most popular dancers is **Pantero**, famous for his ability to pop a steel cap off a beer bottle with his anus. Pantero commands top dollar for his 15-minute private dances involving a four-foot monitor lizard and his pet spider monkey. Tragically, he also recently became the only person known to medical science ever to have transmitted HIV through a peanut-butter sandwich.

One steamy summer night a few months ago, as the club beat cranked like a hot oiled piston and the dancers' jockstraps were stuffed full of one-dollar bills from drunken Anglo sailors, Pantero quickly snatched a couple nibbles from a half-eaten peanut-butter sandwich a coworker had left in the dressing room. Since he had been nursing a rather florid cold-sore scab on his lower lip, Pantero accidentally bled onto the sandwich and left it teeming with HIV. What's worse, he infected the sandwich with Fast-Acting Full-Blown Mexican Brown HIV, an especially harsh strain of the dreaded killer virus.

Within minutes, Pantero was back strutting his stuff under the floodlights while the sandwich's owner, a 19-year-old with *perfect* abs whose stage name is **¡Esteban!**, returned to finish his meal. "When he stuck that peanut-butter sandwich in his mouth, it might as well have been a loaded gun," says Dr. Julio Cesar Chavez Cuernavaca, state physician who monitors STDs among Baja California's sex workers. ¡Esteban!—who until that point had tested clean for everything except genital warts, herpes, and syphilis—notched an astronomically high viral-load score for Mexican Brown AIDS during his next routine monthly HIV screening. The virus's protein structure left a molecular footprint leading directly back to Pantero. Polygraph tests revealed that prior to sharing the sandwich, the dancers had never engaged in sex. "There's no other possibility," Cuernevaca insists. "The peanut-butter sandwich was the primary agent of infection."

Furious at initial rumors that the blood-borne pathogen had been transmitted through sodomy, an angry torch mob of notoriously homophobic Mexican peasant farmers threatened to burn down Maricon's until a local clergyman intervened and explained that the viral transmission was unintentional. Realizing that since they, too, ate the occasional peanut-butter sandwich and were likewise at risk, the peasants calmed down and returned quietly to their humble village.

"You get hungry being an exotic dancer," Pantero explains. "The sandwich was lying there, and I made a decision, and something horrible happened. I got some blood on the peanut butter, he ate the peanut butter, and now he has AIDS. I feel awful about this. If I knew this was going to happen, I would have bought some Ring Dings from the vending machine and eaten them instead."

¡Esteban!, whose coworkers have now taken to calling him *El Cacahuete* (which means "The Peanut" in Spanish), tries to look on the bright side. Prior to eating the sandwich, his negative status was the only thing preventing him from having sex with Pantero. "Now that we're both full-blown," he says with a wink, "we're making up for lost time."

INFECTED: "He got AIDS in my peanut butter!" wails ¡ESTEBAN!

Local Couple Tries New Sexual Position

by Jim Goad
Staff Writer

PASCO, WA—For over 30 years, Eldon and Melba Turteltaub had been using the missionary position—and *only* the missionary position—during their lovemaking sessions.

That all changed late last Friday night, and the couple are still struggling with the emotional repercussions from Eldon's impulsive decision to enter his wife from a different angle.

Last Friday evening, after a fruitful work week in which insurance salesman Eldon, 57, landed a lucrative new contract to insure a local minor-league hockey team, the pair decided to go out on the town and celebrate their good fortune. They ate what Eldon calls "a very nice crab-cake dinner with some jalapeño poppers and gator-bite appetizers" at a local Applebee's restaurant. Upon finishing dessert, they repaired to Applebee's lounge section and ordered a few cocktails.

"The food was spicy, the drinks were strong, and the music was very upbeat, so I suppose I came home somewhat excited," Eldon says. "When we got home, I dimmed the lights, threw on the soundtrack to *Chariots of Fire,* and proceeded to make love to my wife." (Turteltaub estimates that he and Melba engage in intercourse once monthly, not to mention weekly mutual-masturbation sessions.)

After fewer than 20 strokes, Eldon instructed his wife to do something she'd never done in their three decades of marriage—something which resulted in the first whispers of discord to ever sully an otherwise tranquil union: "I told her to get up on all fours, and then I entered her from behind. After about a minute, she asked me to return to our usual method of entry."

Eldon complied, albeit reluctantly. "I was having fun," he says with a self-effacing smile. "I was just, as they say, going along with the flow of the moment. It was a nice change of pace, a little vacation from the normal. I was just winning one for the Gipper. But she's my wife and I wanted to be considerate, so I disengaged and then reinserted myself in the usual way. But at the time, I have to say, I found it rather thrilling. I enjoyed it, but if it upsets Melba, I don't think I'll do it again."

Melba certainly seems upset. A part-time

CURIOUS NO LONGER: Eldon *(left)* and Melba Turteltaub disagree about whether it was a good idea to try the new position.

CPA and volunteer fundraiser who's active in community events and several local charities, she ruefully recalls the meeting in question. She says that Eldon fell rapidly asleep after achieving physical release, whereupon she burst into tears, ran from the room, and made a three-hour late-night call to her mother, who lives in Bellingham. She says her mother implored her to leave Eldon and come live with her, but she has vowed to give the marriage a chance, provided the couple seeks help from a minister or psychologist.

> "You don't need to *try* something to figure out it's wrong. I felt dirty around him for weeks later."
> —*Melba Turteltaub*

"What he did that night shattered my trust in him," Melba says. "It was an adventurous, hasty decision. You don't need to *try* something to figure out it's wrong. I felt dirty around him for weeks later. I'm not a dog. I don't eat Alpo from a food dish, and I won't ever do that again. I don't know why he wanted to do that, or what was so wrong with the old position, and I'm having trouble trusting his motives. First he looks for a new position; next thing you know, he's looking for a new wife. I've invested a lot in this marriage, and I'm not about to give it all up just because my husband wakes up one day and decides to be a sex pervert."

An acquaintance of the Turteltaubs, who asked not to be identified but who lives in a green-and-yellow house directly across the street from them, is shocked at this recent development. "This is the sort of thing that you see on the nightly news," she says, dressed in curlers and a nightgown while clutching her pet Chihuahua. "This is an inner-city thing, not something you'd expect to happen in a quiet town like Pasco. People out here are happy with the regular position. Plus, you remember what happened to Sodom."

It is unknown what percentage of intimate couples actually try positions other than the normal one. Shane Mallard, a licensed sex therapist and professional fire-dancer, says that although such risk-taking behavior may improve a relationship, it can also damage it beyond repair. "There's nothing wrong with getting a little kinky, so long as it doesn't affect your work or family life," Mallard says. "In Eldon and Melba's case, what strikes me as wrong is that he *told* her—rather than *asked* her—to get up on all fours. That's simply rude. There was also some potential for physical harm. For couples well into middle age, a new sex position may put undue strain on their musculoskeletal systems. What's important is that sex-play be safe, caring, and consensual. If Melba doesn't want to receive him from behind, then Eldon should respect that and stop being such a jerk."

The couple's four children, all adults, have not been informed of the event, and the Turteltaubs have asked me to ask our readers not to tell the children about it should they happen to see them.

VAGINAL PALMISTR

FORTUNE TELLER reads LABIA as if they were TEA LEAVES!

THE VAGINAS COME AND THE VAGINAS GO—young and old vaginas, fat and trim vaginas, hairy and shaven vaginas, clean and stinky vaginas. And though the vaginas may differ, they have all come here for the same reason. Behind each of these vaginas, lying on a soft velvet examination chair with her legs strapped securely in leather stirrups, is a woman seeking advice about her future.

Currently inhabiting the velvet chair is a rather inflamed, reddish, saggy vagina belonging to a severely overweight lass in her late teens. She says her name is "Valentina," but I don't believe her. Whatever her real name is, she's a blubbery bundle of misery and despair. Her boyfriend of two years recently dumped her in favor of a thinner specimen. She fears that people are talking behind her back at work. She thinks that her boss is getting ready to fire her. She feels ugly and unappreciated. She can't stop eating— even while spread-eagled and strapped to the chair, she'll stop in mid- sentence to pop another Butterfinger Bite into her eager maw—and she frequently wishes she was dead. She's been desperately seeking answers. She tried astrology, but it never seemed to work. Same with Tarot cards. Same with individual counseling and group therapy. Same with the "Holy Handkerchief" she'd bought for $39.95 from an Internet faith healer. Nothing worked.

Hunched over the girl's vagina and sitting on a dusty Ottoman foot- stool is **Juniper Splatzfus**, self-described "Pudendal Prognosticator." Swaddled in puka shells and a Navajo poncho, with long grey hair and those annoying John Denver eyeglasses, Splatzfus is one of a growing number of alternative health-care practitioners who claim they can tell a woman's future by looking at her vagina.

"Labial soothsaying is not some new crackpot scam," Splatzfus tells me as her 13 cats screech and her two exotic birds squawk inside this tiny office which reeks of Nag Champa and whose interior-design scheme relies perhaps a touch too heavily on fuchsia. "It is an ancient practice which dates before Christ. After bathing in sacred waters, Persian women of yore would read each other's vaginas for sport and pleasure. African witch doctors, after taking nary more than a peep at the labia of a tribal girl on the cusp of puberty, were able to tell with amazing accuracy whether or not she'd remain a spinster. But along came the Christians and the Muslims," she sneers, "with their big-dick macho male Gods, and they actively suppressed this revered ritual of antiquity."

Splatzfus, who holds a degree in Advanced Vaginomancy from Tallulah Bankhead State College in San Luis Obispo, CA, likens vaginal soothsay- ing to better-known and more-respected practices such as palmistry and phrenology. She insists that every woman's labial flaps contain an indelible blueprint for how her life will unfold. "A woman's pussy lips are the road map to her future," she says. "Goddess placed the labia there almost like an owner's manual. You know the little wrinkles and crinkles and creases and folds that make each woman's labia as unique as a pair of thumbprints? They all contain messages. And my job is to decipher these messages and advise the patient accordingly. Every

woman holds a fortune cookie between her legs. My job is to crack open the cookie and read the message out loud."

"Well, you don't go merely on instinct, do you?" I ask skeptically. "I mean, there must be some sort of method to this—like in palm-reading, there's a 'life line,' and its length determines how long the person will live. So tell me a little bit about the method."

"There *is* a method," she says with a giggle, "but it employs sacred knowledge, and if I told you, I'd have to kill you."

"You know, I really, really, REALLY hate that fucking phrase—'If I told you, I'd have to kill you.' It's been used ten million times. It's not funny, and it's not original."

"OK, well," she retreats, alarmed and possibly aroused by my ballsi- ness. "See this here?" she says, holding one of Valentina's labia between her thumb and forefinger and stretching it out to at least a half-foot. "This is a BIG labia. Normally this is not considered cosmetically desirable by our culture, but the wisdom of the ancients tells us that this girl will live a long life. Big labia mean a long life. I also look for wrinkles—lots of wrinkles mean a girl will have many suitors."

She then focuses her gaze on the hapless strapped whale Valentina. "You will live a long life and have many suitors. Family troubles will rectify themselves—give it time. Financial success is on the horizon, but you will need to work hard on it and not lose focus." Valentina seems pleased with the forecast.

"And you can tell all this by looking at her vagina?" I ask Splatzfus.

She gazes at me as if I'm stupid. "You can tell *everything* about a girl by looking at her vagina."

"A woman's pussy lips are the road map to her future."

ex-SLAVES sue DOMINATRIX for REPARATIONS

YAKIMA, WASHINGTON: The ex-slaves huddle outside the courthouse on this chilly, misty Friday afternoon. They wave picket signs, chant slogans, light candles, join hands, and sing spirituals. They are here for justice. For freedom. For equality. And they're also looking for $1.9 million in punitive damages from the ruthless bitch who stole their life's savings and robbed them of their self-esteem.

The defendant in this groundbreaking civil lawsuit is **Ruth Berman** of nearby Kennewick, Washington. For over 11 years, Berman has been better known to the tricks and johns of the area as "Duchess Esmerelda." Among her many clients, Berman gained a reputation as an austere, unforgiving dominatrix "who could make the Vice President eat shit out of a dog bowl." In the lurid advertisements she placed in local smut rags, ads that invariably incorporated fascistic imagery, Duchess Esmerelda claimed that her services included "severe humiliation, infantilization and feminization, psychological and surgical castration, and general all-around ball-busting."

However, it wasn't until a recent ad claimed she was "seeking male slaves" that Duchess Esmerelda ran afoul of the law.

You see, slavery has been illegal in America since 1865.

"I FIND IT HARD TO BELIEVE that in this day and age, slavery still exists in America," says **Max Fischlman**, attorney for the plaintiffs. A hunched, bespectacled man who smells like rancid pesto sauce and whose balding head is partially covered with dry, wild shrubs of pubic-like hair, Fischlman will argue before the court that Duchess Esmerelda's business, as well as those of most of the "tops" in the S&M/B&D sex-worker community, clearly violate the U.S. Constitution's 13th Amendment, which prohibits slavery and involuntary servitude. And, in the same way that many black leaders are urging their constituents to sue for reparations, Fischlman is goading the innumerable "bottoms" in the fetish community to renounce their so-called "masters" and sue them for reparations.

But this isn't involuntary, I shoot back, ready to throw down if I have to. *This isn't like old-time slavery. These people willingly* pay *to be enslaved.*

"That's what makes it so much WORSE," Fischlman counters. "At least the old-time slaves got a free ride." I had no comeback for him. The man was telling the truth.

"SHE TOOK A POO IN MY MOUTH while I was blindfolded," claims a man who asked not to be identified in this article (but whose name, driver's license number, home address, and cell-phone number are available if you e-mail me). He says he was one of Esmerelda's slaves for over three years before Fischlman contacted him and urged him to join the class-action lawsuit against her. "It was the promise of a *lot* of money that unleashed all these memories I'd repressed after my sessions with Esmerelda," the man says as we order corn dogs and lemonade from a food cart outside the courthouse. "She once stuck a cocktail straw up my wee-wee. She made me shave my testicles while I recited nursery rhymes. She attached weights to my armpit hairs and clipped battery cables onto my buttocks. Compared to all that, I'd gladly trade a little cotton-picking and a few lashes of the bullwhip. Those slaves from olden days weren't shit. We're the ones who take the *real* hardcore abuse. I want my money back, and I want my dignity back."

HUMAN BONDAGE IN AMERICA didn't end with the Civil War. And what's worse about the modern "S&M" slavery is that the slaves are actually forced to PAY for their punishment! It's a human issue. It's a sexual issue. It's a political issue. It's a get-involved issue. We need to end the slavery. We need to end the inequality. We need to drag everyone down to our level and learn to live in peace.

SHARKEE'S

AUSTRALIA'S HOTTEST NEW STRIP CLUB!
ALL OF THE DANCERS ARE VICTIMS OF SHARK BITES!

THE GREAT BARRIER REEF IS SAID TO BE SO BIG, you can see it from outer space. Running along Australia's northeastern coast, it teems and burbles and fairly belches forth with a swirlingly pristine psychedelic explosion of aquatic life. But as with all things in this miserable existence, there is a dark and horrifying side. Happy snorkelers are caught unawares, with tragic and often fatal results. As they blissfully flap their rubber feet around in clear sunlit water, they forget that somewhere amid the far-off greenish murk, way out yonder beyond the pretty pink coral and smiling yellow fish, there lurk big sharks with large teeth and bad attitudes and shady intentions. *Ill-willed* sharks. Sharks who don't like people so much.

The Reef, world-renowned for its mean-spirited killer sharks, is also referred to as the "World's Largest Living Organism," so it makes sense that the sandy Australian coast nearby would host the "World's Largest Strip Club Catering to Men With a Shark-Bite Fetish"...perhaps the ONLY strip club catering to this fetish...but definitely "the best!"

Sharkee's Gentlemen's Club, founded in 2002, sits nestled near orange-colored beaches and windswept blue waters about ten kilometers south of the city of Cairns, celebrated worldwide for inventing the Cairn Terrier. The proud and beautiful girls who dance at Sharkee's come in all sizes, shapes, and most races (there's even an aborigine who comes in on weekends), but they all sip from the bitter cup of a tragic legacy which they've worked to their advantage—they've all been attacked by sharks and have survived. Some of the girls were lucky enough to escape with severe scars and mild disfigurement. Others suffered amputation of one or more limbs. And the more severely they're maimed, the more the men seem to like it.

Lavishly decked-out in maritime themes and sea-tragedy memorabilia, Sharkee's boasts a swank menu featuring grilled shark steaks and a drink called "The Hammerhead." They even host an Annual Naked Boat Party and Underwater Dive which heads out into the thick of the Reef. Every year, the party's highlight is when a naked menstruating stripper is lowered into the shark cage.

Sharkee's is owned by **Salty Jack Cheddars**, an ex-wombat poacher and National Boomerang Champion. As a legless stripper spins atop a small brass pole which juts up from the stage floor and is mounted deep into her vagina, Cheddars throws a shrimp on the barbie and says his dream is to install a live shark tank onstage. Although he's faced scathing criticism from numerous Aussie women's groups, Cheddars says he's "fair" to the girls and will not employ any dancers with fresh bite wounds.

"Jack's fair to the girls," says a curvaceously lovely young thing who refers to herself as **The Guppy** and says she's been dancing at Sharkee's since its inception. The Guppy, 27, says she was savagely attacked by a bull shark during a class trip 11 years ago, causing severe scarring on one leg. "Jack's not the problem," The Guppy tells me, "it's the other girls and the stupid customers." She says there is a deep rift between the girls who merely have scars and those whose injuries required amputation, mainly because the amputees garner consistently larger tips. "It hurt a LOT when that shark bit me," The Guppy says, "but not as bad as when guys sit at the rack and don't tip me."

"You wouldn't believe how many guys enjoy looking at naked women who've been bitten by sharks," says **Dingo Bill**, a perpetually drunk and sunburned Sharkee's regular who keeps one eye on me and one on the quadriplegic dancer who crawls across the stage like an inchworm. "A shark bite is the ultimate body modification. I can achieve an erection merely at the thought of a shark biting a woman. There—I just did!"

SHARKEE'S GENTLEMEN'S CLUB...Reasonably Priced Package Tours Available From the U.S. to Australia, Including Airfare, Hotel, Drink Tickets, Snorkels, and Admission to the Annual Naked Boat Party and Underwater Dive. For More Information, Contact jg@jimgoad.net.

Mother-daughter stripping midget teams are commonplace amid the red barns and horse manure that define everyday life out here in rural Pennsylvania. But this spring marked a special date, a milestone for central Bucks County's thriving sex industry—LI'L GRETL SCHRATWEISER turned 18 and became legally empowered to join her mother GRETA (36) and her grandmother GERTIE (53) as part of the "Little Sisters," who are now thought to be the only *tri*-generational team of stripping midgets east of Pennsylvania Dutch Country.

And the most amazing part of all is that *they're all Buddhists!*

Gertie and Greta, even though they're technically mother and daughter, have been dancing as "The Little Sisters" at Kling-a-Ding-Diddle's in Quakertown, PA (right near the Q-Mart) since the early 1990s. Their act, however, has always been more sophisticated than a mere tawdry exploitation of their adorable "little person" status—it has consistently featured juggling, fire-dancing, mutual grape-feeding, and all the parlor tricks that normal strippers do. Their wrestling journey has taken them through oil, hot cream, spaghetti, and mud. On special occasions (and for a hefty fee), they have been known to perform a complicated maneuver they call the "Velvet Donkey." They've even graced the silver screen in an X-rated version of midget classic *The Terror of Tiny Town*, performing simulated 69 on one another over a techno remix of "Follow the Yellow Brick Road" that earned them an *AVN* Video Award nomination for Best Simulated 69 Scene by a Mother-Daughter Team of Little People.

But despite such achievements, Gertie and Greta remained more of an underground cult sensation than a pop-culture phenomenon. In contrast, their success has been sudden and massive since the addition of Li'l Gretl. They've been on *Good Morning, America* and *Charlie Rose*. Even ex-president Bill Clinton is said to be a fan. In a word, they are H-O-T.

"Li'l Gretl brings a young, sassy, unpredictable element to the act which, frankly, was missing before," says Dag Sloat, *wunderkind* editor of *Bucks County XXX*, the most successful of an estimated six free publications distributed throughout the Greater Perkiomen Valley's gentlemen's clubs and erotic juice bars. "Unlike Gertie and Greta—who represent more of the classic-rock generation—Li'l Gretl brings a sensibility that is very urban, very hip-hop, very *now*. And the guys just LOVE her. You never know what she'll do next!" Sloat beams. "She'll come out in these crazy outfits—like a man's tie and a fig leaf—and the crowd just goes *wild*."

"WE HAVE SMALL VAGINAS," Gertie Schratweiser, elder stateswoman of the Little Sisters tells me with a wink when I ask her to explain their appeal to averaged-sized men. "Very small, very *tight* vaginas." A warm-yet-stern woman, Gertie corrects me sharply when I refer to her as a midget. "We are DWARVES," she hisses, her eyebrows arched behind Coke-bottle glasses. "And technically, the proper spelling is 'dwarfs,' but *everybody* gets that one wrong. But referring to me as a 'midget' is like calling an Arab an Israeli. It *just isn't done*. We have normal-sized heads. *They're* little from head to toe." She refers to porn star Bridget the Midget as a "self-hating dwarf" and recalls an onstage catfight between the Little Sisters and the notorious Smalltown Midgets from nearby Reading, PA, which culminated in gunfire. When I ask her to pinpoint the basic dispute between midgets and dwarves, she says, "It's good to know your enemies" and demands that we change the subject.

"The Buddha is looking over us, so it's all good," Gertie says philosophically. She recalls the "tough days" before converting to Buddhism when other strippers would pull tricks such as hiding the Little Sisters' dancer's bags on high shelves so they couldn't reach them. "But the Buddha is watching after my bootylicious ass now," Gertie says. "I was stripping when I had my baby, and she was dancing when she had hers. Even though it's always hard being a single mom, the Buddha is taking care of us."

I finally muster the courage to ask her whether the Little Sisters have ever engaged in incest. "Nice ladies don't tell," she says with a demure eyelash flutter. "But I *will* tell you this—Li'l Gretl is pregnant!"

Thanks for the scoop, Gertie! Hope you're still around in 18 years for the follow-up story!

> THEY CALL THEMSELVES "THE LITTLE SISTERS," BUT THEY'RE ACTUALLY GRANDMA, MOTHER, AND DAUGHTER! AND NOT ONLY ARE THEY DWARVES WHO STRIP... THEY'RE ALL BUDDHISTS, TOO!

WE ARE FAMILY!

A NIGHT AT STINKY'S

Upon entering Stinky's Gentlemen's Club near Jantzen Beach, three things occurred to me in rapid numerical succession:

1) There are naked women here;

2) These naked women are the most *unattractive* naked women I've ever seen in my life;

3) These women are so hideous, I'd actually give them *money* to get dressed again.

These three elements...plus the seductive topper—cans of PBR for only *25 cents*—have paradoxically proven to be a magical business potion for the tiny ramshackle club.

Stinky's Gentlemen's Club, which had teetered on the brink of bankruptcy for almost two dozen years, has turned a profit for the past three business years. Last year, it was among Portland's five most profitable strip clubs. This year, the Portland Sex Academy gave Stinky's a Velvet Clit award for "Industry Comeback Story of the Year." Stinky's secret? A deceptively simple marketing strategy encapsulated in an advertising slogan that has burrowed itself within Portland's collective unconscious as if it were a boll weevil nestled fluffily within cotton:

UGLY WOMEN, CHEAP BEER: C'MON, GET STINKY!

The slogan first appeared in a crude ad campaign which blitzkrieged late-night Portland TV stations for eight straight months in 1999. "If you were a night owl who watched TV back then, you couldn't get away from Stinky's," says Jerry LaBuck, a professional cable-TV repairman, amateur media analyst, and regular Stinky's patron. LaBuck, a tall, amiable, somewhat mooselike Lake Oswego resident, chats with me at Stinky's as we slug down frosty bottles of O'Doul's and watch the crowd loudly urge "Melba," a 73-year-old erotic dancer, to put on her clothes. "Soon after those ads started appearing," LaBuck continues, "everywhere you went, it was Stinky's, Stinky's, Stinky's. 'C'mon, get Stinky!' Everybody was saying it. And the cheap beer didn't hurt, either. The ads made it sound like fun. I started coming here a couple of years ago, and now I actually like it *better* than the places with the good-looking chicks. And I don't mind throwing a five-spot at some old buzzard to put on her clothes. Some of these broads are *nasty,* and I just naturally get caught up in the fun of the moment."

Stinky's, nestled amid junkyards and toxic grasslands in a North Portland industrial no-man's land, is one of the city's oldest strip clubs. It was built in 1947 by Tex "Stinky" Reeves, a one-armed boxer and Impressionist painter who is still listed in *The Encyclopedia of Sexual Records* as having The World's Most Sharply Curved Penis, bending a full 23 degrees from stem to stern. Ironically, for the first few decades, Stinky's was renowned for having the most *beautiful* topless dancers on the West Coast. Stinky's became the haunt of high-rolling mobsters and thrill-seeking high-society members seeking classy adult entertainment.

When Tex "Stinky" Reeves was mangled to death by a construction crane in 1974, his son Biff "Smelly" Reeves, a yoga instructor and heroin addict, inherited the business. Through a series of what he called "costly business decisions"—i.e., the repeated decision to buy heroin with money which should have been spent on payroll, supplies, and taxes—Biff nearly drove Stinky's into the ground. Because of his widespread reputation as a "smackhog," the sort of women who gravitated to Stinky's were, to be kind, Ladies of the Lower Orders. Only the most desperate, over-the-hill, unemployable sort of erotic dancers dared apply at Stinky's. Because of this, Stinky's revenues declined for years. The high rollers went elsewhere, replaced by a brooding, shiftless clientele mainly composed of junkyard workers, incontinent old men, and homosexual serial-killing teams.

Things looked grim for the club until one morning late in 1998 when Biff "Smelly" Reeves, walking through some grasslands near Stinky's, was pecked to death by a flock of hostile pelicans. But what may have been a personal tragedy for the Reeves family turned into a business boon for the club.

When Biff's son, Rick "Stank-Ass" Reeves, acquired Stinky's, no one had much hope for the club's future. With 14 felony convictions for drug possession by the time he turned 21, Stank-Ass seemed cut from the same cloth as his father Smelly.

But as the legend has it, while Stank-Ass sat alone in Stinky's late one night after closing time, "zonked out of my gourd from smoking Mexican tar all night," a vision of his grandfather Stinky Reeves appeared to him. "He just walked right up to me at my barstool," Stank-Ass told a reporter for *The Portland Tribune,* "kind of like with ghosts in the movies, where you can sorta half-see through them, and he put his hand on my shoulder. He said to me, 'My boy, you've got some *really* ugly women here. Make it work for you.' And then he was gone. And then I started writing my business plan: Get the ugliest chicks you can find; sell beer at cost; fill the bar with yahoos who get so drunk on cheap beer, they think it's some kind of conceptual hipster *fun* to throw tens and 20s at ugly women to get dressed; and then charge the dancers 50 PERCENT of their tips off the top in order to compensate for the loss I take on beer and overhead. So far, it's been a fucking goldmine. I haven't even had to kick heroin, and I'm *still* making a profit!"

Yeah, Stank-Ass, but you're also providing a *service.* As I leave Stinky's, I realize I've spent only three dollars on beer and am plastered beyond the ability to speak. I've also spent about 20 dollars on the "unstrippers," but I had a good time doing it. As I drive home swerving between lanes, I realize that for at least another day, I don't want to kill anyone.

THE STRIP CLUB WHERE WOMEN ARE PAID TO GET DRESSED

The women come and the women go, filling this small, damp, vaguely oniony-smelling room with stories of their pain. They cry so many tears that their faces melt into a giant, peach-colored, blubbering Everywoman. Their pain is so real, it's painful to listen. These women are here to share their pain with one another...to honor each other's pain...to envy each other's pain...to nurture each other's pain...to multiply that pain until all they feel is pain...and then to talk about that pain over donuts 'n' coffee at a fat male social worker's basement in Southeast Portland every Thursday at 3 p.m.

"Xena" (center of couch) has been dancing in Portland strip clubs for three years. "I had a great childhood," she says. "My parents never hit me or molested me, so sometimes it's hard to communicate with other strippers." Xena is shown here at a What About Us? support group meeting with group moderator Tom Roberts (left) and a fellow unmolested stripper named "Tabasco" (right).

THESE WOMEN, mostly young and attractive, are among an estimated 13 or 14 members of a local sex workers' support group called **What About Us?**, a nonprofit organization whose literature states:

Just because you were never raped or molested doesn't mean you can't feel pain. It doesn't mean you can't imagine what it felt like. It doesn't mean you should be ostracized by other sex workers who've suffered "real" abuse. We are all women, and an essential part of our womanhood is to suffer and then tell everyone about it later.

"NOW I KNOW WHAT IT FEELS LIKE TO BE BLACK," says "Xena," a stripper who dances at Snapper's in Hood River and Bucky Beaver's in Oregon City. Xena's been attending *What About Us?* meetings for nearly two months after suffering what she calls "a miniature-sized nervous breakdown" when other dancers at her club failed to invite her to an all-night slumber party, pizza feed, and clothing swap. "They said they 'forgot' to invite me, but I know why they didn't," Xena says now. "It's because

WHAT ABOUT US?

"Ginseng" (left) has been a lingerie model for only three months but says she's "shocked at the lack of empathy" she receives from other sex workers when she tells them she was never raped or assaulted.

I was never raped or abused. Because I'm happily married and don't do drugs. Because I've never thrown a rock through a boyfriend's window or cut off all my hair when I'm upset. Because I'm the *weirdo*. The outcast. But these *What About Us?* meetings have given me a new outlook on life, and I've come to embrace the idea that my suffering is every bit as precious as theirs, even though their suffering may have been a little more, y'know, *dramatic*. It's still my suffering and it's still important to me."

"I COULD ALMOST CRY when I hear some of the stories these girls tell," Tom Roberts, the *What About Us?* group founder, tells me later as we kayak down the Columbia River under a gorgeous late-spring sunset. An obese man who's perpetually running his tongue along the outside of his teeth, Roberts says he started *What About Us?* after working for two years as a bouncer at a notorious juice bar called The Oyster's Pearl in Molalla. "After a while, I'd see these girls come in, these lost-looking girls, and I could tell just by the way they carried themselves that they had never been molested as children, and that as adults they were tortured by their abuse-free past and didn't want any of the other strippers to know about it. That's when I decided to get involved in helping the nonabused and the underabused."

"Is that so?" I counter. "Several strippers have told me that you run the support group because it's an easy way for you to meet chicks and exploit their emotional vulnerability."

Roberts says nothing. Instead, he makes a loud coughing sound, continues paddling the kayak, and softly breaks wind.

"I HAVE TWO WORDS for these whiny, unmolested, unassaulted bitches: WHAT and EVER," says Fondue, a stripper who boasts of having been sexually, physically, mentally, and spiritually abused by both parents and all four grandparents and is widely known as The Woman Who Brought Naked Spaghetti Wrestling to Portland. "That's right: *Whatever*. Yadda yadda yadda. See ya, wouldn't wanna be ya! I could care less."

"I think you mean to say that you *couldn't* care less," I politely suggest to Fondue in between sips of my Shirley Temple as we sit at the Ship Ahoy bar in Southeast Portland.

"What?"

"You *couldn't* care less. If you '*could* care less,' that implies you must already care some."

"But dude—*I could care less.*"

"I don't think you understand what I'm saying," I tell her.

"Whatever, dude," comes her sharp-tongued retort.

A SUPPORT GROUP FORMS TO ADDRESS THE UNIQUE EMOTIONAL NEEDS OF STRIPPERS WHO WERE NEVER ABUSED AS CHILDREN

THEY ARE THE LOST SHEEP of the sex-worker flock, these unfortunate dames and lasses who suffer discrimination and emotional estrangement due to a lack of compelling, graphic, disturbing, sympathy-engendering "abuse stories" from their past. Our industry should pull together and quit making the nonabused and underabused feel ashamed. While the lion's share of industry workers can recount childhood events that make the most jaded among us blush with horror and envy, some girls weren't nearly so lucky. We all suffer in various ways and degrees, but few forms of suffering can match the suffering one suffers from never having suffered enough.

Exotic Celebrates a *Century* of Oregon's *Sexual Landmarks*

May, 2002 is a milestone in Portland's sex industry...this month marks **100 years** since the city's **first public erotic exhibition** wowed a prudish P-town crowd who huddled within an opium den in a dark alley near Pioneer Square to watch "Dr. Fitzwater's Dancing Ladies" *(pictured at right)* simultaneously reveal what are thought to be **the first eight publicly exposed nipples** in Oregon's history, marking the official **Birth of Portland's Sex Industry.** Amazingly, in the same month (May, 1902), Transylvanian sex vamp **Lili Dentata** *(pictured at left)* moved to Portland and displayed her ample charms in what is thought to be **the first nude photo session** in the city's history. Here at *Exotic,* we celebrate 100 years of P-Town's sex industry by taking a look back at **100 years of sexual "firsts" in the Beaver State.** We hope you enjoy reading it as much as we enjoyed putting it together!

FIRST PENETRATION SCENE

The frame at right is from *Sirens Along the Willamette* **(1924),** a silent movie filmed in **Clackamas** whose routine plot is suddenly interrupted by a 33-minute hardcore sex scene. The actors depicted at right are **Gunnar Jacksnipe & Minerva Palmetto.**

FIRST "69"

This popular oral-sex position, in which each partner is simultaneously pleasuring the other and being pleasured by them, was first performed in Oregon by **Deltoid & Thumbelina Farnsworth** *(right),* a married couple from **Bend** who did the state's first "69" in **1912.**

FIRST GAY MALE ESCORTS

Portland's first "call guys" were **Thales Hambone & Ike Mendax** *(right),* a muscular pair of sex workers who placed what is thought to be the city's first "men seeking men" classified ad in the now-defunct *Portland Beacon* newspaper in **1933.**

FIRST LESBIANS

Shrapna Kunst & Olga Stegosaurus *(left)* were the city's first openly lesbian couple, working as bartender (Shrapna) and short-order cook (Olga) for over 30 years at **Pinkie's** in **St. Johns,** which opened in **1946** and is thought to be the West Coast's first dyke bar.

FIRST POLE DANCE

Although it's now a staple of every erotic dancer's repertoire, Oregon's first pole dance wasn't performed until **1968** by **Belle Jangles** (above), who is shown here "polishing the brass" at **Mugwump's,** a strip club in **Pendleton** which burned to the ground in the early 1970s.

FIRST BREAST IMPLANTS

Oregon's first fake jugs were borne by **Nita Glansworth** (right), a cocktail waitress from **Scappoose** who underwent a crude plastic-surgery operation in **1957** using hot-water bottles. Tragically, the implants began to sag further and further until Glansworth's breasts actually **fell off** in 1964, requiring major reconstructive surgery.

FIRST TOY SHOW

Using a device she playfully referred to as "Thor's Hammer," Norwegian expatriate **Øona Günterson** caused a scandal one summer night in **1972** at **Salty Dave's,** an **Astoria** gentlemen's club. Local citizens, mostly other women, were so outraged that the Astoria City Charter was rewritten to forbid "the public insertion of blunt instruments into human orifices."

FIRST PHONE SEX

Tortilla Clamato (left), a former calypso *chanteuse* from **Argentina,** left her native country in **1963** and briefly set up a phone-sex operation in a **Klamath Falls** bar. Men would pay her two dollars for the right to "talk dirty" with Clamato from a pay phone across the street from the bar. The phone-sex gig proved wildly successful, but she was soon busted by vice cops and spent four days in the Klamath County Jail, where she became a lesbian.

FIRST "ALTERNATIVE" EROTIC PERFORMANCE

Bunny Gazelle & Tisha Crumbcake (above) lay claim to giving, in their words, the city's first "underground conceptual erotic presentation," a six-hour play called **"El Toro, My Lover,"** which debuted downtown at **Flatch's Cove** at Third & Burnside and played for a week in **1981**. The play revolves around a Midwestern farmer's wife and her sexual obsession for a pet bull in her husband's herd. In the final scene, the bull castrates the farmer character and then removes its costume to reveal that it, too, is a woman just like the farmer's wife, whereupon the two engage in lesbian sex. According to playwright Crumbcake, the show "smashed through the stereotypes and barriers erected throughout 5,000 years of patriarchy and raised serious questions about race, gender, and bestiality in Western culture."

FIRST STRIPPER TO BECOME ADDICTED TO CRYSTAL METH

Bambi Cuidado (left) started dancing at **The Tugboat*** in **Swan Island** during the mid-1970s. In **1978**, she snorted her first rail of crystallized methamphetamine, offered to Bambi by her boyfriend at the time, **Jake Yarbles**, a notorious sex offender/biker/leather craftsman/storyteller/meth cook/arm-wrestling champion from **Prineville**. Within weeks, Cuidado was using speed daily. She has continued using crystal meth every day since then and has progressed from snorting it to smoking it to mainlining it. By 1990, she had lost all her teeth. Last year, she was diagnosed with Hepatitis-C. Despite her health problems, she continues to dance at The Tugboat. So does her daughter, **Chi-Chi** and her granddaughter, **Panocha**.

*("Home of the Original Barnyard Burger")

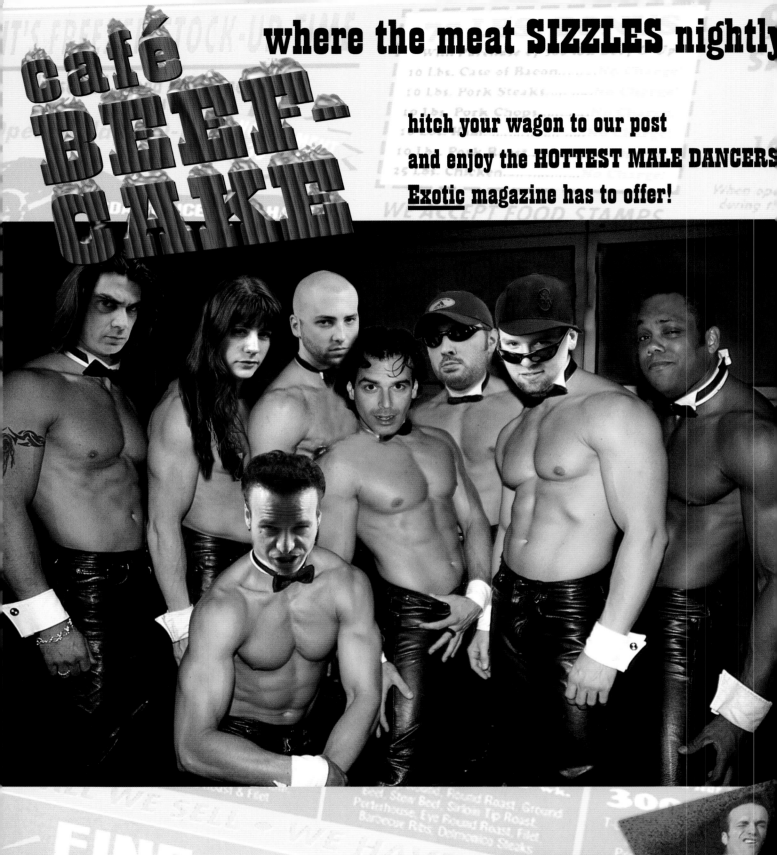

man uses PHOTOSHOP to give himself a bigger penis...

MIRACULOUS PHOTOS of Max Condor before (top) and after (right) he gave himself a bigger penis using the Photoshop software program.

Max Condor of Ketchikan, Alaska, like many other male members of the Chikalit tribe, was born with an exceptionally small penis.

"My thing was so tiny, it's not even proper to call it a penis," Max jokes as we walk down Ketchikan's cold, dusty streets, our senses swirling amid the smells of freshly baked Eskimo Whale Bread and buckets full of fish heads. "It's more like I had a clit with balls. Seriously. It's like, I used to look up at God and say, 'Why did you even bother, dude?'"

Condor says he experienced "a miniature nervous breakdown" one early summer evening during a "nude pool party with some friends" when one of them snapped a Polaroid of him sprawled out on a lounge chair, his measly manhood in full shameful view as if the small pink

Condor took the photo home later that night and, using the popular Photoshop software program loved by millions, he copied a much larger penis from a "gay hunks" website and replaced his own penis with it.

"I decided to superimpose one of those big fat hogs onto my eentsy li'l thing," Condor tells me. "When I saw the finished product, it made me feel better. But the next morning, I woke up with this super-huge boner! I was really packin' some meat! My dick had become as big as I'd made it in the photo!"

We step into an alleyway and Condor shows me his new penis. He isn't lying. It's gigantic.

SCIENTISTS CAN OFFER NO EXPLANATION for how Max Condor was able to give himself a bigger penis using a computer-based image-manipulation program, but there's no denying that he did it. "Max, like many of his tribesmen, used to have what is clinically referred to as a micropenis," says Dr. Augie Saltlick, Condor's family physician since childhood. "Then one day he came rushing breathless into my office, showing me the original picture and then

"Not only did my penis get bigger—it has more *personality*, too!"

a printout of the picture he Photoshopped of himself with a much bigger penis. And during a rigorous physical exam behind locked doors, he revealed to me his newer, gargantuan member. I was shocked, delighted, envious, and tantalized all at the same time! But I can't explain it. Neither can any of my scientist friends. Like you said up there at the beginning of the paragraph, we can offer no explanation for it."

"I CREDIT THE LORD WITH GIVING ME A BIGGER PENIS,"

AMAZING SNAPSHOT of Max Condor and his newer, much bigger, penis.

...and it WORKS!
he actually has a bigger penis! and scientists can't explain it!

fleshy nub was screaming out to be rescued from a giant ocean of fat.

"I saw the picture," Condor tells me, "and when I saw how small my penis looked, I wished that the earth would open up and swallow me whole, almost as if the earth was a giant vagina which I could never satisfy with a penis as frightfully teeny as mine."

Condor tells me as we slowly lick at whale-blubber ice-cream cones while walking through the Ketchikan Downtown Galleria. "Somehow, God was able to shoot that Photoshop picture onto some sort of astral plane or something while I was sleeping...which is sort of the way Santa Claus operates, too...and when I woke up, he gave me the bigger penis I had Photoshopped onto my body."

When I ask Condor why God would be concerned about his genitals, he shrugs and says that he gets "a spiritual feeling that runs through my body late at night when there's no one else around and I take a gander at my new equipment. The reason I think God is behind it all is because not only did my penis get bigger—it has more *personality*, too! I'm not kidding. It has more *spirit*. More *soul*. There's a nobility and a grace to the way this new penis carries itself, and that's why I think it came straight from the Lord."

Max Condor continues to drink heavily and to enjoy an increasingly active social life. Neither Condor nor anyone else has been able to duplicate his results. The makers of the Photoshop software offered no comment because, frankly, we didn't bother to call them.

guide to SUMMERTIME SEXUAL FUN

The heat is on in Oregon, and it's time for us all to sit back, sip a Slurpee, and savor some summery sexual goodness!!! I sure enjoy sex! I sure enjoy summertime! I sure enjoy having fun! I enjoy enjoying myself! And I enjoy putting together these "hot-weather sexual fun tips" for you with the hope that you'll enjoy them, too! Everyone knows that summer was made for sex, fun, and lotsa exclamation points!!!!!!

GET "PUMPED-UP" WITH A "FULL-GENITAL WORKOUT"!

Why do so many Americans become fitness-conscious in the summer? Why do they spend so much money on plastic surgery, tanning booths, exercise equipment, and liposuction? The answer is simple: THEY WANT TO BE MORE SEXUALLY ATTRACTIVE. And so they work on their abs, lats, and delts, huffing and puffing and sweating their way into tip-top physical shape...with one glaring exception. At the end of a workout, rare is the person who "feels the burn" in their genitals. You heard me correctly—in order to be more sexually attractive, people will exercise every muscle BUT their genitals! The "ordinary" muscleman neglects this ever-so-special place. He might have massive, manta-ray back muscles. He might be able to crush cans with his biceps. He might be able to crush walnuts with his neck. But if his penis and scrotum are puny and flabby, what are his chances with the ladies? Thankfully, we now have the **Full-Genital Workout Kit**, which comes complete with barbells, rope, and matching cock and ball rings. Your genitals will thank you—and so will that "special lady"!!!

MANUFACTURER: Nadknockers Unlimited from Walla Walla, WA
PRICE: $99.95

ENJOY A "GENITAL-SHAPED-FOOD PICNIC"!!!

There are two things everyone likes: food and genitals! So why not *combine* the two and enjoy the warm weather by having a picnic composed entirely of food items which in some way are reminiscent of human genitals? C'mon—*treat* yourself! Everyone knows that donuts, peaches, and tacos recall the female private parts...and sometimes "a lovely set of coconuts" is so much more than that...and *don't get me started* about all the food that resembles the male organ! You can choose from among hot dogs, bananas, carrots, pickles, and popsicles just for starters. The mind boggles! The mouth gets sore! Sometimes it seems like everywhere you turn in the supermarket produce section, there's a dick poking you in the face! Imagine the FUN you'll have at the picnic bench, laughing with your friends about all the "oral sex" you're having, while all that the poor folks at the table next to yours can see is that you're eating *lunch!* Ooh, that's *rich!*

RY SOME SUNSCREEN/ MOSQUITO LOTION/ S.T.D. CREAM— IT'S FLAVORED!!!

's a "scorcher" outside today, and you wouldn't be caught dead under that hot soleil without some high-powered sunscreen. Oh, yeah—those pesky "skeeters" are nippin' hard today, so you'd better carry along some mosquito lotion, too. And who knows how many chance sexual encounters are awaiting you at the beach today, so you'd better bring along some STD cream just to be safe, too. Geez, that's a LOT of stuff to carry! But wait, there's a ONE-TUBE solution for all your hot-weather lotioning needs—the **"3-in-1 Summertime Fun Gel"** fights ultraviolet light, mosquitos, and most known sexually transmitted diseases except for the deadly ones! Just find someone to rub it on your back. Then return the favor! And then, as an added treat, you can actually LICK the gel off one another's bodies, because this puppy comes in six exciting FLAVORS! You'll wish that every day came with the threat of skin cancer, malaria, and chlamydia!

MANUFACTURER: Rose City Greaseworks from Portland, OR

PRICE: $8.95

GET WET 'N' WILD WITH A "BACKYARD HIGH-COLONIC LAWN-SPRINKLER PARTY"!!!

Is there anything more fun than a backyard party? Sure there is—a backyard party in hot weather where everyone can run under a lawn sprinkler, giggling like the dickens! But this isn't just any lawn sprinkler, fellas—it provides 1,000 foot-pounds of water pressure that jets up from a hearty pink-plastic tubing device. Just sit on the tubing device for a few seconds, and—*voilá!*—you've given yourself a high colonic! All that meat entombed in your sarcophagus of a colon is instantly BLASTED free! Watch with awe as the black crusty chunks exit your rectum! Not only is it cool, it's cleansing! The **High-Colonic Lawn Sprinkler** also doubles as the world's most powerful prostate massager, delivering an orgasm-inducing 10,000 micro-spurts™ of cool water per second right where you need it the most! You'll pray that summer never ends!

MANUFACTURER: Colonic Solutions from Clifton Heights, PA

PRICE: $499.95

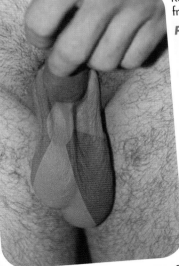

AMUSE YOUR FRENDS WITH YOUR NEW SET OF "BEACH BALLS"!!!

They "won't believe their eyes" when you drop trou and reveal that your scrotum has been lovingly colored like a beach ball! How summery is *that*? This hysterical new gag gift comes with food coloring, a beach-ball stencil pattern, a Scrotal Size Chart so you can determine how large to make the pattern, and an illustrated instruction manual. The **"Beach Balls"** pattern will last 90 days on the average scrotum, meaning you can have a set of colorful, hilarious testicles all summer!

MANUFACTURER: Testicular Technologies from Rahway, NJ

PRICE: $14.95

DEVELOP YOUR CREATIVITY WITH "EROTIC SAND SCULPTURES"!!!

Everything looks better when sculpted into genital shapes, and sand is no exception! Why, just lookit all that dull, flat, beige sand out there just ITCHIN' to be sexualized! As the waves keep pounding, pounding, pounding the sand into soft submission, you can sculpt genital figures that memorialize, at least until high tide comes in, the human instruments of this eternal pounding motion which is, and always will be, the rhythm of life as we know it. Boy, you could really poke an eye out with one of those Giant Sand Penises! And hey—watch out you don't fall into the Giant Sand Vagina!

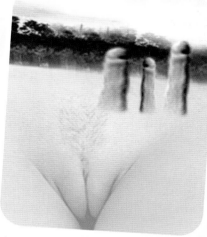

WEIRD SEXUAL PRACTICES

"THE LOCH NESS MONSTER"
One partner defecates in the toilet, doesn't flush, and then forces their partner's head down into the water.

"THE CALIFORNIA BRUSH FIRE"
Holding a lit match to their own anus, the first partner breaks wind, scorching the second partner's pubic hair.

"WEEKEND IN THE DESERT"
The male has sexual intercourse with his partner's armpit.

"THE SONIC BOOM"
Upon reaching orgasm, one partner screams into the other's ear as loudly as they can manage.

"THE SKEET SHOOTER"
The male partner masturbates while standing two feet in front of his female partner, who kneels on the floor, topless. He tries to hit both of her nipples with his cum.

"THE MONKEY GRIP"
The first partner's toes are wrapped around the second partner's penis like a monkey gripping a banana with its feet, resulting in a delightful "footjob."

"THE OLD FAITHFUL"
While having sex, one partner delivers a sharp, unexpected punch to the other's stomach, causing them to vomit.

"THE CHEESE DANISH"
The male squirts his semen into his partner's ear.

"THE THIRD RAIL"
At the moment of climax, one partner grabs the other's hand, forcing their finger into an electrical socket.

"THE KENTUCKY DERBY"
A woman lies naked on her back, holding one fried-chicken drumstick in her mouth and one between her legs. The neighborhood's stray dogs are then let into her room, whereupon they run around her excitedly.

"THE CHIMNEY SWEEP"
Sexual intercourse while both partners have toothbrushes inserted bristle-side-up into their rectums.

"THE DEADBEAT DAD"
In the middle of lovemaking, the male dismounts, gets dressed, leaves, and never calls the woman again.

...AND HOW TO PERFORM THEM

MYTH: Good sex always involves having a simultaneous orgasm with your partner.

FACT: Good sex always involves having an orgasm before your partner does.

MYTH: You can get AIDS from sharing toilet seats, saliva, or utensils.

FACT: You can only get AIDS by sharing these items with my last girlfriend.

MYTH: You can tell a man has a big penis by looking at his feet.

FACT: You can tell he has a big penis if he's ugly, has no money, and still has women hanging on him.

MYTH: Women prefer men with big penises.

FACT: Women prefer tiny penises, referring to them as "cute" and "adorable."

MYTH: Venereal disease is cured if the man has sex with a virgin.

FACT: Sex with a virgin will only cure a man's emotional problems.

MYTH: It takes women longer to reach orgasm than men.

FACT: Women cannot have orgasms, no matter how long I try.

MYTH: I don't have any symptoms of an STD, therefore I don't have an infection.

FACT: Under a microscope, your crotch is a leper colony.

MYTH: Masturbation causes hairy palms, insomnia, impotency, lack of concentration, and blindness.

FACT: Scientists have known for decades that masturbation causes none of these things. It will, however, give you herpes.

MYTH: Most people with disabilities cannot have sexual relationships.

FACT: Many disabled people are able to have vibrant, fulfilling sex lives, but that doesn't mean I want to watch.

MYTH: In gay relationships, one person always takes the role of the woman, while the other partner plays the man.

FACT: Gender roles are never fixed in gay relationships, although one partner always plays the "mean traffic cop" while the other one pretends he's the "speeding motorist."

MYTH: Only homosexuals practice anal sex.

FACT: Only homosexuals practice anal sex with gerbils.

MYTH: Women become lesbians because they have had bad or negative sexual experiences with men.

FACT: Women become lesbians only because they're sexually unappealing to men.

MYTH: You can tell whether someone's a homosexual merely by looking at them.

FACT: You can't really tell whether someone's a homosexual until they start talking.

MYTH: You can't get pregnant during your period.

FACT: You can get pregnant while menstruating, but the baby will never stop bleeding.

MYTH: If your partner fantasizes about someone else during sex, they are not interested in you sexually.

FACT: Although it's emotionally painful when a partner reveals they've been fantasizing about someone else, it doesn't necessarily mean they aren't attracted to you; all it means is that they're much more attracted to someone else.

SEXUAL MYTHS
THE TRUTH ABOUT SEVERAL COMMONLY HELD MISCONCEPTIONS REGARDING HUMAN SEXUALITY

PUG PORN

inside the sinister, glamorous, and lucrative underworld of "pugnographic" cinema

THE SMALL BEAST TWISTS AND GRUNTS AND SQUEALS under the hot camera lights in this cheap motel room while two well-hung human studs put her through the motions. One man stands in the front, one in the rear, sharing their massive manhood with the pint-sized canine. The tiny ogre-faced house pet looks off-camera as if seeking help, panting and howling, grinding and barking, bringing these two men to the foothills of unparalleled bestial delights. Her diminutive-yet-well-muscled haunches straddle the purplish member of the fellow who rides her "doggy style," her compact pug womb choking his man-meat like the tight skin of a big baloney sausage, delivering a level of suction and friction that no human woman can hope to offer. The dog's wide-yet-shallow mouth struggles to contain the other man's throbbing Horn of Love as it prods and pokes and shoves deeper into a throat more suited for Milk Bones than human penises.

The raw, tangy smell of animal sex—human and canine—swirls through the motel room as if generated by a Glade Plug-In™ air freshener. The sweat of human testicles mingles with the juices of a 20-pound pug bitch's vagina, and the pungent intergender, interspecies aromas drive everyone in the room—including the film crew and yours truly, a humble reporter seeking the truth about pornography and its relevance to human spirituality—to disrobe and begin wildly masturbating. Our circle jerk tightens nooselike around the object of our lust, the sourpussed, smushy-faced, rotten little "Chinese Bulldog," while we humans begin a rhythmic chant of "woof, woof" as if we were audience members during a spirited taping of *The Late Show With Arsenio Hall*.

Although we pelt her fawn torso with cum bullets, the pug looks up at us with a wide-open mouth that curls upward at the corners as if she's smiling. She takes our loads like a trouper, and there is something in her expression which vaguely taunts us as if to say, "Is that all you got, Master?"

The pug in question, "Lulu," is a veteran of over eight dozen hardcore adult films featuring live sex acts between humans and pugs. The most recent installment of Lulu's popular video series, *Take it Like a Bitch*, received an *Adult Video News* Award for "Hottest Human/Canine Anal Scene." Although she is barely three years old, Lulu has spent most of her adult life in motel rooms like these, with camera crews like these, taking it in every hole from adult-film actors such as these.

"And she never complains," beams *Take it Like a Bitch* video *auteur* Günter Spätzl, who first spotted Lulu at a puppy farm in Chatsworth, California, and has since groomed her—along with "Bitsy Mae" and the legendary pug whore "Snugglebunny"—into one of the top three female pugnographic film stars in the world. "She never asks for money, she isn't afraid to do black guys, and I know she isn't going to find religion one day and just up and testify against me to Congress," Spätzl says as I sign a model-release form allowing him to use my masturbation scene in Lulu's upcoming video showcase, *Bitch Looks Like a Lady*. "She is the essence of a professional. She's everything an adult-film director could want in his talent."

Spätzl's film *oeuvre*, which includes titles such as *Pugs Gone Wild*, *Flat Face/Tight Ass*, and *Daddy's Got a Bone-Bone*, all fall under the umbrella of "pugnography," a term used to describe a recent explosion of pornographic films depicting interspecies sex between humans and pugs. "Pugs are the perfect canine adult-film stars," Spätzl explains. "Their small size makes them inexpensive to feed, and their ample musculature allows them to endure rigorous sexual activity with a minimum of wear-and-tear. Plus, consumers think they're adorable. They aren't some big scary Doberman that's going to make your average porn consumer feel inadequate, and they aren't so tiny—like a Chihuahua—that a few righteous reamings are going to kill the poor little thing. I've tried other dogs, and no other breed guarantees a hot sex scene better than a pug. It's like they were born to fuck."

"I'd rather fuck a pug than a two-legged bitch any day. The only downside of sex with pugs is with the blowjobs. They tend to bite a little."

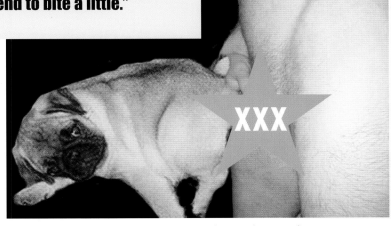

"PEOPLE CALL ME NASTY NAMES all the time because of my film work with pugs," says Steed Bronson, a tanned steroid casualty with a 23-inch penis and an extensive history of starring in pugnographic features. "I've heard 'em all—'pug fucker,' 'puppy lover,' 'doggie dicker'—and after a while, the names just don't bother me anymore. I'm comfortable with my sexuality, and I'm grateful for the opportunity to bone some of the world's hottest pugs."

As we sit in his hot tub sipping Mimosas and watching *Days of Our Lives,* I ask Bronson why he prefers working with pugs over human actresses. "Three reasons," he says, half-coughing as he passes me a joint of PCP-laced marijuana. "First off, they don't speak English. It's not like they're going to ask for your cell-phone number or want a relationship or start bitching you out about how you watch too much football and spend too much time with your friends. Second, I know these bitches are clean—human STDs and canine STDs aren't transmissible between species. Whereas I wouldn't fuck a human female porn star without wearing a scuba-diving outfit, I can power-drill as many pugs as I want without having to wear a condom."

We pause, basking in the champagne, Angel Dust, and therapeutic hot bubbling water. "So what's the third reason?" I finally ask him.

"Tight pussy," he says, winking. "REALLY tight pussy, bro. I'd rather fuck a pug than a two-legged bitch any day. The only downside of sex with pugs is with the blowjobs. They tend to bite a little."

"I AM SHOCKED, APPALLED, OUTRAGED, nauseated, sickened, inflamed, infuriated, and imbued with a sense of bloodthirsty righteous homicidal intent toward all pig bastard humanoids who peddle pug flesh for profit," says Tammy Merkin, director of REPUGNANT, a grass-roots organization which lobbies against pugnography and, according to its Mission Statement, "seeks to abolish, now and for time immemorial, the sexual exploitation of pugs and, by extension, all cute little doggies and kitty-cats."

"I sleep with my pugs," says

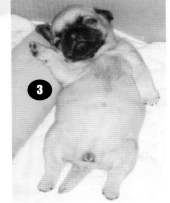

Merkin as we nibble on a coconut-shrimp platter at the Denny's on MLK, "but I don't, you know, SLEEP with my pugs. I see them as warm beings, as caring beings, as loving beings—as beings who are every bit as spiritual as humans, and sometimes even more so, especially because they aren't leaving you every five minutes like a goddamned *man* does—but I draw the line, and I call the cops, when pugs start being treated as *sexual* beings. I believe the Goddess made humans to have human sex with other humans, and for pugs to have pug sex with other pugs, and it grieves Goddess greatly to see humans having sex with pugs, or, even worse, for pugs to have sex with humans."

"How do you propose to stop the problem?" I ask, using a fork to dislodge a fragment of shrimp shell stuck between my teeth.

"Castrate everyone involved in the pugnography industry," Merkin replies without missing a beat. "I'm talking *everyone*—actors, directors, crew members, all the way down to the sickos who stock these titles in their stores and the worthless pieces of darn crap who rent these videos and achieve sexual release thereby. Castrate them all. Get a big dirty meat cleaver and just WHOOSH!—hack off their boy parts. Toss 'em in a dumpster and let a bunch of alley cats just chew on their dismembered guy pieces."

"Anything more constructive than ritual castration?" I ask her, running my fingers through her hair and smacking my lips like a randy mule.

"Sure," she shrugs. "I'd suppose you'd have to kill them all afterwards."

I grow skeptical of her agenda and, indeed, her sanity. "I mean, I've never heard a pug complain about it," I challenge her, "and it's common knowledge that a female pug's vagina will swell in such a manner that a man's penis will get stuck there until the bitch reaches orgasm. If the dog cums, and if she gets a fresh bowl of food and water in the deal, how can you say she's being exploited? Don't we occupy a loftier position in the food chain than pugs, and if so, isn't it the human porn actors who are being degraded here rather than the pugs?"

"It matters not who's being degraded here," Merkin says coyly while slipping me her cell-phone number and a crude sexually themed drawing on a piece of tattered napkin. "As long as living creatures are being degraded somewhere, I'll have a purpose in life."

Those wishing to help end the sexual exploitation of pugs in our lifetime can send cash donations via PayPal to jg@jimgoad.net.

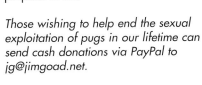

THE NEW (smushed-up) FACE OF BESTIALITY PORNO (clockwise from left) **1. Horny male pug studs await their turn during an all-day shoot with a blonde human adult-film starlet... 2. Tired female pug-porn actress is "fluffed" as she awaits eight hours more of filming under the hot lights... 3. "Bambi Sue,"** title character in **The World's Biggest Anal Pug Gang Bang,** relaxes after taking more than 100 cocks in her ass over the course of 11 grueling hours—a new World Record for a pug!

interview with a

MALE PROSTITUTE

spike "daddy biscuits" fenster:
keepin' it real on portland's mean streets

Daddy Biscuits is a Portland sex-industry legend. He's been peddling his ample manhood on downtown Burnside since Reagan was president. Although we all know him as Daddy Biscuits, he was born Harlan "Spike" Fenster about 30 years ago "somewhere in the Midwest." He came to Portland in the mid-'80s looking for "some fun," and he's been a jovial, easily recognized fixture in the downtown sex scene ever since.

And though he's rumored to wield his mast with a professional's finesse, his skills extend far beyond the boudoir. This is one talented ho we're talking about. His huge, misshapen penis recently starred in *Biscuits 'n' Gravy*, an interracial porno starring actress Gravy Jones. He writes erotic fiction "in a Goth style" and is co-editor of a zine called *'BOUT TIME!!!*, which features nude pictorials of girls who've turned 18 within the last month. He also finds the time to host empowerment workshops, working with other sex activists on behalf of political rights for male prostitutes.

I caught up with Daddy Biscuits at the Subway sandwich store at Broadway and Burnside. Over lunch, we covered a range of topics germane to male prostitution specifically and sex-industry workers generally. I found him to be an engaging, candid interview subject. He seems happy with where he is in life.

But life for one of P-Town's better-known male escorts isn't all fun 'n' games. His eager smile tends to mask a darker, possibly vicious side. He refused to talk about when the FBI shut down his website, DaddyBiscuits.com. "I didn't know the girls were *that* young," is all he'll say now. He also threatened to end the interview when I mentioned the notorious melee which broke out at a local strip club after a visibly drunken Daddy Biscuits interrupted a female dancer's set, commanding the stage and launching into a harangue about how the industry discriminates against male dancers. *(Ed.'s note: Although Daddy Biscuits says he "would like to dance professionally" sometime in the future, he currently only attends Portland strip clubs as a client.)*

Is it true that your father was also a male prostitute?
Daddy Biscuits: Yeah, Big Buck Fenster was his name. Turned thousands of tricks throughout the Northwest. Good man, even though he did some bad things to me. I cried the day he died. My daddy was a male prostitute, and his daddy before him. What, I'm so special and cool that I have to find another line of business?

What about rumors that you were sexually abused by your father?
Most of them are probably true. Daddy wasn't a saint, OK? But we mended our bridges before he died. Worse than anything he ever did was the gang-raping I got at the hands of my uncles and cousins one night during the harvest festival. That scarred me for life. Turned me into a fag for a while, too, but I'm not a fag anymore.

How'd you get the nickname "Daddy Biscuits"?
Because I eat a lot of biscuits. But lately I've been using Metabolife and dropped about 30 pounds. I'm not as fat as I used to be, that's for sure.

Didn't you just become a "daddy" in the literal sense?
Yeah, my son Festus Fenster is two months old. I'm going to try my best to keep him out of the porno industry.

How much money do you make as a sex worker?
Some nights I go home with five bucks, sometimes as much as a hundred. It all depends. It's not as easy to make money as they make it look on the TV. Quite honestly, male prostitution isn't as cool as people think. And sometimes, when conditions get bad, it's hard for me to maintain a sex-positive attitude.

What *won't* you do with a client?
I really don't like blowing guys, but if I have to, I have to. But it's not like I enjoy it or anything. I'll do anal and interracial, but not at the same time. But otherwise, I'm pretty wide open. Fat chicks, old chicks, even large groups of guys if I'm drunk enough—I'll do 'em all, so long as they have money! When things get really bad, I'll do almost anything for a pack of smokes. Or free beer is even better. Just buy me a six-pack of Hamm's cans, and I'm good to go. That shit turns me into a real boner machine.

Describe the moment when you most felt, "I wish I wasn't a male prostitute."
There was this time when I was slipped the date-rape drug at a local dance club. What happened after that was pretty bad.

How does it feel to be a male in an industry dominated by females?
Lonely a lot, sometimes, if you want to know the truth. Some of the things the girl prostitutes say about me hurt my feelings, too, sometimes.

What do you do when you're not doing sex work?
I have hobbies. I make a lot of chicken and salmon jerky in my home dehydrator. See, I don't limit myself to the beef like most guys do. I'm all about the jerky, not just the beef.

What is your stance on terrorism?
I'm against it.

Are there things about you that might surprise us?
I have a passion for Native American pottery. I'm also an Aries. And I like cheese. I'll put it on anything!

What is your motto?
"I know what you want—and I've got it!"

Have you ever been exposed to any STDs as a result of your work?
I got a case of the shingles once.

Any advice to young male prostitutes out there?
Just keep turnin' your tricks and swingin' your dicks, you know? Really, just keep to it and you'll make it in this business, guys. There's plenty to go around, trust me. There will always be money out there for good cock. Good cash for good cock, that's the way of the world. And maybe get yourself a few different costumes, too, because the clients seem to like that.

"I'll do anal and interracial, but not at the same time."

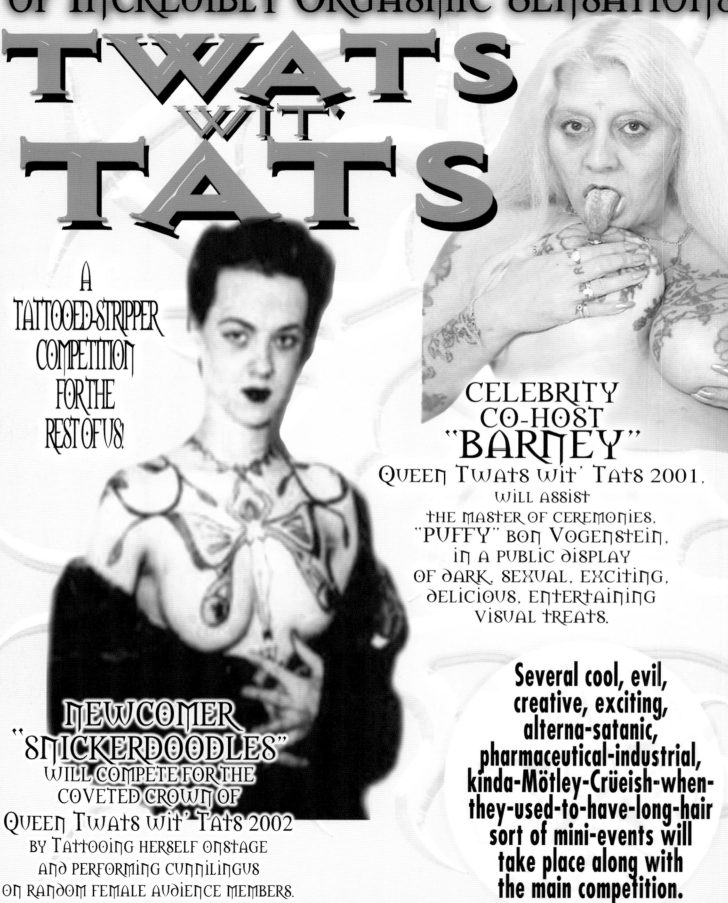

by JOHN BON VOJIRELLI

alcoholic titty

Welcome Back, Pornland, to Destruction and Perversion...With Really Cool, Moody, Rock 'n' Roll Lighting and Lots of Leather Hats

I'm glad to see you all made it through another month and another round of this endless circus of sex, drugs, and rock 'n' roll that is life as we know it in *Alcoholic Titty*. I'm here to piss you off, because I thought it was cool...and I mean in a cool way, not in an asshole way, although it's sometimes cool to be an asshole, don't get me wrong, and anybody who knows me, and a lot of people in this local industry know me, knows that I can be an asshole from time to time, but in a *rock 'n' roll,* '80s-metal-video asshole kind of way rather than just a plain asshole...but as I was saying, my full name is **Baron Lord Don Jon Bon Vojirelli**, widely renowned as one of the most *stylish* pornoad sales representatives in the greater Portland area, and I'm here to piss you off because I thought it was cool when people got pissed off at the stuff **Goad** writes, so if Goad could do it and be cool, I figured I could do it and be cool, too, and so the birth of an Evil New Cool Thing was...um...born.

I like controversy. Controversy is cool. Or maybe it's not cool. It all depends on who's signing my paycheck and what they want to hear. I've got a lot of money behind me now, so controversy isn't very cool to me these days.

You see, I'm not much for consistency. I'm not too big on loyalty. I'll say anything to anybody if I think it will benefit me. My modes of aggression are very bitchlike, indirect, and dishonest. Once you peel off my *Phantom of the Opera* mask, there's really not much in the way of a soul there. I'm not a dumb guy, but I'm a staggeringly *shallow* guy. And it is this emptiness within me, this conscienceless black expanse of pure anti-integrity, which makes me perfectly suited for life in this industry.

I'll have a great time for a few months—none of my old friends, but lots of expendable cash. And then the guys who hired me will realize what a complete fuckup I am, what a scorched-earth disaster my life is. A million dollars a month wouldn't turn *this* train wreck around.

I remember telling Goad about my sellout on the day I signed the contract. I told him that one of the angles I might play is to just milk these new guys for six months or so, drive the local version of their stupid little generic free porn magazine into the ground, and walk away with a lot of cash.

Of course I'll deny it if they ask me about it. How hard is it to lie?

See, even though they're giving me all this money, I'll stab *them* in the back, too.

That's just the way I am. That's just the way life is here in the dirty, lyin', puffy-shirted streets of *Alcoholic Titty*.

◆◆◆◆◆◆◆◆

More Hilarious Stuff About That Dude Who Puts Goldfishes in His Blender

It's 3 a.m. and I'm really fucked-up and I just got back from playing that "Lick my pussy AND my crack" song about 20 times at the club where I DJ, and the magazine's going to press in about six hours and everyone's waiting for me to finish, and I'm really running out of ideas for my column, so I'm going to write some more about **That Dude From That Club Who Puts Goldfishes in Blenders**. He recently wrote me this letter:

Dude:
I broke up with another girlfriend recently, and she really pissed me off, and it just so happened that she had a pet goldfish, too, so I took the goldfish and put it in a blender and turned it on and killed it.
Everybody was crackin' up down at the club when I told them about it.

Thanks for your comments, Goldfish Dude, and here's hoping you don't break up with any more girlfriends any time soon so that we don't have to witness any more tragic, unnecessary shedding of innocent goldfish blood.

That is, until next month when I'm fucked-up at 3 a.m. and need to fill column space.

◆◆◆◆◆◆◆◆

The Top Ten Strippers I Wanna Throw Ceramic Gargoyles At

A lot of HOT sexual activities featuring a lot of COOL people are coming to a BUNCH of clubs near you!

If you know this industry as well as I do, you'd know that there are a lot of people in this industry who don't understand this industry as well as I do. Considering the fact that I have a lot of money behind me now, I think I'm qualified to comment about the people who *think* they know this industry but really don't know this industry at all, at least not as well as they think they do. Some people actually know the industry *better* than they think they do, but I'm not talking about those people. I'm talking about the opposite ones, the ones who don't know the industry as well as they think they do, and those are the ones who make being in this industry a living hell for people like *me,* knowing this industry as well as I do.

◆◆◆◆◆◆◆◆

Has Anybody in the Office Seen My Digital Camera?

First off, I'd like to thank whatever bouncers at **Dante's** hoisted me on their shoulders and carried me up to the office after I vomited all over everyone and passed out inside **Bybee**'s birthday-party limousine a couple of months back. But when I woke up on the back-office couch the next morning, I noticed that my camera was gone. Maybe I left it in the limo. Or maybe at some club we visited that night. I'm not saying someone at *Exotic* stole it, but I *do* have my enemies, so I'm not ruling that out. And it's not like the memory card on that camera was full of nude self-portraits or anything.

◆◆◆◆◆◆◆◆

New Puffy Shirt Purchased for Ink-N-Pink 2003

All you rock 'n' roll vampires who enjoyed the **puffy shirt** I wore during the first three annual **Ink-N-Pink** competitions will be saddened to know that the shirt was irreparably **damaged** during a street altercation involving me, my girlfriend, and several members of a Greek Olympic kayaking team. But everything's cool now…I was able to snag a newer, shinier, *puffier* puffy shirt at **Swashbuckler's** boutique, where I buy most of my alterna-pirate gear. The shirt will be unveiled next year at **Ink-N-Pink 2003: Resurrection of the Puffy Shirt.**

◆◆◆◆◆◆◆◆

Strip Clubs That Suck Because They Won't Give Me Free Drinks Anymore

So I'm pounding down a few boilermakers at **The Brontosaurus Room** out in Gresham, thinking about whether or not I should buy a new pair of cheetah-skin creepers, and I ask **Filbert** the bartender there for another free drink, and he says that I've already had more than my quota since they haven't bought an ad from me in a couple of months anyway, and it got me to thinking about how crazy life in this industry is.

I mean, think about it: I came here years ago with the dream of one day having a stripper girlfriend, and I was able to make that dream come true. Not only that—now I'm even able to play music and announce the *names* of the chicks who take their clothes off, and I'm able to take *pictures* of them and publish them. It's really been quite the porno odyssey for me. Isn't that profound?

But even though I've known Filbert for years, here he is cutting me off from any more free drinks. Sometimes I feel like the people in this industry don't have any loyalty at all.

◆◆◆◆◆◆◆◆

Alcoholic Titty Syndicated in Free Russian and Korean Sex Mags

All my loyal local porno-lovin' slaves will be proud to learn that *Alcoholic Titty*, this very column you're reading right now, is being syndicated in two—count 'em, two—free foreign sex magazines: **Boobs 'n' Borscht** out of Moscow and **Tae Kwan Ho's** from Seoul, Korea. That's right, yours truly, Baron Jonathan von Spookenburger, is now worldwide, baby…meaning that dudes who like to see hot chicks take their clothes off—whether those dudes are little and yellow or medium-sized and white…are reading my deranged ramblings. Cool! That kicks Korean and Russian ass!

◆◆◆◆◆◆◆◆

I Have a Lot of Money Behind Me Now

In case you weren't listening the first couple of times I said it.

◆◆◆◆◆◆◆◆

I Whine Like a Bitch During Sex

At least that's what the kitty-cat from the jack shack upstairs said.

◆◆◆◆◆◆◆◆

My Girlfriend Threw Her Drink at Me Last Night

At the club where we were watching some chicks strip, and it really pissed me off.

◆◆◆◆◆◆◆◆

I Broke Up With My Girlfriend

Last night after she threw that drink on me. That was the last straw. Everything that has gone wrong in my life for the past couple of years has been her fault. It's over. I know I've said this before, but this time I really mean it.

◆◆◆◆◆◆◆◆

I Made Up With My Girlfriend

This morning. I really think she's changed this time.

◆◆◆◆◆◆◆◆

Dude, Our Rights Are Being Threatened

The Founding Fathers of this country shed some serious fuckin' blood so that we could have all the tattooed-stripper competitions and table dances we wanted. You see, back in colonial times, the British were trying to take away our porno, and they were charging stuff like really heavy taxes where you had to do crazy, unfair shit like tip the King a dollar for every dollar you tipped a girl at the rack, and things like where girls weren't even allowed to dance topless on the Lord's Day, and so one day all the guys in the colonial sex industry said, "Fuck this shit, we'll just break away and have our *own* sex industry," and so I think it's really fucked-up that nearly…uhh…200 years later, we still have to fight for the same rights that we thought were already fought for.

The Powers That Be are driven by only one thing—money. Actually, that's the only thing that drives me, too, but I'm driven by it for cooler reasons than they are. And I think it's fucked-up that they're trying to take away our hard-earned, God-given rights to enjoy hot pussy and cold beer at reasonably priced establishments. I think we, as an industry, need to stand up and fight. Fight for your freedom. Fight for your 2-Fer Tuesdays. Fight for the right to pay for sex because you couldn't get laid through the normal channels. Fight for the right to be cool and to wear cool clothes.

◆◆◆◆◆◆◆◆

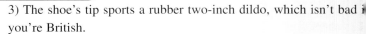
CONSPIRACY SUX

IS THIS VIDEOTAPE FOR REAL? The SUX offices recently received a videotape of the infamous bloodthirsty Puerto Rican night creature the CHUPACABRA forcefully grabbing legendary porn star JENNA JAMESON's arm while Jameson is clearly trying to walk away. Nasty rumors have swirled around the industry for years regarding violence in Jameson and the Chupacabra's tumultuous love affair. Their relationship heated up on the set of 1997's *Fuck Me Like Bigfoot* and has seen its way through one marriage, two children, a divorce, and finally, a restraining order against the Chupacabra. The video shows Mr. Chupacabra stalking Jameson during her recent visit to Barbados. He is seen watching her with binoculars as she suns herself topless on the beach; sitting behind a potted plant while Jenna eats at a seafood restaurant; and following her as she shops for souvenirs. In the frame captured at right, Chupacabra is grabbing Jameson and pleading with her to not call his probation officer to report a restraining-order violation. "Baby, please, please, just talk to me for ONE MINUTE!" Chupacabra is seen begging Jameson on the tape. "We can work this out, baby. PLEASE, baby! Let me see the kids, baby! It doesn't have to get ugly like this!" Jameson was able to summon police, and the Chupacabra was whisked away to the drunk tank. The latest industry gossip is that Jameson has shacked up with a new lover, THE ABOMINABLE SNOWMAN.

GADGETRY SUX

Dildonics Unlimited from Birmingham, England, is the talk of the Sex Gadgets Industry with their new DILDO SHOE PHONE, a sure-fire winner for the North Portland stripper. This delightful contraption serves three purposes:
1) It's a fully functional cell phone, so your meth dealer is never more than a speed-dial away;
2) It's a high-heeled ladies' shoe, sturdy enough for those runways along Killingsworth;
3) The shoe's tip sports a rubber two-inch dildo, which isn't bad if you're British.

The phone comes in two colors: Puckered Anus Magenta and Lime Green. Dildonics Unlimited has scored with another winner here and one lucky SUX reader will win their own Dildo Shoe Phone if they can guess whether or not I dye my hair.

MY LIFE SUX

Lately I've been trying to jump-start my flagging ad sales by trying to smear **EXOTIC**'s reputation. Many of those who know me realize that this is merely guilt-projection, since I've hardly been an angel. While I'm out making my rounds, getting all snootily British about how sleazy my competitor is for publishing SATIRICAL articles, I certainly don't tell advertisers about my *own* arrest for domestic violence in 1992. When I cluck my tongue about an OBVIOUS SPOOF that *Exotic* did called "Adult Films Made by Children," I neglect to tell people that I've had sex with an underaged girl when I was almost 40. Or that I've stolen *Exotic*'s racks all while spreading false rumors about *Exotic*'s staff. Or about the time I attacked someone with a butcher knife in Washington. I definitely won't show THIS *Exotic* article to advertisers while shaking my head about the immorality of Faillace's posse. The truth is, you'd have to look far and wide to find an innocent person in the porn industry—or anywhere, for that matter. And it's usually the ones doing all the accusing who have the dirtiest hands.

The truth is, I'm obsessed with Frank. In a gay way, probably. He's younger than me. His magazine is much bigger than mine. He snags much more pussy than I do. People actually LIKE Frank, while everyone thinks I'm a nebbishy weasel. I love Frank so much, I want to become him, and cloning *Exotic* was my way of becoming Frank. But *SUX* isn't really a clone of Frank's magazine. In fact, *SUX* isn't really a magazine at all. It's a collection of sex-industry ads surrounded by the flattest, blandest, most faceless cardboard editorial filler you could imagine. It is a magazine distinctly devoid of an editorial personality. A robot could have made it. In producing *SUX,* I have managed to create something which is as soulless as I am.

I gotta admit it, I like me some porno. I enjoy looking at all those fancy gals with their big boobies bopplin' out all over the place and their vaginas all spread-open like the mouth of a moray eel, ready to take me inside of itself and show me the sort of rootin'-tootin' night on the town that I haven't seen in a long, long time. I like to look at these fillies' poopers, all round and bouncy and soft, imagining that one day I'll be actually able to insert parts of my body into a girl's derrière without someone calling the cops.

I'm proud to the point of robustness at the fact that I currently use my credit card to subscribe to over three dozen Internet porno sites. I spend more on porno every month than I do on rent, and looking at the pictures of these fine ladies gives me a tingling sense of warmth, community, and a very strong idea of what a vagina actually looks like.

Until quite recently, I've never been disappointed with my porno purchases. Usually, these cool porno websites deliver exactly what they promise—"AborigineNudes.com" features thousands of photos of HOT aborigine women frolicking in their natural element and playing with beach balls...."MormonTwats.com" boasts several galleries of discreet ladies from Utah having polygamous sex with their bearded hubbies while several delighted farm animals watch from afar....And my current favorite, "CafeteriaWoman.org," is the Net's premier location for tasteful naked pictorials of middle-aged women who work in high-school cafeterias.

So let's just say I was more than a little peed-off when I recently subscribed to this "SuicideGirls.com" thing, only to discover that it doesn't have a SINGLE picture of a chick actually committing suicide.

That's right. You heard me correctly, mister. This isn't like some sort of Emergency Broadcast System test where they pretend there's a nuclear war but they're just making sure that all the equipment works. This is the God's honest truth, yo: All of *les jeunes filles* on this bogus website are ALIVE 'N' KICKIN' and doing quite well, thank you very much, and not ONE of them has committed suicide like the advertising materials promised me.

I signed up for a subscription with the best of intentions. "*Cool,*" I thought to myself, "I don't mind shelling out 48 bucks a year to see lots of hot chix swallowing poison and slitting their wrists and jumping from buildings and letting their car run with the windows rolled up. That's easily worth four bucks a month for all the pleasure it would bring me."

But I was duped. Swindled. Hoodwinked. Hornswoggled. They pulled the wool over my eyes and sold me some oceanfront property in Kansas. They knew what they were doing all along, and

I'm sure they're sitting somewhere in their cushy offices with bean-bag chairs, glass-top coffee tables, and secretaries with push-up bras serving all the snacks you can eat, laughing at my misfortune and waiting for the next sucker to come along.

I mean, a lot of these girls are really cute, and they even feature several naked minorities, which I didn't even know was legal. Sure, they're young and skinny, but give 'em a few years and a few turkey dinners and they'll blow up real good and look like actual women. Seriously, if any of them were to come up to me on the street and say, "Howdy, big boy—you wanna slip on back to my place and plop your wiener inside of me until I scream and holler and say, 'Hey, now, that feels kinda good?'," I'd definitely say, "Yeah" and even try to buy them some tasty beverages as we headed back to her crib. I'm nice that way. I'm nice like spice in a bowl of rice.

But I don't like being played like a barnyard fiddle, and that's exactly what I feel like—a freakin' barnyard fiddle. An angry barnyard fiddle. A barnyard fiddle that seeks justice, compensation, restitution, and a sense of fair play.

Instead, I am left with a mossy, grainy, somewhat grapefruitlike taste in the roof of my mouth. It is the bitter taste of betrayal. These chicks can talk the talk, but they don't walk the walk, and they definitely aren't committing suicide like the ads say. This is false advertising, and SuicideGirls.com is filled to the brim with poseurs who, I hate to say it, probably won't EVER commit suicide until the authorities get involved and force them to either shut down or deliver on their promise.

I want a refund.

396 # of suicidegirls, late September 2004

0 # of suicidegirls who've actually committed suicide, late September 2004

suicidegirls.com
all girls, no suicide
what's up with THAT?!?

MY MUSCULAR ASS

I FIRST HEARD THE PHRASE "MY MUSCULAR ASS" IN PRISON (OF COURSE) WHILE AN INMATE WHOSE REAL NAME WAS FRODO (NATURALLY) WAS READING ME A HOT SEXY LETTER HE INTENDED TO SEND TO A FEMALE PEN PAL. AMID THE TYPICAL CONVICT-PORNO-LETTER PASSAGES WHERE HE HAS HER STRADDLING HIS (UNDOUBTEDLY) 13-INCH COCK, SHE GRABS LUSTILY ONTO HIS MUSCULAR ASS. I THOUGHT "MY MUSCULAR ASS" WAS THE SILLIEST THING I'D EVER HEARD, AND IT EPITOMIZED THE INESCAPABLY GOOFBALL TRAPPINGS OF NEARLY ALL CHEESY PORNO FICTION.

EXASPERATED TO THE POINT OF SPITTING BLOOD AT THE INANE "EROTIC FICTION" SPAT FORTH BY MY PREVIOUS EDITORS AT *EXOTIC*, I STARTED A COLUMN CALLED "MY MUSCULAR ASS" INTENDED TO LAMPOON SUCH WRITING. THE ONLY RULE WAS THAT EACH STORY HAD TO CONTAIN THE PHRASE "MY MUSCULAR ASS." WELL, THAT SCHEME ONLY LASTED FOR THREE INSTALLMENTS. THE FINAL TWO COLUMNS PARODIED A PAIR OF THE MAGAZINE'S FEMALE "WRITERS."

1. A SIMPLE COMPLAINT

I awoke this morning with a foul, filmy taste in my mouth. It was the taste of your ass from last night. And I looked over at you, asleep and smiling from the ace rimjob I'd given you before we dozed off, and I felt resentful.

You never eat my ass anymore, and I'm getting upset about it.

In the early days, your tongue was like a plumber's snake unclogging my colon. Back then, we savored each other's intestinal effluvium like two lovers feeding each other black olives on a picnic blanket. We shared each other's asses. We shared each other's dreams.

These days, you wouldn't go near my ass even if I stuffed a fried pork chop between my buttocks. When I ask you to eat my ass nowadays, you just shrug and say you'll "think about it." You avoid my mudflaps as if there were Yosemite Sam "BACK OFF!" insignia emblazoned on them. Truth be told, there is no "EXIT ONLY" sign affixed to my derrière. My ass'd welcome the gentle, probing presence of a caring, loving tongue. But all of a sudden, you have no appetite.

You're very selfish, that's what I think. If I had a nickel for every time I ate your ass and you didn't eat mine, I could pay off the national debt. Relationships should be about sharing, but right now you're only sharing your ass, and I'm only sharing my tongue. Love isn't a one-way street; ass-eating shouldn't be, either. There is no reciprocity in our ass-eating, no sense of fairness. Our relationship's anal inequities push me to the brink of tears. My neglected rectum cries out for some cuddlin'.

Where I come from, when someone does you a favor, it's a matter of courtesy to return it. You scratch my back, I'll scratch yours. You eat my ass, I'll eat yours. It's a matter of basic fairness and human dignity. But maybe I'm from the old school.

My parents didn't have this problem. They licked each other's asses like it was going out of style. Like ass-eating was on sale. Like they got a tax deduction for doing it.

People in the movies don't have these problems, either. You see a happy couple up on the big screen, and you assume they're licking each other's asses, no questions asked.

I've looked at my ass in the mirror. It's a nice ass. I've held a hand mirror right up to my bunghole, and frankly I don't see what's so horrifying that you'd avoid it like you do. What's so disgusting about my ass that you won't eat it out every once in a blue moon? I always use the scented lotions and male douches, so offensive tastes or odors shouldn't be a problem. Would it *kill* you to eat my ass every once in a while? I mean, would it put that much of a crimp in your evening?

From now on, you can lick your own ass, you asshole! Believe me, your ass isn't all that tasty sometimes. It ain't always a cinnamon roll, ya hear me, honey? Your ass isn't as great as you think it is, I'll tell you that. I've seen better. I've licked better. So don't go getting an attitude with me.

I'm just asking for a little consideration. Lick my ass every once in a while, all right? My ass doesn't have teeth. It won't bite your tongue off. The occasional anal 69 would really put the spark back in our love life.

Not everyone you meet out there's gonna be as happy to munch on your fat ass as I am. And that's what bugs me—your ass is flabby, and yet I graciously eat it, while my muscular ass is the very picture of a perfect posterior, yet it sits alone and uneaten.

You just watch—I'll go out there and fall in love with the first person willing to lick my tushie. One day I'll be rolling in clover, my new lover's tongue gleefully lapping at my *tuchis*, while your stinky butt sits home alone, as lonely as my ass is now. My sphincter will be wet and happy, while yours languishes in limbo, unlicked and forlorn.

"EROTIC" FICTION OF A DECIDEDLY UNAPPEALING NATURE

2. FOR THE GOOD TIMES

Thank you, Father Gallagher, for giving me my first orgasm. I'm glad that it was a man of God who popped my cherry. Somehow, it makes me feel cleaner.

Bless me, Father, for I have sinned—with you. Again and again and again. And I don't feel dirty about it. I want to shout it from the mountaintops. I have an evangelical thirst to spread the Good News of your holy, holy, lovin'. You turned me on. You turned me out. You turned this altar boy into an altar man. You made me the whore that I am. You showed me joy. You showed me pain—both physical and emotional—of a magnitude I thought impossible. You reached up under my frock and taught me the meaning of "tough love." As I stood eagerly perched on manhood's hairy cusp, you caressed my muscular ass as if my buttocks were twin golden goblets filled with Christ's blood.

You said that you had spoken with God, and that He approved of what we were doing. You told me we were just sharing the bodies that God had created. You said that God the Father and God the Son did this sort of stuff together all the time when the Holy Ghost wasn't around. You said that God the Father made the Holy Ghost have sex with the Virgin Mary because God was a homosexual who was physically repelled by women's bodies. You called physical intimacy between priests and boys "the eighth sacrament." You spoke of Bible passages that the church had suppressed, passages which told in graphic detail what God *actually* did on the seventh day when He "rested." You said the Bible was using sexual symbolism when it said Jesus "rode into town on a donkey." You mentioned other apocryphal passages which detailed wild parties featuring Jesus and his apostles. "Thirteen men living together, working together, praying together," you'd say with a sly wink. "Think about it. From time to time, they'd need some physical relief."

You were a good man, Father Gallagher—I don't care what they say. You listened to my problems. You bought me things. You left me cute little notes. You played miniature golf with me and took me to the zoo. You taught me Latin and I showed you how to play Nintendo. And we had hot, steamin', Old Testament-style monkey sex. You nailed me in the ass like Christ was nailed to the cross. You split open my buttocks like Moses parted the Red Sea. It was a gas, *mi padre*. Thanks for the good times, dude.

Remember the lazy afternoons by the riverside, sipping sacramental wine and munching on a bag of Eucharists? Remember the time we got kinky with a crucifix? Remember the time we did it right on the altar? Remember the party where we snorted poppers with the Cardinal? Remember the embarrassing trip to the Emergency Room to pry loose the rosary beads from where they were lodged? Remember how turned-on you'd get when I wore the Roman soldier costume? We didn't just have sex. What we did was a form of prayer.

I doubt that rabbis do such things with young Jewish boys. I can't see Buddhist monks doing anal with little Buddhist boys. Muslim clerics, well, I'm not so sure about them. But this I know—you did it with me, Father Gallagher.

When I read about you in the paper the other day, I felt like crying. It's really unfortunate about those sex charges. I'm saddened to see that boys who once claimed to be your friend have grown into men who seek to put you behind bars. I can't see how they can so easily banish so many tender memories from their minds. I remember how it was back then, and they were just as into the sex as you and I were. I hope you beat the rap and continue ministering to the flock. And I hope that one day we can get together, if only for one magical night, and relive old times.

That is, if I'm not too old for you now.

Just kidding, ya big lug.

Call me on my cell phone some time, ya hear?

3. WE ARE SEX-POSITIVE—OF THIS WE ARE POSITIVE

I knew when I saw your eyes across the room that we would share a bed this evening. We both came from out of town, attending a boring business convention in a hotel conference room. And then our eyes met as if by accident, unleashing 10,000 years of hidden animal secrets.

I always love it when I know I'm gonna score.

Smoky bar. Demon jazz. Hot whiskey splashed over cool rocks. Fresh cocktails and stale peanuts. Soft laughter, seductively arched eyebrows. Dirty suggestions, foul innuendos. *Yeah, I'm married, too, but who cares? What they don't*

(CONTINUED ON NEXT PAGE)

know won't hurt 'em! Carpe diem! We finish our drinks, swallow a couple of pain pills, buy some paper towels, and retire to your hotel room to order a few porno movies on the TV.

You tell me all about your childhood and then remove your clothes. You look approvingly at my tattoos and piercings, and I at yours. My wolflike eyes appraise the sensuous garlic-bulb shape of your hips. Your shaven pubis resembles the finest Cornish hen ready for its "stuffing." Your mammoth breasts are a twin pair of football-stadium domes, the fullest nippled flower of your womanhood. Your shrublike hair bears the exotic tropical scents of a really good shampoo and conditioner. The aroma that billows from 'tween your legs is not so bad that I can't handle it.

Our tongues lock together like warring octopus arms. Your frail, understanding hands massage muscles I didn't know I had. My toes curl with erotic tension. We push and grunt and throw each other around the room. Like a sleeping warrior, my maleness awakes and shakes off its slumber. You run your hungry tongue over the most sensitive areas of my penis such as the corona and the frenulum. You nibble on my manhood with the finesse of a professional fellatio-giver, being careful not to bite it. When you stimulate my testicles, I feel tempted to scream with pleasure.

I gently lick the run in your stocking. Your anus puckers as if winking at me. Your well-lubricated vulva beckons me to enter it. You dig your long, catlike fingernails into my muscular ass and mount me like you're the tire and I'm the axle. My cock is a veiny slab of dumb, probing instinct. Your vagina is a whirlpool of tangled emotions, churning, straining, yearning to be set free as I plop my massive rod within you.

My cock is now at full size, all 17-1/2 inches of it. To say my cock is diamond-hard would be unfair, because diamonds are far softer than this. You gasp as I first enter you, but enter you I must. I knock down your door like a DEA battering ram.

Your vagina gobbles up my cock like a hairy, toothless mouth giving me a blowjob. I'm in you, in your heart, between your legs. Daddy's little girl and mommy's little boy are doing something nasty, and the priests and nuns better not find out, or we're both gonna get a spanking. I drill your viscous hole like Jed Clampett seeking to strike some Black Gold, some Texas Tea. You ride me with the aplomb of the most seasoned bronco-buster as I lovingly rub whipped cream and strawberry marmalade on your smiling nipples. Our desperate bodies smack together with the sound of someone slapping a dead trout against a wooden board.

The sweat rolls from your body like hot Jamaican rain off a tin shack. You suddenly jerk back your neck with whiplash ferocity and howl with pleasure, disappearing into a milky white ocean of my cum. You have a million orgasms which, like invisible angels, would all fit on the head of a pin.

When I cum, I shoot my soul into you. My sperm and my spirit now inhabit you. We become one and melt into that strange night. Futuristic lovers teetering over an erotic horizon. Yin and yang, entwined. Plus and minus, reconciled. Plug and socket, feeding electricity to one another. We are sex-positive, of this we are positive.

Maybe there's a difference between making love and fucking, but for now we can't tell.

4. STORIES OF THE SHADOW WOMAN

Dear Shadow Woman:
I'm a faithful reader of your Shadow Woman column.

—A fan of Shadow Woman

I am the Shadow Woman. I lurk in graveyards and delicatessens. I rub the underbelly of the pro-sex literary hinterlands. I dance naked as a jaybird with Ganesha to that crazy swing beat. Sometimes, as a woman, I can sense the toes of a billion pixies doing the Harlem Shuffle on my clit.

I am an outspoken member of the poly, multi, poly-multi, and tutti-frutti communities. I dabble in rimjob academia. I'm schooled in BDSM, water sports, bloodletting, and Nintendo. I dream that one day, Portland [a.k.a. The Town Which Shadow Woman Built] will be filled with sex-positive activists actively having positive sex.

As an American Sexual Being, I have opinions, and I don't care if you don't want to hear them—I'm going to corner you at a party and shout my opinions into your ear. I'm going to tell you things about myself that you really might not want to hear. Even if you act distracted or ask me politely not to go into further detail, I'll blab about my sexuality to anyone within earshot. I'll leave naked pictures of myself on your computer and then ask you what you thought of them.

I am frank, candid, honest, smart, resourceful, and modest. I am so filled with a sense of myself, I don't look where I'm going and often bump into things. It takes so much time for me to take personal inventory, I think I might have to hire an accountant. I am constantly redefining, redesigning, and resculpting myself. On Friday, I'm going to give my soul a high colonic.

I tattooed myself in defiance of the Reagan administration. I pierced my nostril to protest homophobia in bowling alleys. Such *rites de passage* are *de rigueur* in *le monde* of the Shadow Woman.

I want to smell other people's armpits, to bask in their ball sweat and vaginal cheese, to pick lint from their belly buttons and gently lick wax from their ears. I find myself ambling pell-mell down new spiritual paths. I feel vibrant. I feel naughty. I feel hungry, so I think I'm gonna drive to the 24-hour Taco Bell.

I suffered worse than anyone else did in high school. Catholicism damaged me more than it did anyone else. A lot of people don't like me. And it has nothing to do with my personality.

My Cherished Custodian Polopony recently shelled out more than ten grand to a sex-positive alternative dentist in order to give me a shiny new pair of surgical fangs. He also bought me a hot red vinyl corset from Lane Bryant. I wish I had a string of Poloponies.

I suppose I should switch gears and talk about myself. My personal sexuality lifestyle column, "Stories of the Shadow Woman," is read weekly by over 815,000,000 visitors to ShadowWoman.com. My other websites—MoreAboutShadowWoman.com and the amazing floating webcam of Shadow Woman's bathroom, which I've called TheAmazingFloatingWebcamofShadowWomansBathroom.com—have received Golden Vulva awards from the Positive 'Bout Sex Foundation. Don't forget that I'll be speaking at foot-fetishists' convention "Toe Jam 2002" in Des Moines this summer. And in August, me and Brent Williams of T-Cell Times will be hosting a seminar on genital plaster-casting and erotic foot rubs at the Castro Street YMCA. And soon on ShadowWoman.com, I'll post pictures of my recent trip with Polopony to the mall to get photos developed of prior pictures I've posted to ShadowWoman.com.

5. MY DUNGEON IS BETTER THAN YOUR DUNGEON

My dungeon is better-equipped than most dungeons out there. It's a high-tech, state-of-the-art, *classy* dungeon with a beautiful doggy cage and a wonderful set of vintage stirrups. A lot of care and thought went into my dungeon. And although I might charge more for sessions in *my* dungeon than other doms in *other* dungeons do, no one else delivers more bang for your buck in terms of torture, pain, and ritual humiliation. You want a shoddy dungeon, go ahead and pay shoddy dungeon prices and get a half-assed domination session which doesn't even come *close* to destroying your self-esteem—just go ahead and see if I care.

I'm a Pro Dom Top Double-Down Contortionist Butch Femme, and I have been so for over 14 years now. In my platform stiletto heels, I'm nearly eight feet tall and don't look nearly as chubby. I am bold, sexy, and, um, intellectual. The painful fact is that I'm superior, and I'll keep telling you that until we both believe it.

My most recent client was a Gothic bottom-feeding femboy with a shaved chest and a scrotum wonderfully patterned with steel rivets. A disgusting, dirty little boy. A bad little piggly-wiggly. He had seen my website and knew about my extensive background in Asian spanking techniques. He kept up-to-date on my weblog with its frequent reports about my latest dental work.

It was our first meeting. He was a bit disappointed to see me in the flesh, not knowing that I photograph really well.

I was dressed as a Greek Orthodox bishop. He was clad in a diaper and was hovering motionless in my elaborate Suspension Device™.

I had read his application form where he listed his kinks, which mainly involved fresh produce and former Israeli Prime Minister Golda Meir. We agreed on a safety word, which was "nougat."

I removed the acupuncture needles from my autoclaving device and jammed them into his armpits while forcing him to recite Mother Goose rhymes.

He shrieked loudly as I proceeded to clip the battery cables onto his weak little rosebud nips. His screams only drove me toward loftier sadistic delights. His face was red with shame as I applied the cock ring and butt plug, tightening them to maximum tension. The butt plug was in his ass so deep, I was certain its shit-encrusted tip would pop out of his mouth.

I fetched him a bowl of fresh water and a can of Alpo. He barked appreciatively and lapped it up. I then spanked him, called him a bad pony, and refused to give him his candy cane.

I had severely bruised his body with a plethora of pretty little lumps, bruises, and scratch marks. I felt pleased and oh-so-full of myself.

Werner Klemperer-style, I took a long tug from my cigarette holder and proceeded to interrogate him.

"Would you eat my farts?" I asked him.

"Oh, yes, I'd gobble 'em up, Goddess," he slobbered.

"Would you eat my fragrant farts right as they billow from my muscular ass?"

"Yes, I would, Goddess—you already asked me that."

"Don't get snippy with ME!" I yelled at him. "Get me a sandwich," I commanded.

"What kind of sandwich, Goddess?" came his meek inquiry.

"Turkey on rye," I snapped.

The pathetic slug, that groveling human worm-boy, fetched me a surprisingly tasty turkey-on-rye sandwich with a frosty beverage on the side.

I grinned. He cowered. My grin grew wider.

"I will sever your wiener," I told him sternly.

"Oh, do it, Goddess! Sever my wiener!"

"Call me Goddess Sever Your Wiener."

"You are in command, oh lovely Goddess Sever Your Wiener."

When he had reached his credit-card limit, I informed him that our session was over, and my lovely Slavic boyfriend escorted him out.

I went upstairs, popped some food in the microwave, checked my e-mail, and prepared myself a warm bath.

I am so glad to have this sort of danger in my life.

NECROPHILIA

THE LOVE THAT CANNOT SPEAK ITS NAME

(ESPECIALLY IF YOU'RE THE DEAD ONE)

"Every man to his own tastes. Mine is to corpses."
—*French necrophile Henri Blot, quoted during a court hearing*

"I enjoy the cold sensation against the warmth of my own flesh....I've always been physically repulsed by the heat of another living body."

—*Female necrophile Leilah Wendell*

WHY WOULD ANYONE FUCK A CORPSE? Exactly how bored and lonely are you? You can't go on MySpace? There aren't any singles dances where you live? You can't go to charm school or have your teeth fixed? Can anyone possibly be THAT hard-up?

I smelled a dead body once, and I didn't exactly get a boner. I can't (and WON'T) quite put my finger on it, but for me, people lose a certain luster when they're dead. Dead people really let their looks go. For me, the Choir Invisible doesn't hold quite the same appeal as, say, the Dallas Cowboy Cheerleaders.

This is sick fucking shit. Some fucked-up, sickening shit. Some sickeningly, fucked-up-edly, shitty fucking shit. I can see the appeal of nearly all perversions and kinks, but this one I don't get. Not at all. It's not only gross, it's yucky. And not only yucky—it's disgusting. What could possibly be more disgusting? Slurping diarrhea with a straw? Prenatal baby-rape?

I'd rather poop into my own mouth than fuck a corpse. Here are some other things I'd rather do than fuck a corpse:
• Have one testicle removed with ice tongs and no anesthesia.
• Play Russian roulette with a semi-automatic.
• Be head-butted in the balls by a dwarf.
• Drink used-tampon tea.
• Eat dog shit (as long as it's from one of the Toy breeds).
• Eat afterbirth.
• Eat pussy.

So don't go getting the wrong idea. This is NOT an endorsement. I'm offended that you would even think that.

REFERENCES TO NECROPHILIA ABOUND in pop culture, bu I fucking hate pop culture—it's been proven to cause retardation— I won't mention any of those. You wanna go fry the dozen brain ce you have left by watching some more of those faggy Goth monster movies? I won't get in your way.

Although disgusting (did I mention that it was yucky?), necrophilic has been with us as long as there have been dead bodies. In ancier Egypt, according to the Greek historian Herodotus, noble families would wait three or four days before turning a recently deceased family member—especially if the bitch was a hottie—over to embalmers. "These precautions are taken," Herodotus wrote, "because it is feared the embalmers will violate the corpse." Primitiv cultures, most of whom we've blessedly annihilated, tended to be fo of rubbing their genitals up against skulls and jacking off with hume bones. They thought it was a way of communing with dead souls and/or absorbing their sexual energy. Such cultures were very, very stupid, which is why I said it's a blessing that we slaughtered them.

TRUE NECROPHILIA—as opposed to the club kids who slap on corpse paint and black eyeliner—is apparently so rare that there exists scant medical literature on the topic. The most comprehensive report appears to be a 1989 paper released by Dr. Jonathan Rosman and Dr. Phillip Resnick that covers 122 case studies. They concluded that nine in ten necrophiles were male, and, of course, almost always white. Four out of five were heteros. Seven out of ten had above-average intelligence. Half exhibited no discernible personality disorders, with a meager 11% being deemed psychotic They FUCK DEAD PEOPLE, for Christ's sake. What exactly *does* on have to do these days to be classified as psychotic?

Rosman and Resnick (I think they might be Jews) wrote that necrophiles view their prey as spiritually pure and incapable of rejecting them—or of even resisting them. They tend to suffer from abysmally low self-esteem (DUH!) and are usually terrified of being spurned by women. They often turn an overwhelming fear of death into a desire for it. They are invariably control freaks, and people are much easier to control once they stop breathing.

Unsurprisingly, nearly three-fifths of the subjects in their study were employed at places which provided them with easy access to dead bodies.

DAN (NOT HIS REAL NAME, DUMMY) is in his late 40s and toiled for 15 years as an embalmer in central California. He estimates that in the year 2000 alone, he embalmed 1,000 bodies. Dan was eventually fired for refusing to sign a contract agreeing never to talk with the press if he were to witness an act of necrophilia at his mortuary.

Dan says he finds necrophiles loathsome, but he also condemns th death industry's unwillingness to acknowledge that there's a problem He recalls a mortuary meat-wagon driver named Mike, whom he describes as 6'4", 350 pounds, and "pear-shaped." He says Mike "doesn't have a mental editor—he's the type of guy who'll look in yo eyes and say, 'I'd really like to fuck your daughter.'

"There was an [car] accident case, a girl of 14 years who was pretty bad—a lot of stitching and a lot of work to get her ready fo an open-casket funeral," Dan says. "So Mike comes in and he's gawking for a while, and finally he says, 'Nice!' And at first, I thought he was talking about my work. So he said, 'No, I'd DO her, man!' And I said, 'Get the fuck out of here.' I found out later that Mike would touch the vaginas of dead women. I told my bosses, but they didn't want word to get out—they felt that by ignoring it, it wouldn't exist.

"A few weeks after that, somebody went into the Cold Room, and Mike had his pants down, but he pulled them right up. It was a 70-year-old woman in there. We went to the main boss about it. He finally called everyone in, and Mike was gone. We found out through sources that Mike had been given two years' pay to leave and shut his mouth. They made him sign a pledge not to ever go to the media about it. They tried to make me sign it, too. I refused to sign it, and I was let go, too. The follow-up is that one of the fired guys showed up one day and told me that Mike had a little 'accident.' My friend had beaten him down with a beer bottle."

AND YET, GOD BLESS AMERICA, there exist small, smelly, revolutionary pockets out there where a freedom-loving attitude of "Die and Let Live" reigns supreme...where the "struggle" to "pork the bones" is cloaked in PC catchphrases such as "alternative lifestyle"...where living people commune with other living people about their attraction to dead people...where severely fucked-up humans strain with every fiber of their still-living flesh to convince the world (and themselves) that they aren't severely fucked-up.

"It is the grandest wish, that our necrophilic sensuality will one day be freely expressed and practiced, without fear of legal consequences, social ostracism or persecution from haughty, false moralists!" bellows a haughtily moralistic scribe who calls himself "MichiganGhoul" on a website dubbed "The NecroErotic—Necrophilia Online." He lists several "Necrophilic Principles" which read like a corpse-fucker's Bill of Rights. Among these are the God-given "right to engage in [our] orgasmic release of choice as do 'normal' couples." Anyone who opposes—or even questions—such orgasmic release is labeled a "necrophobe." On the flip side, he boldly asserts that cadavers have absolutely no rights whatsoever. The webmaster also features a proud pantheon of necrophilic pioneers as if he was a young black man and Jeffrey Dahmer was Marcus Garvey.

"There are many differences between screwing a live and a dead person which one needs to be aware of," cautions the author of a web page called "Necrophilia for Boneheads." He does make one cogent point which was first brought to my attention years ago when reading about British serial killer Dennis Nilsen: It's not as if the carcass suffers or even has the merest idea of what's being done to it. "Firstly, a corpse will never tell you to get off of it if you're being a bit rough and it will never complain no matter what kinky sexual practices you use it for....If you want a great blowjob then lubricate your partner's mouth, lock it to your preferred width, insert and go for it."

"Westgate Necromantic" is a website curated by a female diddler of the deceased who claims that—forget it. I've had enough. These people are too sick.

ONCE YOU DIE, IT'S *REALLY* TIME TO LAY OFF THE SEX. Let this stand as a living will—I want to be cremated and have my ashes fill the pepper shakers of Denny's restaurants nationwide. But if my final wishes aren't met and I'm spiked up on formaldehyde and stuffed in a pine box, don't try poking anything in my ass, because...well...I truly wouldn't be able to resist.

KING NECRO
CARL TANZLER, 1877–1952

Skull-fuckers are a dime a dozen. To capture *this* scribe's interest, you have to dazzle me with something beyond corpse-cunnilingus. Been there, done *that*. In historical annals clogged with blandly interchangeable carcass-copulators, one nutty old man floats high above the putrefied heap. Anyone can just dig up a cadaver and make whoopie with it, yet it takes a man of rare pathological devotion to climb the craggy cliffs of Mount Weirdo and cop the coveted crown of King Necro.

That man is CARL TANZLER, a Carl Jung-looking German radiologist who formed what may be politely termed an unhealthy attachment with one of his patients. During his youth in Europe, he claimed to have been repeatedly visited by a female ancestor's ghost who showed him visions of his one true love, a raven-haired, dark-skinned filly. After relocating to Key West, Florida, land of Key Lime Pie and sunburned homosexuals, Tanzler's medical practice brought him in contact with a 20-year-old tubercular Cuban hotsy-totsy named Maria Elena Milagro De Hoyos—33 years his junior—whom he instantly pegged as his dream woman. His love was apparently unrequited, which didn't dissuade him from smothering the girl with trinkets, baubles, and endlessly lovey-dovey doodads.

Despite Tanzler's diligent attempts to cure his *inamorata's* TB, she succumbed to the illness within a year, at which point the party *really* started for the quacky doctor. (It's easier to pretend they love you when they're dead.) Tanzler paid for both the girl's funeral and an above-ground mausoleum which he visited almost daily for a year and a half. He even equipped the mausoleum with a telephone in order to conduct "conversations" with her during those unbearable moments when he couldn't be by her side.

One spring night in 1933, his separation anxiety grew too strong, and he plucked the dead girl's corpse from the mausoleum, toting it through the cemetery in a toy wagon en route to his small Key West home.

He strung the girl's bones together with piano wire, replaced her decomposed eyeballs with glass orbs, fitted her with a wig made entirely of her hair, crammed rags within her chest cavity, replaced her skin with wax-coated silk, dressed her in a bridal gown, and fitted her vagina with a paper tube, ostensibly for fucking. He adorned her in stockings and jewelry, repeatedly doused her with perfumes and preservatives, covered her face with a death mask, and placed her in his bed. Such shenanigans went on for seven years until a suspicious relative of De Hoyos made a surprise visit to Tanzler's home. Since Florida had no law forbidding necrophilia, he was charged with grave-robbing, but the charges were dropped because the Statute of Limitations had expired.

Tanzler relocated to central Florida and continued to sell postcards depicting his beloved.

RECTAL FOREIGN BODIES

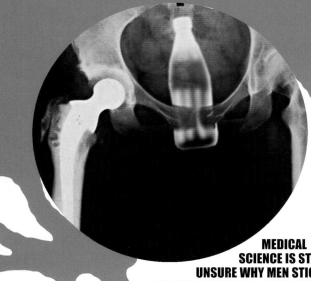

MEDICAL SCIENCE IS STILL UNSURE WHY MEN STICK FOREIGN OBJECTS UP THEIR ASSES. They know that in many cases, it is for the erotic stimulation of the juicy prostate gland that nestles only a couple inches inside the anus. In other instances, it is for masochistic psychological reasons that may only be helped by a psychiatric professional and/or an exorcist. Perhaps it is for both reasons—a sloppy combination of lust and self-loathing. Or it may happen for spiritual reasons that we human peons, in our arrested evolutionary phase, would never be able to comprehend.

What IS known is that many men stick all manner of things inside their asses. And oftentimes, these things disappear down the bottomless rectal pit, causing intense pain and requiring an emergency-room visit. Medical journals are stuffed to the point of bloating with accounts of "rectal foreign bodies" lodged hopelessly up the bunghole and how they were ultimately removed. These stories—seemingly so outlandish that a skeptical mind would dismiss them as urban legends if they hadn't been so exhaustively documented—vary as widely as the array of objects than can potentially fit inside a human rectum. One thing unites them—they are all funny.

IRONICALLY, THE RECTAL-FOREIGN-BODY STORY which has burrowed far deeper inside the American consciousness than any other—the one involving **gerbils**—has never been conclusively documented and must be presumed to be the stuff of fable.

Long rumored to be a favorite practice of gay men, "gerbilling" or "gerbil-stuffing" is said to employ one live rodent, either shaven or not depending on who's telling the story. In most accounts, the gerbil is declawed to avert rectal tearing. A tube is nudged into the rectum, and the gerbil is then placed into the tube, whereupon he trots up into the dark moist anal canal, dancing the Macarena on the prostate gland until he suffocates and his dead body plops out during the host's next bowel movement.

I first heard of gerbilling while living in Philadelphia in the early 1980s. A local news anchor, Jerry Penacoli, was said to have visited an emergency room to dislodge a gerbil that had become trapped inside his tush during some homosexual slap-and-tickle with a lover. Although never confirmed, the rumor did irreparable damage to Penacoli's career.

Similar rumors about public figures emerged nationwide throughout the 1980s, culminating in the most famous gerbilling legend of all, that involving actor Richard Gere. It has been long rumored that he was admitted to an L.A. emergency room for gerbil-extraction. In one version, the gerbil was his own pet, named "Tibet."

Avid researchers, including Mike Walker from the *National Enquirer,* were unable to come up with even a morsel of evidence to corroborate the story. The myth's most plausible origin involves a faxed hoax letter reputedly from the ASPCA accusing Gere of "gerbil abuse" shortly after the film *Pretty Woman* was released in 1990. The fax was refaxed throughout Hollywood, and a legend was born. When confronted by Barbara Walters in 1991 about "salacious rumors," Gere responded with a Zenlike, "If I am a cow and someone says I'm a zebra, it doesn't make me a zebra." OK, Rich, FINE—you're not a cow. And no one's calling you a zebra. But DID YOU STUFF A GERBIL IN YOUR ASS?

An extreme, and obviously false, version of the gerbilling legend involves two male homosexuals who panic when the tiny beast apparently becomes trapped inside one partner's rectum, causing the other partner to light a match in search of it. The flame ignites intestinal gas, causing the match-holder's eyebrows and hair to be scorched.

Due to the gerbilling legend's popularity, someone has undoubtedly *attempted* to do it—but researchers are unsure if it actually works or whether said procedure ever went awry to the point where it necessitated a 911 call or hospital visit. The American Hospital Association even published a book that included the phrase "rectal mass—gerbils" under the category of emergency-room procedures that require 25 minutes to perform. But when an investigator contacted the physician who'd authored the section in question, he laughed and said the editors must have slipped the joke in the manuscript before it went to press.

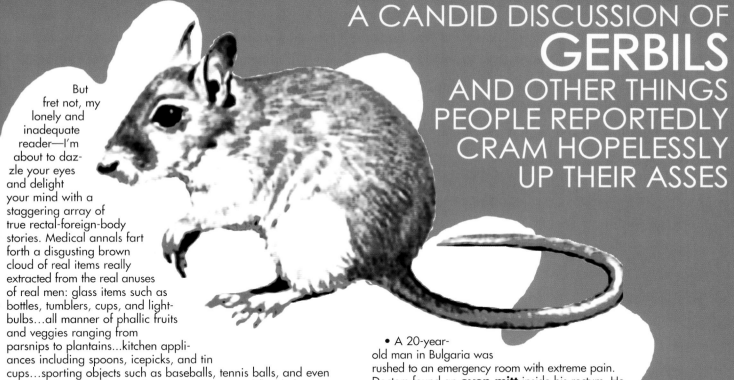

A CANDID DISCUSSION OF
GERBILS
AND OTHER THINGS
PEOPLE REPORTEDLY
CRAM HOPELESSLY
UP THEIR ASSES

But fret not, my lonely and inadequate reader—I'm about to dazzle your eyes and delight your mind with a staggering array of true rectal-foreign-body stories. Medical annals fart forth a disgusting brown cloud of real items really extracted from the real anuses of real men: glass items such as bottles, tumblers, cups, and lightbulbs…all manner of phallic fruits and veggies ranging from parsnips to plantains…kitchen appliances including spoons, icepicks, and tin cups…sporting objects such as baseballs, tennis balls, and even (ouch!) billiard balls…candles, curling irons, and flashlights…axe handles and broomsticks…animal-related items such as a pig's tail, a steer's horn, a "kangaroo tumor," and a frozen fish…seemingly improbable artifacts such as a pair of eyeglasses, a mannequin's fist and forearm, and a plastic bag containing fish hooks…and, yes, even vibrators and dildos. One complainant's ass contained jeweler's saws—29 of them at once. In three extreme cases—involving a shoe horn, a 22-ounce toolbox, and a two-pound rock—rectal foreign bodies have been known to cause death.

Short of mortality, the aspiring rectal inserter risks permanent muscle and nerve damage, infection due to mixing blood with shit, and even scar formation which can prevent him from ever having a satisfying BM again.

Victims are understandably loath to admit why they were shoving things so far up their poop chute that they became stuck. Older men often claim that they were innocently massaging their prostate or dislodging impacted feces when the big OOPS happened. And there's a surfeit of "accidental" sitting upon large objects which somehow penetrated their anuses to the point of no return.

In their selfishly pathetic quest to spare the subject any further humiliation, medical journals tend to avoid identifying factors such as the victim's name and location. Still, we can all enjoy a belly laugh at the following true stories:

• A 65-year-old man admitted himself into an emergency room with a **peanut-butter jar** stuck inside his ass. He claimed that while washing his dog in the shower, he slipped and fell directly onto the jar, which became lodged deep inside his *tuchis*.

• A 69-year-old married man claimed that a **toothbrush** became irretrievably lodged inside his rectal canal after he was using it to scratch his hemorrhoids.

• A 20-year-old man reported to the emergency room experiencing extreme pain after his partner gave him a "**concrete enema**" through a funnel. The enema was topped off with a ping-pong ball to ensure no concrete would leak out while hardening. The cement block, attached to the ping-pong ball, was removed without incident.

• A 20-year-old man in Bulgaria was rushed to an emergency room with extreme pain. Doctors found an **oven mitt** inside his rectum. He suffered rectal perforation not from the mitt, but from a stick he employed to "introduce" the item inside himself.

• An X-ray revealed that a 50-year-old man had inserted a 20-inch **live eel** inside of his most special of places, ostensibly to relieve constipation. The eel caused rectal bleeding and was removed by surgeons.

• A 58-year-old man underwent surgery to have a **soda bottle** removed from his colon. Two years earlier, he had undergone surgery for exactly the same thing.

• Acting on a drunken dare, a 54-year-old man used shaving cream as a lubricant to insert a **100-watt lightbulb** inside himself. He walked around for two days until extreme pain during urination brought him into the hospital. Physicians removed the lightbulb intact.

WHAT CAN WE LEARN FROM ALL THIS? Unless you're an idiot, you should have been born with the wisdom not to stuff lightbulbs up your doody-hole, so I'll stop short of using the hackneyed "Don't try this at home." But we can learn, once more, to laugh at the misfortunes of others. Although perhaps not as extreme as the stories of the man who, "feeling depressed," stuck a lit firecracker in his ass, or the man who committed suicide by firing a pistol up his rectum, these stories mine rich nuggets of humor. And laughing at others is often the only way to feel better about ourselves.

Dirty Words...

ENGLISH	SPANISH	FRENCH	ITALIAN	GERMAN	FARSI
cock	verga	bite	cazzone	Schvanz	kiram
cunt	panocha	la chatte	fica	Fotze	kardan
shit	mierda	merde	stronzo	Scheisse	golole
tits	chichis	doudounes	tette	Titten	pestoon
ass	culo	cul	culo	Arsch	kun
faggot	maricon	tantouze	finocchio	Schwuler	coony
whore	puta	putaine	porca	Schlampe	jende
to fuck	chingar	baiser	fottere	Ficken	kos kardar
fuck you!	que te jodan	va te faire foutre	vaffanculo	Fick dich!	bokoname
blow me!	chupa mi verga	suce ma bite	fammi un pompino	Saugen mein Shwanse	khaayam zireh galoo
clever insult	Chupas las nalgas de monos grandes. (You suck the butt cheeks of large monkeys.)	Si j'avais ta tête a la place du cul j'aurais honte de chier. (If my ass looked anything like your face, I'd be ashamed of taking a shit.)	Se il cazzo avesse le ali, la tua fica sarebbe un aereoporto. (If a dick had wings, your pussy would be an airport.)	Sag deiner Mama ich bezahle sie später. (Tell your mother I'll pay her later.)	Meshosham beh seebillet. (I piss on your mustache.)

MANDARIN	KOREAN	ARABIC	TURKISH	RUSSIAN	YIDDISH
diao	jaji	zib	yarrak	khui	putz
ji bai	boji	koos	kuku	pizda	k'nish
shi	nimiral	zarba	bok	govno	drek
bo ba (huge tits)	ji jis	biz	füzeler	sski	bristen
pigu	uhng-dung-ee	teazak	got	jopu	tuchis
ong xing lian	ddorang	mamhoon	nonosh	goluboj	faygala
ji nv	shibseki	sharmuta	kaltak	blad	kurva
gan tsao	jo ka eun	nik	cakmak	yob	shtup
gun dan	yumago	ana akhan-nethak	siktir git	poshol na khui	ver derharget
a wo deh bang	ko-chu-pal-uh	mus zibii	kukumu yala	pasasee mayu peesku	timtotz li (Hebrew)
o cao ni ba bei zi zu zong. (Fuck eight generations of our ancestors.)	Ni me shi me nuhn il bon chon haam ey soo yong het nuhn dae. (Your mother [grand-mother] swam out to meet the Japanese battleships.)	Kuss ummak bisinaan. (Your mother's pussy has teeth.)	Ananin amina kale kurar sabah aksam mac yaparim. (I would create goals in your mother's pussy and play soccer there day and night.)	Tya mama huyem v rot ebala. (Your mother fucked you in the mouth with a dick.)	Fransn zol esn zayn layb. (Venereal disease should consume his body.)

.in other languages

REAL

SEX TOYS THAT TIME FORGOT
VIBRATORS & DILDOS OF YORE

MEN WILL STICK THEIR DICKS IN ANYTHING, whether it's their own hand, your mouth, an overripe cantaloupe, raw liver, a dead eel, or a hole in the wall. Unlike their delicate, intuitive, empathic, easily bruised sisters, men never seem to have a problem getting aroused and releasing their pent-up libidinal tensions. They may be laughably "dysfunctional" when it comes to pleasing a partner, but almost never when it comes to pleasing themselves. Men never seem to have trouble figuring out how to cum. After waking up one morning at age 13 with a stubborn, angry hard-on, they clutch the baton and start running.

Therefore, the sex-toy industry—with the stark exception of pocket pussies and their *reductio ad absurdum* sex zombie, the blow-up doll—caters almost exclusively to women and their ongoing quest to achieve the blissful muscular release of deep-tissue orgasm. Well, let's amend that—sex toys typically serve the needs of women and *gay men*, because with a little coaxing and some elbow grease, I suppose it's almost as easy to cram something that was intended for a vagina up some hairy jerkoff's pink starfish. Not that I'd know. I mean, I'm flattered that you'd find me attractive, but I just don't *swing* that way. And if you push the matter, I might have to bust out with some irrational, self-hating, homophobic violence.

Where was I? Oh—point being, nine times out of ten, a sex toy's gonna be modeled after a penis rather than a vagina. This occurs for no other reason than the fact that it's easier to design an item based on something rather than on nothing. You might be able to *dig* a hole, but it's hard to really *build* one. When all is said and done, when the chips have fallen and the dust has settled, a vagina is little more than a Waiting Room for a penis. And like I said, when you're hard-up, even a half-rotted cantaloupe will do.

These *faux* penises—which the sex-toy industry is so fond of foisting upon our nation's women with the intent of having them mockingly compare our organs unfavorably to these mammoth inanimate rubber obelisks—invariably fall into one of two categories: **dildos** and **vibrators**. A dildo is a fake penis. A vibrator is a fake penis that moves.

Well, let's clarify that. Vibrators are not *always* phallic. Many times their focus is the clitoris rather than the vagina—the Sweet Pea rather than the Sugar Walls, if you're more inclined to use "street talk." Therefore, unlike the dildo, the vibrator need not resemble any naturally occurring sex organ, because as we all know, Mother Nature purposely avoided designing anything on the male body that would naturally rub up against the clit. It takes you half a week just to *find* the fucking thing on some chicks.

Still, whether phallic or not, the fact remains that most sex toys are designed for women or anal-receptive men, and I'm not sure which is worse.

It may shock you—because, as always, you're pathetically easy to shock—but sex toys weren't invented by ham-fisted, no-neck, Frisco leather dykes sometime in the early 1980s. They are not the noble creation of a plucky cabal of overweight, flabby-titted, sex-positive erotic-fiction writers. They did not magically emerge to coincide with the coining of the term "modern primitives."

No, my chicken-chested, monkey-butted friend, we have always had sex toys. The dildo was invented long before the wheel.

THE ORIGIN OF THE WORD "DILDO" remains unclear. Most experts seem to think it's derived from the Italian *diletto*, which means "pleasure" or "delight." Others peg on the Latin *dilatare*, which roughly translates to "dilate" or "open wide." There's also an old British folk song called "The Maid's Complaint for Want of a Dil Doul," and the words "dil doul" allegedly translate as "erect penis," but fuck if I could find out from what language. Regardless of its derivation, it remains a crass, ugly word—"dildo." It's hard to sound classy and refined while saying it. Try it if you don't believe me.

In Iceland, archeologists have recently unearthed an obvious phallic object which testing has revealed to be 106,000 years old and thus the undisputed title-holder to the much-coveted "World's Oldest Dildo" crown. Carved from whalebone, it is adorned with "goddess symbols" and an apparent menstrual calendar. German rockhounds have dug up an eight-inch "stone phallus" thought to have been used during Ice Age sex parties 28,000 years ago. And ancient Chinese suspected dildos, made of bronze, jade, wood, or ivory, have been found that date as far back as 10,000 B.C.

The problem with many of these Ancient Stone Cocks is determining whether they were indeed double-edged swords, i.e., us

---

"We have always had sex toys. The dildo was invented long before the wheel."

GIGANTIC BOOK OF SEX

both as "sculpture" and as marital aids. How can you tell whether they were only used in fertility parades or whether some troglodyte lass was shoving that stony slab up her prehistoric twat after the harvest festival was over? How the fuck do you tell? Huh? *How?*

Rumor has it that in the Africa of bygone days, dildos were sculpted from dried camel dung coated in layers of hardened resin. I think you'll agree with me that this is disgusting. But it wasn't until we encounter the ancient Greeks—those *freaks*—that we find the spectacle of dildos being crafted solely for penetration of human orifices.

Starting somewhere around 500 B.C., artisans in the Mediterranean coastal city of Miletus began fashioning what they called the *olisbos*—a leather, stone, or wood surrogate schlong—specifically for women. Before going off to war, Greek men sometimes gave their wives an olisbos to stave off the pangs of penile deprivation. And fragments from a third-century B.C. Greek play tell of a young maiden who visits a friend to borrow her olisbos and becomes distraught when informed that her friend had already lent it to another lonely lady.

Renaissance Italians added some twists to the dildo template such as elaborate carvings and the occasional model cast entirely in gold. But as with prior incarnations, these dildos of antiquity were crude, hard, possibly injurious implements that required gobs of olive oil merely to get 'em in.

It was not until the mid-1800s and rubber's vulcanization that mankind entered The Era of the Modern Dildo.

THE ANTIQUE DILDO'S DEATH coincided with the antique vibrator's birth. As early as 1734, the French had invented *le tremoussoir*—a hand-held wind-up toy that produced a vibrating motion on one end—for the purpose of curing a widespread medical condition they liked to call "female hysteria." But it wasn't until the late 1800s that a vibrator industry of absurd proportions emerged amid the clanging steel and smoking rubber of Gilded Age technology.

The idea of "female hysteria"—and I'm not here to argue whether it's *just* an idea or a LIVING THROBBING THING—had

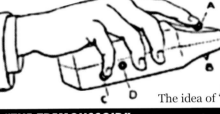

been around since ancient Greek philosophers spoke of a "wandering womb." According to hallowed Greek physician Galen, that wanderin' womb could be repatriated through a medically induced "hysterical paroxysm" evidenced by vaginal contractions and the release of excess, pent-up, stagnatin' pussy juice.

In other words, for a rock-solid 25 centuries—since a few hundred years before Christ up until 1952, when the American Psychiatric Association removed "hysteria" from their list of disorders—physicians took it upon themselves to jack off women to orgasm.

According to some estimates, anywhere from half to three-quarters of an average physician's business in the late 1800s consisted of these anti-hysteria handjobs. Nearly any female complaint would be neatly classified under the "hysteria" umbrella, and thus much jacking was done.

But as we all know, handjobs can be tiring. In 1869, George Taylor invented the "Manipulator," an unwieldy, steam-powered, hand-and-foot-cranked steel contraption that powered a vibrating ball against which a patient ground their pelvis. The Manipulator cut the average handjob time down from about an hour to ten minutes. Taylor cautioned physicians to protect women against "overindulgence."

By 1900, an estimated 100 different vibrators had appeared on the market, most of them confined to the physician's lair. They depended on anything from steam power to gas engines to air pressure to good ol' glowin' coal.

The turn of that century brought a new wave of "portable" models. Although the size of power drills, they were mere hand buzzers compared to the torture racks ensconced in doctors' offices. They boasted snappy names such as the "Gyro-Lator," "Vibra-King," "Vibro-Electra," and "Golden-Glo Vitalator." There were even hand-cranked models resembling pepper grinders.

When Hamilton Beach patented a take-home electrical massager in 1902, the vibrator became only the fifth home electrical appliance, following the tea kettle, sewing machine, fan, and toaster. But by 1917, there were more vibrators in American homes than toasters. Vibrator ads buzzed throughout respectable women's magazines of the WWI era. Marketed as "blood circulators" and devices "for anxiety and female tension," they teased female readers with the prospect of "30,000 thrilling, invigorating, penetrating, revitalizing penetrations per minute" and promised that "all the pleasures of youth will throb within you." The 1918 Sears, Roebuck catalogue peddled a vibrator "That Every Woman Appreciates... very useful and satisfactory for home service."

But when silent porno films of the 1920s began showing women using vibrators in a sexual context, advertisers could no longer hide the vibrator's true use behind medicinal mumbo-jumbo. The vibrator was shamed into obscurity until the 1960s and the Sexual Revolution's wackiness. No longer resembling a rusted steel printing press, the typical vibrator today is a slim pink plastic job the size of a baby carrot.

HAS IT EVER OCCURRED TO YOU that almost all of your problems are rooted in the fact that you aren't getting laid nearly as often as a normal adult human should? And has it crossed your mind that the reason for this is because you simply don't know how to "talk cool" with the chicks? Fret not—I've provided a list of FUN 'n' OBSCURE sexual euphemisms which will have you "making time" with the ladies in no time!

AARDVARKING...Fucking an ex-lover due to boredom or lack of other opportunities

ABSPRITZEN...to ejaculate (German)

ACCORDION...a penis that becomes much, much larger when erect

AGATE...a tiny penis

AGONY..sexual bliss (Jamaican)

APPLE DUMPLIN' SHOP...boobs (archaic English)

ARBOR VITAE...penis (archaic English)

ARTICHOKE...vagina

AXEWOUND...vagina

BABY PASTE...semen

BACKGAMMON PLAYER...homosexual (archaic English)

BADONKADONK...a giant bouncy ass; also, budonkadunk, gadonk-a-donk-donk, gadonkadonk, ga-donk ga-donk donk, and budunk

BAGPIPING...fucking a man in the armpit (19th-Century British)

BAWBELS...testicles (archaic English)

BEAR CLAW...gigantic pussy lips

BEARD SPLITTER...stud (archaic English)

BEAT DAT FACE...to fuck and/or receive oral sex (Jamaican)

BESCHNITTEN...circumcised (German)

BIT OF RASPBERRY...sexy woman (British)

BLANKET HORNPIPE...sexual intercourse (archaic English)

BLOW THE GROUNSILS...sexual intercourse (archaic English)

BLUMPKIN...the act of receiving oral sex while defecating

BOB TAIL...slutty woman or impotent man (archaic English)

BOG QUEEN...gay man who cruises public toilets for sex

BONE SMUGGLER...male homosexual

BRONCO...male youth who is extremely vigorous during sex

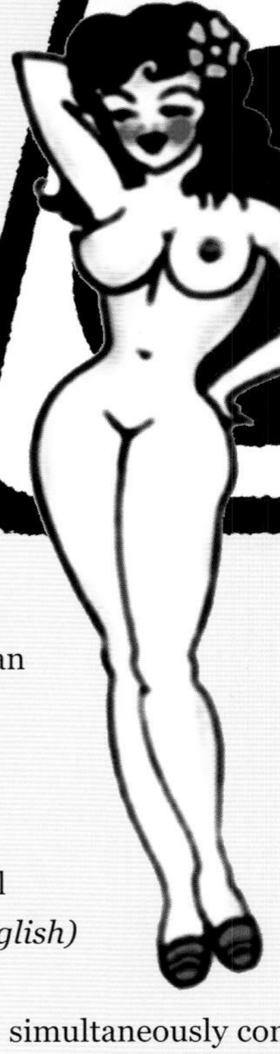

BUG CHASER...a non-infected gay male who deliberately tries to acquire HIV, usually from someone called a "gift giver"

BUMBO...vagina (archaic black British)

BUSHEL BUBBY...big-breasted woman (archaic English)

BUTTERED BUN...having sex with a woman who has just had sex with another man gives you a "buttered bun" (archaic English)

BUZZ BOMB...penis

CASABAS...breasts

CAPTAIN IS AT HOME, THE...I'm menstruating

CAR WASH...blowjob (Canadian)

CHANGE THE OIL...fuck

CHICK-A-BIDDY...young slut (archaic English)

CUNNY-HAUNTED...pussy hound (archaic English)

COCK WAGON...a car designed to impress women

CLEANING UP THE KITCHEN...licking an anus before fucking it

CLEANING ONE'S RIFLE....male masturbation

COOYONS...balls

CRAPPER TAPPER...male homosexual

CRINKUMS...gonorrhea (archaic English)

CULO...ass (Spanish)

DAISY CHAIN...three or more people simultaneously connected by oral sex

DEALYBOB...clitoris

DILLY-BOY...male prostitute (British, 1930s)

DOCK...to fuck

DOLLYMOPPER...stud (British, 1800s)

DOODLE SACK...vagina (archaic English)

DUNG-PUNCHER...male homosexual (Australian 1960s)

DUTCH BOY...a gay man who hangs out with lesbians

EINSTEIN...pubic hair

ETCH-A-SKETCH...playing with a woman's nipples

FLIT...male homosexual

FLYCATCHER...vagina

FONDLING THE FIG...female masturbation

FRENCHIFIED...infected with an STD (archaic English)

FUN 'N' OBSCURE SEX SLANG
YOU CAN USE TO IMPRESS THE CHICKS!

FROGSKIN...condom (1920s Australia)

FUSTY LUGGS...a disgusting slut (archaic English)

FUZZ BUMPER...lesbian

GENTILE DICK...uncircumcised penis

GLAMITY...vagina (Jamaican)

GLEET...gonorrhea discharge (British)

GOLDEN WINNEBAGOS...breasts

GRINDSMAN...stud (Jamaican)

GUBB...semen

GUNCH...to fellate

GWARRY...vagina (South African)

HASBIAN...ex-lesbian

HEDGE WHORE...a prostitute who will fuck you anywhere (archaic English)

HOUSE OF COMMONS...prostitute's vagina

HUNG LIKE A TIC-TAC...has a tiny penis

HYMIE...anus

INDUSTRIAL ACCIDENT...orgasm

JAGS...horny (South African)

KAZOO...ass

KNISH...vagina (Yiddish)

LACE CURTAINS...foreskin

LEATHER CHEERIO...anus

LESBRO...a male who hangs out with lesbians

LOOP-DE-LOOP...simultaneous mutual oral sex; 69

MANTHRAX...semen

MEAT AND POTATOES...penis and testicles

MR. MENTION...stud (Jamaican)

NARROW AT THE EQUATOR...has a tiny penis

NASH...vagina (Jamaican)

NULL THE VOID...masturbate

NUTMEGS...testicles

PEARL DIVER...one who performs blowjobs

PEBBLES...a sexually active underaged female

PEG BOY...a boy prostitute; the word is derived from an actual practice in certain British bordellos during the 1800s of forcing boy prostitutes to sit on wooden pegs to dilate their anuses

PEPPERED...infected with STDs (archaic English)

PINEAPPLE...a male's package

PLAYING CANASTA...eyeballing the crotches of passersby

PROUD...horny (archaic English)

PUMPKIN EATER...pedophile

PUM-PUM...vagina (Jamaican)

PUNTERS...porn addicts; johns (British)

RED WINGS...performing cunnilingus while a woman is menstruating

ROLFING THE PIGLET...male masturbation

SCHLAMPENSCHLEPPER, DER...pimp wagon (German)

SCHMECKEL...penis (Yiddish)

SCROGGING...fucking (archaic English)

SHAKING HANDS WITH THE UNEMPLOYED...masturbating

SHEMPING THE HOG...male masturbation

SKEET...an ejaculatory spurt

SKO...a skanky ho

SLAUGHTERHOUSE...a singles bar that reeks of desperation

SNOW QUEEN...black male homosexual who only dates white men

STRAW...a woman skilled at sex; a female who's good "in the straw" (archaic English)

STROKE THE BLOKE...masturbate

TATERS...breasts

THREE-PENNY UPRIGHT...a prostitute who has sex while standing with her back to a wall (archaic English)

TOPCOAT...condom

TUNTI...vagina (Jamaican)

TURN IN YOUR 'V' CARD...lose your virginity

VAGITARIAN...lesbian

WAGTAIL...a slut (archaic English)

WATER CHESTNUTS...a gay Japanese sailor

WAY DOWN SOUTH IN DIXIE, TO GO...to fellate

WESTERN PATIO...flat ass

WHORE PIPE...penis

WICKET...vagina (medieval English)

WINKTEPI...male butt-sex (Lakota Indian)

YESTERGAY...someone who transforms from gay to straight seemingly overnight

YONI...vagina (Sanskrit)

MAN, I'D SURE LIKE TO BLOW THE GROUNSILS WITH THAT GIRL AND SKEET ALL OVER HER! SHE'S A BIT OF RASPBERRY!

ARE YOU KIDDING? THAT FUSTY LUGGS MAY BE A BUSHEL BUBBY, BUT I'LL BET SHE'S FRENCHIFIED!

The Sad, Lonely World of

BIOLOGICAL SEX FREAKS

For all higher living creatures, nature has drawn a strict, sharp dividing line between two genders. Only lower life forms such as germs and viruses can be considered truly "intersexual."

Sometimes, though, nature fucks up. All human fetuses are initially asexual cumstains, but around the three-month mark, most have the good sense to start heading toward the room marked either LADIES or GENTS. In thankfully rare instances, the wires get crossed, chromosomes misfire, and out plops a sexual monster with genitals that are either deformed or—worse—of indeterminate gender.

Historically, biological sex freaks have been stigmatized and ostracized. When not outright murdered by an angry mob of normals with normal genitals, they were forced to undergo brutal, life-threatening surgical procedures to correct their highly unsexy birth defects.

Their psychosexual scars leave them violated, wounded, and afraid of genuine intimacy, not to mention the shame, distress, self-hatred, and second-guessing that afflict their parents on a near-hourly basis.

It is a sad and lonely world these freaks inhabit. They ARE different from us. Far, far different. As normal, superior, genitally intact human beings, we are duty-bound to look after them. To pity them. We are to reach out with paternalistic condescension across the chasm that separates us from these deformed textbook specimens.

In keeping with such a spirit of inner revulsion masked as patronizing charity, I present to you a Dirty Dozen of genetically induced sex syndromes. Approach with care, and don't fall in love.

DIPHALLIA

AFFECTS: MALES ONLY

FREQUENCY OF OCCURRENCE: 1 PER 2.5 MILLION MALE BIRTHS

SUMMARY: One man, TWO PENISES! In many cases, it is actually only one penis split along the shaft. But the extremely rare "true diphallia" features anything from two distinct dickie-heads to two fully developed urogenital tracts.

HYPOSPADIAS

AFFECTS: MALES ONLY

FREQUENCY OF OCCURRENCE: 1 PER 300 MALE BIRTHS

SUMMARY: The urethral meatus (pee-hole) is located anywhere on the penis but where it should be, almost like the hole on a flute.

HERMAPHRODITISM

AFFECTS: HARD TO TELL

FREQUENCY OF OCCURRENCE:
"TRUE" VERSION—1 PER 83,000 LIVE BIRTHS
"PSEUDO" VERSION—1 PER 500 LIVE BIRTHS

SUMMARY: A "true" hermaphrodite's internal sex organs contain both ovarian and testicular tissue. In some cases, this means a ball on one side and an ovary on the other; in others, it means hybrid beasties known as "ovatestes." To the naked eye, their external genitals tend to be iffy—maybe it's a big clit, perhaps it's a teeny weenie, perchance it's some unholy peno-vaginal mishmash. Pseudo-hermaphrodites have the chromosomes and internal sex organs of only one gender while their external protuberances are, again, anyone's guess.

KLINEFELTER'S SYNDROME

AFFECTS: MALES ONLY

FREQUENCY OF OCCURRENCE: 1.5 PER 1,000 MALE BIRTHS

SUMMARY: An extra "X" chromosome or two leads to above-average height, tiny nuts, low testosterone, sub-par intelligence, sterility, and in some cases, embarrassing man-boobs.

TURNER'S SYNDROME

AFFECTS: FEMALES ONLY

FREQUENCY OF OCCURRENCE: 1 PER 2,500 FEMALE BIRTHS

SUMMARY: The absence of a crucial "X" chromosome results in average adult heights of 4'7", a sad-looking "triangular" face, a short neck that is often webbed, a barren womb, swollen hands, spotted pigmentation, turned-out elbows, and small breasts spaced widely apart with inverted nipples.

MICROPENIS

AFFECTS: MALES ONLY

FREQUENCY OF OCCURRENCE: 1 PER 165 MALE BIRTHS

SUMMARY: The penis is normally shaped and fully functional yet hilariously small. In extremely rare cases—an estimated one in 30 million—there isn't even the suggestion of a penis.

PENILE TORSION

AFFECTS: MALES ONLY

FREQUENCY OF OCCURRENCE: Many men have it to some degree; not considered problematic unless penis is off-kilter more than one-eighth of a turn.

SUMMARY: The penis head and/or shaft is twisted like a corkscrew, for some reason almost always in a counterclockwise direction.

TRIPLE-X SYNDROME

AFFECTS: FEMALES ONLY

FREQUENCY OF OCCURRENCE: 1 PER 1,000 FEMALE BIRTHS

SUMMARY: An extra "X" chromosome causes these "metafemales" or "superfemales" to lag behind the curve in terms of intelligence and emotional maturity. However, this is more than atoned for by the fact that these gals are tall, leggy, buxom, and wide-hipped with super-thin waists.

SCROTAL TRANSPOSITION

AFFECTS: MALES ONLY

FREQUENCY OF OCCURRENCE: Common enough that I could find several disgusting photos of it on the Internet, but not so much that I could find a single estimate of its frequency.

SUMMARY: The penis and scrotum switch places. The ball-sac is positioned above the johnson and resembles elephant ears surrounding the trunk.

PERSISTENT CLOACA

AFFECTS: FEMALES ONLY

FREQUENCY OF OCCURRENCE: 1 PER 20,000 FEMALE BIRTHS

SUMMARY: The rectum, vagina, and urethra converge into one nauseating, funnel-like drainage hole located somewhere in the "taint" area between the clitoris and buttocks. Poop, pee, and vaginal sludge mingle freely. Corrective surgery is costly, complicated, and risky.

XYY SYNDROME

AFFECTS: MALES ONLY

FREQUENCY OF OCCURRENCE: 1 PER 1,000 MALE BIRTHS

SUMMARY: An extra "Y" chromosome gives these "supermales" extra height, testosterone, and acne. They have wide shoulders, thin hips, hairy bodies, and huge balls. Some evidence suggests they are prone toward lower intelligence and higher criminality.

DOUBLE VAGINA

AFFECTS: FEMALES ONLY

FREQUENCY OF OCCURRENCE: 1 PER 1,000 FEMALE BIRTHS

SUMMARY: A superfluous fleshy wall divides the vagina like an oriental room divider splits an apartment in two. Upon loss of virginity, one section stretches and assumes the role of "dominant" vagina. The other half becomes as cramped as a broom closet and thus infinitely more desirable.

ONE HUNDRED
famous quotes about
WOMEN

1. Never sleep with a woman whose troubles are worse than your own. —*Nelson Algren*

2. I trust only one thing in a woman: that she will not come to life again after she is dead. In all other things I distrust her. —*Antiphanes*

3. Man forgives woman anything save the wit to outwit him. —*Minna Antrim*

4. Women like silent men. They think they're listening. —*Marcel Archard*

5. It was a man's world. Then Eve arrived. —*Richard Armour*

6. No man should marry until he has studied anatomy and dissected at least one woman. —*Honoré de Balzac*

7. Only good girls keep diaries. Bad girls don't have time. —*Tallulah Bankhead*

8. Here's to woman! Would that we could fold into her arms without falling into her hands. —*Ambrose Bierce*

9. Women are nothing but machines for producing children. —*Napoleon Bonaparte*

10. To me, girls are just a pain in the ass. —*Brian "The Boz" Bosworth*

11. Good women always think it is their fault when someone else is being offensive. Bad women never take the blame for anything. —*Anita Brookner*

12. Even if man could understand women he still wouldn't believe it. —*AW Brown*

13. Good girls go to heaven, bad girls go everywhere. —*Helen Gurley Brown*

14. Do you know what it means to come home at night to a woman who'll give you a little love, a little affection, a little tenderness? It means you're in the wrong house, that's what it means. —*George Burns*

15. Women hate everything which strips off the tinsel of sentiment, and they are right, or it would rob them of their weapons. —*Lord Byron*

16. Here's all you have to know about men and women: Women are crazy, men are stupid. And the main reason women are crazy is that men are stupid. —*George Carlin*

17. I have always found women difficult. I don't really understand them. To begin with, few women tell the truth. —*Barbara Cartland*

18. The woman who tells her age is either too young to have anything to lose or too old to have anything to gain. —*Chinese Proverb*

19. Never trust a woman, even though she has given you ten sons. —*Chinese Proverb*

20. Women and people of low birth are very hard to deal with. If you are friendly to them, they get out of hand, and if you keep your distance, they resent it. —*Confucius*

21. Heav'n hath no rage like love to hatred turn'd, Nor Hell a fury, like a woman scorn'd. —*William Congreve*

22. Being a woman is a terribly difficult trade, since it consists principally of dealing with men. —*Joseph Conrad*

23. I wouldn't be caught dead marrying a woman old enough to be my wife. —*Tony Curtis*

24. Once a woman has forgiven her man, she must not reheat his sins for breakfast. —*Marlene Dietrich*

25. The gods have sent medicines for the venom of serpents, but there is no medicine for a bad woman. She is more noxious than the viper, or than fire itself. —*Euripides*

26. Terrible is the force of the waves of sea, terrible is the rush of the river and the blasts of hot fire, and terrible are a thousand other things; but none is such a terrible evil as woman. —*Euripides*

27. God gave women intuition and femininity. Used properly, the combination easily jumbles the brain of any man I've ever met. —*Farrah Fawcett*

28. Women are like elephants. Everyone likes to look at them but no one likes to have to keep one. —*W. C. Fields*

29. To find out a girl's faults, praise her to her girlfriends. —*Benjamin Franklin*

30. The great question which I have not been able to answer, despite my 30 years of research into the feminine soul, is "What does woman want?" —*Sigmund Freud*

31. Women are like death: they pursue those who flee from them, and flee from those who pursue them. —*German Proverb*

32. Women and cats will do as they please.

Men and dogs had better get used to it. —*Robert Heinle*

33. Sometimes I wonder if men and wome really suit each other. Perhaps they should li next door and just visit now and then. —*Katharine Hepbu*

34. A thousand men can easily live togethe in peace, but two women, even if they be sisters, can never do so. —*Hindu Prove*

35. Can you imagine a world without men? No crime and lots of happy fat women. —*Nicole Hollan*

36. Man has will, but woman has her way. —*Oliver Wendell Holm*

37. No trust is to be placed in women. —*Hom*

38. There is no fouler fiend than a woman when her mind is bent to evil. —*Hom*

39. Women's intuition is the result of millior of years of not thinking. —*Rupert Hugh*

40. If the wife sins, the husband is not innocent. —*Italian Prove*

41. Nature has given women so much powe that the law has very wisely given them little. —*Samuel Johns*

42. Show me a woman who doesn't feel gu and I'll show you a man. —*Erica Jo*

43. The female of the species is more deadl than the male. —*Rudyard Kipli*

44. In point of morals, the average woman is, even for business, too crooked. —*Stephen Leaco*

45. Age to women is like Kryptonite to Superman. —*Kathy Le*

46. I have nothing against women. As a matter of fact there's something about them that love, but I just can't put my finger on it. —*Jerry Lew*

47. I could sooner reconcile all Europe than two women. —*Louis X*

48. The people I'm getting furious with are the women's liberationists. They keep getting on their soapboxes proclaiming that women are brighter than men. That's true, but it should be kept quiet or it ruins the whole racket. —*Anita Loos*

49. Women should be obscene and not heard. —*Groucho Marx*

50. Anyone who knows anything of history knows that great social changes are impossible without feminine upheaval. Social progress can be measured exactly by the social position of the fair sex, the ugly ones included. —*Karl Marx*

51. A man's women folk, whatever their outward show of respect for his merit and authority, always regard him secretly as an ass, and with something akin to pity. His most gaudy sayings and doings seldom deceive them; they see the actual man within, and know him for a shallow and pathetic fellow. In this fact, perhaps, lies one of the best proofs of feminine intelligence, or, as the common phrase makes it, feminine intuition.

—*H. L. Mencken*

52. Bachelors know more about women than married men; if they didn't they'd be married too. —*H. L. Mencken*

53. Love is the delusion that one woman differs from another. —*H. L. Mencken*

54. On one issue at least, men and women agree; they both distrust women. —*H. L. Mencken*

55. When women kiss it always reminds me of prize fighters shaking hands. —*H. L. Mencken*

56. I expect Woman will be the last thing civilized by Man. —*George Meredith*

57. I don't mind living in a man's world as long as I can be a woman in it. —*Marilyn Monroe*

58. A man who has never made a woman angry is a failure in life.

—*Christopher Morley*

59. I've had bad luck with both my wives. The first one left me and the second one didn't. —*Patrick Murray*

60. Women would rather be right than reasonable.

—*Ogden Nash*

61. Ah, women. They make the highs higher and the lows more frequent.

—*Friedrich Nietzsche*

62. Are you visiting women? Do not forget your whip... —*Friedrich Nietzsche*

63. In revenge and in love, woman is more barbarous than man. —*Friedrich Nietzsche*

64. When a woman becomes a scholar there is usually something wrong with her sexual organs.

—*Friedrich Nietzsche*

65. Woman was God's second mistake.

—*Friedrich Nietzsche*

66. If women didn't exist, all the money in the world would have no meaning. —*Aristotle Onassis*

67. I'm not offended by all the dumb blonde jokes because I know I'm not dumb...and I also know that I'm not blonde.

—*Dolly Parton*

68. Behind every successful man is a surprised woman.

—*Maryon Pearson*

69. There are only two types of women—goddesses and doormats.

—*Pablo Picasso*

70. The woman cries before the wedding and the man after.

—*Polish Proverb*

71. Most women have no characters at all.

—*Alexander Pope*

72. One of the reasons I don't see eye to eye with Women's Lib is that women have it all on a plate if only they knew it. They don't have to be pretty either. —*Charlotte Rampling*

73. A woman is like a tea bag—you can't tell how strong she is until you put her in hot water.

—*Nancy Davis Reagan*

74. There's two theories to arguing with a woman. Neither one works. —*Will Rogers*

75. The reason that there are so few women comics is that so few women can bear being laughed at. —*Anna Russell*

76. Women's virtue is man's greatest invention.

—*Cornelia Otis Skinner*

77. The great and almost only comfort about being a woman is that one can always pretend to be more stupid than one is and no one is surprised.

—*Freya Stark*

78. A woman without a man is like a fish without a bicycle. —*Gloria Steinem*

79. Why does a woman work ten years to change a man's habits and then complain that he's not the man she married? —*Barbra Streisand*

80. Blessed are you, Lord our God, King of eternity, who has not created me a woman.

—*The Talmud*

81. If you want something said, ask a man; if you want something done, ask a woman.

—*Margaret Thatcher*

82. Women add zest to the unlicensed hours.

—*Allen Thomas*

83. I hate women because they always know where things are. —*James Thurber*

84. When I have one foot in the grave, I will tell the whole truth about women. I shall tell it, jump into my coffin, pull the lid over me and say, "Do what you like now." —*Leo Tolstoy*

85. What would men be without women? Scarce, sir, mighty scarce. —*Mark Twain*

86. Women are an alien race set down among us. —*John Updike*

87. If a man is talking in the forest, and there is no woman there to hear him, is he still wrong?

—*Jenny Weber*

88. Marriage is a great institution, but I'm not ready for an institution yet. —*Mae West*

89. When women go wrong, men go right after them. —*Mae West*

90. I only know that people call me a feminist whenever I express sentiments that differentiate me from a doormat or a prostitute. —*Rebecca West*

91. The main difference between men and women is that men are lunatics and women are idiots. —*Rebecca West*

92. Whatever women do they must do twice as well as men to be thought half as good. Luckily this is not difficult. —*Charlotte Whitton*

93. Women: Can't live with them, can't bury them in the back yard without the neighbors seeing.

—*Sean Williamson*

94. All women become like their mothers. That is their tragedy. No man does. That is his.

—*Oscar Wilde*

95. As long as a woman can look ten years younger than her own daughter, she is perfectly satisfied.

—*Oscar Wilde*

96. Every woman is a rebel, and usually in wild revolt against herself.

—*Oscar Wilde*

97. Every woman is wrong until she cries.

—*Oscar Wilde*

98. The only way a woman can ever reform her husband is by boring him so completely that he loses all possible interest in life. —*Oscar Wilde*

99. An exhaustive study of police records shows that no woman has ever shot her husband while he was doing the dishes. —*Earl Wilson*

100. Why are women so much more interesting to men than men are to women?

—*Virginia Woolf*

BATTLE
OF THE

S&M

TITANS

MARQUIS DE SADE
"FATHER OF SADISM"

LEOPOLD VON SACHER-MASOCH
"FATHER OF MASOCHISM"

DOMINANT

SUBMISSIVE

B. 1740
D. 1814

B. 1836
D. 1895

NATIONALITY:
FRENCH

NATIONALITY:
SPANISH,
GERMAN,
& UKRAINIAN

WHO'S THE BETTER WRITER?

WHO HAS HAD A MORE PROFOUND INFLUENCE?

WHICH DUDE WOULD I RATHER HANG OUT WITH

SADE

*Quotes from
Philosophy in the
Bedroom
(1795), by the
Marquis de Sade:*

"Nature has endowed each
of us with a capacity for
kindly feelings—let us not
squander them on others."

"What a weak fellow, this
God! How able he was to
mold all that we know and to fail to form man in his own guise!"

"It has pleased Nature so to make us that we attain happiness
only by way of pain. But once vanquished and had this way, nothing can taste the joy one tastes upon the entrance of this member
into our ass; it is a pleasure incontestably superior to any sensation procured by this same introduction in front."

"Fuck, Eugenie, fuck, my angel; your body is your own, yours
alone; in all the world there is but yourself who has the right to
enjoy it as you see fit."

"To lie is always a necessity for women; above all when they
choose to deceive, falsehood becomes vital for them."

"I ask...how a sincere individual will not always founder in a
society of false people."

"...I should cease to be your friend the instant you were to
become pregnant."

"...there is no doubt that we are much more keenly affected by
pain than by pleasure..."

"Let us no longer be the dupes of this rubbish: We owe nothing to
our parents...."

"Those laws, being forged for universal application, are in perpetual conflict with personal interest, just as personal interest is
always in contradiction with the general interest."

"Is murder then a crime against society? But how could that be
reasonably imagined? What difference does it make to this murderous society, whether it have one member more, or less?"

"I say then that women, having been endowed with considerably
more violent penchants for carnal desire than we, will be able to
give themselves over to it wholeheartedly, absolutely free of all
encumbering hymeneal ties, of all false notions of modesty,
absolutely restored to a state of Nature; I want laws permitting
them to give themselves over to as many men as they see fit...."

"The greatest of men lean toward sodomy."

"May this example serve to remind you that your daughter is old
enough to do what she wants; that she likes to fuck, loves to fuck,
that she was born to fuck, and that, if you do not wish to be
fucked yourself, the best thing for you to do is to let her do what
she wants."

MASOCH

Quotes from Venus in Furs *(1870), by Leopold
von Sacher-Masoch:*

"Whichever of the two fails to subjugate will soon feel the feet of
the other on his neck...."

"Man is the one who desires, woman is the one who is desired.
This is woman's entire but decisive advantage. Through man's
passion, nature has given man into woman's hands, and the
woman who does not know how to make him her subject, her
slave, her toy, and how to betray him with a smile in the end is
not wise."

"But at times he had violent attacks of sudden passion and gave
the impression of being about to ram his head through a wall.
At such times everyone preferred to get out of his way."

"He has only one choice: to be the tyrant over or the slave of
woman. As soon as he gives in, his neck is under the yoke, and
the lash will soon fall upon him."

"It runs—well—one is either very polite to one's self or very rude."

"And every man—I know this very well—as soon as he falls in love
becomes weak, pliable, ridiculous."

"If I am not permitted to enjoy the happiness of love, fully and
wholly, I want to taste its pains and torments to the very dregs; I
want to be maltreated and betrayed by the woman I love, and the
more cruelly the better. This, too, is a luxury."

"Never feel secure with the woman you love, for there are more
dangers in woman's nature than you imagine."

"Man, even when he is selfish or evil, always follows *principles*;
woman never follows anything but *impulses*."

"I seem like a little captive mouse with which a beautiful cat pret-
tily plays. She is ready at any moment to tear it to pieces, and my
heart of a mouse threatens to burst."

"'Very well then, be my slave,' she replied, 'but don't forget that I
no longer love you, and your love doesn't mean any more to me
than a dog's, and dogs are to be kicked.'"

"Pleasure alone lends value to existence; whoever enjoys does not
easily part from life, whoever suffers or is needy meets death like
a friend."

"'Each one of us in the end is a Samson,' I thought, 'and ultimately
for better or worse is betrayed
by the woman he loves, whether
she wears an ordinary coat or
sables.'"

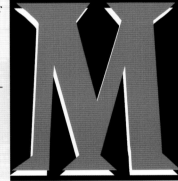

"But the moral?"
"That woman, as nature has
created her, and as man at present is educating her, is man's
enemy. She can only be his
slave or his despot, but never
his *companion*."

"The moral of the tale is this:
Whoever allows himself to be
whipped, deserves to be whipped."

UNDERSTANDING the MALE NIPPLE
object of mystery, fountain of pleasure

The average heterosexual man spends most of his waking hours worried about whether he's a homosexual. Thus, it comes as no comfort for him to apprehend the biological fact that we all began this Grand Journey Called Life as females—nestled inside our mothers' sticky wombs, our ovaries morphed into testes, our clits swelled into cocks, and our nipples...well, they just sort of stayed nipples. They didn't exactly become tits, but they didn't go away, either.

A majority of females are said to derive sexual pleasure from having their nipples rubbed, poked, pinched, sucked, and batted around like birthday balloons. And according to no less noble a source than the venerable JackinWorld.com, at least one in five males enjoys similarly bawdy delights when attention is paid to his udders. His nipples are bona fide erogenous zones which shoot electrical impulses to his brain, which then ricochet straight down to his groin. In extreme cases, these men are able to reach a hearty climax merely through having their man-nips touched.

What are we to make of such men? If they derive sexual pleasure from having their pert, pinkish areolas pinched, are they automatically homosexual? If the slightest feathery touch on their bazooms sends them squealing like a boar hog rutting in mud, should they just come out of the closet? I need to know the answer for personal reasons. Not for me, of course. It's for a friend.

THE WORD "MAMMAL" is derived from the Latin *mamma*, meaning "breast." Most male mammals have mammaries, a.k.a. *mammae masculinae*. There are exceptions, such as the noble stallion and the pesky male rat, who is so macho he emits hormones which suppress nipple growth. But all humans have nipples; we just don't know what to do with them.

We all have nipples, people. Shortly after fertilization, "precursor nipples" form in all fetuses. These proto-nips don't become sex-specific until six to eight weeks post-conception, at which time the hormones kick in to determine gender. Without sufficient estrogen, the fetus becomes a male. Although all infants are born with nipples and milk glands, most boy-nips will never become tits.

Like all things involving Mother Nature, there are cruel exceptions. In rare instances, male infants born with too much estrogen will lactate at birth, emitting what the old wives call "witches' milk." In adult males, hormonal imbalances can also cause a condition known as "gynaecomastia," in which female-style hooters develop.

Modern scientific literature on man-nips suggests they are merely the vestiges of evolution, biologically useless leftovers such as the appendix, tailbone, toenails, and tonsils. As with all these other parts, the nipples do not yet constitute enough of a functional impediment for us to lose them through natural selection.

But unlike all the other parts listed, the nipples serve a definite biological function for one gender, while they seem nearly worthless for the other—unless you value the bawdy joys of human sensuality. The male nipple may be the only part of a man's body whose only discernible purpose is sexual pleasure. It is the male clitoris.

Theodore van de Velde was a Dutch gynecologist who croaked in 1937 and is credited with being the first physician to describe the male nipple as an erogenous zone. Yet despite such clinical endorsements of the idea that enjoying nipple stimulation DOESN'T NECESSARILY MAKE YOU QUEER, pervasive societal prejudice exists toward the practice.

ON THE INTERNET, the soft cooing of New Age hausfraus urging men to "celebrate their nipples" and be "nipple-positive" doesn't help matters, nor do their instructions for female sex partners to "dry-nurse" from their male lovers' teats. Although couched in a heterosexual framework, it just amplifies the Homo Factor tenfold.

Hardcore gay websites featuring inveterate cocksuckers describing male nipples as "chest cocks" and "semi-hard penis heads" likewise provide little comfort to the homophobic male who enjoys having his man-mams tweaked every so often. Detailed instructions about how men can use rubber bands or snake-bite suction cups to increase their nipple size also give pause to the self-doubting hetero. And let's not talk about the one guy who wears bras or the other who fantasizes about having gay males suckle on his lactating dugs.

The fact remains that my friend enjoys having his nipples pinched. And the question remains as to whether or not that makes him a fag.

> **"We all have nipples, people...[but] the male nipple may be the only part of a man's body whose only discernible purpose is sexual pleasure. It is the male clitoris."**

KORO, KORO, KORO!

Being a man is defined by having a penis, but it is also understood that a man is somehow not the *same thing* as his penis and that the penis might be a different creature entirely. Sigmund Freud's "castration anxiety" theory posited that men suffer from the near-constant fear that they will lose their penises and thus cease to be men at all.

While terrifying to those whom it afflicts, castration anxiety is, naturally, very funny to everyone else.

In the phenomenon of **koro,** also known as "genital retraction syndrome," we are faced with vivid, hilarious evidence of Freud's theory in living action. Koro is defined in the *Diagnostic and Statistical Manual of Psychiatry* as an "episode of sudden and intense anxiety that the penis...will recede into the body and possibly cause death."

Although there is scant medical evidence of this ever actually occurring, the textbooks are filled with cases of men injuring their tallywhackers in attempts to *prevent* it from happening by frantically yanking at their cocks with clamps, hooks, weights, and strings.

Koro has been reported for thousands of years, both in individuals and, more enjoyably, in cases of mass hysteria. The word "koro" is thought to be of Malaysian derivation, but debate exists whether its source is a word meaning "shrinkage" or one meaning "turtle head." The Chinese call it *suo-yang* and Thais call it *rokjoo*, with both terms roughly translating to "genital shrinkage."

Its first literary mention is thought to be in *The Yellow Emperor's Classic of Internal Medicine,* a Chinese opus from around 300 B.C., where sudden cock-loss is blamed on a severe deficiency of "yang" essence. Ancient Chinese folklore also points the finger at the *hu-li-jing,* beautiful female "ghost foxes" who have nothing better to do than steal men's genitals.

Medieval European folklore is rife with tales of cock-thieving witches. A 1486 account mentions a witch who cursed a young Bavarian lad so that he "lost his member" and "could see or touch nothing but his smooth body." A century later, a German observer speculated that "a demon dulls the senses and blinds the eyes of those persons who think that their testicles or all of their sexual organs are removed...by the power and skill of Satan." Koro persists in the modern-day West, albeit in isolated cases rather than mass panics. Instead of witches, it has been attributed to epilepsy, brain tumors, strokes, and schizophrenia.

For modern koro epidemics, one must turn to the misty, opium-shrouded East and the Dark Continent of Africa. One of the most widely documented "penis panics" occurred in 1967 in Singapore. Word circulated that a strain of pork which had been inoculated against swine fever was shrinking the ding-dongs of men who'd eaten it. Mass hysteria ensued after the story was reported in newspapers, with more than 500 Singaporean gents delusionally seeking help for their incredible shrinking penises.

In Thailand in 1976, rumors spread that Vietnamese communists had tainted the water supply with a powder that caused penile shrinky-dinking. More than 2,000 Thai men complained of koro-like symptoms until government officials assured them that their dicks were just naturally small.

Public officials in West Bengal, India, quelled a similarly large koro outbreak in 1982 by publicly measuring the cocks of the afflicted.

Mass koro panics have beset the Chinese province of Guangdong since the late 1800s. During a koro attack in 1984–1985, 2,000 or more young Chinamen fell under the delusion that their peenies were retracting into their bodies.

Koro epidemics in Africa tend to add the element of mob violence. In January, 1997, 12 accused witches in Ghana were pummeled to death by crowds certain their victims had cast spells to dwindle the dicky-doos of local men. The mania spread to the Ivory Coast two months later, where superstitious phallocentric hordes murdered an additional seven suspected schlong-attenuating sorcerers.

Similar bursts of violent atavistic mania erupted in Nigeria and Benin in 2001, when at least 24 people were slaughtered by roving packs of locals hell-bent on killing whomever was stealing all the penises. In one attack, eight traveling evangelists were simultaneously burned alive.

Handshakes by a mysterious man known as "Satan's Friend" were largely blamed for a Sudanese koro outbreak in 2003. But in one case, it was said that a man lost Wee Willie by using a comb lent to him by a foreigner.

"No doubt, this comb was a laser-controlled surgical robot that penetrates the skull [and passes] to the lower body and emasculates a man!!" wrote Sudanese columnist Ja'far Abbas, warning citizens that they should neither shake the hands of strangers nor borrow combs from them. Abbas said the penis-melting comb came from "an imperialist Zionist agent that was sent to prevent our people from procreating and multiplying...."

Of course, all of the accusers in all of these cases who were actually examined by physicians were found to have their penises intact and fully functional.

As with most things regarding humans, it's their *minds* we need to worry about.

the wild, wacky, weird Phenomenon of "PENIS PANICS"

Nobody likes a loose vagina. Nobody enjoys a flippy-floppy, slippery-sloppy, honking tuba of a twat. There is no pleasure in a belching basilica of a beaver. I will hear no more of these flatulent, oscillating Jabba the Cunts. If I see another news story where yet another woman "accidentally" lodges a TV set inside her cooch, I'm going to write a letter to my congressman. As a society, we've had enough of ladies with loose laps! Begone with them!

10 tips toward a tighter pussy

Just as all men would rather have a big penis than a small one, all women would rather have a tight vagina than a loose one. If you ask them, this is what they'd say, in these exact words: "Oh, I'd definitely prefer having a tight vagina than a loose one." So let their words be made flesh! Let our fair damsels have tight vaginas! Bestow unto our women tiny constrictor 'gineys which can rip a penis from the root at will. Give to them the sort of taut, snare-drum snatches upon which you could bounce a dime.

A sleek, tight hoochie-noo-noo provides some of the purest pleasures a man can find on this li'l ball o' earwax called Planet Earth. Old-school sex doctors Masters and Johnson, after scrutinizing thousands of penises and vaginas up close, declared that sexual pleasure was directly proportional to how much friction a couple could produce by bumpin' uglies. The bigger the penis or the tighter the vagina, the better the sex. It's a fact. It's also a fact that if you're able to plop your thing inside her without much effort, her hole could probably do with a tune-up. As long as you can get it in, there's no such thing as "too tight."

But it isn't totally about your pleasure. In many cases, a tighter pussy allows the woman to actually feel that thing you call a dick. She might even have an orgasm finally!

But how is the discriminating lady to know which vaginal-tightening regimen is the best for her own vagina and its unique needs? That's why I've provided this list. I've included several practical things which the tight-vadge-obsessed woman SHOULD do and a few impractical things which she SHOULDN'T.

1 STAY YOUNG

There's a reason men of all ages prefer younger women, beyond obvious things such as their fresh skin and pert breasts and refreshing ignorance of the sort of lies which men tell. It's because young vaginas haven't been weatherbeaten by the ignoble ravages of age. "Vaginal relaxation" occurs naturally with time as the pelvic muscles grow lax and your once-fair maiden loses her "honeymoon fit." The vagina increases in diameter. Her twat takes on the gummy looseness of a hippo's mouth, and what you once thought was love dissolves into eternal resentment. However, since there's no known cure for growing old, I'll shuttle you right off to the next tip…

Although you can't stop growing old, every woman on earth who operates above the level of primate retardation is able to avoid producing offspring. Beyond obvious drawbacks such as the fact that kids scream and wipe their shit on the walls and grow up into bitter delinquents who give you a heart attack and make you rue the day you ever had unprotected sex, the li'l nippers' entry into this world is accomplished by the near-total ruination of your vaginal integrity. That ten-pound ball of pink regret blows a cannon hole through a previously pristine pussy. But if you insist on breeding, at least slip your pediatrician an extra 20-spot and have him stitch you back up tight enough to squeeze a Tootsie Roll.

2 DON'T HAVE KIDS

3 DON'T HAVE SEX

Scientists will tell you that the vagina is made of spongy elastic tissue which can shrink or swell to accommodate nearly anything which invades it. They claim it is impossible for a woman to become "stretched-out" or "loose" after having her vagina pummeled by dozens of penises. Don't believe them. A woman's vagina can become irreparably slackened after only one encounter with an above-average wongus.

4 QUIT STICKING THINGS IN THERE

You think that nobody knows you do it? You think that nobody talks about you doing it? You think that it hasn't been, like, the sole focus of our water-cooler jokes for the last six months? Quit sticking things in there. You're gonna blow a gasket.

5 DO KEGEL EXERCISES

Dr. Arnold Kegel was an L.A. gyno-doctor who sure loved himself some tight pussy. His "Kegel" exercises, developed in the 1940s, are the Pilates of the Vagina, designed to tone the pubococcygeus (PC) muscle, eventually allowing any average homely woman to wrap her vadge around a man's cock with python-like force. The PC muscle is the same one which controls your flow of urine. Once you are able to isolate this muscle and strengthen it, you will be able to isolate any man and weaken him.

6 LIFT VAGINAL WEIGHTS

The vaginal-tightening market suffers no shortage of cones, beads, weights, spheres, and steel eggs which any woman can insert halfway up her honey-hole and flex her sugar walls against. They bear such colorful product names as Betty's Barbell, GyneFlex, Smart Balls, and the time-honored Kegelcisor.

7 USE VAGINAL CREAMS

Some "vaginal-tightening creams" contain herbal astringents, some are chemically based, and some contain useless compounds which have no effect on a twat's tautness. Creams containing benzocaine affect the appearance of tightness by numbing the pussy and making it less likely to lubricate, thus superficially seeming tighter. Others feature potassium alum, often used in deodorants, which can actually constrict a woman's hole. It can also cause rashes and yeast infections, but isn't it worth it?

8 VAGINAL SURGERY

Various medical techniques, some employing lasers and others sticking to the cold steel scalpel, are grouped under the life-affirming moniker of "vaginal rejuvenation surgery." Stretched muscles are joined together and "redundant" skin flaps are removed. There is a slight risk of mortality and a larger risk of infection from such procedures. The husband receives a bill for $5,000 and his wife returns home the same day with a vagina which, when fully healed, will be able to crack walnuts.

9 NEUROMUSCULAR ELECTRICAL STIMULATION

An electric prod inserted into the vagina delivers currents which stimulate the pelvic floor and lead to muscular contraction. Over a series of treatments, the woman's tweeter shrinks to a size acceptable to her man.

10 NEOCONTROL THERAPY

A patented technology in which the patient sits in a chair while "highly focused pulsed magnetic fields" roll over their crotch, causing the pelvic-floor muscles to contract. After half-hour sessions twice weekly for eight weeks, the woman walks away with a vagina nimble enough to make change for a dollar.

It produces tremendous sadness among consenting adults. A terrifyingly disheartening experience, it causes great distrust between couples. A neglected, regrettable cubbyhole of human sexuality, it has ruined thousands of relationships.

When a woman's vagina ruins a tender moment with a loud, unexpected expulsion of Cunt Gas, what is the discerning gentleman to do? When the giant slimy clam opens its mouth and belches, what is the proper etiquette? Do you ignore it…or try to console her…or do you tell her how truly repelled you are? Do you try to make light of it with jokes such as, "Who CUNT the cheese?" Or do you immediately get up, get dressed, leave, and never call her again? Do you ridicule her as a cheap hooker filled with rotted sperm? Or do you reply with a friendly fart of your own?

Even if she only does it once, and even if you don't tell your parents or clergyman about it, her slovenly vaginal eructation will always be in the back of your mind, forever destroying any hopes for total intimacy. It's something you need to talk about with your physician and your marriage counselor, and even if they're helpful, the damage may have already been done.

We're talking about pussy farts, gentlemen. Beaver burps. Muff music. The medical term, "vaginal flatulence," sounds like the name of a death-metal band. In England and Australia, where "fanny" is synonymous with "pussy," they call them "fanny farts." Still others call them "varts," a contraction of "vagina" and "farts."

But the most popular slang term to describe vaginal flatulence seems to be "queef." Some say the word is onomatopoeic and describes the sound the vagina makes when it unexpectedly expels air during sex—*queef!* Others say it's a combination of "quim" and "whiff." Others insist the word isn't "queef" at all, but rather "quiff." Or "queeb." Or "queever." Or "quiblet." A correspondent from Southern California says his homeboys call it a "quafe," rhyming with "safe." In eastern Canada it's called a "keiff," rhyming with "knife."

But whatever you call it, at least call it "disgusting."

Though comedians such as George Carlin, Howard Stern, Richard Pryor, and "Dice" Clay have made sport of it, rare is the woman who finds pussy farts funny.

Since it typically happens during moments of sexual rapture, at those rare, blessed moments when men and women share each others' bodies and spirits in the fullness of what it means to be a Sexual Being, the pussy fart is perhaps the single most disgusting and soul-destroying bodily function known to mankind. Unfortunate human realities such as body odor and anal mishaps are the domain of both sexes; vaginal flatulence, like menstruation, belongs in a Realm of Disgust exclusive to the fairer sex. Both male and female genitals can be seen, touched, tasted, and smelled. But only the vagina boldly ventures into the fifth sense, that of sound.

Flurpf! Fwomp! Blurp! Flap! Splat! Thar she blows! A warm, wet, stinky blast from the vaginal steamhole. How charming. How dainty. How thoroughly ladylike. Even without vaginal flatulence, the female procreative organs are a repulsive parfait of mucus membranes intermittently exploding with blood; the pussy fart is the cherry on top, proving forevermore that WOMEN CAN BE ICKY.

So whenever a group of women start raggin' about how all men are disgusting, all you need to say are two words:

"PUSSY FARTS."

The room will become silent. The women will either slink away in shame or attack you *en masse*.

THE PUSSY FART IS SHROUDED in disinformation and misunderstanding. This reporter could find no direct medical texts dealing with the topic of "vaginal flatulence," and this after days of wading through Google.

Surprisingly scant literature exists on a subject acknowledged as so universal. This may be evidence that even doctors are embarrassed that it happens and don't want to think about it.

QUEEFER MADNESS

clearing the air abou
PUSSY FARTS

A physician friend likewise came up with no solid research but instead offered the following opinions:

"I did a MedLine search on vaginal flatulence and found jack diddly. However, based on some personal reflection…it is most likely due to the architecture of the particular vagina. Firm vaginas allow for a tighter seal around the penis, letting less air penetrate into the vaginal vault when the piston-like action of intercourse occurs. This forces air into, and then out of the dead end of the vagina. It would follow then, that loose vaginal muscles will allow queefing to occur. What causes loose vaginas is academic, however, but if a human being has tumbled out of it, or if it's been mercilessly penetrated, logic would indicate these as probable contributors."

A group of women on a post-hysterectomy BBS reported an increase in pussy-farting after their operations, which lends credence to the idea that it's caused by a loose vagina. And a phenomenon known as "windsucking"—basically, equine pussy-farting—occurs among female horses whose cunt-caves have been rendered slack after giving birth.

Several accounts suggest that it occurs most often during "doggy style" intercourse. Many other women report pussy-farting during orgasm. This may be due to the fact that a woman's vaginal muscles expand and contract during orgasm like chimney bellows, sucking air in and then blowing it out.

Pussy-farting is not always caused by sexual activity, because some women claim to get them during yoga squats or other strenuous feats. Through skillful vaginal flexing, many women can actually produce them at will, causing great mirth at slumber parties and in the girls' bathroom.

THERE'S AMPLE CINEMATIC EVIDENCE of such willful vaginal flatulence. Most notorious is perhaps a 1979 Mitchell Brothers film featuring one "Honeysuckle Divine" and her amazing talkin' snatch. A thing of repellent wonder, Ms. Divine's

poony-ya-ya quacks and snorts and breathes and shoots ping-pong balls and blows out candles to the snickering delight of an S.F. grindhouse audience. Another video has circulated for years that was allegedly sent by a wannabe groupie to virtuoso guitarist Steve Vai. For what seems like ten hours, she tries to woo the fast-fingered rocker by making frapping sounds with her sloppy starfucker gash. There are also reports of porn vids wherein a saucy female blows out every flame in a candelabrum with her snatch before drinking a goblet of cum…another where a girl fanny-farts into a flute…even a video called *Amber the Lesbian Queefer*.

But in stark contrast to such willful pussy-farters stand perhaps millions of women who not-so-silently endure the humiliation and social stigma of involuntary vaginal flatulence. What's worse is that there's no way to tell whether a potential mate will be prone to queefing.

It's not like the vagina is a coal mine and you can send a canary in there to test whether it's safe.

I have a friend who, back in his high-school days, dated a gal who once pussy-farted nonstop for a half-minute after he pulled his meatbone out of her.

It was to be their last date. The next day in school, he told everyone of her vagina's didgeridoo-like performance. They all laughed and started making cruel farting noises whenever she'd walk by them in the hallway. She was emotionally ruined and probably became a nun or a stripper.

I ONCE KNEW A GIRL who queefed so much, it was as if her cunt was a set of worn bagpipes hiding under her tartan schoolgirl dress. She had straight black hair, a round face, and nostrils big enough to insert coins in them. And her cunt snorted like a bronco. It was a frickin' whoopie cushion, let me tell ya. She spent much of our relationship speaking through a muff megaphone. She was disgusted and ashamed of her relentlessly belching cuntflaps. It humiliated her to the point of violence on more than one occasion.

Her mortification at queefing was directly tied to the hatred she bore for her vagina, which was directly tied to her guilt, which was directly tied to her low self-esteem, which was directly tied to the lowness of her self. She localized her self-hatred in the act of queefing, rather than the proper place, i.e., her entire being.

And yet, maybe we're looking in all the wrong places, too. One often mistakenly searches for profound answers amid the tangible and pragmatic. As we all know, the vagina is a gateway into the mystical. Perhaps the reason we can find no concrete answers about the pussy fart is that it's hard to find spiritual things stuck amid common, vile concrete.

Is it possible that a pussy fart is actually the voice of the Goddess? Does a queefing cunt serve as some sort of Vaginal Oracle? Is that the voice of the Mother of All Creation speaking through the meat curtain? Is the pussy fart some sort of Lost Chord leading us all into a new gynocratic age? Viewed in such a celestial light, the vagina becomes a spiritual vessel, sort of like a tooth filling that receives radio transmissions. And perhaps the message is urgent, like a dog trying to lead villagers to a child trapped down a well.

Maybe it just sounds like dolphinspeak to us because our technology is too crude, our fall from grace too complete, to ever understand what Goddess is trying to say when she speaks through a pussy fart.

One mouth is never enough for a woman. Maybe we aren't listening closely enough, and maybe there is a message deep inside those talking vaginas, if we can only get past our understandable disgust.

REAL

JEB, 27, IS A GRILL CHEF at a downtown Portland steakhouse. His heavy upper body rests atop skinny legs like a barrel perched on toothpicks. Standing in the parking lot behind his restaurant and wearing a beef-splattered apron, Jeb drags on a cigarette and complains that his girlfriend isn't fat enough.

With tattooed arms, Buddy Holly glasses, and a thick roll of neck blubber, Jeb is no svelte specimen himself. Accordingly, he says he is not attracted to women who are less than 50 pounds overweight.

"My girlfriend is heavy—she wouldn't be my girlfriend if she wasn't—but she isn't heavy enough," Jeb gripes. "She could be bigger. They could always be bigger. I love her the way she is. I'd just love her more if she was fatter."

Jeb says he sometimes masturbates to the idea of over-feeding his girlfriend. Many of his fantasies revolve around escorting her to an all-you-can-eat pancake breakfast and forcing her to masticate until she needs to be rolled out on a hand truck. "I want to make her eat, like, two dozen pancakes and a couple dozen hot links. Loads of grease and syrup and butter dripping every-where, and then, of course, we DO it."

But thus far, Jeb has been unable to cattle-prod his girlfriend into actualizing his darkest wishes. "She eats, sure, but not as much as I'd like. She sometimes gets a little suspicious when I encourage her to just shovel the food down her throat, and she gets like, 'Why do you want me to eat so much?' I once watched her polish off nine Krispy Kremes in one sitting, but still, she didn't finish the whole box of a dozen." Jeb says he's still angry that he had to eat the other three donuts.

"My ultimate fantasy," Jeb leers, "is to be doing her from behind as she's down on all fours in front of an open refrigerator. As I'm drilling her, she's chowing down on a pair of cream pies I've placed in the crisper. I get turned-on at the idea of all that whipped cream smeared over her face. I also like the idea that she's eating while I'm doing her. But my girlfriend thinks that's degrading, so she won't do it, so for now it's still just a fantasy."

Jeb, who grew up with a big butterball of a mom, says his first sexual fixation on an obese woman developed as a child watching the "Lulu" character on the *Hee Haw* TV program. Jeb says he finds female fat comforting—"like a big, soft feather bed I can fall asleep on." He says he likes to nuzzle his face in his girlfriend's teats and belly. He speaks hopefully of a day when he'll be able to get "swallowed up in her fat" as if she were an amoeba and he was a food particle.

"I don't insist that ALL women get fat," he says defensively. "It's not like I'm some kind of pro-fat bigot or something. It's just that I want a special girl that I can fatten up all by myself."

For now, though, it's only a dream. Jeb is forced to nurture his fantasies by visiting feeder porn sites.

THE DISTURBINGLY PROFESSIONAL *DIMENSIONS* MAGAZINE [www.DimensionsMagazine.com], a slick and pop-ular pro-feeder publication, hosts a website that defines a feeder as "a fat admirer who…takes pleasure in the mechanics of the fattening process…a person who gains (sexual) pleasure from the act of…feeding…another person." It defines a feeder's part-ner, the "feedee," as someone who derives similar kicks from being fed. According to the fat fetishists at the Feeder UK website, a feeder's fantasies hinge on snagging a suitable feedee: "What a feed-er dreams of is a per-son who just eats and eats. One who loves themselves fat [and] wants to get fatter and fatter."

As opposed to the boringly political "size acceptance" crusaders and run-of-the-mill "fat admirers," feeders are proactive about their obsession. Feeders fantasize about feeding fat fillies even further. They don't love 'em just they way they are; they want to stuff 'em until they explode.

Watch as the Blue Ribbon-winning livestock gorge themselves silly. Behold the rolling sand dunes of pale blubber. The sickening sacs of suet. The giant pink marshmallows with vaginas buried somewhere deep inside. Snorting, squealing hogs. Bloated freaks. Gluttonous quarter-tonners. Gastric atrocities swelling up like a bag of Jiffy Pop. Watch them blow up to the point where they cease to be Earth Mothers and simply become the Earth.

Sounds disgusting to me, yet one man's puke bucket is another fella's sperm spittoon. For every, say, 100 men who are repulsed by such adipose aesthetics, there's one renegade stroker out there who likes to jerk off after tape-measuring his girlfriend's 50-inch thighs. My mission here is to peel away the layers of flab that obscure understanding and get to the bottom of all these fat-bottomed girls and the men who feed them.

THE FEEDERS ARE TO THE "FAT-ACCEPTANCE" COMMUNITY what NAMBLA is to the gay world—an embarrassing fringe group whose existence taints the larger movement and provides ammo for its enemies. Just when the pro-fat voices were enlightening society about sizeism's evils, along come the feeders pouring heavy cream into some porker's mouth with a funnel, making every chubby-chaser look like a sexual sadist.

Naturally, the shrillest attacks come from the fat admirers themselves, whose chief criticism is that feeders are antithetical to "fat acceptance" since they insist on altering their partners' size. But the feeder's intent, they allege, is far more sinister than mere size-alteration: It is to shackle a woman to a ball-and-chain fashioned of fat, imprisoning her inside a flab wall.

Opponents claim that the feeder/feedee relationship is fraught with abuse. They imply that sadism and control are the only motivations for males and insist that low self-esteem and abject self-hatred are what lure the women. They trot out horror stories of thin, cruel, handsome men force-feeding their partners to the point of immobility, at which point they abandon the gelatinous wretch and move on to new prey.

The feeders and feedees paint a much rosier portrait of their lifestyle than their critics do. They also lament that other size-acceptance weirdos try to distance themselves from the feeders, ostracizing them the same way that mainstream society excludes all fat-lovers. While they concede that the rare dysfunctional feeder/feedee relationship exists, they note that such unpleasant extremes occur with all sexual fetishes and that isolated horror stories shouldn't be used to condemn an entire movement.

Many feeders claim that their orientation is submissive rather than sadistic. They say their pleasure derives not from controlling or harming the feedee, but from tending to her every need like a humble servant—cooking for her, rubbing her feet, massaging her tum-tum, and obsequiously pampering her as if she were a bloated Queen Bee. And if—praise God—the ultimate feeder fantasy of utter immobility is achieved, these valiant lackeys pledge to change her clothes, give her sponge baths, and wipe her bottom, too. "I am emotionally nourished when I am able to please such a woman," writes one feeder. "It seems reasonable to believe that some woman out there might actually enjoy being treated like a goddess."

"They're more submissive than anything else," a 472-pound feedee called Supersize Betsy says of her suitors. "All of them—down to the very last one—have some kind of fantasy of me sitting on top of them or laying on top of them or just enveloping them. To them, it's like being smothered in chocolate syrup.

It's not a death wish or suffocation thing—it's more about being able to feel this femininity surrounding you completely....Us feedees are sexually pretty selfish, because we just want to lay there and be pampered and fed and adored and worshipped."

This is wild, wacky, way-out stuff, ladies and gentlemen. Not that there's anything abnormal about taking pleasure in food. As humans, we learn to enjoy eating years before we have our first orgasm...and for most people, years after our last orgasm. But only a few of us take pleasure in food WHILE having an orgasm.

There are scant pop-culture antecedents for feederism: things such as a 1937 Merrie Melodies cartoon called "Pigs is Pigs," wherein an evil scientist straps down a hog and force-feeds him with a machine (the pig ultimately goes kablooey after eating a final slice of pie) or *Monty Python's The Meaning of Life* (1983), in which a Mr. Creosote finally explodes after gorging himself at a restaurant.

And yet even these examples don't sexualize the act like the feeders do. The feeders act as if stuffing a woman's mouth with food is no different than cramming her vagina with your cock—and since you'd need a two-foot johnson just to get past all the flab, force-feeding often serves as a replacement for hard fucking. The idea of feeding someone until they burst is a warped analogue to an orgasmic release. Food becomes a long endless dick and the girl's alimentary canal serves as a deep, twisting vagina.

MANY PRO-FEEDER APOLOGISTS SLIP into a regrettably pious defense of feederism as some sort of bold political liberation movement wherein feedees, by allowing food to be shoveled down their gullets, are "hedonistic and rebellious" free spirits with "the courage to be fat in spite of society's harassment." A feedee calling herself "Tubular Belle" echoes Patrick Henry's "Give me liberty or give me death" speech in this passage from *Abundance* magazine's website:

As for me, I want to get fatter, and I will, whether you like it or not. The only way to keep me from it would be to put me in jail. Perhaps there are people who would consider doing that, the fear of fat is so intense in some....I and other feedees choose not to cave in to such coercive social pressure against fat....We willingly blaze trails you dare not tread, enjoying ourselves all the while as we (and you, by the way) get fatter.

So is feederism a harmless fetish, a mild perversion, or a murderous pathology? Or is it perhaps all three? Who are we to judge? Who are we to play God? Perhaps it is not up to us, the non-feedlin's, to decide what is normal and what is sick. What I CAN tell you is that while eating my Tuscan Bean Soup and reading some of these online accounts, I came REALLY close to vomiting.

UNTIL THEY'RE IMMOBILE?

People are disgusting. There's no sidestepping that simple fact. For all the sanctimonious belching that attempts to prove human sexuality is a noble and uplifting thing—that it gives us *wings to fly*, even—most of the evidence clearly demonstrates that our desires drag us down to the level of cockroaches.

So-called "normal" human sexuality is bad enough. Blood-engorged cock pounding into slimy vaginal cave—*ewwww!* But when the sane researcher wades past the realm of ordinary hetero coupling into the perverted world of fetishes, fixations, and partialism, it becomes a struggle merely to retain the contents of one's stomach. Can't you people *behave?* I felt like vomiting during this article's entire research phase. You all make me *sick!*

There is nothing on earth so repellent that someone, somewhere, isn't jerking off to the thought of it. Yahoo.com, one of the Internet's most popular search engines and news hubs, allows every psychosexual basket case this side of kiddie-murderers to devote discussion groups to their chosen sexual aberration. At press time, Yahoo! hosted 1,861 groups under the "fetish" classification. I've whittled it down to the 22 groups which I found funniest.

You'll notice typos littered throughout this piece, at least where group names and posts are cited. Except for removing a few passages and replacing them with an ellipsis (...), I haven't edited or corrected anything. This is partially to retain the originals' authenticity, but also because I'm tired of cleanin' up after y'all.

amazoncrush

Describing itself as "the intellectual exploration of mixed wrestling and crush fetish," this group caters to the tastes of the masochistic man who enjoys tusslin' with a woman before she eventually squashes him to death.

SAMPLE POST: *I want a woman, preferably 400+ lbs, to sit on me while she eats twinkies....*

bathroomfetishclub

Let's get the scat fetish out of the way now, shall we?

SAMPLE POST: *I get tueneed on when I see a women sitting on the toilet straining to move her bowels. I like to hear her grunting and then passing what sounds like marbles.*

bears-cigars

Finally, a group for hairy gay men who enjoy looking at pictures of other hairy gay men puffin' away on stogies!

SAMPLE POST: *Any cigar smoking bears near Chicago looking for a smoke, piss and cum swap let me know.*

FUNNIEST YAHOO! FETISH GROUPS

A RIP-SNORTIN' GUIDE TO THE WILDEST, WEIRDEST, AND WOOLIEST PERVERTS ON YAHOO.COM

BeatingTheSmoking-Fetish

A group for Christian men who are trying to overcome an "addiction to watching women smoke." Christian men assist other Christian men in overcoming this odd predilection, and it all sounds pretty faggy to me.

SAMPLE POST: *I struggle with the same addiction. I actually stumbled on your groups page, trying to find Yahoo-groups with pictures/clips of women smoking. I don't know why I have this "fetish", but my fascination with "smoking women" has been going on for a long time. I am very glad that you have this group…it is encouraging to know that a Brother in Christ understands some of what I'm going through.*

DavidGallopsLarkLane-SmellyArmpitsClub

A Liverpool homo who loves sniffin' rank fag-pits hosts this group for other Liverpudlian nelly-boys and their malodorous underarms.

SAMPLE POST: *I just adore the smell of smelly armpits and body odour it is so animal and sexy don't you think? Please make sure you smell under your arms when you come and visit me ! Deodorant is banned in this club, we like the animal smells best. The smellier the better!*

Deaf-Wannabee

On one level, this group caters to the occasional oddball who's sexually attracted to deaf people and/or enjoys wearing hearing aids when they don't really need

them. But on a deeper, far more disturbing plane, it offers networking tools for those who are sexually aroused by the idea of *self-induced* permanent silence. It even offers advice for those who consider "crossing the bridge" by *deliberately* making themselves deaf. The group moderator claims to have "acquired a substantial hearing loss by choice."

SAMPLE POST: *Some…have thought of becoming deaf by choice at some time in their lives but have not yet done so. We have members who wear hearing aids recreationally for fun, others who wear them for need with pride.*

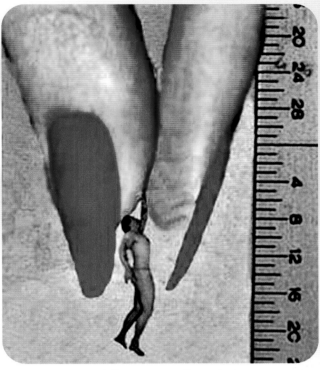

diaper_poet

A typical diaper-fetish group. I could have chosen any of them. They're *all* funny.

SAMPLE POST: *Go to DiaperDad.net to see our expanded free preview section. Diaper Guys and Diaper Gear. Special section on plastic pants… plus new hypno slideshows! A great diaper training technique. Find out about our Diaper Vacations and how to visit our Diaper House. We make guys wear diapers all weekend! Now hiring Diaper Models for the new DiaperDad Diaper Catalog.*

E_C_T

A group for "those that get turned [on or] sexually aroused by the thought of" Electroconvulsive Therapy. It serves not only the needs of the S/M freaks who salivate over the idea of shock treatment, but also those who indulge in "electroplay and electrostimulation" as part of their sexual diet. We learn that "a cattle prod

won't kill you," as well as which classic Hollywood films feature electroshock scenes.

SAMPLE POST: *My boy and I used our Electro Cock Rings for the first time last night. When he came, electricity shot out of his cock, through my asshole and blew the cum out of my cock. I have never came the intensely before. When my boys load shot out of his Cock and into my asshole it felt like a bolt of lightning! I had seen a demonstration in Chicago a couple of years ago and have always wanted to try it. Glad I finally did….I have just ordered an Electro Anal Bullet. I Can't Wait to try it!!! I'm thinking about the electro glove next. Can't imagine how good it would feel to jack off with it or to have my boy play with my ass with it.*

gothfur_mw

"Furries" are people who enjoy sex while dressed in animal costumes. This group specializes in those Midwesterners who dabble in

"the darker side of Furry…[and] support a gothic lifestyle."

SAMPLE POST: *The name's Magnus, (whole alias is Magnus Dingo, but of course no one goes around saying your whole furry alias/name) and I'm obviously a GothFur….I'm a anthropomorphic Aussie Dingo for my fursona. I don't have an avatar for my LJ and FurJournal….Am I the only furson out there in Internet Land that draws/portrays themself WEARING what they actually wear IRL? I find so many fursons who draw all this 'fanart' of their furry selves, yet they don't actually own it. I'm quite the opposite, my fursona's pictures has not been altered or any other accessories added to make me look more 'spehsul & hardxcore'…. Hope I'm welcomed here. =D *Waves a paw to all**

jollygreengiant

For those who fantasize about the Big Green Ass on the Big Green Man from the frozen-vegetable packages.

SAMPLE POST: *One day the great giant, standing more than 50 feet high, felt a little lonely. In fact he was incredibly horny, but there were no female giants, so he did the next best thing. He banged the crotch of a tree. Afterward he regretted it because he got splinters, but the deed had been done. The great redwood tree had been fertilized….Near the top of the tree, was a gigantic pine cone….A sudden gust of wind caused it to fall nearly 200 feet to the ground where it shattered. Hence the untimely birth of the Jolly Green Giant.*

kickmeinthenutsfetish

A meeting ground for nut-kickers and the men who love them.

SAMPLE POST: *sub gay male seeks straight males to kick me in the nuts…i like to be humiliated by str8 guys crawl around while they kick me in the balls they should be laughing most of the time would like ball damage eventually no more creaming for this fag*

ladybusters-anonymous

Yet another one of these electronic watering holes for born-again Christians who, through the power of Christ, have convinced themselves that they aren't perverts anymore. This one's "A Place for Recovering Female Bashers."

SAMPLE POST: *I am a born-again Christian who was once very much into (fantasy) violence against women. I would get off on pictures, videos, and stories about women being hit in the crotch, belly, and breasts. Gradually, however, with God's help and by God's grace, I have come to see how unhealthy, unwholesome, and destructive this particular fetish is….*

nosepinching

"If you get turned-on by the sight of a swimmer wearing a nose clip or a person pinching your nose or holding his or her own nose," writes the moderator, "this site is for you!"

SAMPLE POST: *I remember a scene from Cheers where Sam and Diane grab on to each other's nose at the same time for maybe half a minute, both talking nasally….Hello everyone, I just want some help from you guys here if you know of any movie or cartoon that involves someone's nose being pinched in order to have their mouth forced open. I appreciate it, thanks.*

pukeonmebaby-whenscrewing

An electronic feeding trough for guys and gals who like to sprinkle 'n' splash a li'l "tummy juice" all over their lovemaking.

SAMPLE POST: *Until then we'd been fooling and playing about but as I vomited into her mouth it all changed. We began kissing and rubbing each other. Then we had sex on the bathroom floor - getting covered in slippery slimy puke - totally covered as we threw up a few more times. I've never had such passionate, uninhibited, disgusting sex!!*

pulped

Men who love women who love to beat the shit out of men.

SAMPLE POST: *My wife is a naturally strong woman. Out of experience I can share with you, whenever she beat me up in the past (there always has been a reason though, she never hits or hurts me for no reason) it was utterly painful….Throughout my marriage I have learned the meaning of corporal punishment. I think this is how it should be in every household.*

ruleofthegiantesses

Little Men who want Big Women to step on them.

SAMPLE POST: *All around her, tiny men were scurrying to and fro, looking for ways to please her….It was* deliciously perverted when she realized that even as her giant sole was coming down on them to squish them to grease they had hard-ons and were masturbating as fast as they could....They saw that giant, deadly sole descending on them and they didn't even realize that they were about to die an agonizingly painful death because they were so overwhelmed at her sensuousness and attractiveness that they could think of nothing else.

runningnosefetish

Snot junkies convene to hock loogies on each other.

SAMPLE POST: So her nose is dripping snot and I'm talking romantically to her and our faces are getting closer and closer together. She's still licking up the snot every now and then and I offer to clean her nose for her. I start licking the snot from her top lip until I'm pushing my tongue right into her nostrils -as I hug her she sort of snorts and blows a big load of snot into my mouth.

smellysocksfetish

A place where those good souls who savor stinky socks can network with the arrogant tops who provide those socks for a price.

SAMPLE POST: sniff my rank socks slaveboy....On your knees and sniff my rank socks, suck my toes and eat my toejam. You are only good to lick my feet clean and to give me your fagcash. Will rape your wallet while my huge rank feet are in your face, haha, beg now to get my new pics and videos and pay for my party drinks.

snoringfetishclub

If sawing wood gives you wood or gets you wet...in other words, if you cop a nut at the sound of someone copping Z's...you can meet people here who are just as weird as you are. There's even a section where men provide MP3s of themselves snoring.

SAMPLE POST: i 'm lucky because i have

a girl for a roomate in university, and she snores. The thing is she's goodlooking, and pretty stuck up. she doesnt really talk to me, we just share accoms. anyways for me thats part of the turn on..to watch this beautiful chick snore with her mouth wide open. sometimes when she comes home really drunk and passes out, i know i can also touch her. the first time i touched her, i just put my fingers on her open mouth, and felt her snores. i have also lay down beside her, and put my face right up to hers, to feel her snores on my face. or touching her mouth against mine, i also enjoy pushing her chin down with my finger, so her mouth opens really wide, and she snores way louder. has anyone tried that? it works if you like loud snoring. and i got to touch her tits once. she was passed out drunk, lying on her side, snoring, and her tit fell out the top of her tank top. so i touched the nipple.

swastikaknights

A homosexual stomping ground for Nazi males who love to suck cock and blame Jews. The moderator describes it as a "Man-to-Man

forum for those who believe! Swastika Knights is a Man-to-Man open forum for those interested in NS, WP or the Skinhead movements and desire to share, communicate and network with like-minded Men....The only solution is a NEW ORDER!"

SAMPLE POST (in response to a female intruder who'd insulted the group)**:** What do you know of Odin bitch? The fact that there are only MEN in Valhalla should give you some clue to what's up. And may Odin send all your evil wishes back on you, you mouth breathing breeder dirtbag. Shut up and make some gay babies, that's all you're good for

wheelchairpretendersuk

A corner pub for able-bodied Limeys who are attracted to the wheelchair-bound. Also for Brits who arouse themselves by sitting in wheelchairs and pretending they're crippled.

womeninprisons

Although the name might lead you to believe this group idealizes female inmates, it instead worships females on the *right* side of the law, whether they're wardens, guards, or the psychotic accusers who enjoy putting men behind bars.

SAMPLE POST: my ex girl friend and i love to gloat over all the men that are locked up in prison. i love women governers, haveing all that power is so sexy. my ex girl friend gets turned on thinking about men that will spend the rest of ther lives in prison. i used to make love to her and tell her how horrable it must be in prison, this turned her on so much. we always talked about watching a man get sentenced to life in prison, this would turn us on so much. i think i whant to live in prison, for the rest of my life. while women are on the outside haveing a good time

"There is nothing on earth so repellent that someone, somewhere, isn't jerking off to the thought of it."

fun vagina facts

CANYON CUNT

The largest vagina ever recorded is thought to have belonged to seven-foot-eight-inch Anna Swan (1846–1888), a long-legged Scottish temptress who once plopped out a 26-pound baby, the biggest bambino recorded in world history. Although I was unable to uncover any recorded evidence of her vagina's exact dimensions, it's safe to assume you could comfortably fit a computer monitor in there.

TINY 'GINEYS

The annals of medicine are crammed with accounts of women whose functional adult vaginas were less than an inch in depth. I am engaged in an exhaustive research project attempting to track down these ladies' names, phone numbers, and current street addresses.

Other women are born with little dents in the pubic area rather than fully developed vaginas. Extensive surgery, lubrication, and patience can help ameliorate this problem.

The smallest vaginas, though, are the ones that don't even exist. Roughly one in 5,000 female babies is born *sans* vagina. How, then, do doctors know they're female? I suppose because they complain a lot. But surgeons are now able to fashion fake vaginas for these unfortunate infants.

WOMEN ARE *SO* SENSITIVE

Although most clitorises are far smaller than most penises, they contain twice as many nerve endings as the larger, dumber male organ.

CLITS BIG ENOUGH TO BE DICKS

In 1744, Sir Edward Home described a native woman in the West Indies whose clitoris, when aroused, was thicker than a thumb and three inches long. Around the same time, a Swiss biologist claims to have examined a gal whose swee'pea measured a robust seven inches. And an 1813 account in a French encyclopedia mentions a woman with a 12-inch clitoris resembling "the neck of a goose."

I GOT BUDDHA IN MY VAGINA

Eastern religions seem generally more cunt-friendly than those in the vadge-hating West. For example, Tantric Buddhism pinpoints the essence of Buddhahood—it nestles within a woman's private parts. And the word "cunt" is derived from *Cunti,* one of many titles accorded Hinduism's bitch-goddess Kali.

COCK STRANGLERS

Although the legend of "vagina dentata"—a pussy with teeth poised to rip off the male organ—is known to be a myth, there is some evidence that certain women have vaginal muscles strong enough to clamp down on the male organ and prevent from withdrawing. Known clinically as *penis captivus,* it is thought to be caused by involuntary spasms in the

...evator ani muscles deep in the vagina, which hold onto the penis head and refuse to let it go until it pays child support.

TWICE THE DARKNESS

In rare cases women are born with two vaginas, which, one presumes, would make them twice as annoying.

ORGASMS ARE GOOD FOR YOU

Orgasms alleviate menstrual cramps because the force of the special moment's muscular contractions helps cleanse the woman's dainty bits of the gunky fluids that accrete during her cycle. Orgasms also cure headaches because they release endorphins into the bloodstream.

GIRL JUICES

Like the eye, the vagina is a self-cleaning organ. During a normal menstrual cycle, a woman's vagina will spew forth a total of two to six tablespoons of blood. During ovulation, her punani will burp up one or two teaspoons of liquid discharge in order to clear the cervix of dead cells. The rest of the month, her cooter will spit forth only a half-teaspoon of fluid per day.

A GERM-INFESTED SLIME PIT?

The average human girl-gash is host to 15 different strains of bacteria, "good germs" designed to ward off the renegade "bad germs" which can invade a vagina and make life hell for everyone.

REAL

SCIENTISTS FOR BUSH

Some physiologists argue that hairy vaginas prevent friction and create a pleasant cushioning effect during intercourse. A full bush can also retain vaginal odors which some men find enticing. The longest female pubic hair on record measured 28 inches, which is pushing it.

ONE HAPPY SNAPPER

The world record for most orgasms belongs to a dame who came 134 times in one hour. She still phones me from time to time. The longest continuous female orgasm clocked in at 43 seconds and featured 25 contractions.

I THOUGHT IT WAS THE FIRE EXTINGUISHER

The Hite Report...uh... reported that the phallic object used most often by female masturbators is the candle.

NEW HOPE FOR MEN WITH ONE-INCH DICKS

The first inch of the vaginal canal is by far the most "pleasure-receptive," according to Los Angeles sexologist Patti Britton.

a CUNT by any other name...

a list of several delightful words and phrases to use when you really mean to say "vagina"

Abyss, The	Meat Muffin
Bearded Clam	Moose Knuckle
Beef Curtains	Mother of All Souls
Birth Cannon	Mount Pleasant
Black Bess	Mustard Pot
Bluebeard's Closet	Organ Grinder
Bone Yard	Pecan Pattie
Bum Fiddle	Penis Penitentiary
Butter Boat	Periwinkle
Cabbage Field	Pink Canoe
Cape Horn	Punani
Catcher's Mitt	Pipe Cleaner
Cloven Tuft	Prick Purse
Cock Socket	Quivering Quim
Cod Canal	Red-Haired Lass
Cooter	Rocket Pocket
Cradle of Filth	Rusty Axe Wound
Crease	Sacapuntas
Crotch Cobbler	Salt Cellar
Cum Dumpster	Sausage Wallet
Dead-End Street	Scabbard
Dick Sharpener	Silk Igloo
Doodle Sack	Skunk Guts
Eel Skinner	Slobbering Bulldog
Fancy Bit	Smelly Jelly Hole
Fish Factory	Snake Charmer
Flaming Lips	South Pole
Flesh Tuxedo	Snapper
Flytrap	Sperm Harbor
Foofy Bird	Split Knish
Fun Tunnel	Stench Trench
Furback Turtle	Sticky Bun
Goldfinch's Nest	Sugar Basin
Goo Pot	Taffy Puller
Gravy Boat	Tinkleflower
Grindstone	Trout Basket
Gutted Hamster	Tuna Taco
Hairy Manilow	Twat Waffle
Happy Valley	Under-Dimple
Hidey Hole	Vadge
Hoo-Ha	Vertical Grimace
Jack Straw's Castle	Velvet Glove
Knob Gobbler	Weenie Wringer
Lady Jane	Whisker Biscuit
Lapland	Willy Washer
Lobster Claw	Wound That Never
Madge	Heals, The
Magpie's Nest	Ya-Ya
Manhole	Yeast Cake
Map of Tasmania	Yoni
Mark of the Beast	Yum-Yum

fun PENIS facts

STRAIGHT TALK ABOUT ERECTIONS

A healthy male averages 11 erections per day—nine of them while asleep. After ejaculating, it can take him anywhere from two minutes to two weeks to achieve another erection.

GALLONS OF CUM

The average man shoots one to two teaspoons of cum per orgasm. During his life, he will cum over 7,000 times, resulting in 14 gallons o' jizz, give or take a few drops. Each load contains approximately seven calories, and each spurt whizzes through the air at around 28 MPH.

FROM SHOWER TO GROWER

On average, a limp penis will increase in volume 300% when it is erect. It will also contain more than eight to ten times its normal amount of blood.

BIG 'UNS

The biggest erect penis ever recorded was 13.5 inches. Researchers estimate that fewer than 5,000 men on earth have a penis 11 inches or larger.

SMALL 'UNS

History tells the sad tale of many men whose full erections didn't even stretch out to a half-inch. Scientists refer to this condition as "micropenis," which can be surgically remedied to the point where the sufferer can boast of a still-laughable post-op three-inch schween. For every 35 or so pounds that a man gains, his penis will appear an inch smaller. Napoleon was rumored to be totin' a notoriously small cock, causing him to freak out and attempt conquering the world. The ancient Greeks favored itty-bitty male organs, deeming them more visually pleasing than veiny purple power tools.

THE MYTH IS A TINY BIT TRUE

The Kinsey Report verified the longstanding rumor that black men have larger penises than whitey. The average black male's hard-on measures 6.3 inches, leaving the white man far behind at a pitiful mean of 6.2 inches.

BOYS WILL BE BOYS

Male fetuses can sport wood during the third trimester, according to Ultrasound tests.

SMELLS LIKE A BONER

Aromas reputed to increase penile blood flow: licorice, pumpkin pie, lavender, donuts, and chocolate.

SUPER-DUPER SPERM-SCOOPER

Scientists have recently speculated that the head of the human penis evolved into its current "mushroom" shape in order to scoop rival males' sperm out of the vagina.

SMITE THEIR LAND AND SEVER THEIR PENISES

Around 1300 B.C., victorious Egyptian troops marched home with more than 13,000 severed Libyan penises. Seven hundred years later, Babylonian king Nebuchadnezzar rolled over Jerusalem and sliced off thousands of Jewish weenies.

TESTIFYING ON TESTICLES

In pre-biblical times, men would swear on their own penises. The word "testify" is derived from a Roman legal practice of swearing on one's testicles. The word "penis" comes from the Latin word for "tail."

DOUBLE TROUBLE

In 1609, an Italian physician documented the first case of a man with *diphallasparatus* (two or more penises). This ultra-rare condition has since been found in less than 80 men.

NOT SO PLEASED TO MEET YOU

Australia's Walibri tribesmen say hello by shaking one another's penises.

LONGEST MONEY SHOT

Medical researchers once recorded a man whose wad sailed a staggering 11.7 feet. The best I can manage is to squirt myself in the face every so often.

What's another word for DICK?

Almost everyone enjoys a good **PENILE EUPHEMISM,** so we've compiled some of OUR faves. YOUR faves probably aren't listed because, frankly, we don't like you very much.

ACTION JACKSON
ALBINO CAVE DWELLER
APPLE-HEADED MONSTER
BALD HERMIT
BALONEY PONY
BAVARIAN BEEFSTICK
BEAVER BUSTER
BEEF BUGLE
BIG JAKE THE ONE-EYED SNAKE
BILBO BAGGINS
BLOOD-ENGORGED MAYONNAISE CANNON
BLOW POP
BOB DOLE
BONE PHONE
BOWLEGGED SWAMP DONKEY
BREAKFAST BURRITO
BUSHWHACKER
CAPTAIN WINKY
CATTLE PROD
CHICKSICLE
CHOWDER DUMPER
CORNDOG
CRIMSON CHITLIN'
CYCLOPS
DANGLING PARTICIPLE
DINGUS
DIPSTICK
DOLPHIN
DOODLE DANDY
DOUGHNUT HOLDER
EL CAPITAN
EXCALIBUR
FALLOPIAN FIDDLER
FLAPDOODLE
FLESHY WINNEBAGO
FUCKSTICK
GASH MALLET
GHERKIN
GIGGLE-STICK
GULLY-RAKER
HE WHO MUST BE OBEYED
HEAT-SEEKING MOISTURE MISSILE
HOG
HOMEWRECKER
HOMO ERECTUS
JOJO THE CIRCUS CLOWN
KIDNEY-SCRAPER
KOJAK
LICKIN' STICK
LITTLE WILLY
MEAT MUSKET
MENSTRUAL MINER
MR. CLEAN
MR. MOJO RISIN'
MUSCLE OF LOVE
NEBUCHADNEZZAR
OLD BLIND BOB
ONE-EYED JACK
OVARIAN POOL STICK
PAJAMA PYTHON
PURPLE-HEADED WOMB BROOM
RECTUM ROOTER
SCHLONGMASTER 2000
SCHMECKEL
SNAPPER SLAPPER
SQUIRMIN' HERMAN THE ONE-EYED GERMAN
STRUMPET THUMPER
TACO WARMER
TALLYWHACKER
THUNDERSTICK
TROUSER TROMBONE
VERGA
VERVE PIPE
VLAD THE IMPALER
WEE WILLY WINKY
WHAMMY BAR
WHORE THERMOMETER
WIGGLE STICK
WOMB BROOM
WONGUS

Sexual dysfunctions are distinguished from the broader category of "sexual disorders" in that dysfunctions are manifested *physically*. Whether the root cause is physical or mental, a dysfunction somehow physically impedes the satisfactory completion of the sex act and is therefore pretty fuckin' funny. Although the inability to achieve orgasm without having a Teenage Mutant Ninja Turtle defecate on your face is likewise funny, such a syndrome is fundamentally *psychological* rather than physical, especially if the pervert in question has no problem blowing his load after the turtle poops on him.

The syndromes we'll be laughing at here involve a crippling of the sexual equipment—in all cases except one, the penis. In every instance, what's so goddamned funny is that the victim *wishes* to achieve the cleansing release of a whopping-good orgasm, but their *body* prevents them from doing so. With dysfunctions such as vaginismus and premature ejaculation, the physical problem is rooted in mental conflicts and thus has some hope of resolving itself. With others, tragically—well, tragically for the *sufferers*, yet hilariously for the rest of us—the problem is with the flesh itself and frequently offers a dim prognosis for the victim, his family members, and anyone who's ever called him a friend or lover. *Funny shit!*

PRIAPISM

DESCRIPTION:
A prolonged, searingly painful erection lasting anywhere from four hours up to a few *weeks*. The condition is named after Greek fertility god Priapus, whose never-waning boner was said to be so huge that he could only have sex while standing in an open field.

CAUSES:
Sometimes caused by high blood flow to the penis; ironically, in other cases, it's due to *low* penile blood flow. It can also result from complications due to sickle-cell anemia or the use of certain anti-psychotic medications.

TREATMENT:
In early stages of priapism, decongestant medications can often induce the bone-bone to subside. But once the condition has advanced, blood must be drained through a needle jabbed into the man-shaft. Even then, some of the penile tissue may already be dead. Blood trapped in the penis rapidly grows stagnant, and if left untreated, *penile amputation* may be necessary.

WHY IT'S FUNNY:
It's an erection, but it isn't pleasurable! It's *painful!*

DESCRIPTION:
At the moment of orgasm, semen backfires up into the kidneys instead of shooting out the penis. The cum eventually dribbles out in cloudy urine.

RETROGRADE EJACULATION

CAUSES:
Sometimes caused by medication. In other cases, it's due to conditions ranging from diabetes to prostate or urethral surgery.

TREATMENT:
If caused by medication, the condition will typically subside once use of the medication is discontinued. If due to surgery, well, fella, you'll be squirting joy juice up into your kidneys 'til you die.

WHY IT'S FUNNY:
As with "vaginismus," "retrograde ejaculation" would make a great name for a pseudointellectual death-metal band.

VAGINISMUS

DESCRIPTION:
An involuntary contraction of the vaginal muscles which prevents entry for all foreign objects. Sensing an intruder, the female organ clenches itself so tightly that not even a pencil can nuzzle its way inside. The condition is thought to afflict anywhere from two to six percent of females.

CAUSES:
Daddy or an uncle raped her. Probably her uncle. Equating all penetration with the trauma of blunt-force sexual assault, the vagina shuts down like the door to the Batcave.

TREATMENT:
A lot of teddy bears, soft words, and the gentle, gradual insertion of plastic dilators escalating in size.

WHY IT'S FUNNY:
I enjoy the idea of a pouting vagina that puckers its lips and says, "NO!"

WORLD'S FUNNIEST SEXUAL DYSFUNCTIONS
THE HILARIOUS WAYS IN WHICH OUR BODIES HUMILIATE US

PREMATURE EJACULATION

DESCRIPTION:

Boy gets nervous. Boy shoots his goo way too early. Boy is ashamed. Girl is dissatisfied. Girl tells everyone that boy is a lousy lay. Boy is ridiculed and ostracized by townfolk. Boy moves to a trailer in a wooded area on the outskirts of town, where he eventually kills himself in a grisly satanic ritual involving innocent livestock.

CAUSES:

Almost entirely psychological. In many cases, it's only a matter of youth and inexperience. In several others, it may be caused by performance anxiety when a partner is new and their genitals are unfamiliar. In yet others, it's linked to a complex of psychosexual traumas which would take years to uncover, providing fodder for dozens of additional jokes.

TREATMENT:

A girl needs to gently counsel her lover when he is besieged by the hamsterlike urge to squirt his measly Love Drops within moments of viewing her naked form. She needs to reassure him that he is not an inadequate, despicable, laughable shell of a man who often causes her to have masturbatory fantasies about his best friend.

WHY IT'S FUNNY:

Because whenever someone is told of an incident of premature ejaculation, they laugh. Always.

PEYRONIE'S DISEASE

DESCRIPTION:

severe curvature of the penis which renders ercourse extremely painful or impossible. mong some specimens, the penis is drastically ortened. In rare cases, the penis twists so uch that its underside faces upward.

AUSES:

ften strikes middle-aged men when calcium deposits or scars rm on the highly elastic "tunica albuginea" membrane inside the enis. The hard lumps act as obstacles, forcing the penis to curve ound them while filling with blood, resulting in the banana-or-orse degree of curvature that characterizes this affliction.

REATMENT:

though once stricken with Peyronie's, you are unlikely to ever nder your manhood straight as an arrow again, injections of lcium-channel blockers directly into the penis have shown some omise in softening the penile plaque which causes this heart-eaking—yet sidesplittingly enjoyable, at least from the delines—dysfunction.

WHY IT'S FUNNY:

Look at ol' banana-dick over there! His junk is all curvy like a piece of macaroni!

BROKEN PENIS

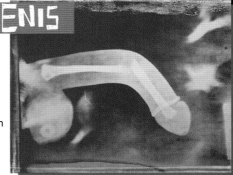

DESCRIPTION:

Inside the penis, the spongy blood bags which engorge during arousal and give the appearance of "hardness" become ruptured, almost always during vigorous sex. A "popping" sound is often heard, immediately accompanied by loss of erection and howling pain. The penis becomes swollen, deformed, and is sometimes said to resemble an eggplant.

CAUSES:

Happens most frequently during the woman-on-top position when the penis accidentally slips out and bends forcefully against some other hard object. This is another good reason for never allowing a woman to be on top.

TREATMENT:

Intensive surgery, although it's not always successful in restoring proper sexual and urinary functions.

WHY IT'S FUNNY:

Hey, look, everybody! This is even funnier than the guy whose penis was curved like a boomerang! This guy's penis is *broken!* Wah-ha-ha-ha! Dude's motor won't crank! And there's no way to fix it! Must suck to be him!

REAL

WHATTA WAY

THE MORBIDLY EROTIC PHENOMENO

DEATH DURING SEX

The French, those fucking pussies, refer to the orgasm as *le petit mort*, which translates as "the little death." Cultures throughout world history have believed that with each puddle of cum, a man coughs up a teaspoonful of his life force, never to be replenished. Each "little death" cumulatively leads to *le grand mort* and a burial plot.

The Romans, those oily homosexuals, used the Latin phrase *mors osculi* when referring to cases where humans suffered the Big Death while trying to achieve a Little Death. Literally translated, *mors osculi* means "death in a kiss."

I call bullshit on such a romantic interpretation of death-during-sex. One suspects that having a partner die while you're fucking them would tend to ruin the mood. There he was, pumping away like a jacked-up Viagra Rabbit, huffing and puffing and sweating and sticking his tongue out, when he suddenly collapsed like a big pink sack of dead shit over your horrified, squirming body. At first you thought that perhaps he was only exhausted, but after a full minute you realized that his heart, rather than his cock, blew a load. His mouth hangs open, his skin turns a sickly grey, and his limbs stiffen. You finally muster the strength to roll his rhinoceros-sized bulk off your trembling naked body. And then you make the two phone calls you dread: one to the police and the other to his wife.

MOST OF US WHO AREN'T ENTIRELY RETARDED are aware of death-during-sex...or at least death-*right-after*-sex...in the animal world. The male black widow spider, like many unfortunate oppressed males throughout the insect demimonde, breathes his last buggy breath shortly after shooting his wad. The male praying mantis is likely to have his HEAD EATEN while shagging a lady mantis. And there's an ultra-rare mammal (only 20 or so females are thought to exist) in Uganda called the "wandering devourer." To perform intercourse, male devourers must CLIMB INSIDE the female's giant vaginal cavity. Upon completion of the sex act, the female devourer gets hungry and EATS the male.

In Hollywood, the cabal of shadowy figures who rule things have not been reticent to feature death-during-sex as part of the decadent, bread-and-circuses show which they use to keep our minds off the REAL enemy.

The final scene of ultra-morbid motion picture *Looking for Mr. Goodbar* features Diane Keaton being stabbed to death by a sexually confused psychopath who is unable to achieve an erection with her. And having sex with Madonna leads to an old codger's demise in the 1993 film *Body of Evidence*.

Death-during-sex has likewise featured in the plots of television shows ranging from *Hill Street Blues* (the roll-call sergeant dies while having sex with a woman); *As the World Turns* (handsome man dies while screwing beautiful woman); *NYPD Blue* (a man dies while fucking a sheep that network censors insisted wear a pink ribbon to indicate it was female); *Melrose Place* (cruise-line owner Tony "The Fish" Marlin expires while shagging Lexi); *The Tick* (a superhero named The Immortal dies whilst in congress with Captain Liberty); and the pro-homosexual propaganda piece *Will and Grace* (a fat man named Stan gives up the ghost, squashing a British girl beneath him).

So why does it happen? Despite isolated freaky cases (such as the Romanian soccer star and his girlfriend who died of carbon-monoxide poisoning while fucking in their car and the Japanese woman who suffered a fatal arachnoid hemorrhage while masturbating with a carrot), death-during-sex can usually be blamed on four main culprits: **heart attacks, embolisms, autoerotic asphyxiation,** and **murder**. Study the list carefully, and I'm sure you'll find a method that suits you!

HEART ATTACKS

Although they account for less than one percent of all cardiac fatalities, heart attacks are probably the leading cause of death-during-sex among adults. Interestingly, statistics in both the U.S. and U.K. indicate that three-quarters of all fatal heart attacks occurring during sex happen with persons *other* than one's primary partner. This is due to the incontrovertible fact that sex is always more exciting when you're cheating.

EMBOLISMS

An ultra-rare cause of death-during-sex recently documented by British doctors in which air bubbles get absorbed by uterine wounds into the bloodstream. Documenting over 20 million pregnancies between 1967 and 1993, researchers found 18 cases of embolism-induced death occurring in the weeks directly following delivery. This is one of the main reasons why physicians counsel couples to avoid sex for roughly six weeks after delivery. There are also documented cases of fatal embolisms caused by sex *during* pregnancy, when air gets trapped between the fetus and the uterine wall. But since sex during pregnancy and *any time thereafter* is inherently disgusting, this is a human tragedy which could logically be avoided.

AUTOEROTIC ASPHYXIATION

Accidental death due to cutting off one's oxygen supply during masturbation is thought to account for a third of all adolescent hangings and 6.5% of all purported teen "suicides." Experts estimate that 250 to 1,000 Americans, most of them teenaged males, die accidentally this way every year. These estimates may be conservative, because the family members who find their precious sons hanging from a belt strap with a monstrous erection and surrounded by hardcore gay porn mags are likely to tell everyone it was a straight suicide rather than a kinky act gone horribly wrong.

In *Justine,* the Marquis de Sade described how the victims of hanging would get erections and often ejaculate. In *Waiting for Godot,* the characters debate whether they should hang themselves, because at least it'd give 'em erections.

Oxygen deprivation apparently gives you a KILLER bone-bone and leads to the sort of orgasm over which you'd mortgage your house. Practitioners refer to it as "scarfing," "breath play," and "terminal sex." They almost always rig their self-strangulation contraptions with some sort of slipknot or rescue device; it's when these devices fail that they accidentally strangle themselves to death.

"Being reminded of death should be erotic for most of us," writes one autoerotic-asphyxiation advocate. "We should get moist and hot and hard at the thought of it....One has only to take a small further step to recognize that this transcendence of time and space is a form of psychic death. To be swallowed up by blackness is an exquisite pleasure. It is to know ecstasy, but it is also to die."

Remind me NOT to have sex with this person.

MURDER

Chiefly the domain of sexual psychopaths and freaky-deaky pervatrons who garner extreme pleasure from crushing the life out of someone. True-crime books abound with tales of rapist-murderers, both hetero and homosexual, strangling and hammering their way to sexual ecstasy, stabbing their prey with a knife after they've commenced stabbing them with their dick.

It's possible, but unlikely, that someone could accidentally strangle a partner to death during sex. Joseph Micale of Syracuse, N.Y., recently pleaded guilty to criminally negligent homicide for strangling his wife to death with a telephone cord while fucking her. Rough sex sometimes unravels into something worse, and— BOOM! There you are cleaning your cellmate's toilet seat with your toothbrush.

Apart from their immediate family members, NO ONE REALLY CARES when an anonymous dirtball peasant dies during sex. The story might be good for a few days' worth of chuckles, but ultimately any person who trudged through life as a nobody will become even more of a nobody upon their expiration. The cruel, lacerating fact is that they don't exist anymore, and within a few years, there will be strong doubts as to whether they existed in the first place.

Pope John VII

We are Americans. We only care about the celebrities. And so it goes that when someone dies during sex, we only really care if the victim enjoyed some measure of fame and/or power in the years preceding that fateful day when their heart gave out before their rocks got off.

As with death-during-sex cases among the hoi polloi, nearly all of the following incidents among the rich-and-famous are alleged. Unless YOU were having sex with **Attila the Hun** at the moment he died, you can't really be sure that's what killed him, now can you? What's generally accepted is that the barbarian conqueror died while partyin' hard during his wedding night. Whether it was rough sex or, as is more commonly alleged, a nasal hemorrhage that took his life was a secret which probably died with his betrothed, a saucy German maiden named Ildiko.

Attila the Hun

There are likewise rumors that the **Prophet Muhammad**, founder of Islam, died while engaged in sex with an underaged girl. It is said that the disciples and wives who discovered his body were startled to find that his penis was still hard. This is undoubtedly a viciously untrue rumor started by the infidel foes of Islam, and I'm saying this only because I have enough enemies and don't really need some terrorist camel jockeys launching a personal jihad on my ass.

Five Catholic popes are said to have croaked while in the act: **Leo VII** (936–939), **John XII** (955–963), **Leo VIII** (963–964), **John XIII** (965–72), and **Paul II** (1467–1471). The latter was thought to have been strangled by his partner, but I could find no evidence whether said partner was a chick or a dude.

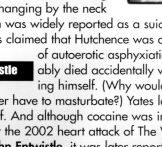
Felix Faure

A popular anti-czarist myth claims that Russia's **Catherine the Great** (1762–1796) was crushed to death under a horse while having sex with it. What's more likely is that she died on the toilet of a cerebral hemorrhage while straining to poop.

In 1899, France's president **Felix Faure** died while receiving a blowjob from an eager *jeune fille*. The woman went into shock when she realized he died, then suffered lockjaw and had to be rushed to the hospital in order to pry her mouth from the dead president's penis.

Some historians believe that the deaths of U.S. Presidents **Warren G. Harding** in 1923 and **Franklin Delano Roosevelt** in 1945 were also due to fellation from frisky *femmes fatale*. It is commonly believed that **Nelson Rockefeller**, Secret Leader of the World, died while fucking his mistress in 1979.

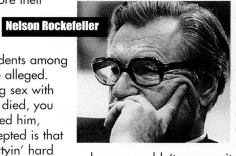
Nelson Rockefeller

Greasily dashing Hollywood B&W era actor-studs **John Garfield** and **Errol Flynn** are believed to have expired in mid-hump, as is film director **Ernst Lubitsch**, who directed classics such as *Ninotchka* and *Heaven Can Wait*. In Lubitsch's case, heaven couldn't even wait until he shot his load.

Lubitsch died while having sex with a prostitute. Once-brilliant/now-deceased comic **Richard Pryor**'s father met the same fate, ironically in the same brothel where Pryor's mother worked. Curly-haired actor **Matthew McConaughey** has claimed that his own father died while mom and dad were doin' it.

Super-buff martial-arts star **Bruce Lee** is said to have died while having sex with a spunky li'l Hong Kong lotus blossom.

The pop-music world writhed in pain and agony in 1997 when it was announced that **Michael Hutchence**, singer of INXS, was found hanging by the neck in a closet. His death was widely reported as a suicide, but his girlfriend Paula Yates claimed that Hutchence was a practitioner of autoerotic asphyxiation and probably died accidentally while pleasuring himself. (Why would rock stars ever have to masturbate?) Yates later killed herself. And although cocaine was initially blamed for the 2002 heart attack of The Who's bassist **John Entwistle**, it was later reported that his ticker blew while he was rutting a stripper.

Michael Hutchence

John Entwistle

FAMOUS PEOPLE WHO'VE (ALLEGEDLY) DIED DURING SE

MASSACHUSETTS

Women throughout the state are forbidden from being on top during sex. It's against the law for anyone to sleep naked in Salem motel rooms.

MICHIGAN

Detroit couples are only allowed to have sex in a car while parked on their own property. Men in the Motor City cannot legally "ogle" a woman while driving past her. In Clawson, a lonely farmer can legally "sleep with his pigs, cows, horses, goats, and chickens."

MINNESOTA

Men in Alexandria, MN, can be forced by their wives to brush their teeth before having sex if their breath stinks of sardines, garlic, or onions. Men throughout the state are forbidden from engaging in sexual acts with birds and live fish. (The law makes no mention of dead fish.)

MISSISSIPPI

All sadomasochistic acts are *verboten*, including theatrical and literary depictions. This is obviously a new law, since it didn't stop slaveholders from whipping their slaves back in the day.

MISSOURI

Corsets are forbidden among the merry women of Merryville, because "the privilege of admiring the curvaceous, unencumbered body of a young woman should not be denied to the normal, red-blooded American male."

MONTANA

Couples who have sex in their front yard after sundown in Bozeman are required to wear clothes. Likewise, women in Helena who choose to dance on saloon tables must be wearing at least three pounds and two ounces of clothing.

NEBRASKA

Anal sex is punishable by up to 20 years in the Big House. Hotel guests in Hastings, NE, are forbidden to be naked. The hotel owner is to provide them with nightshirts, which are required by law to be worn during sex.

NEVADA

Are you a state lawmaker who's thinking about wearing a penis costume during a legislative session? Forget about it—it's illegal.

NEW JERSEY

"Mutual masturbation" between men could yield the perps up to three years in the pokey. In Liberty Corner, a possible jail sentence faces couples who accidentally honk their horn while having sex in a car.

NEW MEXICO

All oral sex is illegal and can yield up to ten years in prison. In Carlsbad, it's OK for couples to have sex in their car during a lunch break, but only if their vehicle has curtains which prevent onlookers from witnessing the act.

NEW YORK

Fathers in Staten Island are not permitted to call their son a "faggot" or "queer" in response to alleged "girlie behavior." In Manhattan, a $25 fine may be levied against flirtatious men who turn around on the street to look "at a woman in that way."

OHIO

Cleveland women are not permitted to wear patent-leather shoes because they may reflect their underwear. Women in Oxford are forbidden to strip naked in front of a man's photo.

OKLAHOMA

If you're a woman in Schulter, don't even think about gambling while nude. And if you're a man in Clinton, you could be arrested for masturbating while watching a couple have sex in a car at a drive-in.

OREGON

In Willowdale, men are not permitted to utter profanities during sex.

PENNSYLVANIA

Female toll-booth collectors—but not males—are prohibited from having sex with truck drivers while working in their toll booths.

SOUTH DAKOTA

Couples are forbidden from having sex on the floor between beds in all Sioux Falls hotels. Oral sex brings a possible ten-year bid in the pen. Prostitutes throughout the state are forbidden to turn tricks inside covered wagons.

RHODE ISLAND

State law describes oral sex as an "abominable, detestable crime against nature" which could yield up to a decade behind bars.

TEXAS

All pigs in the town of Kingsville must refrain from copulating on airport runways.

UTAH

Women in Tremonton are prohibited from having sexual relations with men while in a moving ambulance. If convicted, the offending female will have her name printed in the local paper. Throughout the state, sex with animals is legal unless it's done for profit.

VIRGINIA

Patting a woman's ass in Norfolk could land you in jail for two months. Having sex in a moving motorcycle sidecar has likewise been

(CONTINUED ON NEXT PAGE)

strange sex laws

abolished in Norfolk. In Romboch, sex is only legal if the lights are off. In Lebanon, a man cannot legally kick his wife out of bed.

WASHINGTON, D.C.
Missionary style is the only sexual position allowed by law.

WASHINGTON STATE
Seattle women who sit on men's laps while riding a bus or train must place a pillow between themselves and the man or risk six months in jail. In Auburn, it is illegal to have sex with a virgin—even if you've just married her.

WISCONSIN
Men in Connorsville must under no circumstances fire a gun while their female sex partner is having an orgasm.

WYOMING
One must never encourage anyone under 21 to masturbate, under penalty of law. In Newcastle, couples are prohibited from having sex inside a store's meat locker.

FOREIGN

BOLIVIA
Men in Santa Cruz are forbidden from having threesomes with a mother and her daughter.

CHINA
While in a hotel room, it is only legal for a woman to be naked in the bathroom.

COLOMBIA
In Cali, a bride's mother must witness the first act of intercourse between the married couple.

ENGLAND
You can't have sex on a stationary motorcycle in London, you can't do it "on the steps of any church after the sun goes down" in Birmingham, and female clerks in Liverpool are only allowed to go topless while working in a tropical-fish store.

GUYANA
Nude swimmers in Georgetown are to be painted head-to-toe and dropped off outside of town.

HONG KONG
Women in Hong Kong who catch their husbands cheating are only allowed to kill him with their bare hands, but they are permitted to kill the other woman by whatever means necessary.

INDONESIA
Masturbation results in decapitation.

JORDAN
Husbands are required by law to engage in sex "with the wife at least once every four months."

KUWAIT
Men are prohibited from lustfully staring at statues of women and female animals.

LEBANON
Men are permitted to have sex with female animals, but indulging in carnal relations with male animals yields the death penalty.

MEXICO
The death penalty may be served upon all males in Durango who so much as touch their wives during the first 12 days from the onset of menses.

PANAMA
Homosexuals are castrated and then exiled.

PERU
Sex with alpacas is forbidden. Unmarried men are forbidden to cohabitate with female alpacas. A law dating to 1583 metes out the death penalty for homosexuality, bestiality, and pedophilia.

POLAND
Bestiality in Krakow is illegal. Three strikes brings a bullet to the head.

URUGUAY
Husbands who catch their wives *in flagrante delicto* with another man can either kill both of them or cut off his wife's nose and her lover's balls. All men in Montevideo who have sex with their wives during menstruation are to be fined and given 200 lashes in public.

VENEZUELA
Unmarried men and women in Valencia are forbidden to have sex with deformed people and anyone widely considered to be an "idiot."

ALL THE GAY BEASTS OF THE FIELD

THE SLURPING SOUND WAS FAMILIAR, but my ears hadn't prepared me for what mine eyes were about to see. I had spent nearly every waking minute of the previous six weeks attending to my female pug's nine hungry puppies, alternately bottle-feeding them and making sure that Mama Pug let them hang off her nips long enough to get a hot, nourishing meal. It was exhausting work—by the time the ninth one was fed, we were right back at the top of the batting order. I had fallen asleep on the couch as the pups cuddled together in a big box on the floor.

The slurping sound roused me from my brief siesta. I immediately figured someone was nursing, but I was startled to look in the box and see Mama Pug was nowhere to be found. Instead, to my incredulous horror, I espied one male puppy feverishly BLOWING another! This is the sort of apparition for which a lifetime of psychological counseling and spiritual training could never prepare you, but I had to believe what my eyes were laser-beaming into my brain. Little "Johnny Boston," one of the smaller pups, was bobbing his head up and down on the micro-mini-cock of "Da Priest" with the diligence of someone who faced a jailhouse beating if they resisted. Da Priest, for his part, languidly lied on his back, legs spread and head lazily pointed toward the side as if enjoying a foot rub.

Since neither one of them seemed remotely interested in stopping their faggy little song-and-dance, I found it my duty as a caregiver to immediately separate them. Alarmed, angry and ashamed, I pondered the implications of this sordid act for which the medical books and wildlife specials had not prepared me: Were two of my puppies homosexuals? And if so, how would this affect their market value?

Homosexuality among animals is as natural as a shiny red apple on a big green apple tree. Despite galaxies of evidence to the contrary, there still exist some mentally deficient Corn Nuts who believe that homosexuality is unnatural, citing as Gospel fact the myth that God's beasts of the field are too macho and law-abiding to ever dabble in same-sex pleasures.

Au contraire, my kind, closeted friend. The historical record teems with case accounts of tawdry homo behavior among the lower orders. A massive book called *Biological Exuberance* claims that at least 470 species have been observed committing same-sex acts ranging from fellatio to cunnilingus to handjobs to pussy-bumping to "swordfighting" and full anal penetration. Many of these acts result in orgasm for one or—hopefully—both partners.

Female elephants have been observed using their trunks to diddle each other's big rubbery elephant snatches. Lady monkeys and hedgehogs routinely muff-dive. Male dolphins have been known to fuck each other's blowholes and stimulate one another's naughty bits using "sonic pulses." Lesbian seagulls form girl-only colonies off the California coast while randy West Indian boy manatees engage in all-male orgies. From the Agile Wallaby to the Bean Weevil, from the Indian Fruit Bat to the Mountain Dusky Salamander, from the Southern Green Stink Bug to the Yellow-Backed Chattering Lorikeet, from the humble Tsetse Fly all the way up to the majestic Sperm Whale, it seems that all of God's creatures are prone to a little faggin' off. And refreshingly, they do it without any of the annoying self-labeling so peculiar to humans. You might see orangutans blowing each other, but they'd never identify themselves as "queer." They're just blowing each other and having a good time.

Homophobes and troglodytes struggle to dismiss such obviously GAY behavior as either a display of social dominance, a friendly "greeting," or even a case of mistaken identity. But when you consider that orgasms occur, and that mutually affectionate and protective same-sex "relationships" often persist for years among animal couples who have ample access to the opposite sex, it seems plausible that homosexuality might even be an *orientation* among certain furry freaks.

This makes no sense from a Darwinian perspective, since evolution dictates that all sex aims at procreation. But it may make sense in that homosexuality lessens sexual competition and may even facilitate social order. Consider the fact that "gay" animal couples have been observed hatching others' eggs and raising the young'uns, often with more success than "straight" couples. And never underestimate the social-bonding value of a good BJ.

Well, just because it's natural doesn't make it right, say the critics. *After all, animals have been known to eat their young. Incest, gang rape, and pedophilic acts are also common among those pesky varmints.*

What is unnatural, you ask me? Nothing. What's wrong with any of it? I can't say.

But beyond all the animal gay-play, and even out past where the murderous baby-eating incestuous Prairie Dogs roam, there's another practice that exists both in the human realm and the animal kingdom: Lifelong committed heterosexual relationships. The only difference? It occurs with LESS FREQUENCY than nearly all of the sick acts listed above.

HOMOSEXUALITY IN THE ANIMAL KINGDOM

Whiskey Dick

the role of intoxicants in erectile dysfunctio

More than anything else, men fear impotence. They know that even one limp-dicked episode can have drastic, life-altering results. At the very least, the poor fellow's unsatisfied lover will go blabbin' to all the girls in town that he's a dud in the sack, leading to embarrassment, job loss, severe social ostracism, and a life of eating potato chips in front of the TV on Friday nights. That's at the *very* least. At worst, we're talking about murder-suicides and an eventual episode of *Forensic Files.*

And yet most males reading this, if they bear the merest scrap of honesty within their horny, fatty-acid-strangled hearts, would admit that at least once in their lives, they have suffered the abject humiliation of **erectile dysfunction**, known in some circles as **"not getting a boner."** Judging from our extensive marketing research regarding our readership, it's safe to assume that in many of your cases, there's a correlation between **drug use** and subsequent **bedroom failure**. I know this to be true because intoxicants are spread throughout the sex industry like tar on a rooftop.

Living as Sanctified American Adults in a free nation that bombs whomever the fuck we WANNA bomb, we ingest intoxicants primarily for PLEASURE. It simply FEELS GOOD to slam down drinks, shoot up heroin, and sit around in a drum circle puffing on a hookah with a bunch of smiling, socially conscious friends.

Our stinking lust for pleasure is likewise fulfilled in the sex act and its bawdy carnal delights. For the average male—or, in my case, the *above*-average male—the brain floods with Happy Juice whenever we're sticking it to a chick like a sand shark burrowing deep inside a wet pile of beachfront property.

Sex and drugs. Two roads leading straight to Pleasureville.

Combined, sex and drugs are the chocolate and peanut butter of sensuality, a Reese's Cup of unbridled indulgence and satisfaction. Drugs, as all of us know from hard experience, are often used to *enhance* sex. Behold the foofy hipsters wearing their chic clothing at all the trendy nightspots, readying themselves for the rigors of alterna-coitus by toting a cigarette in one hand and a martini in the other, slinking off to the bathroom to snort poppers and rocky piles of Peruvian Marching Powder. You know the type—they pout their lips and flutter their eyelashes. They soak their brains in red wine, green bud, and China White.

Sex and drugs. Drugs and sex. It's a Pleasure Train.

Usually.

The fun is often derailed, though, when the drugs get in the *way* of the sex. It's almost as if the drugs get *jealous* of the sex and try to prevent you from having a threesome with it. Given the right dosage, alcohol and certain drugs can impede or even prevent an erection by altering blood flow to a guy's ding-diddy-dong. Sip a li'l too much sauce or toot a li'l too much blow, and you might find that your once proud Love Loaf is reduced to a soft, watery blob of uncooked pizza dough. Or just keep drinking and smoking like you've been doing, and you'll be flaccid in a few years, anyway.

But since I care about you like no other writer on earth is even CAPABLE of caring, since I've invested considerable prayer, emotion, and ball sweat in the idea that one day you'll actually FIND a girl willing to go home with you and that once you're there, you'll be able to *perform* with some level of rudimentary adequacy, I'm going to hold your soft little hand and guide you through the potential hazards of drug-induced impotence.

> **FACT:** "Whiskey Dick" is the actual name of a town in Oregon about 20 miles no of Madras.

> "Sex and drugs. Drugs and sex. It's a Pleasure Train. Usually. The fun is often derailed, though, when the drugs get in the *way* of the sex. It's almost as if the drugs get *jealous* of the sex and try to prevent you from having a threesome with it."

Alcohol

In Shakespeare's immortally faggy words, excessive drinking "provokes the desire but takes away the performance." Nary a man among us, and scarcely even a boy, can honestly claim they've never been "too drunk to fuck." Through the ages, how many millions of drooling drunken males have vainly tried to squash their wormy-soft anti-erections inside their repelled lovers' 'giney-holes? How many brave lady citizens have toiled for hours, their jaws sore from sucking on their sloshed boyfriends' soft candy cocks?

Long-term alcohol use ravages the liver and fries the nervous system. The neural connections between the pituitary gland and the genitals are damaged. Testosterone plummets, leading to the syndrome referred to as "Whiskey Dick" or, in the U.K., "Brewer's Droop." In severe cases, the hormonal damage wrought by alcohol can even cause men to grow breasts. *Ewww!* Prolonged alcohol use damages penile nerves and can cause permanent impotence, even if the person quits drinking.

So keep drinking, assholes, and give me your girlfriend's phone number while you're at it. She's gonna need me in a few years.

CT: "Crystal Dick" is the actual me of a Program Assistant at e University of Louisville.

Tobacco

Although nicotine is so pervasive that few consider it a drug, it is actually the most addictive psychoactive compound known to mankind, the only intoxicant which a user craves a mere half-hour after receiving a fix. Studies have shown that smoking as few as two cancer sticks before sex will cause a dramatic decrease in blood flow to the peeny-ween. Chronic tobacco use permanently impairs circulatory function, leading to a smoker's hack and a limp noodle—one more reason to quit the World's Dumbest Habit.

Marijuana

Reefer's proponents tout its alleged aphrodisiac properties and its use by herbalists throughout history to cure impotence. But the Assembled Enemies of Stoners Everywhere cite studies claiming that long-term tokers risk a permanent drop in testosterone, the resultant penile limplitude, lower sperm counts, and possibly even an embarrassing case of THC-induced man-boobs. They claim that chemicals in marijuana play havoc with the brain's neurotransmitters, leading to impotence, heartbreak, and always forgetting where you left your keys.

I disagree (except for the part about the keys). I've smoked BALES of the shit over the years and don't have problems raising *my* joint.

Cocaine

Coke's legendary status as Feel Good Sexual Space Candy is at least partially deserved, yet there exists a dark side...a shame-riddled side...a *droopy* side...which threatens to strike the genital regions of males who either do too much at one time or even 1,000 little bumps over a long time. Although moderate doses affect neuro-transmitters in a way that boosts sexual performance, additional blasts may actually reverse the chemical equation. Blood flees the penis, leading to 1,000 shriveled rock-star cocks surrounded by 3,000 yawning hookers.

Amphetamines

The tweaker world—a dazzling, loving, wondrous, sun-drenched community of caring souls who seek to get through life AS QUICKLY AS THEY FUCKING CAN—refers to meth-induced impotence as "Crystal Dick," an exasperating thimble-sized shrinkage of the wiggity-wang that maddeningly coincides with a Neanderthal sex drive.

Like its older, richer, more well-liked brother cocaine, the decidedly déclassé family of speed variants can have conflicting results on sexual performance. Depending on a man's tolerance, he's either hammering nails in the wall with his dick...or he's trying to find it with a magnifying glass.

Heroin

Who *cares* whether or not junkies can get it up?

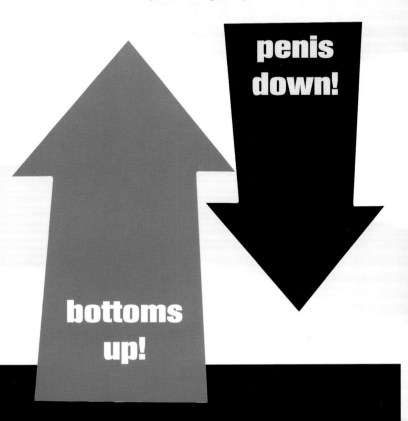

penis down!

bottoms up!

Round and 'round went the big fucking wheel,
In and out went the prick of steel.
Until at last his wife she cried,
"Enough, enough, I'm satisfied."
—*"The Fucking Machine," from* The Dirty Song Book *(Jerry Silverman, 1982)*

LARGE-BREASTED ASIAN WOMAN howls with pleasure at the orgasm-inducing thrusts of a "fucking machine."

A cyber-nightmare stalks the American male's virility. The inevitable collision of sexual perversion and technological innovation has produced a new wave of "fucking machines"—motorized devices designed to achieve tireless, high-speed penetration of the human vagina and other, even dirtier, orifices. And what's more unsettling, these electro-powered metal-and-rubber monsters are being marketed to women and gay men—the two most dangerous elements of our society.

As a human male with a human penis, I am offended. No matter how many sit-ups I do or protein shakes I drink, I still can't compete with the greasy, steely stamina of these horny automatons. No matter how many handfuls of Viagra, Levitra, and Cialis I jam down my gullet, I still can't muster 300 thrusts per minute until the electric company shuts off the power.

This sense of my relative physical frailty, the humiliating knowledge that I can't satisfy a woman of *my own tribe* with the same piston-pumpin' ferocity as a pile of nuts, rubber, and bolts, is what informs and fuels my rage against the fucking machine. I am jealous of its stamina and, yes, maybe even its looks.

The granddaddy of fucking-machines websites, **www.fuckingmachines.com**, shows crude animated GIFs for a slew of motorized hump-contraptions with scary names such as "The Intruder," "The Trespasser," "The Hammer," "The Predator," and—my favorite name—"The Drilldo." Watching these perpetual-motion appliances pumping away with locomotive fury was a shamefully emasculating experience for me. The home page for **www.fuckmachines.net** only rubs more salt in my wounds:

These women experience pure penetration and unrelenting vibration for the first time in their lives. They control the speed of the penetration. They control the depth of the penetration. They control the intensity of the vibration. They fuck like they have never fucked before. It's a beautiful thing to watch—orgasm after orgasm!

A man who builds fucking machines for a living describes their technical advantages over the human male:

With fucking machines…you can easily achieve more penetration stimulation than possible in any other way. My normal fucking machines might have a stroke up to 6", and up to 300 strokes a minute….One based on a reciprocating saw (my "Hole Saw") can easily do over 2000 short (1-1/4") strokes a minute. Not a chance any human can match any of that….

The website for a product called the "Jetaime," which resembles a padded barrel with a dildo sticking up through it, lists "REASONS WHY JETAIME IS BETTER THAN A MAN," which they claim is "Adapted from the Cucumber Book":

JETAIME is at least six inches long … JETAIME stays hard for as long as you need … JETAIME never suffers from performance anxiety … JETAIME will never make a scene because there is another JETAIME in the house … JETAIME will not leave dirty shorts on the floor.

"My wife came over and over again," writes a fucking-machine manufacturer regarding his spouse's first ride on a mechani-cock. "She scratched me 'til I almost bled."

"It saved my marriage!" enthuses one satisfied customer's online testimonial. "[The machine] serves as the other male partner my wife always fantasized about (double penetration, a huge black cock, etc.), but that I would have never accepted with a real guy. And much safer, too (no STDs, no danger of her falling for the other guy, etc.)!"

"My wife cannot believe this machine," burbles another happy cuckold. "She has ridden it every day for up to

RAGE AGAINST THE FUCKING MACHINE

A BRIEF, HURRIED GUIDE TO A FRIGHTENING NEW WAVE OF MOTORIZED PENETRATION DEVICES

3 hours...wow! Every orgasm is a '10.' She's hornier than ever...."

In a discussion of fucking machines posted on **soc.sexuality.general**, one man shares my fear of imminent sexual obsolescence:

With all these mechanical dicks hanging, lunging and/or pumping all over the place, has the male penis, the actual embodiment of straight and hard, become obsolete? Have we, as men, lost our claim to the title of pleasurers of women?...It is my pride and joy that I can get women off like they never have gotten off. But what good am I if she can have all of the above done by a machine?

IT'S DIFFICULT TO MAP OUT a history of the modern fucking machine. Although motorized sexual gizmos have existed as far back as the late 1800s, a discernible trend of electronic penetration devices only seems to have emerged as recently as the mid-1990s.

In her book *The Technology of Orgasm*, Rachel Maines chronicles over 50 sexual-stimulation applicances developed before 1900, all under the medical guise of curing women of "hysteria." These ranged from small, hand-cranked doohickeys all the way up to giant steam-powered thingamajigs which necessitated a crew of laborers in a separate room to feed them with coal.

But between then and now, lost in a tangle of vibrating bullets, magical eggs, and battery-powered marital aids, there exists a sort of Dark Age regarding the genesis of the modern fucking machine. The makers of the "Sybian," which might be regarded as more of a high-tech vibrator than a full-on penetration gadget, claim the idea for their squirming dildo-on-a-barrel device was hatched in the early 1970s and finally began development in the mid-'80s.

"I don't think any specific invention started the modern boom," claims a man calling himself "Sartan," who began building fucking machines in the mid-1990s and sells models crafted from such items as toolboxes and attaché cases. "There certainly aren't any components involved that couldn't be found or swapped at the turn of the prior century, if you didn't mind steam as a power source."

Sartan is the most articulate and passionate of the new crop of fuck-machine builders, these pioneers who meld sexual fetishes with tool-shop savvy, who mix the Marquis de Sade with Bob Vila. They engage in a kinky techspeak revolving around pivot points and linkage, of converting rotary to linear motion, of stroke length and thrusts per minute.

"My own fascination with machine toys is twofold," Sartan writes on a Usenet discussion board. "First (and probably primarily) is the mental aspect...helpless before the machine, as it were. A machine, as opposed to a human, is relentless. Relentlessly consistent and mechanical. It doesn't ever get tired (as long as it has a continuous duty motor), doesn't quit, you set—it goes. I routinely use my fucking machines on my wife for several hours at a time (it's a power trip thing for me)....It's a huge turn-on to watch Jenni getting fucked by a machine."

This theme of using fuck-machines to indulge sexual sadism is even more evident in one post on a gay-bondage newsgroup: "I've heard stories of mechanical fucking machines that you can attach a dildo to and flip a switch—and fuck forever. Just imagine the look on a poor boy's eyes when after he's been tied down securely, the machine comes out—one that never tires, and is always indifferent and deaf to cries for mercy."

FOR REASONS OF UNBRIDLED VANITY and a bottomless sense of insecurity regarding my place in the cosmos, I worry about these so-called "fucking machines." I fret that the more these metallic beasts become popularized, the less currency I will hold as a sexual being. Painfully aware that I cannot compete with these apparatuses on the physical plane, I agonize over the fact that I will finally have to develop personal charm and act nice to women.

I asked a female friend whether she was aroused at the idea of these newfangled electro-studs, and, at least for the record, she denied that they moisten her lap. "I can't get turned-on by anything that doesn't have a heartbeat," she told me, possibly lying.

In an online discussion thread regarding the socio-sexual implications of fucking machines, other women tend to agree with my friend's sentiment: "How can a machine kiss you and hold you afterward?" one of them gently asks. "It's the touch contact that is just as, if not more, satisfying than sex and multi orgasms. Only another person can provide this."

"You're human," counsels another. "You have a warm body. You have a mind. You can speak. You can smile, laugh, massage, cuddle, whisper sweet things, etc., things that a machine cannot."

That all may be true, Toots, but I can't wiggle my pickle 300 times a minute and keep it up forever. And that is why point, set, and match go to those goddamned fucking machines.

It is generally accepted that God is a male, and as such, it must be assumed that He has a wonderful penis. In the vibrantly throbbing multiplicity of his creations, He has also fashioned all manner of animals, and He has bestowed upon most of them a wonderful penis all their own.

Lord knows how many animals Noah crammed on his ark, but we *do* know they filed in two-by-two, with each male animal toting a unique, divinely fashioned penis.

Let us take a moment to reflect on the variety of cocks our Lord has made—whether they come equipped with spines, hooks, knobs, twists, or bulbs—and let us be profoundly thankful.

To most marsupials, He has given a bifurcated penis, which splits into two columns like antennae.

To the gentle dolphin, He has given a marvelously useful penis which operates like a prehensile tail, enabling the highly intelligent creature to probe the ocean floor like a blind man searching for cigarette butts.

To the American skunk He has given an 'S'-shaped

penis, and He has gifted the lovable wallaby with a sexual appendage shaped like an ice-cream cone.

To the pig He has given a corkscrew-shaped member which moves with a rotary action and ejaculates once it is snugly within the female pig's corkscrew-shaped vagina.

To the banana slug, especially a pimpin' breed known as *Dolichyphallus* ("giant penis"), He has given a member equal in size to the rest of its body. And He has endowed the lowly barnacle with a johnson roughly 20 TIMES the rest of the barnacle. Lady barnacles, rejoice!

Our creator's handiwork is evident in the formidable schlong of the daddy longlegs spider, which measures roughly two-thirds of its entire body length. Scientists in Scotland recently unearthed a daddy longlegs fossil containing what is believed to be the world's oldest extant penis, a spider dick nearly 400 million years in age, blowing away the previous record-holder, a 100-million-year-old penis belonging to a tiny crustacean known as an ostracod.

God has included a literal bone within the "boners" of many mammalian species, and to the rest of us He has given a blood-engorged flesh sac which only *approximates* a bone, at least when I take Viagra.

Thank you, God, for all of these penises. Thank you not only for my criminally tasty penis, but also for the mystical, life-giving penises of all the birds in the air, the beasts in the field, and the fishies in the sea. Our penises all point toward heaven and thank you.

ASIANS, THOSE HAPLESS LAST-PLACE-FINISHERS IN THE HUMAN-PENIS SWEEPSTAKES, routinely ingest animal cocks in order to enhance sexual potency or revive a flagging libido. Cruising the back alleys of most Chinatowns throughout America, one finds dusty old stores which peddle potions containing all manner of animal cock—tigers, wolves, seals, deer, ostriches, goats, snakes, and even the cuddly li'l gecko lizard so beloved in current TV car-insurance commercials—ground into pastes, potions, pills, and soups which promise enhanced sexual performance among humans. China alone is thought to import at least 30,000 seal penises every year for such purposes. In 1993, Chinese officials seized 731 seal and deer dicks which black-market weenie vendors were attempting to smuggle across their border.

OF COCK

THE FROSTY ISLE OF ICELAND, home to the midnight sun, glorious hot springs, and that shrieking psycho cunt named Bjork, also boasts what is thought to be the planet's only "penis museum." Nestled in the town of Husavik, the Icelandic Phallological Museum contains over 100 specimens of animal cock, representing all of the island's mammalian species save two—the human and the dolphin.

Not to fret, though—an Icelander named Pall Arason, described as "very far from being modest," has willed his penis to the museum upon his death, provided that it be removed from his still-warm corpse before the blood clots in order that it can be injected with fluids to keep it forever erect.

Cruising the museum, one finds a staggering array of animal wee-wees: a tank containing 29 whale dicks; a dried bone from a skunk's cock; a tanned bull penis fashioned into a whip; a jump rope equipped with animal-dick handles; a bow tie made from whale-schlong leather; a coat rack with animal-cock legs; a "penis mini-bar"; and a smoked horse *schvanz* donated by surviving family members of an Icelander who used to eat such items "as a treat."

Yum! Think I'll fix myself a horse-cock sandwich!

AN ANIMAL PENIS TO SUIT EVERY TASTE

1. Happy boy elephant gets his "hang" on;
2. Male whale enjoys life to the fullest;
3. Dried whale penis from the Icelandic Phallological Museum;
4. "Thor," a giant dildo modeled after a horse's cock by the kind folks at Zeta Creations in West Virginia.

"BROWNBEAR" AND "TIGGER" ARE THE PROPRIETORS of Zeta Creations in West Virginia, which to my horrified knowledge is the world's only manufacturer of dildos modeled after animal penises. Cruising their website (www.furcen.org/~zetatoys), one marvels at the love and detail invested in plasticine re-creations of canine, equine, ursine, feline, and aquatic phalluses. The site boasts a sharply curved kangaroo dildo (for going "down under," the ad copy explains) and promises an alligator dildo in the near future.

"It's hard to explain to someone else what it feels like to have a bear cock slide slowly in," reads their promotional literature, "or feel the slick curve of a dolphin penis gliding in and out. You'll just have to find out for yourself."

Uhh...think I'll pass.

The testimonials from satisfied customers should induce nausea in most sane readers:

I haven't felt this good since my 1st time with a male K9 lover.

Received "Smokey" the new bear dildo from "Zeta Creations" today, and it is quite fun to use.

I like the design and feel of the raccoon cock, but the curve is a bit much for me to take the whole thing, but I'll keep trying. ;)

I just got 'Squirmy' from you recently. I have to say...it's wonderful!

I purchased your Grand Pup toy, and I've enjoyed using it very much. It gets used as often as I can manage. =)

IT'S A WIDE, WIDE WORLD OF ANIMAL COCK OUT THERE. As long as there are animals, there will be animal cocks—getting hard, shooting their jizz, and creating more animals, roughly half of whom will have *new* animal cocks. It's all part of God's master plan. Thanks, Big Guy!

PEOPLE ARE PERVERTS,
thus there are potentially as many paraphilias as there are things in the universe.
The word "paraphilia" is derived from the Greek *para*, meaning "beyond," and *phile*, meaning "love." A paraphilia, therefore, is a way-out kind of love. It is typically considered abnormal or socially deviant, and faggoty "mental-health experts" consider it an impediment to "emotionally meaningful" relationships.

According to David Rosenham and Martin Seligman, authors of *Abnormal Psychology*, paraphilias typically involve one of three categories:

1) Objects not usually considered sexual;
2) Sadomasochistic scenarios revolving around humiliation;
3) Sex acts forced upon the unwilling.

What follows is a list of individual paraphilias, followed by a very brief description. The list employs shorthand to avoid redundancy.
Each ellipsis (...) can be replaced by the phrase "sexual arousal through an abnormal fixation on." So when you see...

NECROPHILIA ... the dead
...you are to fill in the blanks inside your tiny pinhead and read it as:
"Necrophilia *is sexual arousal through an abnormal fixation on*
the dead." Got it? Good! I love you! I fixate on your
crusty toenails and masturbate to the thought
of them as you read this!

A

ABASIOPHILIA ... crippled or physically impaired persons

ABLUTOPHILIA ... bathing or otherwise washing oneself

ACOUSTICOPHILIA ... sounds

ACROPHILIA ... heights

ACROTOMETOPHILIA OR **ACROTOMOPHILIA** ... partners with amputated limbs

ADELOPHILIA ... feigning disinterest in sex

ACUCULLOPHILIA ... circumcision

AGALMATOPHILIA ... naked statues and mannequins

AGONOPHILIA ... partners who pretend they're being raped

AGORAPHILIA ... the great outdoors, especially having sex in 'em

AGREXOPHILIA ... others' knowledge of one's sex life

ALBUTOPHILIA ... water

ALGOPHILIA ... pain

ALTOCALCIPHILIA ... high heels

AMAUROPHILIA ... a partner whose sight is impaired either by darkness or a blindfold

ANASTEEMAPHILIA ... a partner whose height is significantly different than one's own

ANDROMIMETOPHILIA ... a female partner pretending to be a man

APHEPHILIA ... being touched

APOTEMNOPHILIA ... fantasizing about having a limb amputated

ARACHNEPHILIA ... spiders

ASPHYXIAPHILIA ... loss of oxygen through being strangled by oneself or one's partner

AUTAGONISTOPHILIA ... having others see one's genitals incidentally or accidentally rather than intentionally

AUTASSASSINOPHILIA ... exposing oneself to potentially fatal situations

AUTOABASIOPHILIA ... fantasizing about being crippled

AUTOASSASSINATOPHILIA ... fantasizing about being murdered

AUTOGYNEPHILIA ... cross-dressing

AUTOMYSOPHILIA ... fantasizing about making oneself filthy

AUTONECROPHILIA ... fantasizing about being a corpse

AUTONEPIOPHILIA ... acting like an infant and/or being treated as one

AUTOSCOPHILIA ... observing one's body, especially the naughty bits

B

BASCULOPHILIA ... being rocked and cradled as if one was an infant

BELONEPHILIA ... pins, needles, and other sharp objects, especially being pricked by them

BIASTOPHILIA ... surprising and sexually attacking a stranger who resists

C

CANIDAEPHILIA ... dogs

CARPOPHILIA ... the feeding of fruits

CATAGELOPHILIA ... being ridiculed

CATHETEROPHILIA ... catheters and catheterization

CHOREOPHILIA ... dancing

CHREMASTISTOPHILIA ... being robbed or forced to pay blackmail money

CHRONOPHILIA ... age discrepancy between oneself and one's partner

CHRYSOPHILIA ... gold

CLAUSTROPHILIA ... being confined or trapped in a tiny space

COLPKINOPHILIA ... underdeveloped breasts

COPROLALIA ... "dirty talk"

COPROPHILIA ... touching, smelling, seeing, or eating poo-poo

COULROPHILIA ... clowns

CRUROPHILIA ... legs

CYPRINOPHILIA ... slutty women

CYPRIPAREUNIAPHILIA ... hookers

D

DACRYPHILIA ... a partner's tears and/or the sight of a partner crying

DENDROPHILIA ... trees, particularly as phallic symbols

DERMAPHILIA ... skin

DIAPHANOPHILIA ... see-through garments

DISCINCTOPHILIA ... fucking while partially clothed

DISHABILLOPHILIA ... undressing for people

DYSTYCHIPHILIA ... accidents

E

ECDYSIOPHILIA ... watching people strip

ELECTROPHILIA ... electricity

EMETOPHILIA ... puke

EPHEBOPHILIA ... teenagers

EPROCTOPHILIA ... flatulence

EROTOPHONOPHILIA ... lust killing

A FREAKY LOVE KIND OF LOVE
THE A-Z LIST OF PARAPHILIAS

F

FLATUPHILIA ... the flatulence of others
FORMICO-PHILIA ... crawling things, especially when they crawl over one's genitals

G

GERONTOPHILIA ... geriatrics
GLUTOPHILIA ... buttocks
GONYPHILIA ... female knees
GRAOPHILIA ... geriatric women
GYNEMIMETOPHILIA ... one's male partner impersonating a female
GYNOTIKOLOBOMAS-SOPHILIA ... a woman's earlobe

H

HAPTEPHILIA ... being touched
HAMARTOPHILIA ... breaking laws or committing sins
HARPAXOPHILIA ... being robbed
HEMATOPHILIA ... blood
HEBEPHILIA ... teenagers
HIEROPHILIA ... sacred objects
HIRSUTOPHILIA ... armpit hair
HODOPHILIA ... traveling
HOMICIDOPHILIA ... fantasizing about a partner or a stranger being murdered
HOMILOPHILIA ... hearing or giving lectures
HOPLOPHILIA ... weapons
HYBRISTOPHILIA ... criminals, especially violent ones
HYGROPHILIA ... bodily fluids

I

J

K

KAINOTOPHILIA ... change
KAKORRHAPHIPHILIA ... failure
KERAUNOPHILIA ... thunder and/or lightning
KINESOPHILIA ... exercise
KLEPTOPHILIA ... stealing
KLISMAPHILIA ... enemas
KNISSOPHILIA ... incense
KOPOPHILIA ... exhaustion
KOROPHILIA ... young males

L

LACTAPHILIA ... milk-producing breasts
LAVACULTOPHILIA ... staring at a person in a bathing suit

M

MACROPHILIA ... giants and/or oversized objects
MAIEUSIOPHILIA ... pregnant women, particularly those ready to drop
MAMMAGYMNOPHILIA ... tits
MECHAPHILIA ... machines
MELCRYPTOVESTIMENTAPHILIA ... black panties
MERINTHOPHILIA ... being bound
MICROPHILIA ... small things
MIXOSCOPIC ZOOPHILIA ... watching animals fuck
MORIAPHILIA ... telling dirty jokes
MYSOPHILIA ... filthy, soiled things

N

NANOPHILIA ... short partners
NARRATOPHILIA ... telling dirty stories
NASOPHILIA ... touching a partner's nose
NECROPEDOPHILIA ... young dead people
NECROPHILIA ... the dead
NEPIOPHILIA ... infant partner
NEOPHILIA ... new things
NORMOPHILIA ... acts considered normal
NOSOPHILIA ... a partner's terminal condition
NYCTOPHILIA ... darkness and nighttime

O

OCHLOPHILIA ... being in a crowd
OCULOPHILIA ... eyeballs
OSPHRESIOPHILIA ... odors normally thought to be unpleasant

P

PARTHENOPHILIA ... taking someone's virginity
PEDIOPHILIA ... dolls
PEDOPHILIA ... children
PHALLOPHILIA ... giant cocks
PHOBOPHILIA ... fear
PHYGEPHILIA ... escaping or being a fugitive
PICTOPHILIA ... sexual pictures or films
PILIPHILIA ... hair
PLUSHOPHILIA ... stuffed toys
PODOPHILIA ... feet
PSYCHROPHILIA ... being cold
PUBEPHILIA ... pubic hair
PUPPETOPHILIA ... blow-up dolls
PYGOPHILIA ... buttocks

Q

R

RAPTOPHILIA ... fantasies of raping someone
RHABDOPHILIA ... being beaten or whipped

S

SALIROPHILIA ... ingesting someone else's sweat or spit
SAPOPHILIA ... researching paraphilia
SARCOPHILIA ... flesh
SARMASSOPHILIA ... kneading flesh
SCATOPHILIA ... eating jizz that has been ejaculated into an ass
SIDERODROMOPHILIA ... trains
SOMNOPHILIA ... having sex with a sleeping stranger
SPECTROPHILIA ... ghosts or mirror images
STATUOPHILIA ... statues of naked people and nude mannequins
STIGMATOPHILIA ... tattoos and scarification
SYMPHOROPHILIA ... watching a disaster that one has caused

T

TAPHEPHILIA ... being buried alive
TELEPHONE SCATOPHILIA ... OR **TELEPHONICOPHILIA** ... making obscene phone calls to strangers
TELOPHILIA ... intercourse without foreplay
THANATOPHILIA ... death
TIMOPHILIA ... gold, money, and power
TRAUMAPHILIA OR **TRAUMATOPHILIA** ... wounds or traumas
TRICHOPHILIA ... hair
TAPHOPHILIA OR **TAPHEPHILIA** ... being buried alive
TRIPSOPHILIA ... being massaged

U

UROPHILIA ... all things piss-related

V

VACCINOPHILIA ... being vaccinated
VELOPHILIA ... bicycles
VICARPHILIA ... stories of other persons' exciting lives
VOMEROPHILIA ... puke
VORAREPHILIA ... cannibalizing someone or being eaten by them

W

X

XENOPHILIA ... strangers or aliens
XYROPHILIA ... blades and razors

Y

Z

ZELOPHILIA ... jealousy
ZOOPHILIA ... animals

NUDISM

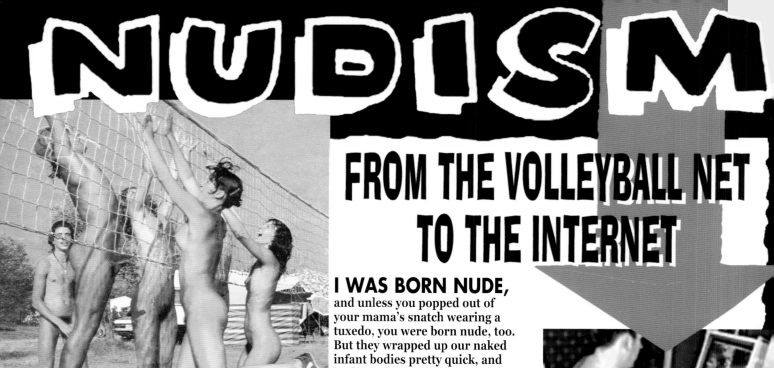

FROM THE VOLLEYBALL NET TO THE INTERNET

I WAS BORN NUDE, and unless you popped out of your mama's snatch wearing a tuxedo, you were born nude, too. But they wrapped up our naked infant bodies pretty quick, and in the end, they'll likely bury us in clothes.

As a kid of around three or four, I'd sometimes do a little dance after getting out of the shower before getting dressed. I called my dance "The Nude Dance," and it consisted of a basic two-step with my arms swinging back and forth in front of my wee naked frame. Amused by my naked jig's gleeful innocence, my teenaged brother even wrote a song called "Do the Nude," whose lyrics consisted entirely of the mantra "Do the nude, and a-do the nude" repeated while I danced. Even my parents were amused by my Nude Dance, because I was obviously too young to realize people shouldn't be nude at all, much less *dance* about it.

I grew up fascinated by cheesy nudist culture in the 1970s, dovetailing as it did with long-gone trash-sex phenomena such as streaking (running nude in public—sort of a form of nudist terrorism), wife-swappin' swingers, and male "flashers" in trenchcoats (what the hell happened to *them?*).

As an adult, I've been publicly naked at an all-male health club in Stockholm (keep your wisecracks to yourself), a nude beach in Copenhagen, and sundry "clothing-optional" hot springs across the American West. When coworkers weren't around, I've even had occasion to trudge through the *Exotic* office naked as a porn-peddlin' jaybird. Unless it's too cold, I always sleep naked and spend much of the time in my apartment without one thread of evil textiles to cover my pink skin. I often lift weights nude while looking at myself in the mirror. For lucky naked partners, I will even sometimes perform my hilarious "penis dance," and a good time is had by all.

BUT IT'S TOUGH BEING NUDE in a world where everyone wears clothes. Everyone who's "civilized," at least.

Clothing. You either wear it or you don't. Clothes change everything. Clothes are so anthropologically important, it's silly. Clothing is a social dividing line almost as all-encompassing as gender. More social significance is accorded clothing than just about any other material item. So many invisible walls fall to the ground along with one's clothes. We attach so much absurd importance to clothing to the point where we've convinced ourselves that nudity, rather than clothing, is what's unnatural or deviant.

LIFESTYLES OF THE NUDE 'n' FAMOUS

Proponents of social nudism, eager to prove that their lifestyle is not solely the domain of utopian cuckoo birds and shady-minded swingers, point to a strong historical tradition of nudism among the famous and powerful.

They reach nakedly back toward antiquity and point to pro-nudist sentiments expressed by classical giants such as **Plato** and **Thucydides**, the latter of whom argued that nudism elevated the Greeks above the fur-clad barbarians.

They cite favorable comments and glowing reminiscences of bein' nude amid the work of fruity Jersey poet **Walt Whitman**...Italian ceiling-painter **Michelangelo**...self-absorbed Frenchman **Jean-Jacques Rousseau**...pious back-to-nature goober **Henry David Thoreau**...insufferable playwrights **George Bernard Shaw** and **Eugene O'Neill**...and obsessed-with-giant-white-things novelist **Herman Melville**. They note that throughout **Mark Twain**'s *The Adventures of Huckleberry Finn,* considered by many to be the greatest novel written in English, Huck and Nigger Jim [hey, pipe down, that's what TWAIN called him, not me!] raft down the mighty Mississip' buck-naked, and nobody has a problem with it. They say that even one-man kiddie-book factory **Dr. Seuss** was a practicing nudist who published positive comments about his so-called "naturist" lifestyle.

Many influential American politicians practiced a nudist lifestyle. **Benjamin Franklin**, one of our country's Founding Fathers and a singularly unattractive man, took daily naked "air baths." **John Quincy Adams** was said to have taken a swim *sans* clothes in the Potomac every day while he was president. **Theodore Roosevelt**, also a habitual presidential skinny-dipper, once swam naked with a visiting French diplomat. *Bully!* Slain chick magnet **John F. Kennedy** is alleged to have held high-ranking meetings while naked in his bathtub and surrounded by assistants, all of whom were clothed. Jowly goat-roper **Lyndon Baines Johnson**, purportedly proud of his endowment, also would meet with his clothed subordinates while he was in the *nyood.* LBJ also reportedly held skinny-dipping pool parties at the White House and would frequently greet outside guests such as Frank Sinatra while defiantly unclad. Greasy morose tragic clown **Richard Nixon** was also alleged to have held White House meetings without a stitch of clothing on him. And in an intriguing meeting of the political and entertainment worlds, there is also a rumor that crazed-with-world-domination **General Douglas MacArthur** and pro-Nazi cartoon mogul **Walt Disney** once skinny-dipped together at a beach in the 1960s.

Modern celebs known to have practiced social nudism include neurotic chick singers **Alanis Morissette** and **PJ Harvey**...sun-poisoned good-timey musician **Jimmy** "Cheeseburger in Paradise" **Buffett**, who claims that his whole family practices nudism...superdupersupermodels **Elle MacPherson** and **Christie Brinkley**...forgettable actresses **Lynn Redgrave** and **Bridget Fonda**...and Muslim-slurring animal-rights lunatic **Brigitte Bardot**.

Nudity. So simple and yet so powerful. The naked body, when revealed, is both more and less than what we had imagined. So much hinges on its suppression. If the world were to suddenly turn all-nude, catastrophic social meltdowns would result. Clothing, since it cages our sexuality, is essential to our idea of being civilized. God may not have always told us that nudity is bad, but the King does. He always does. He needs us to quit fuckin' around, get dressed, and start building the roads.

But mandatory social clothing has only been a very recent blip in human development. It has existed for less than one percent of the entire timespan of the slapstick comedy called Humans on Earth. It wasn't until the loom was invented in China about 6,000 years ago that clothing became an option. Until then, the whole world was a nudist colony.

Nearly all cultures of antiquity, and many world cultures today, practiced public nudism. Most pagan societies incorporated nudity into their rituals. The ancient Egyptians walked around nude, as did as the Greeks, especially in their homoerotic-by-inference nude sporting spectacles. The Greeks were even known to WAGE WAR in the nude. The Roman public baths were all-nude, as were many European public baths throughout the Middle Ages. European families often slept in the same bed naked.

Ferocious, repressive anti-nudity sentiments grew as Protestantism took hold throughout Europe, culminating in the Victorian Age, when people didn't even talk about body parts in mixed company. Even piano legs were often required to be covered, lest they suggest the shamefully seductive female leg.

ALTHOUGH THE PRECISE MEANING ELUDES ME at the moment, there is surely great significance in the fact that the country which invented the modern nudist camp also invented the modern concentration camp.

In 1903, a German named Richard Ungewitter published a 104-page treatise extolling the virtues of mixed-gender public nudity. The same year, inspired by Ungewitter's book, Paul Zimmermann opened *Freilichtpark* (Free Light Park) in Lubeck, Germany. Considered the world's first modern nudist camp, the park remained in operation until 1981. Faithful to Teutonic control-freak tendencies, the park's overlords dictated ironclad laws for its members. Meat was forbidden. So were cigarettes and alcohol. All park guests were required to wake up early and undergo two rigorous hours of exercise under an instructor's whip.

Germans referred to the nudist lifestyle as "Free Body Culture." The nudist meme proved infectious, and 20 years later, experts reckoned that 50,000 Krauts were practicing a lifestyle which included marching around naked at least some of the time.

In 1929, a German nudist named Kurt Barthel immigrated to these shores and founded the American League for Physical Culture, whose purpose was to spread the nudist Gospel. Nudist colonies emerged across America in the early 1930s, aided by the 1933 formation of The National Nudist Conference, which later changed its name to the American Sunbathing Association. By the mid-1930s, there were an estimated 80 nudist colonies in America, some of which are still operating. Camps such as the "Sea Island Sanctuary" (founded on Cat Island off South Carolina's coast in 1932) and "Sunshine Park" (established by a Baptist minister in New Jersey in 1935) practiced a cooperative lifestyle with vegetarian diets and lotsa nude sports. But despite nudism's utopian/egalitarian pretensions, membership in many early camps was only within reach of the wealthy.

(CONTINUED ON NEXT PAGE)

NUDISM

To the clothed world, the nudists might as well have been Martians. Nudist colonies faced frequent police harassment, public ridicule, and evangelical outrage. Even so, pasty white mammaries and wrinkly white penises continued to flap defiantly under the open American sun. In the 1950s, courts decided once and for all that the idea of a cloistered nudist colony harboring consenting adults was perfectly legal.

Utopian nudist-colony culture became diluted (purists would say polluted) by an unwashed influx of free-lovin', hard-druggin', mass-orgy-havin' hippie culture in the 1960s. Public nudism became increasingly sexualized, more of a vulgar mass movement than an underground folk religion. It devolved from its lofty Edenic origins, becoming a haven for seedy swingers and pedophilic predators and thrill-seekers of all stripes. The culture of nude beaches and love-ins and Woodstock and smokin' hash oil naked in redwood hot tubs invaded the pristine culture of astringent nude diets and wholesome naked family living and 500 mandatory daily nude Jumping Jacks. Essentially, the hippies murdered the first wave of American nudist colonies.

The nude establishment (yes...sigh...there really is such a thing) has struggled to resurrect American nudism from the sex 'n' drugs image that has tainted it since the '60s. High-financed, tightly regimented nudist "resorts" catering to upscale couples and families constitute the modern Acceptable Face of American Nudism. Except for the clothing policy, many of these neo-nudist resorts are indistinguishable from high-tech health clubs. They offer nude swimming, nude ping-pong, nude water skiing, nude badminton, nude dining, and communal nude Macarena lessons. Nudist-friendly travel agencies offer nude cruises and nude travel packages.

The American Association for Nude Recreation, currently the nation's largest nudist club, claims 50,000 members. Its bland-as-shit website tries its best to portray a safe/anti-septic/desexualized/family-oriented strain of nudism, with obvious reasons. Modern Nudism equals Big Bucks, and any intimations of nude meth-pipe circles or nude mud wrestling with children would only hurt business. Entrepreneurial nudism's mouthpieces offer stats claiming that the ranks of the American Nude are growing by 20 percent yearly. They cite polls stating that

Americans are growing more tolerant of nudism.

SIDESTEPPING THE IRONY
of using computers to go back to nature, nudists have taken to the World Wide Web in order to proselytize their lifestyle and network with similarly nude individuals.

From what I can gather after reading a few dozen of their websites, nudists consider the "textile world" alien to their sanctified world. They view it as a corrupted, predatory, automated, sex-hating, fascistic mainstream *Überkultur* filled with meanies, a world whose violence and neuroses and fast-food wrappers and fall from grace are all rooted in the fact that its members AREN'T NUDE IN PUBLIC ALL THE TIME. Nudists use the word "textile" as both a noun (*he's a dedicated textile*) and an adjective (*it's a textile beach*), and it's usually used with some level of pejorative malice. Nudists refer to the textile world's pathological tendency to wear clothes as "clothes-obsessiveness" and "clothes-compulsiveness."

These days, many of the Socially Naked tend to shun the words "nudist" and "colony" altogether. Instead, they label themselves "naturists" who congregate with "traveling clubs" or at "resorts." It's a conscious distancing measure from any sleazy/creepy/cultish associations people might attach to both the terms "nudist" and "colony." Just like San Franciscans hate it when outsiders call their city "Frisco," modern self-described "naturists" frown upon usage of the term "nudist colony," because it makes the inhabitants sound like mindless ants.

That's really too bad, and I'm sorry to have to hurt their feelings, but I just can't use the word "naturist" seriously. I don't like the way it rattles off my keyboard or rolls off my tongue. It's pretentious and not nearly as sexually suggestive, in an erotically pre-porno way, as the delicious term "nudist." I prefer to use "nudist," and I'll call those freaky nude bastards nudists whether they like it or not, fuck them *and* their stupid colonies.

Nudists defend their lifestyle with the zealotry of the folk religionists they are. They say that social nudism relieves psychological stress, and they'll show you medical studies to prove it. They'll show you another survey that proves group therapy is more effective when conducted in the nude. They'll cite statistics that say nudists are typically richer and better-educated than your average textile-wearing drone. They say that nudists, rather than being sexual deviants, are statistically less likely to commit sex crimes or incest and engage in extramarital affairs than the sickos in the textile world.

They claim that clothing is a breeding ground for bacteria. They say one's skin needs to breathe, to absorb and excrete, and that clothing subverts many of the skin's natural functions. They claim that full-body exposure to sunshine insures a higher absorption of Vitamin D, essential to the immune system. They assert that nudity improves fertility, clears psoriasis, and prevents Lyme disease. They say that basking nude in the sun fights many types of cancer, even skin cancer. They say that clothes impede the body's circulatory, reproductive, and lymphatic functions. They say these ball-smashingly tight blue jeans I'm wearing right now could possibly lead to testicular cancer.

The devoted nudist feels, deep in the bottom of the sockless toes he squishes in the grass, that he lives in a fundamentally more moral, equal, and honest world than those in the textile world. Employing desiccated

MILESTONES IN NUDIST CINEMA

grey-pubed leftist jargon and pompous, Francophilic gobbledygook amid feely-meely googly Edenic let's-all-mush-together-in-a-gooey-protoplasmic-Love-Soup aesthetics, the nudist theorist proposes a loftier, more spiritually advanced mode of living which is available to anyone simply by droppin' trou. But don't be fooled—his form of nudism aspires to much *more* than mere triflin' nakedness—it seeks to create a utopian society, to champion the struggle for women's freedom, and to maybe even smash the patriarchy if there's any time left after all that other stuff. He proposes a world which accepts...nay, *celebrates*...the human body, with all its warts, rashes, sagging flesh, ingrown toenails, and swampy ass-stank.

THE NUDIST WORLD, despite all its delusions of philosophical grandeur and human uplift, will forever remain a severely *tacky* world characterized by goofy jokes, by *Elmer Fudpucker at the Nudist Colony* comedy albums, and by zany nudist-camp cartoons depicting a guy who can carry two cups of coffee in his hands and a dozen donuts on his boner. 'Tis a world encapsulated in irritatingly clever catchphrases such as "Skin does not equal sin" and "I've got a brand nude attitude!" and "We are nude, not lewd" and "Grin and bare it!" It's a world filled with an uncomfortably high quotient of pervy weirdlin's who, if it weren't for nudism, would be into, oh, *Star Trek* to satisfy their lonely itch for communal belonging.

In many ways, nudism is also the natural-born enemy of pornography. Nudism proposes that *all* of us should be naked, while porno posits that only a *few* of us should. That's a monumental difference. Porno depends on the general societal suppression of nudity, or it wouldn't be special enough that people would pay for it. Much of the sex industry's wealth is actually dependent upon the mainstream *suppression* of nudity. If nudity were commonplace, it wouldn't be so "exotic," and guys wouldn't actually PAY just to see a woman's bare tush.

I tend to side with the pornographers. My main beef with social nudism, apart from the oceans of aesthetic cheese, is the undeniable, proven-by-science fact that some people SHOULD be hung-up about their bodies. I'm currently seeking evidence for my anthropological thesis that clothing was initially invented not as vain, peacock's-feathers-style adornment...nor for weather-related reasons...nor to hide a sense of naked shame...but solely as punishment for unattractive people.

I *love* my body. Yours, I'm not so crazy about. There are so many people I wouldn't want to relate to on a nude level. If I don't even want to look at them clothed, why would I want to see them with their shit all up-front and in my face? I don't feel so swell about Utopia if it means I have to be naked along with everyone else.

Still, the warm wind feels great on my exposed skin. But for now, I'll raise the fence around my *own* garden of Eden and frolic there. Me and m'woman'll practice our own private brand of Antisocial Dystopian Nudism. I like the idea of nudity for me...but not for thee. Or as a lady friend succinctly phrased it when I asked for her thoughts on nudism, "I don't need to look at somebody else's junk."

Until the late 1960s, the only LEGAL way for Americans to ogle the naked human form in print and on movie screens...well, the naked *Caucasian* form, anyway, since *National Geographic* had no trouble showing dark-skinned "primitive" nudes... was via the purposely non-erotic genre of **nudist magazines** and **nudist-camp movies**.

Films featuring naked adults frolicking at nudist camps began to emerge in the early 1930s, coinciding with the first wave of American nudist-colony culture. The early films are typically imbued with a pompous, classically naturist, *Triumph of the Will*-styled conviction that nudism will bring about a worldwide elevation of humanity. **Elysia: Valley of the Nudes** (1933—*foreign-language poster pictured at right*) was filmed at a California nudist colony. The film begins with a producer's statement that "Our purpose is to show the benefits derived from bathing the body in the sun and air. Our hope is to show that the rapid growth of the Nudist movement throughout the world is based on health—both of the body and mind." The film's plot (some nudist-camp films have plots, some don't) concerns a newspaper reporter who's assigned to write about a nudist camp and winds up *joining* it. Other early nudist-colony movies include **This Nude World** (1932), a documentary featuring European and American nudist colonies...**Hesperia** (1937), filmed at an Oregon nudist camp that would later become Squaw Mountain Ranch...and **The Exposé of the Nudist Racket** (1938), which melds *Reefer Madness*-style scare-tactic anti-nudist narration with, of course, footage from the evil camps themselves. At one point, the film's narrator makes an unflattering comment about a portly female nudist.

In 1954, New York authorities banned **Garden of Eden**, filmed at a nudist camp, because it allegedly portrayed nude humans in "unwholesome sexually alluring positions." The film's distributor appealed an initial court decision, and in 1957 the state court ruled in the film's favor, with one judge arguing that "nudism in itself, and without lewdness or dirtiness, is not obscenity in law or in common sense." The decision made it easier for wider commercial distribution of nudist-camp movies, and exploitation directors pounced on the opportunity, unleashing countless whimsically naughty "nudie-cuties" for the commercial market in the late 1950s and early 1960s.

B-movie legend Herschell Gordon Lewis produced nudie-cuties such as **Nature's Playmates** (1962), **Daughters of the Sun** (1962), and **Goldilocks and the Three Bares** (1963) before single-handedly inventing the slasher-movie genre with 1963's **Blood Feast**. Recently deceased cult director Doris Wishman was one of the nudie-cutie's savvier exploiters, concocting clever stunts such as transplanting a grindhouse stripper onto nudist-colony grounds and filming her—nothing illegal about *that*— in **Blaze Starr goes Nudist** (1965) and setting a nudist colony in outer space in **Nude on the Moon** (1961).

Since full-frontal cinematic nudity was considered legally obscene in America until 1968, the nudist-camp films were always careful to artfully conceal the subjects' genitals, especially swingin' weenies. A strong distinction should be drawn between **nudist** films and the **pornographic** films which immediately succeeded them. By definition, a nudist film prohibits any equation of nudity with sex. You'll see nude adults playing volleyball and rowing canoes (known as "canuding" among initiates), but you won't see any remotely amorous activity. When legal decisions allowed for naked onscreen sexuality in the late 1960s, the nudist-camp genre quickly expired, stampeded to death under increasingly bold cinematic eroticism and, finally, hardcore.

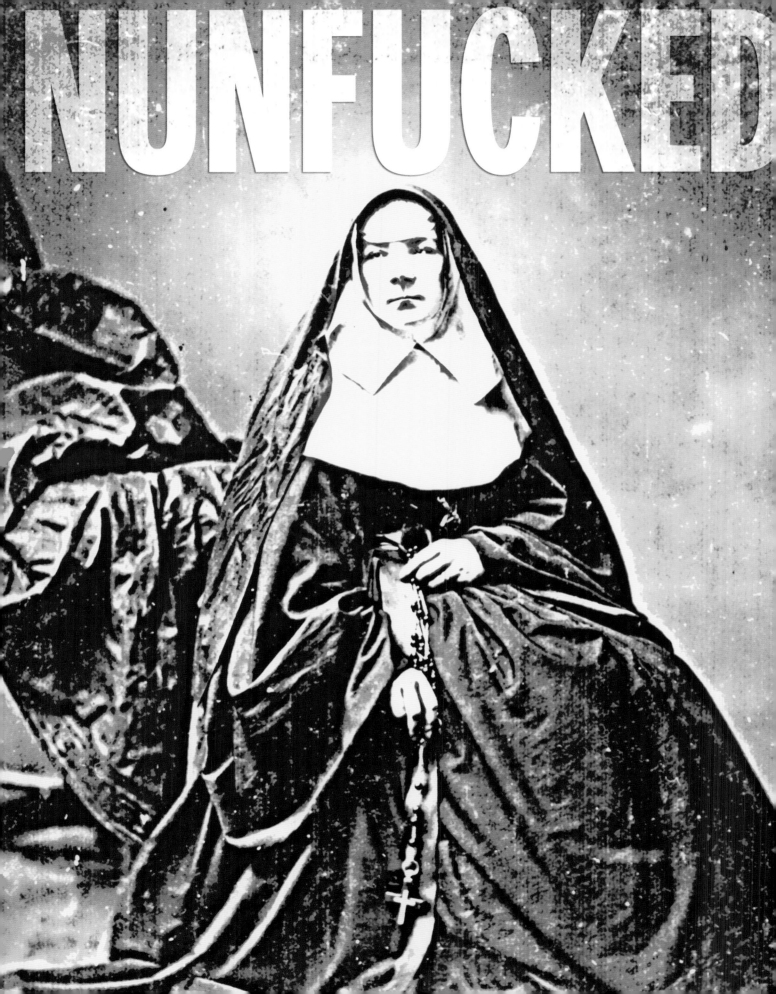

In February 1999, St. Mary's Church in suburban Boston celebrated its 125th anniversary. Cardinal Bernard Law oversaw the festivities, including a mass where parish children were summoned to the altar for a special blessing.

Sister Ann Daylor, a Dominican nun and St. Mary's director of religious education, glowingly told a reporter that the celebration would launch a yearlong program in which the Catholic young'uns would learn "the importance of their place in the future of the parish."

Oh, you got *that* right, Sister.

In December 2002, Cardinal Law would resign amid allegations that he covered up child sexual abuse committed by priests in his flock. The Cardinal's sagging, pale, piggish visage was splayed all over the media as an emblem of the exploding pedophile-priest scandal.

But less than a month before Cardinal Law resigned amid blinding flashbulbs, Sister Ann Daylor—the nun who predicted that children would play a crucial role in her church's future—was quietly placed on leave. She had been accused of sexually abusing a fifth-grade girl almost 40 years ago, a charge that she denies.

While an estimated 300 American priests were removed from duty during 2002 for similar reasons, Daylor is thought to be the only American nun relieved from her post last year due to sex-abuse charges.

A recent statement by the Leadership Conference of Women Religious (LCWR), an organization representing

abuse," claims Cait Finnegan, a Pennsylvania resident who says she was "sexually abused by a Sister of Mercy for several years."

"There are obviously more nuns than priests or brothers, and more kids in their charge for much more extended periods of time," Finnegan says. "One need only do the math."

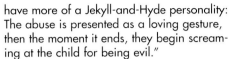

Although one rarely hears about it, there are dozens of documented cases of nuns sexually abusing children, most of them girls. Some cases suggest a level of sadism far beyond anything that priests have been accused of doing.

In the past decade, more than 100 nuns have been publicly accused of sexual misconduct with children in the United States alone. Over a dozen lawsuits have been filed in the U.S. alleging sexual abuse by nuns. Most have been settled out of court. But there is no evidence that an American nun has ever been criminally prosecuted for sex crimes.

Most estimates peg society's quotient of female sex offenders at roughly 5% of the total. Some put the percentage as high as one quarter of all sex predators. But even when women are accused of sex crimes, they are much less likely than males to be prosecuted. And they are almost never convicted.

have more of a Jekyll-and-Hyde personality: The abuse is presented as a loving gesture, then the moment it ends, they begin screaming at the child for being evil."

Such a pattern of "fondle-then-punish" is echoed in a recent Australian case where a woman claimed daily sexual abuse at a Catholic girls' home 30 years ago. She said the nun would digitally penetrate her, beat her with a blackboard ruler, call her parents and tell them she'd been bad, then send her home, where she'd be punished all over again.

Hill speculates that people have a hard time believing that nuns can be sexual predators "because women have not been regarded as sexual beings for so long, for much of history, I guess. If you're not a sexual being, you cannot possibly be a sexual predator."

And if women can't be sexual predators, goes the logic, then men certainly can't be their victims. On an Internet message board for a group calling itself SNAP (Survivors Network of those Abused by Priests), one anonymous poster recently claimed he has been rendered a self-loathing, drug-addled homosexual adult due to a nun's sexual abuse of him in grade school. He alleged that at age six, a nun wrongly accused him of looking up a girl's dress in the schoolyard. He said she led him to a private room and snarled that "boys who look up little girls' dresses should have their little dickies spanked." He claimed she slapped him hard across the face several times, forced him to drop trou, and then poked at his li'l-boy genitals with her cane, calling his penis a "horrible thing that boys have and it makes them do awful things!" She then allegedly forced him to wear a paper sign with the word PERVERT written on it and then paraded him in front of other students, who jeered at him until he "wanted to die."

"YOU ARE PATHETIC," came the unsympathetic response from a woman, a self-proclaimed survivor of sexual abuse by priests. "I am sick of men feeling sorry for themselves...GET OVER IT BIG BOY...did the nuns put something inside of you like what happened to me? No, they didn't, did they?...Putting focus on nuns instead of rapist men? This website is pathetic...and you women who support this are playing into their hands."

E HIDDEN STORY OF SEXUAL ABUSE BY NUNS

America's 75,000 or so nuns, claimed that its ranks were "deeply troubled" by the snowballing pedo-priest debacle. Yet the LCWR refused to sign a recent Bishop's Charter condemning clerical sex abuse, arguing that it didn't apply to nuns. Similarly, a nun-led group in the Philippines recently made public a report they wrote detailing "sordid disclosures about sexual abuse by [Filipino] priests."

To many, the nuns appeared bold for "speaking out" and "taking a stand" against pedophile clergymen. But to some of their alleged victims, the specter of finger-wagging nuns is bitterly ironic. "I must admit this boils my blood almost more than the initial

One study showed that six out of every seven victims of childhood sexual abuse by women are not believed when they first tell their stories.

Ashley Hill is the author of *Habits of Sin: An Exposé of Nuns Who Sexually Abuse Children and Each Other* (Xlibris Corporation, 1995), which might be the only book in world history devoted exclusively to sexual abuse by nuns. Hill claims a nun molested her when she was seven.

"I believe that among the nuns, the level of mental illness runs deeper than with the priests," says Hill via e-mail. "To me, it seems as though the abuse by priests is more along the lines of sexual gratification, whereas with the nuns, they often seem to

In 1994, nine male ex-residents of the Holy Childhood of Jesus School in Harbor Springs, Michigan, went public with allegations of sexual abuse by the Sisters of Notre Dame. The abuse, allegedly ranging

NUNFUCKED

said to have occurred throughout the 1960s and into the early '70s. Bed-wetters were reportedly forced to wear their piss-stained sheets on their heads like turbans. One former resident charged that one nun came in almost nightly and would lie on top of him…for starters. The nuns reportedly would refer to the boys, all of whom were Native Americans, as "heathens" and "black savages."

At the nearly embryonic age of three, Joey Barquin remembers being dragged into a closet by a nun at St. Joseph's Orphanage in Burlington, Vermont. He says she yanked his trousers down to his feet and began groping his preschool penis. When he tried to pull away, he says she forcefully grabbed his balls and ran an unidentified sharp item between his thighs. "Next thing I know," he was later to tell a reporter, "there was unimaginable pain, and there was just blood everywhere." He also alleges that one nun had a habit of arousing him to the point of erection and then burning his penis. Barquin claims that he still has anal scarring from repeated rapes at the orphanage. He says the abuse only stopped when he was adopted as a five-year-old in 1953.

After Joey made his accusations public 40 years later, an estimated 100 other former residents of St. Joseph's also came forward with tales of being abused by nuns there in the 1940s and '50s. Their compiled stories became what Barquin called "the Schindler's List of Vermont."

At four years old, with his mother dead and haunted by vague memories that his father had hung himself, Paddy Doyle was sentenced to 11 years at an Irish industrial school run by the Sisters of Mercy. His "crime," according to the state, was "being in possession of a guardian who did not exercise proper guardianship." In essence, he was declared a criminal for being an orphan.

In his book *The God Squad* (Raven Arts Press, 1988), Doyle recounts a creepy incident of a nun jacking him off at age six:

She held my limp penis in her hand and drew back the foreskin. It hurt slightly but I was too scared to say anything….She moved the skin backwards and forwards until I had an erection. A sensation I had never experienced swept through my body, causing me to squirm and writhe involuntarily. When it had passed I sobbed uncontrollably, frightened at what had happened.

Doyle's punishment extended to a series of brain operations with the stated intent of fixing a defective foot. Many of the operations were unnecessary and probably experimental, rendering him crippled as an adult.

"In a recent article I wrote for an Irish newspaper," Doyle says via e-mail, "I made the comment that wherever you have vulnerable people, you will have predators. Who or what can be more vulnerable than a child who is institutionalized and under a fear of terror of being punished by the 'predators'—in my case, the nuns, in whose care I had been placed?"

In an Irish TV documentary called *States of Fear,* another survivor of the Catholic industrial schools echoed Doyle's terror: "The one good thing about Christmas Day was that there was no sexual abuse on Christmas Day."

Perhaps the most sensational claims of nuns goin' "up in it" come from the Land Down Under. In the late 1990s, a wave of Australian adults surfaced with accounts of having suffered monstrous childhood abuses at Catholic orphanages.

At Nazareth House near Brisbane, children were allegedly subjected to savage beatings for such infractions as being left-handed or opening their eyes while praying. A woman named Lizzie Walsh, from "fondling to intercourse," was who'd been a child resident of Nazareth House in the 1950s, recounted tales of being vaginally raped by a nun with a flagstick "to get the Devil out of me." When another nun found her sitting in a pool of her own blood after the rape, she reportedly chided Walsh to clean up the mess and return to class. Walsh also says nuns refused to believe her claims of being raped by two priests. Amid allegations of having been made to drink her own urine and eat vomit, Walsh also claims to have been force-fed the feces of a sexually predatory nun.

Bobbie Ford, another alleged Nazareth House victim, corroborated tales of nuns raping girls with "broomsticks and flagsticks…to get the Devil out of them." She also tells of nuns rubbing Vicks onto girls' pre-pube crotches in order "to get their puberty hair to grow." Ford claims that while a child at Nazareth House, she was imprisoned in dark cells for days and was once hung naked by her wrists for hours. She also recalled an incident where nuns shoved a guinea pig down one girl's pants and forced her to remain still while it nibbled on her crotch. Other alleged victims of Nazareth House told of being forced to kiss dead bodies. Some were reportedly warned that if they told anyone of the abuses, the Devil would turn into a dog and rip their throats out.

As far-fetched as some of these claims sound, there appears to be solid supporting evidence. "The story of Lizzie Walsh at Nazareth House is beyond understanding," concedes Bruce Grundy, a journalism professor in Brisbane who has written extensively about abuses in Australian orphanages, "[but] I know the Lizzie Walsh matter was presented to the police. I saw her statement….With respect, we are NOT talking about hysterical people," Grundy says. "I have surveyed scores of them, read their files and their psychologist's reports, and cross-checked their claims with others. I have sat and listened while they have cried, hour after hour, grown men and women. Dozens and dozens of them."

Grundy, who says that his reports have outraged Church officials but that "no one sued," claims Nazareth House was "a shocking place for some of the kids. Absolutely beyond belief….The nuns seemed to specialize in physical and psychological cruelty, torture, and terror….There was a sort of madness that singled some out and others not….The psychological warfare they waged against [a girl named] Helen Forde at Nazareth makes Machiavelli a saint."

Grundy also wrote a detailed report regarding lurid allegations against Sisters of Mercy at a children's home in Neerkol, northern Queensland. The abuse, reportedly spanning a 90-year period beginning in the 1890s, included: a red-hot poker applied to a girl's bare back in order to "exorcise" her; children raped by priests with nuns' consent and even direction; forcible toenail-removal with pliers; a nun forcing a girl's leg down into boiling water; a pregnant girl being forced to take judo lessons until she miscarried; and live naked floggings of children in front of the entire school.

Grundy recounts one allegation of a nun sexually abusing a boy at Neerkol: "At Christmas, the Neerkol kids used to be taken down to the beach for a holiday. A boy wanted a drink and went to a tap, [then] put his mouth in his hand under it and turned it on. He washed a wasp (or a hornet) into his mouth. It stung him in the back of the throat. He was in agony for hours and was sent to the dormitory.

"That night he was still sobbing in bed. A nun came and took him to her room, took him to bed, and, I suspect you call it rape, but, whatever, she had sex with him. It was a bit of a shock for the boy, since sex was something he had not encountered before. There were no witnesses, so there is no corroboration."

In contrast with the blunt concentration-camp brutality of the orphanages, there exists a pattern of nuns sexually abusing those placed under their care in pastoral or "teacher's-pet"-style situations. These cases, while seemingly more benign, tend to involve high levels of psychological manipulation. They often feature relationships lasting several years, and because they sometimes bear a quasi-romantic flavor, it is difficult to discern where consent ends and abuse begins.

In 1989, a Minnesota woman filed a lawsuit claiming that Sister Georgene Stuppy "regularly and repeatedly engaged in unpermitted, harmful, and offensive sexual contact" with her over three years beginning in 1978 when she was 13 and Stuppy was in her 40s. Strangely, Sister Stuppy admitted to engaging in sexual contact with the girl but acted surprised that anyone deemed it sexual—she always considered it a "spiritual" thing. The case was settled out of court.

A woman named Jill Thornton was given my e-mail address from someone at Broken Rites, an Australian anti-clergy-abuse watchdog group. Jill tells me that in 1980 at age 40, she entered into a "Therapeutic Relationship" with a nun acting as a psychologist. But it was an odd sort of therapy, Thornton says, one which "was described as working on skin to skin...with the client." Thornton says the counseling, which lasted over 12 years, "included seeing clients in bedrooms, using the bed. I was a 40-year-old adult; however...I always regressed during these 'touching sessions'....[This] nun came in...with only knickers underneath, at times. The grooming procedure was very subtle over a number of years. As I became 'more adult,' I began to resist this form of therapy."

Although Jill is reluctant to share details (but really, isn't the "knickers" thing plenty?), she says she has recently made a complaint of "indecent assault" to Australian police, who are deciding whether there is sufficient evidence to prosecute the nun. "SHE WILL HAVE TO ANSWER BEFORE THE POLICE AND NOT HIDE BEHIND THE LEADER," Jill ominously tells me in all-caps letters via e-mail.

Thornton claims that her prolonged sexual abuse led to "a complete nervous breakdown....I sat in a chair for a year not able to care for myself." She has since learned to deal with the trauma by becoming "an advocate to others in Australia, including nuns who have been sexually abused or raped by nuns."

Sometimes, as Thornton alleges, nuns even reach out and touch other nuns. The book *Habits of Sin* claims that nun-on-nun sexual abuse is used as a coercive tool for establishing convent hierarchies, even for fucking your way to the top. Young nuns willing to indulge the Mother Superior's ungodly tastes might just find themselves awarded that peachy post-grad scholarship.

A Kentucky lawsuit recently filed by a former nun hinges on similar accusations. Emily Feistritzer, now in her 60s, claims that as a schoolgirl, she was molested by a nun who was grooming her to be a nun, only to be molested again by other nuns after she actually became a nun. Whew! The suit alleges that Sister Eugene [real name Rosemary Imbus], Feistritzer's eighth-grade teacher, "repeatedly sexually molested" her, which involved "unwanted and lewd touching...of the plaintiff's breasts, attempts to undress her, kissing her and actual or attempted vaginal contact." It also claims that Sister Eugene pawed at Feistritzer's privates while she was dressing as a postulant.

Feistritzer's lawsuit also claims she was molested by two nuns upon entering the convent in 1959. It alleges that a certain Sister Christopher committed dastardly acts such as "attempting to forcibly have sexual contact with her...forcibly undressing her, and...having unwanted sexual contact with her."

There's a somewhat indirect strain of sexual abuse by nuns which might properly be called "nuns-as-pimps." Such cases involve nuns facilitating or overseeing rape and molestation committed by others. One allegation against a Sister Philomena at Australia's notorious Nazareth House orphanage says she handpicked child victims for a pedophile priest, knowing he'd rape them. At the Neerkol orphanage, nuns were said to have "loaned" children at Christmas to known pedophiles who'd made large cash donations to the home.

In 1999, Sister Dominic, an Irish nun whose real name is Nora Wall, was sentenced to life imprisonment. She'd been convicted of holding down a ten-year-old girl's ankles, allowing a homeless man to rape her. The act allegedly occurred on an unnamed date in 1987 or '88 at St. Michael's Child Care Centre in Cappoquin—the same place where Paddy Doyle says a nun masturbated him in the early 1960s. Wall's victim, Regina Walsh, testified about the alleged rape in court. She claimed to have suffered repeated sexual abuse at Cappoquin from ages nine to 12. She called Sister Dominic "evil to the bone" and "ice cold."

Sister Dominic's conviction—and, mind you, it's the ONLY criminal conviction on record of a nun for sex abuse which this reporter was able to find after exhaustive research—was quickly overturned due to a minor point of prosecutorial misconduct, one which appeared to have little to do with the evidence against the nun.

So as it stands, there is no record...or at least none I could find, and none that the experts knew about, either...of a nun ever being convicted of a sex crime and serving time as a result.

It's hard to make a sex beef stick against a nun. In many cases, the alleged atrocities occurred decades ago, so evidence is hard to obtain. Memories are lost, blurred, or worse, "recovered." And nuns exist in a cloistered world that thrives on secrecy even more than the Mafia. Nuns move around. Nuns change their nun names to other nun names, and sometimes you never know their "real" names.

But in contrast with an almost utter lack of criminal indictments against sexually abusive nuns, victims have made some headway with civil complaints.

In Vermont, the church made cash settlements in an estimated five dozen cases involving St. Joseph's orphanage, where Joey Barquin claims to have suffered a bloody scrotum at age three. At least a dozen of these settlements are thought to have involved sexual abuse.

In Australia, church officials doled out an estimated $1 million total in settlements to over a dozen women who'd claimed physical and sexual abuse at Nazareth House. There were also settlements regarding abuse at the Neerkol orphanage, but secrecy clauses prohibit further disclosure.

In America, the Catholic church has reached settlements regarding claims of sexual abuse by nuns in New York, Georgia, Minnesota, and Massachusetts. There are also pending lawsuits alleging sexual misconduct by nuns in Rhode Island, Massachusetts, and Kentucky.

Despite all the settlements, not once has the church admitted liability for sexual abuse by nuns, nor does the word "sorry" seem to surface in any of its official statements. Payments of hush money aren't legally an acknowledgment of guilt, so I have to state here that it's possible no nuns ever molested anyone.

It's possible.

But not likely.

"I don't think we are close to having a handle on this problem," Ashley Hill says. "It is only beginning to unfold. This issue is about where the priest scandal was 25 years ago—just emerging."

NO ONE IN THEIR RIGHT MIND WOULD ARGUE that the idea of anonymous high-risk sex with a total stranger isn't exciting. EVERYONE knows it's exciting. There is something undeniably appealing about impulsive rutting unburdened by the dreaded word "relationship" and all the torture/drudgery it implies. The one-night stand, at least for one night, frees the captive blackbird from his dirty cage. With the implicitly fleeting nature of such a genital *tête-à-tête*, there is no emotional melodrama, no annoying teardrops, no wide-eyed recriminations. You both know why you're there, and you don't give a fuck about their soul, their dreams, their interests, or EVER meeting their parents. A one-night stand is something that only "cool guys" get to enjoy—mobster guys in blue sharkskin suits with big hairy dicks and padded expense accounts.

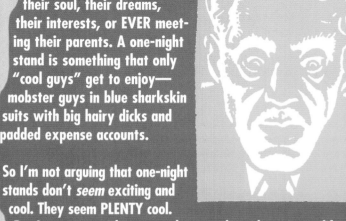

So I'm not arguing that one-night stands don't *seem* exciting and cool. They seem PLENTY cool.

But I can count at least two dozen such incidents in my life, and for me the sex was only decent—not great, mind you, and certainly not artery-blowing—in only two of them. And I'd reckon ALL these girls would say I'm a lousy lay, if I even made it to the point of insertion. Instead of the intrigue and heated embraces you read about in those dime-store novels, I left a slug's trail of prematurely blown wads and sad, stony impotence.

There is nothing inherently wrong with the one-night stand until you enter ME into the equation. I am a paranoid part-time sociopath who walks around inside prison walls made of flesh. I am petrifyingly nervous around new sexual partners, and I only start to warm up with someone after a half-dozen or so encounters with them. So these unlucky dames never got to taste the true glories of physical intimacy with me. I present these stories, highlights of ten one-night encounters, merely for your amusement.

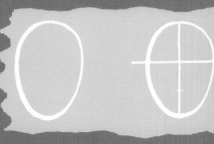

♥ As the dark, salty Atlantic waves crashed nearby, I learned a surprising and invaluable trick to ensure a woman will fuck you: Act like *you don't care* whether she fucks you! I laughed to myself while working this maneuver on a dumb-but-nice blonde girl I met at a bar one summer night in Wildwood, New Jersey. We were both drunk, and during our slobbery make-out session in the parking lot, she expressed some shy hesitation about walking under the boardwalk and "going all the way" with me. A few aloof shrugs and "sex-isn't-importants" on my part, and we were 69'ing in the dark sand. While walking 'neath the boardwalk, I crunched my head on a concrete beam and was bleeding, but I didn't want to tell her and "ruin the mood." I also didn't inform Blondie I'd shot my wad all over my leg about two seconds after we undressed. While I lapped away at her downy vagina and tried to hide the white fluid on my leg and the red fluid on my forehead, she kept blaming herself for failing to get me hard.

♥ A butch girl I knew from college who vaguely resembled Mickey Dolenz of rock combo The Monkees. She had a very hairy pussy and dark brown circles under her eyes that made them look as if they were poking out of an unwiped anus. It was my last night in Philly before moving to New York, so we rented a hotel room and decided to "go for it." Amid a flood of hotel-room artificial light, I suffered humiliating shrunken erectile dysfunction all night long, peppered with her repeated question, "What's *wrong* with you?"

♥ After ten years of marital fidelity, I decided it was high time I cheated on my wife. I met a very large young girl with rosy cheeks at a local bar, hoisted her into a cab, and pointed the driver toward the nearest hotel. During our post-coital pillow talk, she spoke openly of how her boyfriend had mistreated her. This, naturally, hastened my arousal. I fucked her again, for a grand total of one minute's worth of fucking.

♥ She had a bald eagle's pointed face, yellow buck teeth, thinning brown hair, and she drove a semi truck for a living. Can you say, "Boner Mountain"? She mounted me on top and had some seriously strong hip-thrust action—that is, for

...five or so seconds it took me before reaching climax. ...hen she broke the tense, silent "afterglow" portion of our evening with laughter, I asked if she was laughing at my performance, but she denied it. I gave her a friend's phone number and told her it was mine.

♥ The fattest girl I've ever fucked. Possibly ...e fattest girl *anyone* has ever fucked. But with her ...nt pelican nose and utter lack of charm or intelli...nce, she would have been hideous without even a ...oplet of blubber. When she took off her clothes, it was ...e pulling the string on an emergency life raft—she ...tantly ballooned up to twice the size. When I climbed ...p her bulk, it was like laying on a jiggly waterbed. ...early got seasick. I had serious difficulty finding her ...gina. Once the evil portal was located, I squirted a ...y raindrop of cum within a nanosecond. During our ...forgettable night of rapture and ecstasy, she warned ...e that she didn't want to become "just another ...e-night stand." After I'd successfully ...oided her for weeks, she confronted me ...a bar and reminded me of her warning. ...elt afraid, but in the end, she became ...t another one-night stand.

♥ A highly intelligent pharmacist ...th monster boobs I met in San ...ancisco while touring. She fed me ...armaceuticals and allowed me to ...ter her "special place" four times. She ...as on the rag at the time, and I felt like ...ruthless conqueror as I roamed around ...r apartment naked, my bloody cock ...ngling in front of her face while she ...lked to her live-in boyfriend over the phone.

♥ It was a blazing Portland summer night where ...e orange moon was so big, it spanned Burnside and ...t clipped on both sides by the buildings. I dragged ...freckly, frizzed-out thing from Dante's upstairs into ...e infamous *Exotic* back room and let the frosty air ...nditioner roar. When I leaned in to orally pleasure ...r, I caught a sharply unpleasant whiff of something. ...e moment my tongue touched down upon her teeny ...nk pinto bean, she uttered the word "shit." She ...eant to say, "Shit—that feels good," rather than ...hit—that's what you smell," but I couldn't help ...aking the connection.

♥ A libertarian political candidate with frightfully large melon breasts. I performed cunnilingus on her curvaceous frame while reclining in my girlfriend's bed. (She was away on vacation.) I rapidly came inside my tightey-whiteys and didn't tell her. Instead, I kept my underwear on, then lied and told her I like to eat pussy all night.

♥ In sociological terms, this is the most interesting of my one-night stands. It was a few years ago at 4 a.m., and I'd recently arrived back to my tiny apartment from a marathon magazine-deadline session. Exhausted, I'd taken my shoes off and was wandering around clad in my windbreaker, white socks, and a white mustache from a late-night vanilla protein shake—in short, I was looking SEXY. A knock came on the door. It was a black stripper who lived in my building. She was obviously smashed. "Can I come in?" she slurred. *Um, sure.* "So," she said happily, tearing off her clothes to reveal a pair of mammoth coconuts, "I hear you're a Nazi." *No, well, that's not true.* It didn't matter if it was or wasn't. She was already naked and in my bed. Things transpired that evening, my friends, which would permanently disqualify me from membership in several top-flight white-supremacist organizations. In the morning, she smelled like garbage. I don't mean she smelled foul—she smelled precisely like a sodden brown bag filled with orange peels and coffee grounds that had been left out too long in the sun. I'm not implying it had anything to do with her blackness, only that she smelled like garbage in the morning. You didn't smell what I smelled, so you're in no position to judge.

♥ I can't even tell you about this one. It's too dangerous. Like, on my skin. Her old man would kill me, and it wouldn't be the first time he did something like that. Lifelong insufflation of crystallized stimulants made his wife look twice her age. In my defense, I will say that no man on earth has ever been able to resist the "I'm in town and would love to fuck you" pitch.

my one-night stands

TRYING TO MAKE SENSE OF WOMEN WHO LOVE

THE NIGHT I GOT OUT OF PRISON, some friends took me to a hipster-thronged Portland bar for dinner. After having spent more than two years alongside violently muscular convicts, the first thing I noticed in this smoky little tavern was how pathetically inadequate all the males looked: slump-shouldered, brown-sweater-wearing, bespectacled alterna-ferrets with tousled hair and not a whisper of Butch about them. It was as if the ladies—all of whom seemed strong and confident by comparison—had siphoned all the testosterone from the boys like sipping banana daiquiris with a straw.

Let's be succinct and say my crime involved a woman who tried to break my spirit but could not. More specifically, my crime may be fairly depicted as particularly hostile to all women, since they all seem to take these sort of things personally: I had hit my girlfriend back. I hit her back hard. My crime had been widely publicized in the area, as well as my unflinching stance that I felt not a speck of remorse. When any-one, male or female, systematically tries to destroy you, I see nothing wrong with punching them in the face—especially when they punched you first.

When I was ejected from the prison gates like an overdue abortion, I wondered whether I'd ever get laid again. What I'm about to tell you will sound like hollow, delusional bravado to the phalanxes of pussy-flogged limp-dicks and eternally PMSing rat-snatches who clog our freeways and supermarkets, but a few wise souls out there will sense I'm speaking the truth: I NEVER GOT SO MUCH PUSSY IN MY LIFE. And every one of the women attached to those pussies was aware of my crime. I was 37 when I went to prison. In the meager six years since being sprung loose, I've had at least FOUR TIMES as many women than I did in my ENTIRE LIFE before incarceration. Removing my first 18 virginal years from the equation, I've been sampling new gash at a rate nearly 13 TIMES the pace I'd set before I was arrested. If, just for fun, you were to include my early life, the rate skyrockets to 2200%. It's as if I'm a member of KISS on tour.

At more than twice the age of what's presumably my sexual peak, I'm more appealing to women than ever. My newfound pheromonal pull was surprising and a bit disturbing: The worse my public image, the more pussy I got.

On the face of it, this makes no sense. I am known, perhaps primarily, as a misogynist. In a sensible world that doesn't spin backwards on an upside-down axis, most women should have fled from me. Quite the contrary, oh, my little sponge cake: The girls, as Flavor Flav once said, were "on my jock like ants on candy." I certainly wasn't young, so I must infer that the reasons for this startling turnabout are psychological. I will speculate about why this is. I may be entirely wrong, but speculate I must. Unlike most women I've met, I'll allow the possibility that I'm wrong.

MORE THAN 20 YEARS AGO as I was earning an ultimately worthless journalism degree, I'd been dating a girl who was a distant cousin of William Shatner's, and, unfortunately, she looked a bit like him. I was a young, dumb, predictably liberal college boy who had tried my best to be a sensitive—dare I say it, *feminist*—male. But despite my attempts to please, appease, wheedle, and cajole this less-than-fair maiden, she grew bitchier with me at every turn.

Upon graduation, we embarked upon what was supposed to be a six-week European vacation, but our ceaseless bickering led to a split-up only three days into the trip. In that bygone era before cell phones and the Internet, she was somehow able to track me down at a youth hostel in Berlin three weeks later. Annoyed to the point where I decided not to be a nice boy anymore, I acted like a dick to her over the first day of our reunion. To my surprise, the meaner I behaved, the nicer she became. The less I acted as if I needed her, the more she seemed to need me. By that point our union had run its course, but as I left alone on a train headed for London, I'll always remember the look of loss and aban-donment on her face as she stood on the platform and realized she'd bitched me out of her life.

I kept that lesson in my pocket and have whipped it out when needed—which was often—ever since. It was not a principle I wanted to be true, but it works with almost scientific precision. I wish the world operated along some half-baked principle of fairness—when you're nice to people, they're nice to you. Reciprocity is a wonderful concept, but it's only applicable in a severe minority of cases. Everyone else is busy playing hunter and hunted. Against my better wishes, I discovered that romantic relationships are like a balloon in that one side swells up when the other gets squeezed. From then on, I decided not to get squeezed.

That is not a popular stance for men these days, although, as noted, it works wonders. These idiot guys who make googly eyes at women and fall all over themselves trying to make them happy are the same ones who will *never* make them happy. On a deep, immutable level, many women realize how nonsensical their gen-der can be. Women disdain men who worship them because they realize how acutely silly that is. In world history, has a woman ever lubricated after being called a goddess? I doubt it, but I'll bet you a few ladies have lathered after being told to shut the fuck up. Submissiveness is not sexually appealing in anyone regardless of their gender, but I must say it wears better on women.

And yet, desperate for pussy and horrified of being called bad names, most men will eat shit until their guts burst. Throughout

BAD BOYS

my life, I've observed that female partners in marital or otherwise long-term unions tend to view it as their birthright to degrade, harass, and insult their men in ways which would automatically bring out the Abuse Police if a man were acting similarly.

For all we hear about evil, "controlling" men, my lifelong observation has been that it's the *ladies* who seek to control and dictate their partners' actions, while the guys bumblingly seek to appease them or at least get out of their way.

Around the time of my horrible, horrible divorce, wifey-poo kept mentioning some study that had just been released claiming that the relationships which lasted were those in which the men obeyed the women. But although I've sampled dozens and dozens of vaginas in my life, I never found one which was so enchanting that I desired to act like an obsequious slave-boy around it.

How you guys put up with their endless whining and teardrops and hypocrisy and recriminations is beyond my ability to grasp. Who the fuck wants to hear her cackle and squawk forever? Not I— nay, not I. The joke is sadly true: Men die younger than women because they *want* to.

Granted, there exist rare relationships where both partners seem mutually respectful. But I don't believe these constitute anywhere near a majority. As in most human interactions, it's a power struggle, and the men generally seem to concede power to the women. But riddle me this: How many wives seem genuinely *hot* for their husbands? Not many, right? They insist on taming their partner, but once this is accomplished, they resent them for it. Once the pretty male butterfly is trapped under glass, he loses his beauty.

Women speak with forked tongue about what they want. The hole in their mouth says one thing, while the one between their legs says quite another. They may want a good boy for money and protection, but they want a bad boy to fuck them. I'd never say that women want men to beat or murder them, but many of them seem to find the *potential* highly arousing. They at least want to know

there's a little bit of animal left in you—a lot of animal, even better.

When nature designed genitals, it was clear which gender was supposed to be the active partner and which the passive—which one was supposed to do the fucking and which was supposed to get fucked. It's solid v. liquid. Hard cock/wet pussy. Plug and socket. All the misguided human-sexuality classes in the world won't alter this basic evolutionary fact. When that rare man strolls by in lockstep with nature, the women flock to him.

So although I've adopted a hardass stance for most of my adult life, getting out of prison seemed to be the icing on the cock. Here, as Travis Bickle said, was a man who would take no more. And in response, the women took numbers and stood in line.

Poor deluded dolls— they all think they're the ones who will change me. I'm a "challenge" for them. No matter how honest and explicit I am about my intentions, I've never found a woman who doesn't feel she has the Lucky Charms that will make me hers forever. So it's an inherently unstable game I play. Once they realize they may never capture their prey, they get nasty. That's when I leave.

I am lucky to live in a time when vaginas are in ample supply. There is no Vagina Famine. There are more holes out there to fill than you could possibly conceive. You could start counting right now from the number one and keep counting your entire life, and you'd drop dead before you put a dent in three billion. Genitals are replaceable, but you'll find it's nigh impossible to replace your dignity once you've given it away so cheaply.

I tote around a set of balls that, if swung properly, could demolish buildings. I shave my balls just so you can see how big they are. In the war between the sexes, most men surrender without a fight. But I won't be taken alive. They might kill me, but until that point, they'll never tame me. I'll give them all the inches I have, but otherwise I won't give an inch. I'll stick it to them hard and good and long, but I won't stick *with* them. Their one and only prayer is that someday I'll care, but I won't. And that's why they want me.

IT'S MY GIRLFRIEND CALLING.

I can tell it's my girlfriend, because it's the only girl I'm currently fucking whose REAL NAME is displayed on my cell phone when she calls.

Mistress #1, who slept with me last night, is identified as my friend Steve when she calls. Mistress #2 pops up on the display as my good buddy Phil.

I make sure that no other potential fuckdolls have my current number. Instead, I give them my old voicemail number and let them think I don't answer my phone very often. I check for their calls about once a day and always feel better when they've called.

Cell phones are made for cheating. My camera phone is also good for taking pictures of my cock, which I forward to my e-mail account and then on to other women in the hope that I'll have more and more covert affairs without my girlfriend's (or mistresses') knowledge.

I currently have 19 pictures of my cock loaded on my web server…the first one was taken by my girl-friend as I reluctantly posed in her bed. At the time, I felt like I loved her. And yet while she was sleeping, I e-mailed the picture to a dozen girls. Half of them I'd already fucked; half of them had already made clear they'd fuck me if we were ever within striking distance of one another.

And though my girlfriend had a habit of grabbing my cock, closing her eyes, and chanting the word "mine," I would have shared that cock with a dozen other women…or a dozen times a dozen.

So long as she doesn't know.

I want her to *suspect*, but I don't want her to know.

There's too much trouble when they know.

That's why I've spent the last three hours washing the bedsheets and sweeping the floors and emptying the wastebaskets and running long strips of clear packing tape over the couch and pillow covers, hoping I caught every last long strand of Mistress #1's hair. And just when I thought I'd cleared all the evidence, I took a piss and saw one of her hairs stuck to the toilet. And while showering all of last night's sweat, cum, and girl-juice off me, I found one of her hairs tangled around my fingers.

Can't ever be too careful about hair evidence. I could sweep the place 100 times and I know there'd still be one renegade strand out there.

After Mistress #1 left a couple hours ago, I hung pictures of my girlfriend back up all over the apartment. I vowed that when she came over, I would not accidentally call her by one of the other girls' names. I turned off my cell phone's ringer and removed all suspicious middle-of-the-night calls from "Steve" and "Phil" from its history log. I cleared my e-mail inboxes and outboxes of all flirtatious and/or explicit correspondence with other ladies, especially the married one who flew cross-country to stay at a hotel a block away so I could fuck her. I purged my web browser history of Mistress #1's naked pix and weblog, plus the blogs of the girl in Minnesota who says she pretends it's me when her boyfriend's fucking her and the gal in the Bronx who actually PayPal'ed me $25 for the privilege of seeing my cock pictures.

It becomes impossible to hide all the evidence. My girlfriend and I were in my bedroom a couple weeks ago, and I'd done an immaculate cover-up job except for the big crumpled ball of cum-encrusted paper towels sitting on the dresser.

I know she saw it, but she didn't say anything. Not like the hell she gave me about a month ago for the big scratch on my left shoulder.

"Your other girlfriend give that to you?" she taunted while biting my flesh around the scratch, creating a strawberry patch of hickey-like "turf marks" as a warning to all other females. "Tell the ugly cunt I said to stay away from you."

I told her the truth, which is that my psychotically hyper dog had scratched my shoulder while leaping up to kiss me. But she wasn't buying it, and she bit me some more.

In my long years of cheating I've found that when women *suspect* you they're usually right, but when they're certain they have you nailed on evidence, they're almost always wrong.

I once had a girlfriend who found a pair of panties under our couch cushions, and—whatever God is out there can strike me dead if I'm lying—I had no idea how they got there. I'm telling the truth about the panties, but even you probably don't believe me. And that's my problem. Nobody believes me about anything anymore. And after reading this, there won't be a woman on earth who'd ever believe me about anything again

Last thing I do before answering my girlfriend's call is hide my notes for this article. When she asks me what I've been doing all day, I can hardly say, "Writing an article about cheating on you."

4:39 a.m.….Still awake from one of the girl-friendliest days of my life. Spent the afternoon in bed with Stephanie. Then Grace and Sheena from the vintage store came up to the apartment for a bit. Then Paula knocked on the door and drove me down to Dante's. Then Trina came into Dante's roaring-drunk and forcibly tongue-kissed me more than once….Then Paula pulled

MY CHEAT

WHY I'VE LOST FAITH IN

me next door and, for the first time in my life, I was forcibly kissed by two girls in the same day….Then Linda called. Then Lori called. Then the second Linda came into Dante's and gave me her number. That's some level of "action" with eight girls in one day. I'm sick. I need to work more.

—My diary entry, April 3, 2003
(names have been changed in the interest of self-preservation)

HAD THE ABOVE PARAGRAPH BEEN WRITTEN BY A HIGH-SCHOOLER, it may have borne a goofy charm. But the fact that I scribbled it when I was comfortably into my 40s bespeaks a rare level of chumpy immaturity.

More than a year after writing that passage, I still find my fingers stuck in too many pies. I'm not proud that I'm a triflin' man and a serial philanderer. A sociopathic pig-dick. An infantile, trashy bum. It makes me feel all ghetto, and not in the cool, MTV kind of way. I know it's juvenile. I know it's contemptible. But I don't know whether it can be cured.

I mean, I promised myself I'd be a good boy at least while writing this article, and I couldn't even do that. I nailed Mistress #1 last night and Mistress #2 the night before. And as I'm typing this, if some naked chick were to fall out of the sky and land on my cock, odds are that I wouldn't pull her off it.

The Byzantine Dating Maze I've constructed for myself, my seeming inability to stick with one woman and keep my dick in its holster the rest of the time, has reached a point of absurdity that finally drove me into therapy. For one hour a week, I blab to a woman about my troubles with women, my all-scorching brush-fire drive to have as much sex as possible while avoiding loneliness and commitment.

Let's just say I have a bad history with women. Imagine the worst, because it's far worse than that. I'm a serial faller-in-lover. I fall in love easily, fall out of it even easier, and fall in love with someone new while the old relationship is still flailing and half-alive. I start off collecting their love letters and wind up documenting their death threats.

I'm a strong man. I can usually last a few hours without female company. After that point, I become achingly, gnawingly, desperately lonely. It always feels worst when the sun goes down and I realize no one will be sleeping next to me tonight. My crushing fear of romantic isolation sends me out into the darkness, seeking to pair up, to find a body, any warm body, to drag home next to me. Soon enough, sooner than I'd prefer, I'll enter a postmenopausal void of pain and decay. Loneliness is the true death, and I flee it like a shrieking woman.

But as much as I fear being alone, I also dread being smothered. I use women to stave off loneliness, but I never let them get too close. I walk a tightrope strung between loneliness on one end and suffocation on the other. I'll keep one girl at arm's length until I find another one within arm's reach.

I believe in love. I know I've felt it. And I've found a way to destroy it every time. Love…when it's good…is the best thing in the world, the only thing that feels better than sex.

But love is unstable like plutonium, and I won't allow myself to get hurt. So I wrap myself in armor and seek love. I'm a steel-claw-equipped lunar land probe, scuttling over cold rocks looking for someone to cuddle.

I'll risk STDs and legal charges, but I won't risk a broken heart. Better to be a bastard than a sucker. I have found, against my better wishes, that the nicer you are to women, the less they desire you. Their pussies are likelier to lubricate if you forget their name than if you send them flowers. If you were to become the sensitive guy they say they want, they wouldn't want you anymore. So I never spend money on them. I never make the first move. I never make them feel remotely secure that I'll be around tomorrow. And precisely because—not in spite—of all this, I've never been dumped.

"He's a great fuck, but emotionally unavailable," one of my exes told another girl. "He's absolutely worthless as a human being, but the best fuck of my life," said another. I savor such comments.

WHY CAN'T I BE HONEST WITH THEM? Most of them wouldn't fuck me if I was honest. So I maintain the charade. I don't trust myself to be trustworthy. And I don't believe that absolute trust is possible. During nasty breakups when all the mean things are said, you realize that most of your suspicions were right. There's always SOMETHING—even if it's only a mildly negative opinion—that you're going to hide from them and something they're hiding from you. You really can't share everything. If you told the whole truth, the whole world would fall apart.

And no matter how much you love somebody, somebody else will catch your eye. It's nature's way, and it turns the idea of love into a sad, sick joke.

Dad never cheated on mom. They stayed miserably together for nearly four decades until cancer gobbled him up like a Pac-Man food particle. I observed firsthand their faithfulness. And their unhappiness.

I never cheated on girlfriends as a teen, mainly because none of those blessed unions lasted for more than a few weeks.

And I can proudly announce that as an adult, I never cheated on my first long-term girlfriend.

And, uh, that's about it.

I don't think it ever *occurred* to me to cheat on her. We had shacked up as college students for a little over a year. When it inevitably crumbled, we still shared an apartment lease but would time-share the place, each living there one week at a time.

When she found a Cyndi Lauper cassette I'd borrowed from my new girlfriend, she smashed it to pieces with a hammer.

I noted the tremendous power one could wield over a woman

(continued on next page)

ING HEART

TY ABILITY TO BE FAITHFUL

by introducing another woman into the picture.

Less than a year later, as Cyndi Lauper girl grew bitchier and more demanding, I wound up cheating repeatedly on her with a big-booty black girl.

I felt a savage electric thrill the first time I did it, stealing away with her and another couple for a weekend in New York City, feeling her lips against mine as the spring air rolled over us in the backseat in some Staten Island badlands, getting off on the fact that this would all hurt my bitchy girlfriend. And when we finally broke up, I made sure to tell her all about Big Booty, and I relished the pain in her eyes and how she implored me to never do that to another woman again.

Big Booty naturally became my girlfriend, until I met the first girl I ever felt I truly loved. I broke the news to Big Booty over the phone. I felt bad about it, but not bad enough.

About a year into my relationship with First True Love, I got a drunken late-night call from my former college girlfriend. She told me that while we'd been together, she'd fucked my best friend when I was visiting my brother in Florida.

I felt bludgeoned and naked and furious. What felt the worst was having been patronized, that they did something behind my back and kept it secret from me because I presumably wouldn't be able to handle it. I felt betrayed and infantilized and erased.

And it was that night I decided to marry One True Love, certain she'd never do anything like that to me.

She didn't. Over nearly a dozen years, she didn't.

Of course, I did it to her. I stayed faithful for ten years. And then, after all of the lust and most of the tenderness had been squeezed dry, I went on the prowl. When I finally told her about my first dalliance that lasted longer than a one-night stand, she demanded a divorce. "I never even thought about cheating on you," she said, looking straight in my eyes. "I would rather have been split in half with an axe."

Speaking of axes, when I got divorced and cheated on my new mistress-*cum*-girlfriend, she used a wooden axe handle to smack the skull of the girl I'd cheated on *her* with, requiring a hospital visit. I was conjuring the forces of chaos by cheating on my god-damned *mistress*, the first eruption of the multilayered infidelity which has pockmarked my later years.

THERE ARE SEVERAL REASONS WHY I CHEAT. Sex. Boredom. Spite. Ego.

If my girlfriend begins withholding sex, I feel a near-moral obligation to cheat on her. Or even if she doesn't and her pussy's starting to taste a little stale, I'll get some action on the side. If she's being bitchy, I'll subvert her attempt at domination by fucking someone else. If she's trying to make me jealous, I'll fuck every girl she knows. Or if some other girl is making moves on me, nine times out of ten I'll take her out for a test drive.

A freelance writer's life provides ample time and little money. I don't have many belongings, so I measure my riches in women. I collect them like dolls; the more dolls in my collection, the better I feel about myself. The vagina is a wonderful thing. Some are better than others, but most are fairly spectacular. But none is so good that it made me forget there are more than three billion other vaginas out there. Women wield considerable power over men due to

the fact that we like their pussies. But the surest way to short-circuit this power is to continually remind women that their li'l fishy isn't the only one in the ocean.

I met my girlfriend and the two mistresses in the same bar. All three of them had boyfriends when they met me. And all three of them made the first move, leaving their boyfriends when I took the bait. At different times, I've called each of them my girlfriend. And I've cheated on all of them with all of them.

Mistress #2 was my girlfriend for a year and a half. A few weeks after we broke up—and after I'd neglected to change the locks on my apartment—she busted in on me and Mistress #1 only seconds after we'd finished rutting. She lunged at Mistress #1, who narrowly escaped down the hall in her panties. Screaming, she kicked my shins, smashed a coffee pot against the wall, threw all of Mistress #1's belongings out the window, and then summoned the strength to carry my mattress out of the apartment and into a nearby parking lot.

I felt so bad seeing the pain in her eyes, I dumped Mistress #1 and made Mistress #2 my girlfriend again.

Months later, when Mistress #1 saw me walking downtown hand-in-hand with Mistress #2, she cried so much I dumped #2 and made #1 my girlfriend again.

And then for a while, I was calling both of them my girlfriend.

Then I met the current girlfriend and dumped both of the others.

The current girlfriend and I were evenly matched in terms of narcissism and our indefatigable will to make our partner jealous. She never let me forget about all the B-level rock stars who wanted to fuck her, and I made sure she knew about all the literary groupies who were batting their eyelashes at me. Possible infidelity became the obsessive focus of our relationship, and many was the night we spent together not because we enjoyed one another's company so much, but merely to prevent the other from cheating.

For more than six months, I was faithful. But at one point during an argument when we'd gone for a month without having sex, I told her I was headed back home to fuck the best piece of pussy I'd ever had—Mistress #1.

My girlfriend threatened to call the cops and tell them I'd raped her.

She apologized days later, after I'd already shagged Mistress #1…and Mistress #2…dozens of times. And I took her back.

For most of the summer and into the fall I juggled all three of them.

Then two weeks ago…after I'd started writing this article…we quarreled into the night, finally spitting out that we'd been cheating on one another with exes for months.

Within an hour, Mistress #1 was back in my bed.

And now she's no longer Mistress #1. She's my girlfriend again.

The old girlfriend sent me relentlessly nasty text messages about my new ugly pudgy loser prostitute stripper satanic girlfriend until I finally changed my phone number. And although I hadn't contacted her, she then e-mailed me a threat to take out a restraining order against me.

Right now the new girlfriend is across town, and I'm not sure what she's doing.

And I'm here all alone.

And here's my cell phone and the Internet, just begging to be used.

METHTURBATION BLUES

There is no dignity in what I'm about to share with you. Few things in the world are less classy than smoking crystal meth. Speed is the bastard child of the drug family, cocaine's ugly retarded stepbrother. Like alcohol but unlike almost all other illegal drugs, it causes brain damage. Yet maybe twice a year, when all my booty calls are out of town or otherwise engaged, I'll motor over to a female friend's house and ask her to light me up. I do this not because I enjoy being more agitated than I naturally am, nor because I savor the idea of being awake for 93 straight hours, but because it gives me the rampaging sex drive of an adolescent stegosaurus.

She'll dip into her bag using a knife blade, pull out a tiny pile of yellowy slush, fill the little glass bulb at the end of her pipe, and run the flame under it as I inhale a half dozen or so bronco snorts of pure white smoke. It tastes like hair spray and hits the brain instantly. All warm-cheeked and excited, I bid my friend adieu and head home quickly for a robust round of self-pleasuring.

It once took me six straight hours of masturbating BEFORE I was able to get it up. The last time, it took me TEN hours. All of this, mind you, while I was screamingly horny yet pitifully limp, a single-minded Sex Cyclops consumed with rutting mammalian instinct.

The larger my speed-induced lust, the smaller my penis. It becomes a pink rosebud. A decorative curlicue resting featherlike atop a miniature birthday cake. A whisper of a penis. At best, the *implication* of a penis.

Flopping and flailing, tugging and yanking, rolling my micro-burrito between my thumb and forefinger, I desperately Google "Hairy Asian Pussy"..."Big Black Tits"..."Shaved Mature Naked"...but am unable to focus on any single image long enough to construct a suitable fantasy. I click rapidly from one photo to the next, accidentally smearing vitamin E oil on the keyboard and mouse, all through the night until morning's cruel rays mock my soft, greasy loins.

I'll finally manage a pathetic micro-gasm while still half-hard. It resembles a tiny worm vomiting its lunch. I will then make lists for a day or two before finally falling asleep.

The upside is that I become hypersexual for a solid week after crashing, with hearty, vein-laden erections and orgasms so intense it feels as if I'm pulling cartilage out through my perineum. This becomes handy when the booty calls start meowing outside and begging for a saucerful of milk.

SMOKING TWEAK MAKES THE SPIRIT WILLING AND THE FLESH WEAK

Squirtin'!

is FEMALE EJACULATION real... ...or is it just PISS?

As the fat warthog's snatch spewed a geyser all over my face, dripping down onto the couch and soaking the carpet to the point that it made a sploshing sound when I stood up and stepped in it, I realized that this cheating housewife wasn't kidding when she warned me she "squirted" every time she had an orgasm. A basic "sniff test" determined that this fluid was not, as scoffers have suggested, a rude expulsion of urine. It was dark in the room (I couldn't bear to look at her pockmarked, makeup-caked, prematurely aged face), so I was unable to determine the fluid's color. However, I was certain that the watery substance bore none of human pee-pee's unmistakably acrid stench. It was odorless—although, sadly, her vagina was not.

A week later, as I rutted her in my laughably tiny studio apartment, Miss Piggy closed her eyes, tensed her vadge muscles, and shot forth another fire-extinguisher's worth of fluid, soaking my balls and the tasteful pink futon which lay beneath us. This whale's blowhole was always puking fluid.

She was my first squirter. I soon dumped her as if she were a piece of poop plopping from my buttocks, although it had nothing to do with the squirting. In fact, the squirting was the only remotely interesting thing about her.

Roughly two years later, at a time when my self-esteem had become sufficiently elevated to afford sexual congress with a slimmer, sexier, younger lass, I was squirted upon again. She was a diminutive sprite with snake tattoos whose vagina worked like a speed blender. The little chippie was riding me on top as I lay on my wildly sexy fake-leather couch when she suddenly closed her

eyes and buckled forward as if punched in the stomach. Immediately I felt the warm fluid soaking my shaven testicles and dripping down 'tween my butt crack, eventually leaving a pizza-sized stain beneath the sofa cushions. Again, the fluid was odorless. Snake Girl marveled that this had never happened before. She said the orgasm felt different—more intense—and that at the point of climax, she envisioned a golden spinning symbol which I won't identify for fear of offending our Jewish readers.

She was my second, and, as of this writing, my last squirter.

I made the mistake of relating the latter tale to a pathologically jealous girlfriend, who became furious at the idea that my finely crafted penis had induced such a wallopingly aquatic orgasm in someone. "You must like being pissed on, huh?" she taunted me. "You're pretty sick. Why don't I just piss on you, since you seem to like it so much?"

"It wasn't piss," I gently countered. "It was 'female ejaculation.' Some girls can do it, some girls can't," I stated with cool indifference, letting my eyes communicate pity that she was one of the unfortunates who couldn't squirt.

And yet, as is often the case when I haven't reached my thrice-daily masturbation quota, a faint hint of self-doubt crept into my battered skull. What if Jealous Non-Squirting Girlfriend was right? What if there is no such thing as "female ejaculation"? What if I'm a simple rube who's been hornswoggled by the sex-positive carnival barkers who've convinced me that these wet-'n'-wild episodes were something more than cruel jokes perpetrated by women who couldn't do the proper thing and wait until they skipped off to the loo before unleashing their bladders all over my nutsac?

DETERMINED TO GET TO THE BOTTOM OF THIS, I did what I normally do when I have an hour left on deadline and am unprepared because I've spent most of the month fucking other guys' girlfriends—I hastily Googled the topic and have messily compiled my findings in the hope that you'll see them as something other than the shoddy research and half-baked conclusions they invariably represent.

"Research has demonstrated that all women ejaculate a substance through the urethra that is not urine," states Beverly Whipple, president of the American Association of Sex Educators, Counselors and Therapists, and with such a windy title, the bitch damn sure better know what she's talking about.

This Mystery Sauce, this tsunami of girl-cum, is mentioned throughout ancient literature. It was alluded to as early as the 4th century B.C. by a writer who distinguished between a woman's "red and white fluids." Aristotle, sex-crazed horndog that he was, made note of vaginal eruptions which were odorless and left no stain on his finely laundered Greek sheets. Such fluids were also cited by Roman author Galen, of whom I know little and about whom I care even less. The American Indians, bless their vanquished souls, spoke of the "mixing of male and female fluids" during the sacred act of intercourse. In 1672, Dutch physiologist Reigner DeGraaf observed that Dutch chicks would often expel "large quantities" of fluid through their urethral ducts during sex and that it was analogous in pleasure to male ejaculation. "During the sexual act," DeGraaf wrote, "it discharges to lubricate the tract so copiously that it even flows outside the pudenda. This is the matter which may have been taken to be actual female semen."

Vaginal explorer Ernest Grafenberg, discoverer of the "G-spot," wrote in 1950 that proper stimulation of the now-infamous lima-bean-sized pleasure button would often result in "large quantities of a clear, transparent fluid...not from the vulva, but out of the urethra in gushes."

However, it wasn't until the 1980s that researchers finally got the bright idea to *analyze* this "female semen" to determine exactly what it was. Studies conducted by two clowns called Whipple and Perry determined that the liquid bore some similarities to urine, but compared to piss, it was much lower in creatinine and urea and much higher in glucose and prostate acid phosphatase, components which are commonly found in male ejaculatory fluid. This fluid originates from the Skene's glands (a.k.a. the G-spot or, in some circles, the "female prostate") and is chemically similar to male semen except for the sperm.

Some researchers believe that all females release some ejaculatory fluid during orgasm, but since it may comprise less than a teaspoonful, it often becomes mixed with their vaginal lubrication and passes unnoticed. However, one researcher found a woman who ejaculated TWO CUPS of girl-goo in one shot. Another physician studied a woman who expelled nearly a QUART. Yowsa bowsa holy cowsa! Would you like a donut with that, honey? Can I get you some Gatorade so you can rehydrate?

The Internet is a bastion of unholy squirting websites, many featuring videos of dubious authenticity showing women spouting Old Faithful-style blasts of cunt-vomit from their holes. In some cases, these women are probably urinating rather than squirting female ejaculatory fluid. In others, they cram their vaginey-holes with water or other fluids before filming and then try to pass off what amounts to a vaginal enema as an authentic squirting episode. Websites with fancy-pants names such as "Real Squirt," "Squirters TV," "Squirt Crazy," "Pussy Squirting Carly," "Nasty Fetish," "Jacking Teens," "Sexy Gushers," "Teen Gushers," and "Drippy Slits" cater to the sick lusts of men who somehow find the sight of vaginas spouting off like garden hoses to be arousing. Porn *auteur* Seymore Butts made a pretty penny with his *Squirters I* and *II* videos. And somewhere in the mix, the ubiquitous Ron Jeremy is getting his mustache wet and cashing in on the trend.

SO MY JEALOUS EX-GIRLFRIEND WAS WRONG. I do not enjoy being pissed upon. I am not a sick man nor some sort of gutter pervert who basks in female waste products. I am not now, nor have I ever been, someone predisposed to wallowing in urine. I am, in fact, a meat-eating, pussy-hunting American male who is surprisingly virile for his advanced age, a man who is able to induce aquatic cataclysms in at least two of the dozens of vaginas I've sampled since being paroled. *I* am not the one with the problem. *My ex-girlfriend*, in fact, is the one with the problem. It was her problem for thinking that I had the problem...rather than her. She's the one with the problem. Not me. Just wanted to make that clear.

But a broader, more troubling question emerges: What are we as Americans to do about female ejaculation? More importantly, how can we prevent women from educating themselves about it? I, for one, consider it dangerous for females to feel this much pleasure. In a very real way, I almost would *rather* it be piss.

When I was a small boy...and I need to clarify that I was a small *heterosexual* boy, whereas now I'm a full-blown hetero-sexual *man* who enjoys intimate relationships exclusively with women, lest any of you wisenheimers get the wrong idea...but any-way, when I was a small boy, I used to spend lots of time wondering about house pets owned by black people...were the *pets* black, too?

By the same tortured reasoning, when a gay chef in a gay bar cooks a hamburger, is the *burger* gay, too? And what about the person who eats it?

I have heard of these so-called "gay" people and their mysterious practices. I have heard of their boisterous Pride Parades and their disproportionate influence in the fashion industry. I have heard of their Judy Garland biog-raphies and Bette Midler videocassettes and Laura Branigan CDs. I have heard of their amyl nitrite and their Tony Awards and their clean teeth and their pet poodles and their well-oiled armpits. I have heard of their cock rings and their golden showers and their quiver-ing prostate glands. I have heard of their turd-encrusted penises and saggy sphincters blown-out like inner tubes. I have heard of their analcentric politics and their jagged glory holes and their virus-laden seminal fluids.

Very interesting, these gay people. But why are they called gay, when not all of them seem happy? Must be the same reason there's no ham in a hamburger.

We already know that lesbians subsist on a diet of potato chips and cheap beer, but what about male homosexuals? Do gay men eat the same sort of food as real people? The hamburger is a good place to start. It is more quintessentially American than, say, anal fisting. So what about the gayburger? How does it differ from the burgers produced by Giant Heterosexual Corporations?

I needed to know. So I decided to set my prejudices aside and sample some of Portland's homosexually oriented burger fare. I had my fears, of course. I was scared about rampant rumors of Secret Gay Sauces and vindictive homo-terror-ist chefs. I was reasonably certain that, despite my leather jacket and trim appearance, the gays would be able to tell I was an inter-loper. And I made it clear, in NO uncertain terms, that I wanted NO mayonnaise or melted cheese on my gayburgers.

Most of Portland's gay restaurants, and thus most of Portland's gay hamburgers, are clustered around "Vaseline Alley," the notorious homosexual ghetto tucked like a greasy salami in Downtown P-Town's backside. I have heard murmurs that the city's health inspectors are afraid to set foot in Vaseline Alley.

But not me. I needed to taste this forbidden meat.

I expected to find dingy S&M dungeons whose walls were spackled with dried seminal fluids and crusty feces smeared like chocolate cake frosting. Instead, I found pleasant, polite, color-coordinated, well-groomed dining experiences. If it weren't for the pumping disco music, exclusively male clientele, and muscular, well-tanned waiters, one might think these were regular het bistros.

All told, I ate three gayburgers in three different gay restaurants. To my relief, they were the BEST FUCKING HAMBURGERS I'VE EVER EATEN!!! They were thoroughly delightful taste treats, and I can say this without compromising my masculinity in any way. After all, enjoying a gay hamburger is not tantamount to engaging in sexual congress with a gay man.

The main difference between the gayburger and the hetero burger is that gayburgers are much bigger. Lots more meat. For some inscrutable reason, gay men seem to enjoy shoving huge slabs of beef into their mouths.

There I sit, eating my gay ham-burger. Gay patrons look over at me as I wrap my eager mouth around a giant hunk of meat. The gay people smile at me. I smile back courteously, my twinkling eyes saying, "I don't care what sort of blunt objects or furry rodents you shove up your ass—that's a *damn fine hamburger!*"

I am proud, and more than a little relieved, to report that never once did I achieve an erec-tion during my dining experiences, nor was I in the least bit titillated by all the sweaty, muscular manflesh swirling around me. Plus, no one tried to convert me, and I appreciate that. I didn't even have to make it clear that I didn't wish to suck anyone's penis or penetrate their anuses.

I learned some very important lessons from all this...

I began to slowly realize that gay people are almost human. Gay people eat food, too. And they need love, respect, self-empowerment, dignity, and a sense of connectedness just like people who *don't* insert gerbils into their rectums.

Merely because they indulge in practices which God clearly con-demns doesn't mean that they aren't like us in many ways. And even though they're going to hell unless they repent, that doesn't mean they don't experience what might properly be called emotions.

Gay people have hopes and dreams and bank accounts and mortgage pay-ments. They drive cars, take showers, and sleep in beds. They slather shampoo on their hair and sprinkle talcum powder on their achin' tootsies. They breathe the same air as us and flush their toilets into the same sewer system.

And they eat hamburgers. Delicious, oversized hamburgers!

Anyone who can cook such a bitchin' burger doesn't deserve to be herded in gay concentration camps or persecuted for their alternative lifestyle or strung up to die on lampposts or labeled with nasty, unfair nicknames such as "pole-smoker," "rump-wrangler," "peter-puffer," "ass jockey," "butt pirate," or "cum-guzzlin' Nancy-boy."

Although I might recommend that gay people be forced to use separate drinking fountains and restrooms, I am not ashamed to assert that they deserve equal treatment under the law.

Gay people enjoy a good hamburger just like the rest of us. No...make that a GREAT hamburger. Right on, you gay people!

Stand up, gay people, and be proud of your hamburgers!

my EROGENOUS ZONES

Will you PLEASE pull my cock out of your mouth and realize there's more than one way to give me pleasure? I have no problem with your abject schween-worship, but what about the REST of me? Doesn't THAT count for something? It's not all about the cock, darlin'. Sometimes I need some SPECIAL touchin', too. My body is a colossal pink island of nerve endings yearning to be stroked, pinched, and caressed. Don't you want me to have a better orgasm? Don't you want me to call you again? Sure you do. My pleasure is your business. So with my uncanny foresight and boundless regard for your well-being, I'm providing this road map of my "special places." Study it. Then tape it to your headboard.

EARS

Every millimeter of both ears is ultra-sensitive, especially the hole. Breathe and moan into my lonely erotic audio-coves, but please, fair child, do not scream. Cram your tongue in one ear and plug the other with your finger. It will strengthen my penile rigidity and might even increase the volume of my ejaculation.

ARMPITS

Fear them not. Many ladies find the faint aromas which flutter from my well-groomed underarms to be a pheromone-spiked butterscotch sundae. Run your fingers through these nectar-laden nests and, if you're truly devoted to pleasing me, lick them. If you ride the thin line between touching and tickling, if you walk without trepidation into my Secret Jungle of Happiness, you've made a friend for life.

NIPS

These non-lactating vestiges of an embryonic womanhood—beyond which I was wise enough to evolve—serve no other purpose than to feed my carnal delight. Rub my gentle rosebuds 'tween your thumb and forefinger. Lick my nips as if they contain essential nutrients. Nibble lightly if you must. Tune these radio dials straight toward a station called PLEASURE, but don't pinch too tightly or you may get an involuntary slap.

COJONES

Also called yarbles, balls, nuts, testes, or, in Yiddish, "testicles." Your vagina cannot give life until it is first given to you from my testicles, where little baby sperm are made. I tote around a nice shaven semen-satchel, a freshly shorn Easter basket, a clean pink suitcase. Touching them with your hands doesn't do much for me. So lick them. Flap, flip, and flop your tongue all over and around them. Earn your keep, woman.

BEHIND KNEE

I never heard of anyone citing this as an erogenous zone before, and if I did, I must have ignored them. Behind where my knee bends, there's a pleasure pocket, the soft white underbelly of my unreasonably muscular legs. The lighter the touch here, the better. Touch or kiss softly, lest you offend me.

ANUS

If God didn't want you to play with my ass, he wouldn't have placed so many neurons there. Lightly touch the areas around the anal areola. Use your finger or, if you're really drunk, your tongue. But you don't wanna try sticking things in there. My mother tried, and she's dead now.

gay 'bout me!

my sexual fantasies about myself

My lover awaits me every night in my bed. Under the soft, velvety moonlight, I approach him. Cool shafts of lunar light accent his strong arms, his vaguely Jewish nose, and his burning blue eyes. He is the perfect man, a man among men—almost as if Adonis, Montgomery Clift, and Stone Cold Steve Austin got together and figured out how to make a baby. There are other men, to be sure—about three billion at last count—but there are no other men who I'd like to, you know, do. But not only do I want to do him, I want to do him and do him, and after that, do him after he's been done. I want to De Doo Doo Doo, De Da Da Da him. I want him so badly, I could pop a load right here and now. We both know that I am here for his pleasure. He can smell my lust as if it's a day-old baloney sandwich and winks playfully, beckoning me to slip under the tasteful, zebra-striped sheets.

To my horny delight, I observe that he has already "pitched a tent." I reach under the covers an forcefully grab his pink burrito. Squealing like a Vietnamese pot-bellied pig, he arches his back ecstatically as if struck with a bug zapper.

"Do you like when I do that?" I ask him with equal measures of playfulness and super-playfulness.

"Oh, yes," he gasps as if running to catch a bus, "I lllloove it when you do that!"

"Do I know how to touch your pee-pee better than anyone else touches your pee-pee?" I query him like a schoolteacher ready to flunk a student if he doesn't give the correct answer. "In other words, am I the best pee-pee-toucher you know?"

"God, yes," he painfully grunts as if a chicken bone is lodged in his esophagus, "you're the tops! The very tippy-tops! The zip-a-dee-doo-dah tippety-tops! And I'm not just saying that!"

"Howzabout if I pinch your nipple?" I beseech him.

"Thanks for beseeching me," he says. "Yes, please—pinch my man-nip as if it were a strawberry you were testing for ripeness at your local produce store. Pinch one, then the other, then the first one again, 'til they stand firm and pointy like pinkish Hershey's Kisses."

As I squeeze his nips, he flaps and flails like a speared fish and makes a screeching sound not unlike that of th giant pterodactyl in those Japanese monster movies. He's havin' a GOOD time.

"How about your armpits, laddie?" I ask. "Should I gently run my fingertips around your armpit area, hovering ever-so-slightly above the soft, pale skin as if I wer a fat old grey-ponytailed lady in a poncho performing Reiki healing?"

"I would never be able to talk to you again if you didn't pay some erotic attention to my ultra-sensitive armpit area," he admonishes me. "I wouldn't send you birthday balloons, and I'd erase your number from my cell phone."

Fearing such abandonment, I move my bony, veiny, ten-years-older-looking-than-the-rest-of-me fingers around his armpit area like a gentle wind softly blowing the sands of the Sahara. He screams as if being stabbed repeatedly by a gang of street toughs, only his screams are those of pleasure...I think.

"Would you like it if I sucked your dick?" I ask, growing as bold as a used-car salesman. "Would it feel good if I just wrapped my lips around your Love Pole and started chowing down as if it were a spicy hot link and I were a Mexican migrant worke on a 15-minute lunch break?"

"There is nothing on earth—nor on Mars or Venus—tha I would love more than if you were to suck my dick," come his earnest reply. "If you were to suck my dick, it would be as if a giant slingshot sent us catapulting into the astral plane, where nose hairs never grow and you can eat all th donuts you want without gaining weight. But both you an I know that this will never happen. You will never be able to suck my dick."

"WHY?!?" I pout, as if told that Santa wasn't real.

"Because you just aren't limber enough," he says.

"How hard is it to suck someone's dick?"

"Almost impossible," he counters, "if it's your own dick, Jim."

"If I were able to clone myself, I'd marry myself in Hawaii or the Netherlands, or wherever it is that allows same-person marriages."

"Whatever do you mean?" I ask, flabbergasted.

"I mean, NIMROD"—he sits up, quickly losing his erection—"that this is only a dream, and you're only having sex with yourself."

"You mean that YOU'RE ME?"

"That's right, Einstein—I'm you, and you're me. I am he as you are he as you are me and we are all together."

I suddenly awake, hard as a rock, and finish the job... sadly, with my hand rather than my mouth.

I DIDN'T NEED TO LOOK FAR to find my perfect lover. I didn't need to look at all. He's always been right there, under my nose.

If I could clone myself, the first thing I'd do is have sex with myself. I'd grab myself by my greasy hair, shove myself into bed, and launch into the most perfectly symmetrical '69' in world history. Who knows my dick better than I? Who, indeed, has touched it more than I? Who is more intimately involved with my brain's pleasure center than I am? Who knows when to go harder or softer, faster or slower, like I do? Aided by the miracle of cloning, I'd become my own sexual biofeedback machine, lost in the forbidden joys of onanistic solipsism.

If I were able to clone myself, I'd marry myself in Hawaii or the Netherlands, or wherever it is that allows same-person marriages. I'm my perfect match. I not only grasp my physical needs, but also my emotional needs. No one else could possibly understand me as well as me and myself understand each other. I know and accept all of my darkest secrets. I'd never get into a fight with myself due to miscommunication. I would take care of myself, and myself would take care of me in turn. I'd walk hand-in-hand with myself, strolling through an apple grove, telling myself jokes.

I wouldn't kick myself out of bed, I can tell you that much. I fancy myself. When I see myself walking down the street, I get a tingly feeling. When I catch a glimpse of myself in the mirror, I think, "Oooh—I wants me some of that!" I'm a complete fag about myself...but nobody else. I don't want to have sex with other men, because I can't see how it would be pleasurable. I don't like the stink of men. Don't like their bodies. Don't share many of their interests or insecurities. I am disgusted by other men yet tantalized by myself.

Opposites attract? Not in my case.

I am attracted to a man—myself.

But I'm not technically gay.

Just gay 'bout me.

As a friend once said to me, "What's the only thing cooler than Jim Goad? TWO Jim Goads. And what's cooler than two Jim Goads? Nothing. There is *nothing* cooler than two Jim Goads."

It would be arrogant for me to disagree.

You can call me all the homo names you want, and I still wouldn't want to have sex with you—only myself. Me and my good pal Sigmund Freud have found that the biggest homos are ALWAYS the ones who make a point of telling you they aren't homos, always the ones who are calling everyone ELSE homos, always the ones who are obsessed with homosexuality far more than any out-of-the-closet homosexual. So go ahead, ya repressed nelly-boy—tell me you've never touched a dick. Not even your own, right? And pretend you've never tried—and failed—to suck on your own wang-a-dang-diddly-dang, you lying Fag-a-Tron.

Civilization is built upon the fact that 99% of men are unable to suck their own dicks. If most guys were able to do this, as the joke goes, they'd never leave the house. Our entire infrastructure would crash to the ground as most men sat at home, eternally gobbling their own cocks.

Only one percent of men are said to possess the magical combo of penis size and spinal dexterity to be able to self-blow. If a dog licks his balls because he can, it follows that the only reason men don't suck their own dicks is because they can't. There's a rumor, probably false, that the ugly-girl-looking rocker Marilyn Manson had one or more of his ribs removed so he could auto-fellate. And there's an online joke that speculates Adam—the first man—originally had his rib removed for similar reasons.

Sucking my own dick would bring closure...the circle would be complete. I would become Ouroboros, the snake eating its own tail, a self-sufficient mythic creature eternally reproducing through mitosis and auto-fellatio.

Let the yoga classes begin!

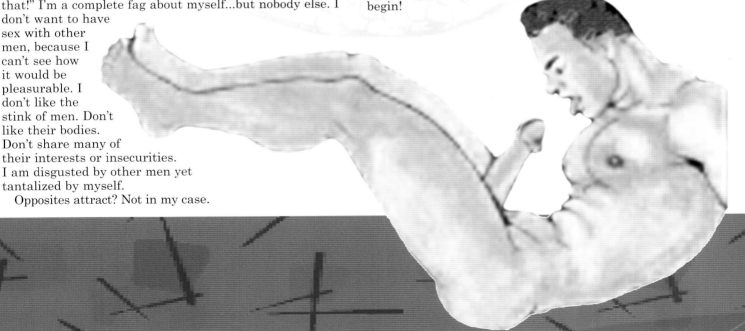

Hey, bird dog get away from my chick
Hey, bird dog you better get away quick
Bird dog you better find a chicken little of your own
—The Everly Brothers, "Bird Dog"

IN 1950S GREASER SLANG, A "BIRD DOG" was someone who raided the chicken coop when the rooster wasn't around, making off with the hen...or at least some of her eggs. It's a guy who pursues a girl even though—or maybe because—he knows she has a boyfriend.

I have gleefully played the role of Bird Dog throughout my adult life, with one notable twist that is both nobler and more sinister than the ordinary situation—I let the girls pursue *me* even though they have boyfriends. I have never...no, not once ever in my life...consciously made the first move on a woman, whether or not I knew she had a boyfriend. I'm too afraid of rejection to be so bold. But none of this has stopped them from making moves on me.

I've counted nearly a dozen situations from my past—11, to be exact...I *wish* it was 12, because it sounds much cooler to say "a dozen," but in truth it is only 11—where women in allegedly "committed" relationships went a-fishin' for me and I swallowed the bait. In three of these cases, the hussies were married!

For years, all of the girls who would eventually become my girlfriends—ALL of them—had boyfriends when they first met me. And ALL of them initiated our first sexual contact.

They usually dump their boyfriends immediately, even though I've made no promise. They seek sex from me and then, for some reason, they want a relationship. Some of them invariably become my girlfriends, but it's never as exciting like it was at first, when I was the Other Man.

I'M A BAD BOYFRIEND AND A GOOD FUCK—the perfect combination for a Bird Dog. It's a good life and it's a fun life, but it's also a dangerous life. I am here to provide you with a service, but I am not your daddy, your boyfriend, nor even a person who likes you very much. I'm just the one who leaves you walking bowlegged when I'm done.

I'm not looking for a relationship. I'll just help you feel good for a few hours before I kick you back into your boring little world.

When one is bird-doggin', the second most dangerous risk you face is the possibility that the girl's boyfriend or husband could hunt you down and kill you.

But the scariest risk of all is that she'll fall in love with you, leave him, and then go psycho when you explain that you never intended to play "Boyfriend and Girlfriend" with her.

RARE IS THE COUPLE that can maintain lust for one another year after year. After a while, the desire dries up like an old seahorse.

One by one the ladies would come to me, all with the same lament.

They'd sigh and tell me that they love him, but they're just not excited by him sexually anymore.

"He's a nice guy. I just don't want to fuck him."

Who knows what killed their lust? Maybe it was the rigors of cohabitation, the hundredth time she heard him fart on the toilet through a closed bathroom door. Maybe he snores or has smelly feet or rotten breath or doesn't wipe himself as thoroughly as he should.

These men aren't necessarily evil or irresponsible. They are something far worse. They are dull. They are men who deliver financially and emotionally, but not sexually. They bring home the bacon but not the sausage.

Because of this, I fuck the girls extra-hard. I send them home sore. They know why they come to me. I provide them with a service. I'm here to help.

In each case, I'm flattered and aroused at the idea of being able to satisfy them in ways their boyfriends can't.

God blessed me with a nice body and a wonderful penis and an attractive scent in order to give

THE PERILS AND PLEASURES OF FUCKING ANOTHER MAN'S WOMAN BIRD

the ladies pleasure. If I can give them something better, why should I feel guilty?

Let HIM wash the dishes and fix the refrigerator. Let HIM pay the bills and drive her to acting class.

I don't mind being the male equivalent of a mistress—a "mistress"? A "mister"? Were it not for its innate precariousness and instability, it would be the perfect situation for me.

REMEMBER ALL OF THE BOYFRIENDS and husbands—some fat, some bald, some underendowed, but all of them pathetic.

The bespectacled poet/father.
The pug-faced drummer.
The silent metalhead.
The mopey Injun.
The ugly sport fisherman.
The chubby alcoholic closet queen.
The cokehead magazine editor.
The mildly well-known artist.
The clueless Alabama businessman.
A bunch of other Faceless Angry Shlubs.

I feel sorry for all these men, but never sorry enough to regret what I've done or to stop doing it again.

I didn't feel bad as I walked around his San Francisco apartment buck-naked while she talked to him long-distance in Europe.

I didn't mind having her husband stare at me dejectedly across the dinner table at Thanksgiving, knowing that sooner or later I'd be fucking his wife just because of the way she was looking at me and talking to me.

I don't mind when she squints and tells me she's still "getting used to the size."

LOOK, MISTER, IT ISN'T MY FAULT that your lady came to me for sexual relief. She approached me with a problem—one that YOU, not she, created. I've tried her out a few times, and there's nothing wrong with her sexually. She's certainly not the best that I've had, but it's not like any of her parts are broken, either. So if you were having bad sex, I can only blame it on you.

It's not like I want to be her boyfriend. I'm not stealing anything of yours—I'm just *borrowing* it from you. Maybe she's a little worse for wear and tear, but hey, that's not my problem.

Don't be angry with me—I'm just a happy fella lookin' for a good time. And don't be mad at her—she's only seeking the satisfaction that comes from being in the arms of a *real* man. Be angry with yourself, my friend. *Mon frere. Mi amigo.*

If you had sufficient size…or finesse…or a delicious aroma like I do…you wouldn't be facing this pain and humiliation right now.

So don't try to kick my ass. You'd probably lose, anyway, just like you lost the battle for her pussy. That pussy is mine. I've taught it to meow, to sit and roll over, and to stand at attention on its haunches.

I'll bet she's been less bitchy since I started fucking her, right? So what's the prob?

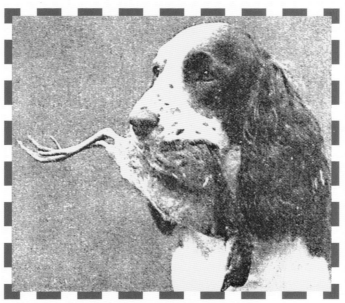

Look at it another way: She was hungry 'cause you've been starving her, so she comes to me for a seven-course meal. Why would you be angry with me for feeding the woman you love? Why are you not angry with yourself for refusing to feed her?

She, not I, was the one who kept referring to you as stupid. She was the one who kept calling you a loser. She was the one who said that you wouldn't be able to find her G-spot even if you had a flashlight and a miner's helmet. I have no beef with you. If anything, I feel sorry for you, because your girlfriend is kind of a cunt.

Look, I did you a favor. She's an untrustworthy, mean, conniving, self-pitying whore. We both know it. And she isn't even that good-looking or skilled in the sack. No offense to you, of course. I'm sure that compared to what you're used to, she's fine.

But I've got other eggs to snatch and other chickens to catch.

Doggin'!

test-driving viagra

Whenever a new drug comes out, I just have to try it. Back in '86, it was crack. Rock-cocaine scare stories were all over the news, so naturally I drove up into Harlem, scored a butter-colored gumball-sized rock, and went to the Catskills with my girlfriend. We puffed crack from a glass pipe and went to watch Jewish nightclub comedians, my heart pumping so ferociously that it felt like a balloon trying to squeeze out between the slits in my rib cage.

Recently, the drug-of-the-moment was Viagra, a PILL which gives you a more robust erection, or at least an erection where none was before. The butt of a million retarded jokes and the subject of hilariously gauzy TV ads with 60-year-old codgers symbolically *square-dancing again* with their pruny-dry wives, Viagra was a drug I was just itchin' to try. Using my extensive underworld connections, I was able to secure a small stash of Viagra in both pill and liquid form.

There are three types of women in the world: blondes, brunettes, and redheads. I determined that I would test-drive the world-famous Boner Drug with one girl from each tribe.

I would not, of course, tell them I was under the influence of this notorious erection-raiser. That revelation would be saved until...well...*now*.

THE REDHEAD

DESCRIPTION: She's a diagnosed sociopath with tattooed boobs. Giant full-moon eyes. Short, round body. A smart girl. Mensa material. A bit of a chameleon, too: sometimes bespectacled and preppie, sometimes all Gothed-out and silent-movie-star-lookin'. We'd had sex a dozen or so times before.

> "This is the meaning of life: To have a cute little gap-toothed truck-drivin' blonde girl from the South hold your cock in her hand and use the word 'big.'"

She has a tangy, sour-tangerine smell that I find erotic. Her hair is dyed a bright rusty color, so that qualifies her for the redhead's role.

Her boyfriend hasn't been giving it to her. In fact, they've been going out for something like four months and have NEVER had sex.

That's where I can help.

She swings both ways and has recently arranged a threesome with her, me, and a stripper. That's why I don't mind when she forgets her wallet whenever we eat breakfast.

MY VIAGRA EXPERIENCE WITH HER: She called me up and said she was taking a "personal day" away from work, which means she wants to come over and have sex with me. There's an incomparable thrill knowing that someone is on their way over to your place strictly for the purpose of having sex with you.

I pop two 50mg Viagra tabs about a half-hour before the time I told her to arrive. While sudsing my genitals in the shower, I notice them starting to swell. Then I feel all flushed and horny. I feel drugged in a pleasantly speedy way, rollin' along like a hyperventilatin' caveman in cocaine/amyl nitrite-styled white-water rapids. I feel supercharged.

While leaning over my kitchen sink and shaving, I accidentally brush my cock up against the sink, causing it to become erect. This is like high school all over again, where even featherlike contact with another object would cause massive penile engorgement.

She gets over to my crib and says, "I have to tell you—it's my period, and we can't have sex."

My Viagra-enhanced boner doesn't want to hear this.

"Oh, we're *having* sex," I insist. "One way or another, WE'RE HAVING SEX."

I never act this way normally, but I'm taking orders from a really hard, really angry penis.

Red seems aroused by my forcefulness.

We start fumbling around on the bed. I grab her hand, place it on my granite-hard bulldog cock, and say, "I'd like to PUT this somewhere."

"Where do you want to put it?" she asks, somewhat guardedly.

"How about your ASS?" I suggest with an arched eyebrow.

She pauses. "Well, if you have lube, then sure."

With a hop, skip, and a jump, my naked body and thick boner bouncing up and down all the way, I'm in the kitchen, fetching some aloe-coconut oil from under the sink. I slather a greasy handful onto my lobster-red cock, get in bed, and lay on my back. She sits down on that cock, wincing and groaning.

My pole is easily hard enough to jam it right up that ass without struggling or bending. Frankly, I enjoy her expressions of pain. That's what she gets for being on the rag. It feels good to be stuffing myself up her ass.

Harder, thicker, veinier. I'll give her something for a girl to hold onto. A lightning rod with which to ground a skittish female. One has a weird sort of power over another person once you've been in their ass. I think you all know what I'm talking about.

I drill her butt for a LOOONNG time. I finally cum in her poop chute. When she dismounts to go to the bathroom and wipe up, I shampoo all the doody off my schlong in the kitchen sink and then treat myself to a bagel. While munching on the circular doughy treat, I check out my naked self in the mirror. My hangin' hammer looks impressive. My dick's lookin' REAL good tonight. NICE.

After another round, Red and I go out for coffee and ice cream. I feel ecstatic. I feel at ease. I feel rubbery. I feel witty. I feel things more intensely. And I think the Viagra has something to do with it. It would make sense that a drug which is powerful enough to give Bob Dole a woody would have some euphoria-inducing effects.

Red tells me that I have a "friendly penis" and that she's becoming obsessed with it.

Sweet afterglow. We loll around in bed amid the dewy sort of bliss you only see in '70s ads for douche products. I'm happy that I'm a man and she's a woman. The feeling in the room is THAT corny.

THE BLONDE

DESCRIPTION: A tiny skinny miniature Tonya Harding doll with a beautiful gap in her teeth and naturally blonde hair she sometimes wears in pigtails, making her look about six years old. She drives a truck and is from the South. We have very little in common besides a very strong mutual chemical attraction. Once we get close enough to one another to sniff the pheromones, it's almost maddening.

HER boyfriend of four years (I *love* being a male mistress) is only delivering the groceries to her once a month, and that's where I come to the rescue.

MY VIAGRA EXPERIENCE WITH HER: Blondie says she feels guilty even *making out* with me and doesn't want to fuck me until she moves out on her boyfriend. But this doesn't stop her from calling me to hang out a few times a week for insanely passionate dry-humping sessions.

For some reason, I'm sure we're going to fuck tonight.

I swallow a vial of liquid Viagra in the bathroom of the Matador, a bar where Blondie has been tankin' herself up all night on beer and mixed drinks. She looks like she weighs about 20 pounds, so it shouldn't take much to get her plastered.

She gets so drunk, she forgets where she parked her truck. It takes an hour in freezing February weather to find it. When she finally starts driving, it's the wrong way down a busy one-way street.

When we get back to my pad, I'm fairly limping around with a steel-hard observatory-telescope erection. We plop down on my bed and start making out teenager-style. I pop open my belt buckle, unzip my tight jeans, take my diving-board-hard cock out, and place her hand around it. Li'l Jimmy seems twice as thick as normal. It's so hard, so bloody full of blood, it's comical.

This is the first time she's made contact with my prong, and I'm glad she's feeling it in the vibrant fullness of its tumescence. I wanted to give her a really good first impression. While she's grabbing it, I distinctly hear her say "big" or "so big." Joy and happiness! This is what it means to be a man. This is the meaning of life: To have a cute little gaptoothed truck-drivin' blonde girl from the South hold your cock in her hand and use the word "big."

But the little C.T. still doesn't want to go all the way, what with the guilt and all. So we make out for about three hours, her hand on my crankshaft all the while, whispering in my ear that one day we'll fuck so much we won't have the strength to get out of bed.

We fall asleep together. When I fall asleep, my cock is hard. When I awake two hours later, it's still hard. Blondie has to be at work. She gathers her belongings and is gone.

About two seconds after she leaves, I start jacking off with Tasmanian Devil ferocity. I cum so hard that I splat my face twice—one squirt on the forehead, one on the chin.

THE BRUNETTE

DESCRIPTION: A six-foot-tall salty marshmallow from Arkansas with a beautiful hot pale body. Crow-black S&M bangs hanging over huge blue eyes. Thick muff and great sense of humor. She gets a nice slick of sweat going in bed, and I love licking it off her ivory skin. I can't think of anything bad to say about the girl. I like her so much, I'm kind of glad she doesn't live in Portland, because I'd probably lose my head about her, and I hate when that happens.

Although she's quite the tasty snack, she hadn't had sex in over two years before flying up to Portland last summer for the express purpose of having sex with me. And it was great...I'd almost forgotten *how* great until she flew up recently to remind me.

MY VIAGRA EXPERIENCE WITH HER: Around Valentine's Day, we decide it's high time she fly in for another three-day snugglefest with me.

I drop two 50mg Viagra tabs right after picking her up at the airport. We go back to my apartment, which is roughly the size of a desk drawer, and get busy. I power-fuck her hard and long, then pull out and squirt all over my ugly beige carpet.

But I'm not sure the Viagra makes much of a difference in this case. She stays for three days and we fuck a lot, and a few of the sessions are better than the Viagra-fortified one. The drug just didn't match the natural juices that are flowing between us. "God, you made me cum so much," she exclaims after one particularly sweaty round. I MADE her cum so much, as if she had no choice in it. This is the only thing a man wants to hear. This is his fundamental project. Hearing a girl say, "you made me cum so much" is one of life's greatest treasures, regardless of whether one's stiffie was chemically enhanced or *au naturel*.

[I'd like to apologize to Blondie, Blackie, and Red if they see this and are embarrassed. Sorry if I kinda used you like guinea pigs and stuff. You're all top-flight gals, really good sports. And have I told you lately how pretty I think you are? No, "pretty" isn't the word—you're BEAUTIFUL. All right? Don't get pissed. Look, girls, nobody knows who you are...just me...you...and now every strip-club-crawling deviant in the greater Portland area. And hey—at least it proves you actually read *the magazine like you told me you did, right? I'll buy the next breakfast, OK?]*

MOTHER NATURE'S VI

did somebody say, "horny goat weed"?

a partial list of PLANTS & HERBS which, at one time or another by one idiotic culture or another, were thought to contain aphrodisiacal properties:

African Evergreen Tree • Agave • Angel's Trumpet • Anise • Ayahuasca • Basil • Belladonna • Betel Palm • Borrachero • Brunfelsia • Calamus • Cannabis Sativa • Cardamom • Cayenne • Chan-Su • Chili Peppers • Cinnamon • Clove • Coral Tree • Coriander • Damiana • Date Palm • Ephedra Nevadensis • Epimedium (a.k.a. "Horny Goat Weed") • Fennel • Fly Agaric • Garlic • Ginger • Ginkgo Biloba • Ginseng • Gotu Kola • Guarana • Henbane • Horseradish • Irish Moss • Kava-Kava • Licorice • Lotus • Lovage • Maca • Mandrake • Morning Glory • Muira Puama • Mustard • Nutmeg • Nux Vomica • Parsley • Poppy • Puncture Vine • Qat • Rosemary • Sage • Sandalwood • Saffron • Sassafras • Saw Palmetto • Scopolia • Sea Bean • Stinging Nettle • Sunflower • Tongkat Ali • Vanilla • Vervan • Wood Rose • Wormwood • Ylang-Ylang • Yohimbe

Before we get started, I need to make clear that there's nothing wrong with me, my penis, or my sex drive. All three of us are doin' mighty fine, thank you very much. In every way—*beyond* every way—I am a fully functional adult American male whose organ snaps to attention whenever I command it to do so. With smiles on their faces and songs in their hearts, my hundreds of regular female sex partners will attest to the fact that I leave them satisfied in every way, and that includes "Greek" and "Roman" if they're so inclined. Just the other day, one of my lady friends said, "Wow! You really have a hard penis, and you are a splendid sexual performer who gives me the sort of thunderous, robust orgasm I seek." Those were her exact words. Another lady companion put it this way: "Your penis is always hard and big, and it contributes to my endless sexual satisfaction, including an orgasm each time we make love." Despite my advanced age, I'm fit as a fiddle and not too old to cut the mustard. I can probably kick your ass, and I can do more pushups than any of you yellow-bellied punks. I lead the lazy, leisurely life of a freelance writer. I sit around all day, measuring my cock and scribbling notes on a pad. Sound like fun? It is, my bitter, workaday friend—it is.

Therefore, I'll tolerate no snickers, nor titters, nor any hardscrabble foolhardiness from any of you upstart rapscallions regarding the idea of my possible sexual inadequacy. My hard penis stalks the misty night like a sand shark seeking a bellyful of algae, or whatever it is that sharks eat. Maybe it's seaweed.

My interest in erection-enhancing compounds is purely that of a *journalist*. The fact that I've already written three *separate* articles about Viagra, Cialis, and the "urethral suppository" lovingly referred to as MUSE should in no way give the reader the impression that I'm desperately seeking a chemical cure for a humiliating, debilitating, lifelong sexual dysfunction which has scarred my personal relationships and led to several unflattering comments written on the bathroom walls of local establishments which advertise in *Exotic Underground*. Nor should the fact that, in *each* of those articles, I wrote about the respective Penile Wonder Drug's life-giving effect upon my *own* penis—added to the fact that in *this* article, I'll be doing exactly the same thing, except the love potions I'm swallowing are all-natural this time—lead anyone to believe that I'm lying when I say that my penis operates fine without any of the ointments, creams, lotions, pills and injectable "miracle cures" to which I subject it daily.

So when I walk into Fred Meyer and plop down a bottle of Yohimbe capsules, a bottle of Saw Palmetto softgels, and a bottle of Horny Goat Weed/Maca pills, I look at the cashier as if to say, *"Research,* honey. This is all just for research. I'm a journalist. I'm researching whether this sort of quack medicine has any effect on the sort of losers who can't get it up."

ON A LARK A FEW MONTHS AGO at a gas station, I bought a little foil-wrapped package bearing a picture of a ripped male torso and the words TOP GUN.

Inside were two capsules containing, among other herbs, some "Horny Goat Weed," so called because Chinese farmers noticed that goats who grazed near this plant tended to bust out and get busy and do the wild thing and get jiggy wit' it.

A SHORT JAUNT INTO THE ALLEGEDLY BONER-INDUCING JUNGLE OF NATURAL APHRODISIACS

AGRA

An hour after swallowing the capsules, I was rutting my girlfriend like a horny goat. Rather, my penis was more like a mighty ram's horn, crashing against the rock-hard mountainous walls of her shrub-riddled nether regions. She screamed with delight, and I complimented the gal on her taste in men.

Was I experiencing the famous "placebo effect," with my mind playing tricks on my dick? Was this TOP GUN product merely a Horny Sugar Pill which made me feel sexy merely through the *suggestion* that it could make me feel sexy? Or was there actually some *substance* to the idea that we already reside in Eden, and Jehovah God has provided us with all the plants, herbs, and wacky berries we need to bust a nut like there's no tomorrow?

THE WORD "APHRODISIAC" is derived from Aphrodite, the Greek goddess of—I don't know, the vagina or something. It is said that she was born amid sea foam that issued from—I'm too tired to make this up—"the genitals of Uranus." She apparently was quite the slut, and her birth legend gave rise to the idea that seafood has lust-inducing properties.

In one form or another, it is thought that humans have used aphrodisiacs for 60,000 years, which is a hell of a lot of boners when you really sit down and think about it. The Book of Genesis alludes to Rachel's use of mandrake root as a fertility drug. The Kama Sutra recommends boiled ram or goat testicles mixed with milk and sugar to spice up one's love life. The ancient Greeks enjoyed the alleged libido-enhancing properties of a wild orchid called *satyrion* so much that they plucked the frail flower out of existence. The Roman poet Ovid wrote an entire book of aphrodisiac recipes called *Remedies for Love*. Witches in medieval Europe would smear a purportedly aphrodisiacal paste containing mandrake, belladonna, and henbane inside their vaginas using a broomstick, giving rise to the "flying on broomsticks" myth. And as recently as the 1960s, it was thought that green M&Ms could make you horny.

Although the FDA concluded in 1989 that there is no evidence of any natural so-called "aphrodisiacs" having an effect on the human libido, Americans plop down countless millions every year in search of an herbal Magic Bullet to enhance the act of makin' whoopie.

I BOUGHT THE HORNY GOAT WEED/MACA MIX because I'd already had success with the goat weed and liked the ring of the word "Maca," also known as

"Peruvian ginseng." I added the Saw Palmetto because it tunes up the prostate, the Fountain of Male Pleasure so cruelly buried in the anus. And all the research I'd done pointed toward Yohimbe, an African tree bark, as one of the most reliable herbal erection-enhancers.

About ten days ago, I began gobbling twice-daily doses of these reputed boner-boosters. I promised myself that I would not experience psychosomatic arousal as a result of knowingly swallowing pills alleged to render me a Fuck Monkey. I would attempt to carefully monitor my physical performance, as well as my "erotic mood," with the highest level of clinical skepticism. I wanted to be cynical. I wanted it not to work.

But the first night, as I was plowing the gentle lamb who shares my bed, I had the sensation that my erect penis was a proud tree root reaching into dark, moist jungle clay. I felt bold, primitive, and, dare I say it, *black*, although I have far too many freckles to actually *pass* as black in real life.

Over the ensuing days, I felt more confident, more tactile, more sexy, and definitely more hard. And there were none of the headaches or feelings of cocaine-level poisoning that accompany a Viagra binge. It was all free 'n' easy, my friend, all natural 'n' smooth...and hard. Harder and harder.

HUNDREDS OF OLD PICKLE JARS line the dusty shelves of this Chinese herb emporium in a Chinese section of town the locals refer to as "Chinatown." About 30 jars in a row are classified in the TONIFYING YANG section, which is Far Eastern fancy-speak for STUFF THAT GIVES YOU A BONER. There are dried seahorses. Seal testicles. Several types of deer antler. And all manner of herbs which li'l Chinamen use to make their dicks a li'l bigger.

I buy an ounce of epimedium leaves (Horny Goat Weed again) and a gram of ground deer antler. The gentle clerk instructs me to brew the mix in six cups of water for a half-hour and drink the resulting mess as a tea.

(continued on next page)

why "spanish FLY" can make you die

PERHAPS THE MOST FAMOUS APHRODISIAC OF ALL is the notorious "Spanish Fly," derived not from a fly but from **green "blister beetles"** indigenous to Spain and France. But although the bug also calls France home, you never hear anyone call it "French Fly," because that would just sound like a Chinese man trying to say "French fry," confusing everyone. What used to be sold as "Spanish Fly" (before its sale was made illegal in the U.S.) typically consisted of crushed-and-powdered beetle carcasses. The li'l green critters contain a compound known as **cantharidin**, which inflames body tissues and often results in a persistent erection that is not perceived as sexually pleasurable by the, um, "erectee."

Cantharidin is so corrosive that it is sometimes used as a wart remover. Taken even in small doses, it can induce vomiting and potentially blister the urethra, leading to bloody urination. Genitals get scarred…kidneys fail…men die.

Nevertheless, a Roman empress named **Livia** (b. 58 B.C.) dosed other members of her royal family with Spanish Fly, thinking it would force them into committing sexual acts with which she could later blackmail them. And hoping that it would inflame their loins, the **Marquis de Sade** heavily laced some candy with Spanish Fly and fed it to a pair of French prostitutes, who became violently ill. Facing criminal charges of poisoning, the wily de Sade fled to Italy.

The greenish beverage tasted like a mixture of lawn clippings and countertop cleaner. It was a much higher dosage of Horny Goat Weed than I'd become accustomed to from the gas-station capsules. And let's not forget all the deer antler sprinkled in there like libidinal pixie dust. Yet, because I am a rugged journalist and will do anything for the scoop, I drank it all down, anticipating a near-orgasmic rush and the inexhaustible sense that I could sexually satisfy a female blue whale if the need arose.

Hours later…nothing. No perceptible effect from this hearty concoction. One would tend to believe that a raggedy old store in Chinatown carries the REAL aphrodisiac herbs, while the capsules you buy in gas stations are filled with sawdust and rat droppings.

Not so, apparently. Back when I didn't expect much of any sexual effect from the foil-wrapped TOP GUN capsules and the bottled Fred Meyer herbs, I was a bronze Mandingo warrior using my steely weenie as a scythe, mercilessly ripping through milady's vaginal thickets.

But when I anticipated a rip-snortin' horny bronco blast from the real-deal Chinatown herbs, my penis rustled not a whit more than usual.

Because the shit hit me when I least expected it—and likewise, because it did nothing when I was certain it would—I must conclude that the placebo effect had no bearing in my case. I can also infer two more things: first, that at least some of these herbal cock-inflaters deliver precisely what they promise, and second, that I think the guy in Chinatown ripped me off.

•••••••

THE WAY TO A MAN'S COCK IS THROUGH HIS STOMACH

A jolly litany of foods purported to heighten the sex drive:

ALMONDS
APRICOTS
ARTICHOKES
ASPARAGUS
AVOCADOS
BANANAS
BEEF
CARROTS
CAVIAR
CELERY
CHOCOLATE
CUCUMBERS
DATES
DONUTS
EEL
EGGS
EGGPLANT
FIGS
FISH
FOIE GRAS
FROG'S LEGS
GOOD & PLENTY
GRAPES
HONEY
KELP
KUMQUATS
LICORICE
M&Ms
MANGOS
NUTMEG
NUTS
OATS
OKRA
ONIONS
OYSTERS
PEACHES
PEPPER
PINEAPPLE
PINE NUTS
POMEGRANATES
SQUASH
STRAWBERRIES
SWEET POTATOES
TOMATOES
TRUFFLES
TURNIPS
TURTLE
WALNUTS
WHEAT
WILD GREEN OATS
WILD LETTUCE
ZUCCHINI

3 Coins in the Condom Machine

can one achieve MAXIMUM INTIMACY and ABSOLUTE PLEASURE using coin-vended novelty items purchased in dive-bar restrooms?

So you're stinking-drunk in some crusty low-rent bar bathroom, fumbling through your pocket for three quarters to buy a rubber with which to safely bone some skaggy barfly ho whose mascara is as thick as Groucho Marx's greasepaint mustache.

You're in luck. You forgot to do laundry, and there are five bucks' worth of quarters in your pocket waiting to be wasted. So, your head swirling amid the scents of cheap cologne, mothball-smelling urinal cakes, and freshly dumped Skid Row poopie, you keep feeding coinage into the machine's cold, scuffed-steel mouth. Every time you insert three quarters and twist the handle, a small, cellophane-wrapped package plops emotionlessly out of the machine. Every packet is adorned with brightly colored '70s-style artwork and screaming headlines that guarantee so much pleasure, it might be painful for you.

You buy rubbery items:

"SUPER STUDDED LUBRICATED PREMIUM QUALITY CONDOM... Electrify Her with studded rubber nubs...DRIVE HER WILD WITH PLEASURE!..." and "GLOW IN THE DARK RING OF PASSION...EXCITE HER! STIMULATE HER!...."

You buy creamy, oily items:

"Enjoy That Moment of Pleasure Together with CLIMAX CONTROL...A NEW REVOLUTIONARY LOTION DESIGNED TO PROLONG INTERCOURSE..." and "DELICIOUS LOVE DROPS...Flavor Your Lovemaking Experience..." and "VANILLA FLAVORED PERSONAL LUBRICANT WITH GINSENG FOR INCREASED SENSITIVITY."

You buy goofy little temporary tattoos featuring "dangerous" imagery such as cartoon spiders and scorpions:

"Body Play Tattoos...TAKE A WALK ON THE WILD SIDE...FOR A BOLD NEW YOU!...The Ultimate in Fun & Fantasy... BE WILD...BE CREATIVE...PUT THEM ANYWHERE!..."

You buy dirty little pictures designed to enhance your arousal:

"Sneek-A-Peek...Totally Erotic Photos... Your Own Private Stripper," which describes a series of naked photos of chicks with suspiciously lush vintage bushes whose nudity is superimposed with scratch-off fake bra and panties which you rub away with a nickel, only to watch her undergarments magically reappear after a few seconds.

You buy joke items:

"OVER THE HILL CONDOM—LIFETIME SUPPLY— CONTENTS ONE—FOR THOSE WHO AREN'T AS GOOD AS THEY ONCE WAS AND ONCE MORE WOULD PUT THEM SIX FEET UNDER..." and "THE ORIGINAL Slick Willy COMMEMORATIVE CONDOM—Meets Presidential standards set by the White House—Sure way to avoid embarrassing dress stains—Designed for a full cover-up."

NOVELTY MIDGET TEENIE WEENIE TICKLER

The Rocking Position
We have the Arabians and their "ships of the desert" to thank for this erotic import. This position allows frontal caresses between the partners while they gently rock to a prolonged orgasm aided by the swaying of camels.

You buy purportedly educational items, such as the tiny, Cracker Jack-box-toy-sized "Exotic sexual artistry FROM AROUND THE WORLD!" booklet which illustrates a dozen sexual positions and their countries of origin.

You scoop up your cache of Lovemaking Aids and escort your quarry back to your moldy studio apartment, where intense pleasures and scorching intimacy erupt as you snap on a glow-in-the-dark Casper the Friendly Ghost condom atop which you've applied a pink studded tickler, with "intimate gel" rubbed on one of your nips and "love drops" on the other, and a smiley face daubed on your tummy in strawberry-flavored edible neon body paints. You both giggle at the bawdy cleverness of the "pecker stretcher" joke while doing the "wheelbarrow position" as instructed by the tiny booklet, and she doesn't even

"Haven't you always wanted a glow-in-the-dark cock and an ass that tastes like vanilla and ginseng?"

realize you've been fantasizing about the hairy-lapped, Farrah-feathered chippie whose scratch-off panties you just rubbed away with a nickel.

Sound like fun? Haven't you always wanted a glow-in-the-dark cock and an ass that tastes like vanilla and ginseng?

I wanted to sample these forbidden pleasures for myself, so I blew a roll of quarters. I should note that the cellophane wrapping is way too tight on most of these packages, and one risks losing one's erection in the process of opening a novelty item intended to augment said erection. As part of my research, I employed the services of my trusty female assistant, who says the ribbed rubber and luminous studded tickler did nothing to intensify her pleasure. The prolong cream mildly deadened my penile sensations, but nothing major. We couldn't bring ourselves to use the banana-flavored condom, but I tasted it, and it tasted sweet and banana-y, and this doesn't make me a fag, I swear. The flavored neon body paints had the texture and taste of strawberry cake frosting, which is pleasant, although hardly aphrodisiacal. The only item which seemed to help was the flavored body drops, which seemed to contain some Ben Gay-style heat-enhancing compound that for some reason actually got the blood flowing in all the right places. But overall, the most noticeable effect these novelties had on our lovemaking was that we were both laughing during sex.

And then I wondered about the people who *don't* find this stuff silly. What about the losers who are so socially retarded that they learn about sex from a beat-up steel machine in a germ-pit public bathroom? What about the social cripples and terminally homely? What about the sexual untouchables?

God bless them.

God bless the people who can just have sex without attaching meaning to it, who are aroused at the very mention of sex, who find all dirty jokes funny, no matter how cheesy. God bless the people who are just idiotic, ugly, and drunk enough to enjoy these items at face value.

I wish I was like that. It'd be a relief to be an animal.

Sex has meaning, but its meaning is biological rather than personal. People who have sex shouldn't write about it, and people who write about sex shouldn't have it.

In search of...the
PROSTATE

For proof that God has a cruel sense of humor, one need look no further than the fact that He hid the male G-spot about three inches up every man's ass.

By day, the prostate is a walnut-sized gland exclusive to males. Its job is to produce seminal fluid. But at night, it becomes a fun-loving, rebellious, attention-seeking, *naughty* gland that is always primed and READY FOR ACTION.

Of course, when men get older, the prostate gets all bloated and football-sized, leading to humiliating impotence and infantilizing, diaper-necessitating urinary dysfunction...and, in many cases, death. Prostate cancer ain't no fun. No way. In fact, even the *idea* of prostate cancer is a turnoff. And I wouldn't want any of you to associate the humble prostate gland, which, when in its prime, is a li'l red panic button that can launch atom-bomb-sized orgasms, with unpleasant things such as chemotherapy and spinal injections, so I'd better steer the conversation back toward pleasure—rather than flesh-searing, never-ending pain—quickly.

Since the prostate is composed of roughly the same cluster of tissues that form the female G-spot, the term "male G-spot" is scientifically accurate. In fact, the entire anal area is the second-largest bundle o' nerves in the human body next to the genitals. And since the prostate gland butts up (no pun intended...well, yeah, it was) against the root of the penis that extends up inside the body, a.k.a. the "penile bulb," it is crucial to male pleasure.

But even though most men might realize there's a Fourth of July fireworks show just waitin' to explode 'tween their buttocks, the very idea of crossin' into that section of town implies weakness and

PROSTATE

homosexuality, if the man in question doesn't consider the two things synonymous already. Having one's anal portal penetrated in *any* way is considered submissive and unmanly. It's almost as if once you open your sphincter, all the Fag Spirits come screeching out of it, forever faggifyin' you. That's the primary reluctance that most males, at least in the prostate-hostile West, harbor regarding ANYTHING ass-related. They defensively chirp that their ass is marked EXIT ONLY just so no one thinks they're a fag, not that anyone would anyway, because they sure don't act faggy, at least not in public.

Over in Japan, wives massage their husbands' prostates as if they were taking out the trash, and the men enjoy better orgasms and drastically lower prostate-cancer rates. And no one calls them fags. People might say they have little dicks, but no one calls them fags.

THE INTERNET, BLESS ITS ASS, fairly bubbles over with helpful tips on rectal fun. Much of it consists of New Agey jibberty-jabber, rendered that much more hilarious because they're talking about ASS: beautiful crystal anal wands and Tantric sphincter-contracting exercises and rectal acupressure points and letting one's significant Yin diddle up the murky passageways of your Yang and jamming one's finger up one's butt to get the ol' chakras goin'. Along with upbeat tips about anal beads and vibrating eggs, right there amid stomach-churning chitchat regarding the "pubo-rectal sling" and the sigmoid colon, and somewhere in the vicinity of a stern warning that a perforated rectum can be fatal, some self-ordained Internet assmaster counsels us that:

You need to work with your anus. When you do anal play, you need to get re-acquainted with your anus....We have to learn to communicate with the anus, and communication is a two-way street....

Umm—I think I'll *pass* on the two-way communication with my anus. The day my anus talks back to me is the day I voluntarily depart this sad planet, OK?

Still, whatever Higher Power designed the male body made sure that the prostate gland was a throbbing crystal ball of sensitive nerve endings directly related to male sexual pleasure. And the Creator's intentions were apparently fag-neutral. It's not as if homosexuals have sensitive prostate glands and no one else. *All* guys are sensitive there, so that either means:

1) All guys are fags; or
2) Enjoying prostate stimulation doesn't make you a fag.

At least that's how it looks. I'd really hate to find out this late in the game that I'm a fag. I'd have to change my wardrobe and everything.

CURIOUS ABOUT THIS MAGIC BUTTON lodged somewhere up my poop chute, I did some research about the prostate gland and its association with male sexual pleasure. The following is a hodgepodge of quotes from a handful of pro-prostate propagandists:

Because this gland has so much nerve conduction to the area, it's easily aroused, often resulting in an intense orgasm....It can reputedly stimulate orgasm if it is massaged, much like the vaginal G-spot can....Massage of this gland by your finger will produce some of the most delightful sensations your partner has yet to experience....When gently stimulated, the many nerve endings located there can intensify feelings of sexual arousal, actually heightening sexual sensitivity, taking him to new heights of pleasure...[and] super-heightened sexual ecstasy....Pressing or rubbing it...causes the penis to swell and engorges his erection even larger....[It] creates an intense pleasurable sensation for most men, [resulting in] crashing orgasms.

See, I'm TOTALLY down with having an engorged erection and crashing orgasms. I don't think I've ever had an orgasm that crashed in my life. That sounds really good...so good, I don't even mind if people think I'm a fag for inserting something up my butt. *You think I'm a fag, huh? Well, at least my orgasms crash, tuff guy!*

If what the experts say is true, there are some *neurological realities* here that have nothing to do with sexual preferences. At least I don't think they do, and even if they do, those crashing orgasms sound so fucking good, I'm not sure it matters.

I'm so fucking secure with my butchness, my meaty pulsing machismo-laden butch-osity, that I'm not threatened by the idea of a hot girl squeezing

GLAND a.k.a. "The Male G-Spot"

her finger in my ass in search of this hidden jungle temple which the Sages of Yore claim is the key to a white-hot blinding orgasm.

Being a rock-hard pimp daddy is fun, but sometimes it's OK to just sit back—which is what I decided to do—and let *her* grab the joystick for a while. As one writer on the Internet put it regarding prostate massage:

Obviously, this is a great way for your woman to show her appreciation for all that you do in bed and let you be in pure receptive mode, something that all men find relieving and absolutely delightful.

Or as another writer put it, certainly not plagiarizing the first:

Obviously, this is a great way to let your partner be in pure receptive mode, something that many men find a relief and a delight.

THE CLOSEST THAT MOST MEN GET to a prostate massage is when their family physician jams a cold, latex-covered, petroleum-jelly-smeared finger up their ass and takes a few sharp pokes around in search of abnormalities.

The closest I got—well, I guess I went *all the way,* actually—was last night with this curvy hot redhead girl. She's kind of a freak and I guess I am, too, and we're both hyper-confident about our ability to get each other off. After I fucked her hard enough that she copped a half-dozen or so nuts, she asked me when *I* was going to cum. I stopped thrusting and calmly explained my editorial mission—I was in search of my prostate gland—and she agreed to help me find it.

With some coco-aloe oil and some gentle nudging, her middle finger was in. It was initially uncomfortable, but then...then...*then*...she touched upon something. I told her to keep touching it there. Yeah, right *there*. She was kissing me all over and telling me how sexy she thinks I am. My hard hard HARD cock—wow, the veins NEVER bulge THAT much—was dribbling mad wet pre-cum all the way down the shaft. And when I finally came, BOOM! Shots rang past my head and onto the pillow.

It was a crashing orgasm.

And I'm not sure I'm able to articulate it clearly right now, but I think I've stumbled upon the prostate gland as some new source of male political power. Just like women copped an attitude once they discovered their clits and G-spots, there must be some way we can work this prostate thing into something that annoys and threatens females as much as their discoveries have annoyed and threatened us.

Nah. They'd just laugh and call us fags.

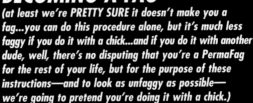

"PROSTEE THE HAPPY PROSTATE GLAND" a cartoon figure designed to help men relax and enjoy the sensual delights lurking a short distance up their rectums.

HOW TO STIMULATE YOUR PROSTATE GLAND WITHOUT BECOMING A FAG

(at least we're PRETTY SURE it doesn't make you a fag...you can do this procedure alone, but it's much less faggy if you do it with a chick...and if you do it with another dude, well, there's no disputing that you're a PermaFag for the rest of your life, but for the purpose of these instructions—and to look as unfaggy as possible—we're going to pretend you're doing it with a chick.)

1) get that ass clean

take a shower. if you're kinky, give yourself an enema, but again, if you start doing things like that, you're veering toward crossing the international border of a nation known as Fagland.

2) find some lube

yeah, I agree, the idea of having a wet hole between your legs is sort of feminine and, sure, faggy, but unless you think rectal bleeding is groovy, it's a good idea to make sure that the, uh, toboggan track is waxed.

3) get in position

on-your-back-with-a-pillow-under-your-ass is probably the best. on-your-side-with-your-knees-up-toward-your-chest might show up as a radar blip back at Fag Control Tower. and on-your-knees-with-your-ass-in-the-air will assure you a Lifetime Fag Gold Card, with all the benefits it implies.

4) relax

if you keep tensing your sphincter muscles like that, no one will be able to get a toothpick in your ass, much less a finger. why so tense—afraid someone will think you're a fag?

5) insert finger

meaning, of course, have the HOT CHICK you're with insert HER clean, well-lubed finger slowly and gently up your poopie-hole. if you're on your back, her palm should be facing the ceiling. she should continue the slow insertion until she's up to her second knuckle or, if you can stand it, a little further. once she's up that far, she should curl her finger upward as if making a "come hither" gesture. to her, the prostate will be felt through the rectal wall as a small, spongelike lump. to you, once she finds it, the prostate will feel warm and oddly pleasurable.

from this point on, you'll both have to negotiate what feels best. many men report that prostate stimulation is enhanced while being blown or jacked off.

if the idea of any sort of anal penetration gets your Fag Fear Flag a-flyin', one can indirectly stimulate the prostate by pressing in sharply on the "grundle" area between your anus and your testicles. if you hadn't noticed already, your hard penis extends up into your body toward that area and ends near the prostate gland.

have fun, you jackoff! and I won't tell anyone you're a fag!

MY TEENAGED CELEBRITY CRUSHES

linda blair

debralee scott

bernadette peters

I was a Catholic schoolboy...and roughly the same age as Linda...when she became possessed by Satan in *The Exorcist* (1973). I yearned to be alone up in her bedroom, where she'd shove a crucifix in her pootie and tell me my mother sucks cocks in hell.

Yeah, the face is a bit like something from *Planet of the Apes*, but this freckled party girl encapsulated the mid-'70s glam-slut ethos even better than bucktoothed drug baby Mackenzie Phillips. She had a raspy voice, and many was the night I fantasized about cumming all over her feathered hair. She was perfect as Brooklyn high-school tramp Rosalie "Hotsy" Totsy on several 1975 episodes of *Welcome Back, Kotter,* and she also starred as the sister of the title character on the brilliantly warped mid-1970s nightly soap-opera spoof, *Mary Hartman, Mary Hartman.*

An almost unbearably cute blonde Betty Boop with breasts large enough to feed a small South American nation. She still looks fantastic, although she must be about 90 by now.

carol kane

Bushy hair, dark circles under her eyes, and one of the most beautiful faces I've ever seen. For years I've thought she was the hottest celeb on earth. She is best known as Latka's wife on the TV show *Taxi* rather than as a featured player in my masturbatory delusions.

I first realized I was able to make sperm shoot out of my cock sometime in the mid-'70s, back in the Greatest Decade America Has Ever Known and Ever Will Know, back during the Good Old Days of snuff films and angel dust and swinger's parties, back when even the president had sideburns and smoked pot, back when I'd sit on the toilet in my parents' bathroom with the AM radio turned up loud, feverishly tugging at my virgin crankshaft, my brain pan awash in implausible sexual scenarios that often featured me and the ladies, at least half of whom are Jewish, who surround this interminable run-on sentence.

barbra
-reisand

o one thinks she's an
nnoying yenta more than I
o, but publicity stills such
the one at right for *The
wl and the Pussycat*
970) led to my first-ever
ornographic dream at the
awn of my adolescence.

A million times hotter than Bettie Page, whom she resembles.
Was one of the *Hee Haw* girls and was married to Hugh Hefner.
I'm not sure
if she had
any
talents
or
not.

barbi
benton

penny
arshall

Wonderfully sexy
overbite. Honking Jew
York accent. Big nose,
hot '50s chick look
amid all the blow-
dried Farrahs of the
'70s. Much more
humpable than the
pinched, goyish Cindy
Williams, her costar
on the unreasonably
popular *Laverne and
Shirley* TV program.

No singer
has ever
sounded
sexier than duckfaced Donna
on eternally beautiful Euro-
drone classics "Love to Love
You, Baby" (1975) and "I Feel
Love" (1977). She was the first
black woman I ever thought
about while masturbating and also
the first black woman I realized
was able to have an orgasm.

donna
summer

linda
lovelace

The first true porn star, best known
for gobblin' cock like she was at
an all-you-can-eat Cock Buffet in
Deep Throat (1972). Everyone in
America knew she stuck dicks in her
mouth at a time when everyone in
America knew chicks weren't
supposed to stick dicks in their mouths.
Years later, when I found out she
fucked a dog in one movie and
claimed her husband abused her for
years, it only added to her charm.

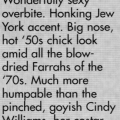

madeline
kahn

Sexy funny Jew babes
are the tops with me,
and Madeline Kahn was
perhaps the sexiest and
funniest, if not the
Jewiest. In performances
as the German-songbird-
with-Jungle-Fever Lili von
Shtupp in *Blazing
Saddles* and as the bride
of the title character in
Young Frankenstein (both
1974 masterpieces by
Mel Brooks), she man-
aged to be both painfully
funny and so sexy, she
almost left a stench on
the screen. The news of
her recent death actually
saddened me, which
rarely happens when
celebrities die.

SUMMERTIME IS HERE, AND THERE'S A HEAT WAVE IN MY PANTS. The sun makes plants grow. It does the same thing to my dick. My penis grows like a proud cornstalk, reaching toward the sun. My balls hang low enough that I could stumble on them. Those balls drop like mangoes from de mango tree. My sperm are so big and healthy, you can see the little tadpoles with the naked eye. My loins belch forth semen like so much pollen. I run naked through the cornfields, eagerly distributing my cum as if it were free detergent samples. Summertime conjures the latent sensualist in me. It is my personal mating season. My time of the season for rutting. In the summertime...when the weather is fine...I would like to jauntily ram my penis inside every woman except the very old, the lame, and most of the infirm. And so I offer this paean, this *hommage*, to my summertime sexuality.

I was conceived in late summer and born in early summer. I grew up battered by the harsh East Coast seasons. I only recently returned after two decades out West. I lived in L.A., where it's always a mild ashen summer, and then Portland, with three months of dry sunshine followed by eternal rain. Having been deprived of the East's

violent seasonal changes, I hadn't thought much about the weather's influence on my sex drive.

Back here, my body runs hot and cold with the weather. Like a frail flower, I blossom in the summer and hide in the winter. My genitals shrink in cold water and cold weather. East Coast winters are a time of reflection and learning. The wintry clouds form a giant wet blanket over my ding-dong. It's too bleak and frosty to think about taking off my clothes, even in bed.

But here I am, in sun-dipped early June, with the mosquitoes a-buzzin' and the humidity so thick, I could cut a cube of it for myself with a pair of scissors. Pollen is squirting forth like projectile diarrhea. Today is gloriously warm and wondrous. It's as if Tom Sawyer had a bucketful of sunshine and the whole world was a wooden fence he'd been forced to paint. As the days grow longer, all I want to do is squirt my goo everywhere as if I was sandblasting sheetrock.

Part of it is undoubtedly the heat. There's a reason we refer to a sexy person as "hot" and a nonorgasmic woman as "frigid." Clothes fall to the ground as the temperature soars, and I catch glimpses of all the sugary ripe girlflesh that had remained cloaked during the cold months.

a Heat Wave in my Pants

as temperatures soar, so does my sex drive

But more than anything, it is the hot, stinking, swampy jungle *humidity* that conjures the lust inside me and makes me feel so butterlicious. The summer air is moist like a vagina. It leaches the sex drive from my marrow, manifesting as sweat on my skin. Motoring eastward across the Mississippi River last year, I could actually SEE the humidity like a giant grey wall. East Coast humidity is virtually a fourth dimension. And it is like Viagra that Mother Nature sprays on my body.

Tonight will be the night. The lush wet valley teems with lightning bugs and thunderstorms, with moths swarming under streetlights as the horny crickets chirp. I will leave the cold bedroom air-conditioner hum and walk outside in the middle of the night clad only in flip-flops, a wifebeater, and some shorts, my low-slung balls swinging in the balmy evening breeze. High as hell, my lady friend and I will drive on dark country roads with the windows rolled down. And as we park and walk deep into the woods, I will make her keenly aware of what this weather does to me.

in praise of Mature Women

"Older women are beautiful lovers," runs the lyric to a whiny '80s C&W song, and for the longest time I didn't want to believe it. Most males just aren't tantalized by floppy wine-skin jugs, stretched-out chicken-rubber twats, parched-creek-bed crow's feet, and thinning grey hair.

But lately, in the spirit of investigative journalism, I've been doing some hands-on research of the topic, and dagnabbit if the song isn't true! It's TWUE, it's TWUE! Old babes got it goin' on!

Most males are unaware that when it comes to the erotic arts, psychology is at least as important as physiology. Older women achieve their beautiful-lover status through the wonderful synergy of emotional hardness and sexual savvy. They've been through the drudgery of marriage and child-rearing; thus they suffer no delusions about pipe-dreams such as "love" and "everlasting commitment." The "pipes" they dream about are of a much more literal nature. Holy Menopause, do they love to fuck.

With younger lasses, what you gain in perky boobs and taut skin tone is easily outweighed by minuses such as obsessiveness, babyish tantrums, high-pitched voices, that ANNOYING habit of snapping their bubble gum, and woeful inexperience in relationships...and in the sack.

Not only do young chix want babies and commitment and terrifying scenarios such as the Vaginal Exclusivity Clause known as marriage, they can't smoke pole like the older ladies can. Can't puff a peter with nearly the same finesse. Can't gobble a bone with the desperate abandon of a shark in a feeding frenzy.

Although her body may be falling apart, at least the seasoned Woman of Age knows what to do with it. She knows what makes her feel good, and she knows what makes men feel good. Dicks have passed these hard-working Methuselitas like trains through Grand Central Station. And I'm not bothered by this. I'm not a jealous man. I'm confident of my skills in *les arts d'amour*. I'm actually turned-on by the idea that their vaginas have acted as airplane hangars for hundreds...or thousands...of penises before mine parked there. I'm not intimidated by the fact that enough cocks have been jammed in their mouths to stuff the Alaskan Pipeline. These are all good things.

Because the brutal fact, the one that younger women would like to keep secret, is that experience breeds skill. One of my mature partners manipulated my penis with her FEET while I was orally pleasuring her Venusian Mounds. And I don't mean she just diddled the thing or tapped at it with her toes—she had my rod in a real fuckin' MONKEY grip with her feet and was feverishly pumping the thing! Amazing! No younger chick on earth would even THINK of attempting such a stunt. Such feats of derring-do only come with hard, long, agonizing experience. A decades-long process of sexual trial-and-error stuffs an old bag's Bag of Tricks with innumerable such erotic gems.

Looking for a mature lady friend? I usually meet mine in smoky karaoke bars. Their husky voices, their whisky breath, their yellowy teeth (dentures?), their hard-luck stories, their pathos-laden attempts at shoveling makeup on their faces and whipping their hair into just-seen-a-ghost enameled perfection...these are all turn-ons for me. Buy 'em a couple drinks, hold them close on the dance floor during "Love Lift Us Up Where We Belong," and in a few hours you're in the bedroom of their spacious homes where they live alone with their cats and a truckload of bad memories, stroking their liver spots with your fingers and sharing tender moments.

And then, after you've plastered their sagging frames with cum a few times, comes the best part: They tell you to go home. They have business to conduct and doctor's appointments to attend, and they have no time for cuddlin' and cooin'. It's what I've always sought in life: a woman who will kick *me* out of bed when it's all over.

AS I LEAF THROUGH THE SEXUALLY CHARGED PICTORIALS in adult men's magazines, I'm often left with the cold, shadowy feeling that something's missing. Or, rather—something *isn't* missing—namely, a tooth. To remedy this, I will hoist a pen and carefully blacken out a tusk in the young lassie's grille...mmm... *there*. That's better. That's much, MUCH better. It's SO much better that I am compelled to wrap my paw around my cock and aim for that little black gap in her mouth.

A few years back I spent a long, torturous night with a red-headed heifer who had big taters and a tiny brain. This, mind you, was a REAL woman instead of the ink-on-paper holograms which you convince yourself are real while you pathetically jack your knob atop your piss-encrusted, stray-pube-covered toilet seat. But this particular portly specimen seemed more interested in gobbling the caramel-coated snack foods I'd purchased for her than in having anything approximating good sex. She jacked me off and I jacked her off, then we commenced to snoring. Even the seedy hotel atmosphere, which is usually wildly erotic for me, failed to spark the mood.

The next day we returned to her crib, and as we were lounging about in our undergarments, she removed a prosthetic tooth from top-row center and launched into an agonizingly dull 45-minute explanation of how she'd had the tooth fashioned by an ortho-dontist. But I wasn't listening to what she had to say. I was spell-bound, staring at that glorious gap. Golden choirs of heavenly, harp-playing cherubs flew through that li'l hole in her mouth.

I thought, "Why the fuck didn't she take out that tooth last night?" I knew that if she'd removed the horrible fake incisor the night before, I'd have been hard as granite and slam-ming her cranium against the headboard with my furious, flamenco-influenced hip thrusts.

I had a similar orthodontic sexual epiphany back in the winter of '99 at the Oregon Correctional Intake Center on my way to

prison. We were herded into a classroom, handed #2 pencils, and instructed to fill out a 567-question personality test by an unre-markable-looking woman who, I reckon, was in her mid-40s. She wasn't bad-looking—slim and proper with neatly clipped bangs which swung back and forth while she walked up and down the aisles handing out the tests—but there wasn't anything out-standing about her which raised my drawbridge, either. That is, until she parted her lips and smiled...and revealed a set of steel braces. Blinding, divine, whiter-than-white, ultra-luminous fluo-rescent light flashed off those wondrous braces. It was an Erotic Valhalla for me.

I have other dental fetishes such as an affinity for bucktoothed women with that cute little bunny-rabbit overbite which pushes out their lips and makes it look as if they've been sucking cock all their lives. And speech impediments caused by dental problems, such as lisps and the oh-so-sexy whistling "S," are also the tops with me.

Naturally, there are limits to this fetish. I don't want her to be toothless. A mouth full of rotting tombstones isn't a turn-on, either. Dentures don't do a thing for me. The idea of her drooling all over my cock with her bare, bleeding gums doesn't exactly spin my spurs. I don't want some rotted-toothed sea hag with purple, green, and black teeth slurping on my Love Rod, if that's what you were asking.

Perhaps there's something wrong with me, but how can some-thing be wrong when it feels so right? My raging tumescence for orthodontically challenged females undoubtedly has a psychologi-cal basis, but if the fetishist were to come to terms with the roots of his fetish, t'would cease to be a fetish, t'wouldn't it? And so I waddle onward, brazenly straddling the line between fetish and perversion. Yet it occurs to me that any sort of orthodontic irregularity calls attention to a girl's mouth, which in turn calls attention to what that mouth is good for.

If a woman has a set of perfect, gleaming choppers, it makes it easier for her to bite you. And maybe that's why I like a girl with dental problems. It gives her a sweetness and vulnerability, a goofy, childlike smile which conjures warmth and cuddliness; by contrast, a woman with a grille that would do a Great White Shark proud is more likely to be emotionally distant and domineering. I don't like perfect women. They don't need love. For me to be interested, the girl has to be damaged in some way. A girl with dental problems likely has more problems than that.

Peut-être I suffer from a silly, fatal romantic streak which makes me think I'm emotionally equipped to con-jure an invisible Tooth of Love where no real tooth exists, or that my overbearing affection will prove to be an ersatz set of emotional braces that will straighten out the poor girl's soul. In my own delusional way, I'm not that much different from Romeo, Valentino, or that dude who selflessly threw his jacket over the mud puddle and let the bitch walk over it, ruining a perfectly good jacket.

in defense of women with BAD TEETH

I only saw my mother's bush once, and I've never fully recovered. I was so young and small that her pubic region hovered above my head on that fateful evening when I wandered into the bathroom unannounced and stumbled upon the disturbing apparition of her pasty white skin and that BIG BLACK JURASSIC-PARK BUSH. I was startled and frightened by what I saw. There seemed something evil about the wadded knot of blackness between her hips. It was as if I had walked into a lost episode of *Star Trek* and some parasitic Tribble had attached itself to mommy's crotch. At first, I was unsure whether she needed my help.

Neither of us said a word, and after a moment of youthful silence, I spun around, left the bathroom, and went back to my Etch-A-Sketch.

Mom's dead now, which should quell most of the cynics out there alleging that I want to fuck her. In truth, I don't miss her at all. And the only thing I like about the old bag is that she never took a razor to her nether regions.

Some men like big asses. Others like big boobs. And I like big bushes. The bigger the bush, the harder my cock.

I realize that my tastes are not currently fashionable. I'm aware that I risk severe social ostracism by declaring my fondness for the hirsute vulva. Nowadays, most men and women seem to favor a *mons pubis* that is at least partially shorn. Partial, I guess, is better than total. The Hitler mustaches and landing strips and Mohawks and five o'clock shadows are bad enough; some foolhardy gals take it to the extreme and shave their womanhood down to a shiny wet peach *sans* the fuzz.

But human genitalia are not the most attractive thingies. The vulva, like the penis, is not a visually appealing organ. It has none of the aesthetic grace of a Grecian urn or a '57 Chevy. A bald vagina is no more attractive than a bald head. It looks like a kangaroo fetus, all pink and slimy and squirmy. Like a battlefield after nuclear war. Like an open, dripping wound. Like a wad of wet, chewed-up bubble gum. A sheared snatch looks as if it's undergone chemotherapy. Put a wig on that thing. Cover that hideous thing up. Comb the hair over to cover the scar. Cover the scar. Cover the goddamned scar.

I don't merely want a nice light carpeting of fur down there...not a light dusting of snow...I don't simply require *coverage* down south in the Golden Triangle; I want VOLUME. I require something three-dimensional. I'm not satisfied with gentle, unassuming tufts; I want a BUSH. I want it to look as if a frickin' tarantula is sleeping on her crotch. I want something you can lose your car keys in. I want a bush you can grab and pick her up with. I want a chick to be like the Jimi Hendrix Experience down there. I want her to look like Fidel Castro, Abbie Hoffman, or the Smith Brothers (of cough-drop fame). I want her lap to be covered with a fleece of chick-fur so dense that a hairbrush gets stuck in it and she has to resort to an Afro pick. I want some righteous shrubbery down there. A tumbleweed between her legs. A luxuriant briar patch of female chaparral. I like it shaggy. Furry. Woolly. A lush, gnarled, tangled, black Brillo pad. A matted, stinking, soppy mass of dreadlocks.

A long-whiskered vulva bespeaks fertility. Fruitfulness. Health. Sensuality. Like darkest ground coffee or a huge, resinous tobacco leaf, a full, healthy bush reaches toward the sun and greets the new day.

Don't think I can't hear you chuckling. You say I'M the freak?!? Hey, at least I dig it the way nature *intended* it to be. You want your gal to shave her bush? Why don't you insist she shave her fucking *head,* too? And why not cut her nipples off while she's at it? T'ain't me who has a fetish—it's all you sorry goofballs who want your girls to shave down until they look like kindergarteners.

All you smacked asses who shudder at the thought of a full, lovely bush are nothing more than brainwashed, kiddie-porn-lovin' conformists. Thirty years ago, you all would have recoiled at the idea of a shaved snatch. Ain't it hilarious how you ALL, in UNISON, suddenly changed your taste, you spineless, craven maggots? You easily molded dumbfucks. You pathetically endowed robot hamsters. Don't you see? You've all been psychologically conditioned by a pedophilic cabal of Madison Avenue child-molesters. These fruity homo ad execs have made the bush—that fullest flower of womanhood—into something unhip and disgusting. They have force-marketed small-breasted, skinny, bushless women onto the American consumer because it reminds them of the little *boychiks* whose tiny pink puckered starfish they crave so dearly.

Maybe I'm wrong. Maybe there's nothing wrong with being sexually attracted to shaved snatches...and maybe there's nothing wrong with being sexually attracted to eight-year-old girls. Why don't you just go fuck a Girl Scout, eh, Johnny Boy? Why don't you just slap a diaper on that hairless beaver while you're at it, Chief?

If you enjoy ladies with crew-cutted snappers, you are not only a pervert, you're a sinner. A shaved bush is irrefutable evidence of a sinful lifestyle.

A vast, bounteous, three-dimensional, *bushy* bush is what God almighty, in His Infinite Fucking Wisdom, intended Earth Women to have. The Lord Jehovah provided the birds of the air with fluffy, pretty feathers...He provided the clams of the sea with hard protective shells...He provided the trees of the forest with thick, rich bark...and He provided the human vagina with an ingenious natural camouflage.

If God wanted us to stare at naked bald vaginas, he wouldn't have gone to the trouble of infusing a woman's DNA code with instructions for constructing a bush, nor for *RE*constructing that bush every time some foolish sinner is reckless enough to shave it. The fact that a bush grows BACK is evidence of God's will in action.

The Lord God, in his pricelessly greasy generosity, bestowed women with bushes, and it took the sinful arrogance of wretched humans to shave it all away. When you shave that bush, you are hoisting a weed-whacker against the Garden of Eden.

I ALWAYS VOTE FOR BUSH

Nothing ruins a moment of intimacy worse than hot gobs of bright red blood shooting out of your cock at the moment of orgasm.

I speak from terrifying personal experience, but I speak both literally and metaphorically. Everything is a metaphor, if you only squint hard enough. If you keep still and let the connections reveal themselves, the symbols become as vivid as blood gushing from your prick. Sometimes one's body expresses things that mere words couldn't convey. And so it was when I ejaculated blood, which happened on three occasions in late 1989.

The first time was the scariest, following as it did only weeks after touring the Trinity Site near Alamogordo, New Mexico, staging ground for the world's first atomic-bomb blast. The Feds only open the site to tourists one day a year. A desolate, hours-long, droning car ride through parched desert scrub will get you there, and once you're there, you wish you'd never come. The place looks like a small gravel parking lot with an A-bomb monument the size of a large tombstone. No crater, no obvious devastation, no awe at man's destructive power. After being savagely underwhelmed, my wife and I went soaking in some nearby hot springs.

Back in our musty Hollywood apartment a few weeks later, she was giving me the standard Friday-night after-work handjob. I was lying on my back, my manhood pointed toward the ceiling. And as I erupted, the fluid came out fire-engine red rather than pearly white. It gushed rudely upward like red-hot magma from Mt. Vesuvius.

Talk about ruining the mood.

Blood from my dick? I knew I was intense, but this was ridiculous.

We both worried about possible nuclear contamination from the Trinity Site and from my balls having been soaked like hard-boiled eggs in those irradiated hot springs. I feared that at any minute I'd sprout to 60 feet tall, swaddle myself in a giant diaper, and destroy Las Vegas *à la* The Amazing Colossal Man.

Alarmed that I'd suffered isotope sickness and the onset of testicle cancer, I got a referral for a urologist. Urine Man's office was on Vermont Avenue near Sunset Boulevard in Hollywood. Cheap hookers. Filthy sidewalks. Rough trade.

The waiting room was like an auditioning center for circus freaks: cheerful clubfoots, whiskered women, and dwarfish men. It appeared as if the entire cast of The Doors' *Strange Days* album cover had simultaneously come down with urinary-tract infections and were awaiting treatment. The receptionist, an obese woman with canary-colored hair and thickly penciled eyebrows, handed me a large kidney-shaped steel pan and instructed me to piddle in it. As I entered a dimly lit broom closet-*cum*-bathroom, I noticed that the pan already contained dried crusty stains from some indeterminate ex-fluid.

And then I was ushered into see Doctor Piss, who had the nervous manner, thinning blond hair, and foggy spectacles of a Nazi physician who'd been banished to ply his trade in Venezuelan jungles. In Dr. Mengele's steamy examination room, as he shakily inserted a latex-swathed finger in my rectum and clumsily gave me a reach-around, tugging angrily at my limp knob in an attempt to squeeze some pre-cum onto a dirty glass microscope slide, I noticed several flecks of dried blood on the walls from his former frolics with other patients.

It was not a good place to be.

My darling physician said that bloody ejaculates are usually caused by either cancer or burst capillaries from rough sex.

An X-ray revealed no cancerous growths, which left rough sex as the culprit, which was kind of implausible, seeing as I was married.

A month or so later I squirted blood again, but it was more a purplish-brown color than the original flaming red. I called the Nazi Butcher, and he said it was probably some residual blood from the original popped vessel. In another month it happened again, but this time it was a dark violet mixed with the color of natural cum, sort of a vanilla-boysenberry swirl.

And that was the last time blood ever shot from my penis, at least as we go to press.

But I never got a definite answer as to what caused it. The doctor could only speculate. As can I.

Whence the bloody cum? Was it from rough lovemaking, or was it cancer?

And why should anyone expect ME, of all people, to be able to tell the difference?

See, that's my problem—I always mix the two. Love and blood. Cum and cancer. Affection and death. Kisses and bruises. The parents who gave me life and wanted me dead. Self-preservation and self-destruction are like tangled vines inside me. Trying to untie the knots has proven fruitless.

Am I revealing too much if I admit to you that I'm confused?

I'm SO fucked-up about love. So tortured and damaged and torn-up. I know that I need it, and yet it always winds up hurting so bad. I hurt so much from riding the churning yin-yang carousel of love and lovelessness, it fucking immobilizes me.

It was my heart which pumped that blood through my cock. And matters of the heart consume all my thoughts.

How many years...decades...of my life were spent just trying to capture or recapture the feeling of being loved? How much energy was expended in running from the cold-vinegar feeling of lovelessness? Right now, I'm on the verge of tears even thinking about it.

Love hurts, but not as much as the alternative. I'm so needy for love, I remain in situations that turn carcinogenic. I need love more than I need anything else, and yet it always winds up bloody. There are idiots out there who think domestic violence has nothing to do with love and that promiscuous people aren't emotionally needy.

Groping around in the dark, my task is to prevent the blood from ever coming back.

There is no worse feeling on Earth than love gone wrong.

Feels like blood shooting out of my cock.

FAKING THE MALE ORGASM

My testicles are very nice and shapely, but they can only produce so much Elmer's Glue, if ya know what I'm sayin'. And there are times, often after I've popped a half-dozen loads over a lazy afternoon of balling some nameless, faceless cum-bucket, where I'm able to lift the tube of Pepsodent but can't manage to squeeze any toothpaste out, if you catch the cut of my jib. After an hour of aimless thrusting, fucking doesn't seem so fun anymore. Suddenly, fucking conjures images of blind rodents burrowing inside damp underground tunnels...of soggy toothpicks poking between tartar-laden teeth...of a dirty rubber plunger seeking to unclog a toilet...of colonoscopes probing for rectal tumors.

One doesn't want to appear...unmanly. And one most definitely doesn't ever want to hurt a lady's feelings. What I DO want is for it to be over...please, holy bleeding Jesus Christ, let it be over. And so on those grim occasions, I'll roll back my eyes, emit a token grunt, and pretend as if I've blown my wad. And my lady friends have never been able to tell the difference.

Much has been written about premature ejaculation, yet there's a sinister Conspiracy of Silence regarding its Evil Twin Brother—delayed or nonexistent ejaculation.

It is perhaps the greatest, most pervasive Unspoken Truth in Western Civilization:

Men fake orgasm. A lot. And yet cultural taboos and prejudices prevent us from talking candidly and openly about it.

As research for this important, groundbreaking article, I asked several adult males whether they've ever faked an orgasm, and all but one of them responded in the affirmative, and he was a little weird, anyway. The men I queried...no, wait, I don't like that word "queried"...sounds too faggy...the men I've *quizzed* regarding the Faked Male Orgasm (FMO) usually said it was because they were disgusted with their partner. Their FMOs were typically isolated occurrences involving one-night stands when they suddenly sobered up enough to see the stretch marks or smell the stench.

So why did these gallant knights fake it rather than confront the maiden with an unpleasant truth?

To spare her feelings? Only indirectly. Most of them, in typical swinish boy-pig oinkety-oink fashion, seemed breezily unconcerned with her "feelings." But they ALL seemed highly fretful about what possible damage the spurned woman might inflict on them once her feelings were hurt.

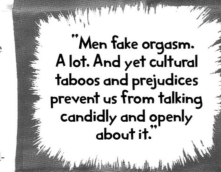

"Men fake orgasm. A lot. And yet cultural taboos and prejudices prevent us from talking candidly and openly about it."

We've all heard the salty sailor's joke stating that women fake orgasms because they think we care. So why do men fake it? Because we KNOW they care.

Because, simply, anyone who's able to rub two brain cells together knows that women are childlike, irrational, hyperemotional, immature, vicious, vindictive, petty, unfair, poopie-faced creatures, and to imply that they can't draw the venom out of your Love Fang—EVERY fucking time—is just too much truth for their fragile little china-doll hearts to handle. To imply that her inflamed, slimy Pleasure Orchid may not be the Blue Ribbon-winning flower she fancies it to be will ultimately only bring suffering on you rather than on her. To claim that her vagina is anything other than a Golden Honey Palace is to invite pain upon yourself. Undeserved pain, but pain nonetheless. A woman who feels less than desirable is fully equipped to rain hellfire on the chump who made her feel that way.

It never occurs to her that she might be unable to satisfy you. It just isn't part of her psychological makeup. It doesn't compute. *Huh? Say what? Not satisfy you?* she'll ask, failing to understand the situation's simultaneous gravity and hilarity.

And yet it *is* funny...when a female fails to reach climax, the male is blamed, but when a male can't seem to pop open another creamer to dump in her coffee cup, the male is *again* blamed. The male *always* gets blamed. That's an unfortunate fact of our culture, and one with which I'd counsel all young boys to familiarize themselves.

'Tis relatively easy to fake a male orgasm while wearing a condom, so long as the rubbery device is disposed of with swift discretion. But an unsheathed penis will find it difficult to emulate a jizz-load. Unlike the female orgasm, the male orgasm leaves a "footprint," as it were. Emotions are easy to fake...bodily fluids, not so easy. One cannot impersonate a bodily fluid the way one can fake the exaggerated grimaces and turkey-gobble sounds of male ecstasy.

If you choose not to wear a rubber and your woman is the suspicious kind prone to doing regular "dipstick checks," you may have a problem. Inserting an alien fluid into her vagina when she isn't looking presents several difficulties, and one should never underestimate such tasks' formidability. Should one stash a turkey baster near their mattress? This is a matter of personal preference, and a subject on which I am not legally authorized to comment at this time.

But without fear of violating the conditions of my parole, I can make this statement: The Veil of Silence which enshrouds Faked Male Orgasms has persisted for far too long. It is time for us to raise the curtain, to pierce this invisible hymen.

Our strength, kind gents, may lie in withholding our precious fluids. Just as women seem to relish the psychological power that comes from the fact that our bony, cylindrical wee-wees don't always deliver them to Shangri-La, we boyfolk may get a lot of mileage from letting the ladies know that their furry li'l snappin' turtles don't always close the deal for *us*, either.

So next time, guys, don't fake it. Instead, pull it out, shrug your shoulders, and blame it all on her. Please, God, blame it all on her....

TAKING PICTURES of my PEEN

A LONG TIME AGO IN A LAND FAR AWAY, there existed a crude Polaroid of me naked as the day I was bee-eye-bucky-bo born, sitting up on my knees atop a hotel bed with a full-fledged boner and a gleaming smile. I had encouraged my wife of the time to shoot the photo because I was highly aroused and figured that my penis would look gigantic.

It did not. It looked like a shriveled pink egg roll. I was mortified. I destroyed the photo and swore that I would never allow anyone to see photographic evidence of my apparently pathetic manhood ever again. I also became highly cynical and insulting of male porn stars—I depicted them as tacky and stupid, which may have been accurate, but it was merely a thin cover for my obvious jealousy of men with big schlongs who weren't afraid of showing them.

About ten years later, I hooked up with a young girl who was uniquely fixated on my cock. It was a new experience for me, and I found it intensely arousing. She just couldn't shut up about how big and beautiful it was—and she'd been around the Maypole quite a few dozen times, so she knew about cocks—and one night as I was standing outside the Fred Meyer taking a piss, she snapped a candid picture of me in all my urinating limpitude. I was happily surprised with the results. I was totally soft, and the thing was twice as long as my thumb.

It would be nearly another decade before I became involved with another Portland Cock Queen. She, too, had quite a few Frequent Flyer Miles, and she, too, became obsessively enamored of my peen. As I lay in her bed one night, hard as a rhino, she grabbed her Polaroid camera, the flashbulb popped, and she gleefully presented me with a picture of a man with a REALLY BIG HARD DICK. She'd giddily show the photo to friends around town as if she was a hunter and my cock was some 12-point buck she'd tagged.

My entire attitude about pornography changed the second I realized that I had what it takes to be a porn star. I scanned the picture and uploaded it to a private folder on my website, e-mailing the link to several of my booty calls, ex-girlfriends, and potential future fuckdolls who'd flirted with me online.

THE DAY I LEARNED TO USE A CELL-PHONE CAMERA TO MAKE PORNOGRAPHY OF MYSELF

Encouraged by the response, I purchased a cell phone with a built-in camera and dutifully began snapping photos of my fully erect bone-diggety-bone.

There is nothing artful about these photos. They are total meat shots focused right in on my long, fat, hard, shiny, and very, *very* pink penis. I blessedly don't have one of those ugly brown or purple *schvanstukers*.

You can see my face in two of the photos—the original Polaroid and one other shot—but my face isn't important here. This is self-made pornography, and my cock is the porn star here. In some pics, it truly is the White Whale. It even looks huge in the little desktop icons.

I stopped at 19 pictures, because I knew that if I kept on going, I'd fall into the Porn Hole and do nothing else for the rest of my life. It's been over two years since I've added a new picture to the folder, yet I comfort myself knowing that my big hard cock is out there in cyberspace, waiting for interested women to ogle it. I never foist these photos on anyone. I don't forward the links to a girl until after there have already been some explicit sexual overtures on her part. But great God in heaven, do I get HOT just thinking about their reactions…

"Scary big penis…hung like a black man…Are you kidding me? WOW!…Your cock is a weapon…Big, gorgeous cock…" And from the woman in France, a simple, savory "BIG." Many girls wrote elaborate fantasies of what they'd like to do with it. Some of them said it's a bit intimidating and they're not used to one of that stature.

Another one said she and her girlfriend were squealing like schoolgirls as they looked at it together. And the best reactions were the cases of initial disbelief, insisting I must have enhanced myself using Photoshop or a body double. Such comments were incredibly exciting to me.

Even more thrilling is when one of them contacts me out of the blue a year or two later, begging to see more. The idea that they're sitting there dreaming about my cock to the point where they suddenly appear out of the dark, purring and meowing at me? HUGE turn-on for me. And the thought of them touching themselves to orgasm while thinking of the pornography I've made for them? I could touch myself right now just thinking about it.

Let's just say I enjoy being on the receiving end of cock worship. I have no objection to a woman viewing me strictly as a sex object. I don't care whether she likes—or even *notices*—my "mind," my "spirit," or my "self." Does she like my *cock*? Many times, that's all that matters.

Friends have griped about my dirty little habit, insisting that such a level of narcissism makes me gay. Hey, I may be gay, but it's for completely different reasons. You never hear anyone calling a woman who photographs herself nude and shows the pictures to men a "dyke," do you? Isn't it sort of sexist to insist that only women are expected to be vain? I can't *believe* how misogynistic and homophobic some of you people are.

In a fair, sane, just, free, EQUAL world, heterosexual men will be permitted to act like narcissists without having to face ostracism and derision. My experience has led me to conclude that there are only two types of people: exhibitionists and those who have something to hide. Allow me to project my warped, isolated experience onto the entire world and conclude that the only people who don't want to be porn stars are those who fear they wouldn't be very good at it.

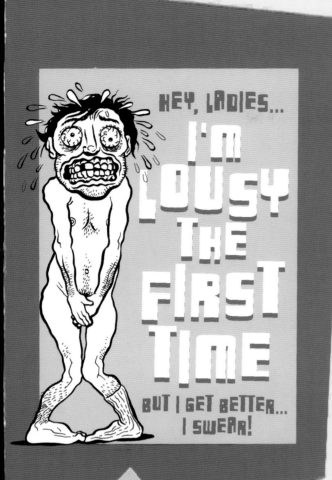

HEY, LADIES...

I'm LOUSY THE FIRST TIME

BUT I GET BETTER... I SWEAR!

MY LIFELONG STRUGGLES WITH PERFORMANCE ANXIETY DURING THE FIRST INTIMATE ENCOUNTER WITH A WOMAN

Dearest Dollface...Schnookums...Honeybucket...Doodlebug... Sweet Tits...Cockbiscuit...oh, my inestimable Li'l Love Lozenge and Spicy Hot Pocket of Steamingly Unrestrained Carnality, I have to warn you:

You'll be very, very disappointed the first time you have sex with me. It gets rapidly better once we're over that hump, but the inaugural experience will have you thinking I'm some sort of gay impotent retard. If my performance was a Broadway play, I'd close on Opening Night every time.

Yes, I realize you find me attractive, and yeah, I know you've seen the un-retouched photos of my stunning cock, and indeed, you've stood close enough to me that you're aware of my irresistibly sweet musk, so you're not sure what the problem could possibly be, but there's a problem. Trust me, Cunt Dumplin'—there's ALWAYS a problem with me the first time.

You'll try to assure me that it's *always* awkward the first time, but I'll be way *beyond* awkward. I'll be like some sort of sexual polio victim. We'll make out for a half-hour, and you'll be hot and wet enough to boil pasta, but then you'll wonder why I'm totally limp when my clothes fall softly to the floor. Somewhere down there, hiding amid the pubic hair, will be my penis. It's not only flaccid—it's *retracted.* A frightened snail. You'll suck on it and yank on it and spend all night trying to coax the groundhog out of its burrow, but to no avail. During more first encounters than I care to recall, I've spent from dusk 'til dawn completely mortified, lolling around naked without ever achieving an erection.

In the event that I actually get it up, I will not last long, at least not inside you. One time I actually shot my load in my *underwear* while only half-erect. Try explaining *that* to a new paramour. And the poor girls, bless their hearts, attribute my jackrabbit-styled preemie spurting to the idea that I'm overwhelmed with *lust* for them. HA! They fail to distinguish between sexual excitement and solipsistic terror. In my lifetime, there have been—what?— about 50 of these "first nights." And all told, I've probably lasted less than an HOUR inside these women—CUMULATIVELY.

It's not you—it's me. I know that sounds like I'm feeding you a line, but it's true—it's never been about you, always me. It's *never* you, no matter how objectively disgusting you are. If I'm in the right mood, I can get it up for dead rodents. My immobilizing first-time performance anxiety has nothing to do with how attractive I find you—I'm equally nervous with hot, curvy bombshells and lifeboat-sized pig-monsters. Whether I'm wildly attracted to you or repulsed by your very existence...whether I find you brilliant and charming or if I rank you lower than a trilobite on the evolutionary hierarchy...no matter. First Timer's Disease is always there with me.

I am not a relaxed person. I don't feel comfortable being in the same *room* with most people, much less naked with them. I surround myself with an invisible force field, and the first time someone enters my radar, all sorts of alarms start flashing. Not only am I cripplingly aware of the other person's presence—it's as if I'm performing for the Super Bowl Halftime Show.

You can diagnose me as having a fear of vaginas and the women who surround them...or of being plagued with doubts regarding my adequacy...but those fears would stick around beyond the first encounter or two, wouldn't they?

Up in my brain, I understand that performance anxiety is counterproductive. The more I fret about a good performance, the worse I perform—and the less I care, the better I am. It's a scientific law. My mind realizes this, but my meaty loins are still clueless.

I have absolute confidence in my size and technique—it's just a matter of getting over that invisible "hump." Once I get in the groove, I'm a fuckhammer. Women whose steel-trap snatches have grappled with hundreds of cocks tell me—without my asking—that I'm the best fuck on the planet. We'll do it on the couch, and I'll ram you so hard the couch moves from one end of the room to the other and back before you plead with me to stop because you can't handle any more orgasms without fainting. These are actual quotes from satisfied customers:

Jesus Christ! Do you know any way to fuck but HARD?

Sometimes it's so intense, I just want to get out of the way.

You need to pull out, or you're going to kill me.

But these are all women who, for whatever reason, decided to sleep with me a *second* time. They agreed to hold my hand, engage in pointless chitchat, and wait until I felt comfortable enough to pole-vault over the "hump."

So just pretend I'm Little Bo Peep the first time, because the Big Bad Wolf is waiting right around the corner.

For as long as I could remember, I had wanted to lose my virginity. I had yearned to cast aside my innocence since I'd been born. It would have been no skin off my ass, as they say.

Losing one's virginity is Mother Nature's Bar Mitzvah—the day you truly become a man. It is when God reaches down and unlocks the gates to the Garden of Eden, allowing you to walk around inside and hit on chicks. It is when your flower bulb opens its petals and disgorges its pollen into the moist tropical air. You clasp your lady's soft, milky hand and run naked under the Tahitian sun. Pineapples and coconuts fall all around your heads as you rut like wild boars. Multicolored parrots sing a sweet song as they sail swiftly through the summery sky.

It is the new rising of the sun. The first blossom of springtime. The urge to create. The muddying of clear blue water, perhaps, yet it is also the whitewater-rapids rush of positive change and spiritual rebirth. You become a little less innocent, yet in some weird way, a little bit taller and thus closer to God. It's a lot like the life-altering ascension from Webelo to full-blown Boy Scout.

It would have been nice if poppin' my cherry had been a positive, life-affirming experience like that, but it wasn't.

Fuck, I would have been glad if it had been *traumatic*. If it couldn't have been pure and beautiful, I would at least have liked for it to have been cheap and ugly. I wouldn't have minded if it murdered my innocence and severely damaged my chances of ever getting into heaven. It might have been sorta cool if it left me crumpled in a ball at the bottom of a hot shower, crying for mercy and never, *ever* feeling clean again. I think it would have been sexy if it plunged me deep into drugs, violence, devil worship, and the occasional bout of prank-calling. I'd have nothing to complain about if the vagina was a black portal sucking me straight down into a life of dissolute debauchery and spitting me out the other end like a piece of street trash blown away by the dirty, dirty wind.

I wanted it to be *special*—either really good or very bad—rather than what it turned out to be, which was quick and ordinary.

It wasn't until I lost my virginity that I realized you don't really cross over an invisible bridge and become something new—only an *ex*-virgin. The English language has no true antonym for the word "virgin." Some would suggest "whore" or "slut," but such terms don't really apply to everyone who is no longer a virgin. The website thesaurus.com lists "defiled, sullied, [and] abused" as antonyms for "virgin," yet such harsh epithets seem like a blanket indictment of anyone who's ever had sex. Other searches yielded words such as "unchaste," "unpure," and—my favorite—"seasoned." I like the ring of that. It's as if you have some sort of spice on you for the rest of your life.

But alas, my experiences were not nearly so spicy. They had all the flavor of Saltine crackers with all the salt removed.

I'm honestly not sure when I technically lost my virginity. I guess it all hinges on how you define a "virgin." If it means any act of vaginal penetration, even if your balls are tiny grape nuts that haven't dropped yet, then I was 12. If it means post-pube full-bore ejaculation mode—known in street lingo as "P.-P.F.-B.E.M."—then I was 18.

At the age of a dozen years on a warm Easter Sunday, me and a male partner-in-delinquence trotted the neighborhood slut—also 12—down near some sewer pipes in the woods behind our tract houses. This girl was a drug addict and race-mixer long before such things were considered as cool as they are now. I was mesmerized by the snotlike secretions glistening between her legs and the fluffy tufts of black hair right above the glistening slit. I stuck my little pink pre-pube bone-bone inside her and just lied there motionless for about a minute before confusedly dismounting. I had no pubes, no cum, no orgasm, and no grasp of concepts such as thrusting.

It would be six more years of agonizing teenaged celibacy—and 10,000 jerkoff sessions—before I'd get the chance to poke another vagina. I had just graduated from high school and was enjoying Senior Week down at the Jersey shore. Sunburned and drunk, I bedded a girl who was blonde, rosy-cheeked, and rather plump. What was her name? Kathy? Katey? Peggy? Porky? Something with a 'y' at the end, I'm sure of it. I lasted all of 12 seconds. I quickly got dressed, my cock still slimy and smelly as it rested inside my tightey-whiteys, and rushed down to the boardwalk to indulge in the superior pleasure of carnival rides.

LOSING MY VIRGINITY

was not the glorious, sun-dappled experience i had hoped it would be

Though I've had dozens of partners and thousands of sexual experiences since then—ranging from the terrifying to the sublime—I can't help but feel as if life has cheated me by giving such a crucial rite of passage all the excitement of a trip to the DMV. Thanks, life—you can *really* be an asshole sometimes.

the auto-suck

As a teen in the pro-PCP/serial-killing/child-porn 1970s, I used to visit a dirty little smut store down near the Philly Greyhound station. In the back pages of HUSTLER's well-thumbed back issues, past the pictorials of Gloria Bunker look-alikes tugging on their saggy beef-jerky labia, there were ads for a delightful device called the "Auto-Suck." Its charm was simple: Plug one end into your car's cigarette lighter, fasten the other end on your dingus, step on the gas, and hit the highway for automotive blowjob fun!

I remember the apparatus resembling a black-vinyl pocket pussy powered by a spring device that robotically gnawed on your knob. Across from the dusty bookstore where they'd let me peruse the nudie mags without buying anything, there was an even filthier store that sold "marital aids" and other Rube Goldberg-style sexual appliances, but you had to be 21 and I'd lost my fake ID.

Turns out the store was part of a chain owned by the Doc Johnson sex-toy empire, makers of

...it sucks

the selfsame Auto-Suck. Their old downtown Philly "marital aids" shop recently closed, but Doc Johnson continues to make the Auto-Suck, and I'll be hornswoggled if I didn't comb most of southeastern Pennsylvania 'til I found a sex emporium that still sells it.

The 2005 Auto-Suck model looks nothing like I remember it from HUSTLER. Fully assembled, it's the size of a hair dryer and about as loud. The handle is fashioned of black plastic that's so cheap, it's probably imitation plastic. And the attachment is a clear rubber-gel cannoli with a pinkish "mouth" on one end. It resembles a freshwater hydra or a baby albino eel—SEXY!

And who exactly is supposed to be able to fit their penis inside the rubber cannoli? Pygmy children? Fully limp and shriveled-up on a misty October night as I barreled down a dark road in my unbearably sensuous minivan, I was unable to insert even the tip of my flaccid maleness inside the Auto-Suck's eel mouth as it loudly whirred.

Most girls never have the finesse and seasoning to suck on you hard enough, but the Auto-Suck is even worse. Its low-grade vacuum suction is so understated, it feels like a whisper. If you enjoy the sensation of a three-mile-an-hour wind softly rustling over your penis, this may be your perfect companion for those long, lonely nights, trucker.

But it did nothing for me. After finally managing to squeeze my still-soft prick tip through the creepy synthetic portal, I tried jiggling the machine around to try and stir some interest in my loins, but the rubber attachment kept falling off.

My sexual frustration turned to rage, then quickly to laughter, and then settled into a profound pity for the sad sacks who depend on such contraptions. How long has it been since any man who thinks this feels like a blowjob has actually HAD a blowjob?

The Original World Famous Auto-Suck
Manufactured by Doc Johnson Enterprises
Mine cost $26.99, but I've seen them priced anywhere from $19.95 to $39.99

when
the tender, erotic side of corporal punishment
SPANKING isn't WRONG

Spanking is such a ubiquitous part of popular sexual fantasy and roleplaying that we often lose sight of how truly sick and depraved it is.

While commonly viewed as harmlessly naughty fun, it invariably features unpleasant themes such as sexual violence, incest, and psychological power games—none of which seem so frickin' benign when you put down the studded wooden paddle and think about it.

In my long life with its checkered sexual history, I've fantasized about myriad sordid scenarios while touching myself, but I've only proposed a grand total of TWO fantasy scenarios to actual partners. One of them involves me chopping wood while topless and wearing tight jeans. The other one involves spanking. I refer to as the "Oatmeal Fantasy," and it runs something like this:

I'm a greasy, sweaty, middle-aged widower whose wife recently died in a fiery car crash, leaving behind a daughter so young that she still eats from a high chair. I work all day in a used-car lot, clad in a cheap leisure suit and reeking of cheaper after-shave lotion. Back when the wife was still alive, I used to spend afternoons at the horse track, but my needy young daughter now makes such trifling pleasures impossible.

After a long, fruitless day at the car lot, I rush home in time to make a quick dinner for my daughter—a pipin'-hot bowl of nutritious oatmeal. I place the bowl on her high-chair tray, but she immediately throws the entire bowl onto the floor, creating a huge mess.

I lose my temper. The dead wife, the demeaning job, the bratty child— it's all too much.

Trembling with anger, I take the child roughly in hand, place her over my knee, and deliver a spirited spanking. After a minute of uninterrupted slaps to her posterior, I'm able to peek through my rage and see that she's crying.

This little, innocent girl is crying. The only thing still pure in my world is crying. I instantly stop spanking her and become remorse-stricken. I begin crying, too...and apologizing.

I pull down her panties and begin kissing her everywhere that I hurt her. It's all a blur of tears and red buttocks and kisses and apologies....

TECHNICALLY, THAT'S WHERE THE FANTASY ENDS. I've never gotten any further with it. By that point, the girl who's listening to it is either masturbating furiously or calling me a pervert.

My fantasy never involves actual children, only a willing adult partner who's pretending she's my child. Still, it involves elements of violence, guilt, and incest. I must also note that I've never actually enacted the oatmeal fantasy, although I haven't lost hope.

But does the fantasy itself constitute some sort of sexual thought crime? Is it possible for spanking to ever be anything BUT wrong? And is it ever truly possible to have fun without feeling that you're doing something wrong?

Since almost all living adults were spanked at least once as children, it is the disturbing sexualization of childhood punishment which threatens to taint all grown-up "spank play" with pedophilic overtones.

But what about non-playful spanking? What about whacking your kid's ass for disciplinary purposes? Is that unavoidably sexual, too? James Dobson, a pro-spanking Christian psychologist and author of *The Strong-Willed Child*, seems hell-bent on spanking the will out of any child who expresses even a wisp of it:

A spanking is to be reserved for use in response to willful defiance, whenever it occurs....When a youngster tries this kind of stiff-necked rebellion, you had

better take it out of him, and pain is a marvelous purifier...the spanking should be of sufficient magnitude to cause the child to cry genuinely....Real crying usually lasts two minutes or less but may continue for five. After that point, the child is merely complaining....I would require him to stop the protest crying, usually by offering him a little more of whatever caused the original tears.

Well, then! The Marquis has spoken! One odd consistency I've noted while poring over the vast literature of spanking is that sexual overtones tend to INCREASE in directly inverse proportion to how feverishly the speaker DENIES that spanking is sexual. While websites devoted to bawdy, ribald, consensual spanky-poo between adults seem annoyingly unerotic—making me want to punch the participants rather than spank them, because their entire aesthetic platform is *très* **WRONG**—passages such as Dobson's fairly drip with real, raw, menacing S&M psychology.

Debate continues to rage, mostly between fundamentalist Christians and the rest of the world, as to whether corporal punishment is ever beneficial for children. In almost any conceivable case, I feel that spanking a child is **WRONG.** The evidence overwhelmingly suggests it is detrimental to a child's emotional development and that it is far preferable to confine them in the sort of plastic crates designed for transporting small animals.

THE ELECTRONIC SEA OF FILTH called the Internet hosts thousands of spank-obsessed sites, blogs, and discussion boards. Much of it gets rougher than a simple cheek-reddening slap or two. We're promised Russian teens confined in woodsheds, bent over the knees of dusty old borscht-smelling men-swine who whip them with birch sticks until the stripes on their bloody buttocks resemble grill marks on a hibachi hamburger. This is, of course, **WRONG**—only because I find it aesthetically ugly, not because I waste any teardrops about the Russian teens or their precious little "emotions."

For similar reasons of purely aesthetic (rather than moral) distaste, I object to "female supremacist" depictions of smirking dominatrixes mercilessly ass-flaying slump-shouldered, ball-gagged males. To each their own, I suppose—masochism is never wrong if I'm never the masochist. I don't get aroused through being hurt or insulted. In fact—I swear to Christ—I once achieved an immediate, towering erection after a woman conceded that I was *right* about something. But hey, if strong-woman/weak-man is your scene, and if that's what you need to muster a bone-bone, by all means allow thy Goddess to slap thine ass silly, Puffball. But the idea of some muscle-marbled cuntflap trying to dominate me feels plumb **WRONG**. My mama was the last woman who's ever gonna spank THIS ass.

SITTING AT THE FOOT OF THE BED, I firmly place her small frame over my knees. Her naked ass is up in the air, aping the rear-entry receptive sexual position of most female mammals. I roughly pull her panties down to her knees and deliver a series of stinging slaps to her rump with my bony left hand.

It doesn't really matter *what* she's done wrong, and I honestly couldn't tell you. But we both concede that she's a human being, so she's always doing things that are wrong. And the only way to make things right again is for her to lay over my knee and accept her punishment.

With each slap comes a soft little whimper—so girlish in tone, so different from her assertive, intelligent, everyday self. SMACK! *Unnnh.* SMACK! *Ohhh.* She arches her spine with each slap. Once or twice she acts as if I smacked a little too hard. Within a minute, her ass is rosy-red. Though she may be in pain, it doesn't seem as if she's suffering. I stick a finger between her legs, and she's sopping-wet.

We both reach quick, satisfying climaxes. Over the next few hours our interactions are sweeter, easier, and more playful. Things are now in order again. A natural sort of balance has been achieved. Our dark little power game was some form of exorcism. **NOTHING WRONG** about that.

Who's to say where "healthy sex play" ends and incest-themed violence begins?

Only one person: ME.

There is only one universal moral principle, only one Golden Rule that is engraved on all our hearts: Things are only wrong when other people do them.

FIVE SECONDS OF BLISS

What pitiful creatures we are. Mother Nature places us on a giant stage and then laughs at us. She gives us bodies that often betray us in nasty, nasty ways. We are animals, but we are also something more than animals, and it's this "something more" part which always ruins sex. You never hear of impotence or premature ejaculation in the animal kingdom.

Performance anxiety, the perpetual affliction of the sexually insecure, works a cruel, wicked inversion upon its victims. With mathematical precision, *concern* for one's performance works in inverse proportion to the *actual* performance that results. Self-consciousness, for all its good intentions, works against you. Sex is always worse when you're worried about making it better.

I've been a limp noodle and a quick shooter. I've been horrifyingly impotent, my cock a wrinkled baby turtle afraid to poke out its head. There was a time...recently...when, naked in bed with a girl, I came all over my leg even before I had a chance to stick it in her and then had to try and clean up the mess before she noticed.

What's worse than not being able to get it up or cumming too quick? How about cumming too quick before you've even fully gotten it up? That happened to me about a year ago at a cathouse just south of Reno.

I'm a white guy who doesn't feel guilty for being white, but I also enjoy having sexual relations with Negro women. I had Jungle Fever back before it was cool, byaaaatch! Black women smell like honey, candle wax, and a hint of chicken soup, and that's all right with this here peckerwood. I like black chicks and they like me, so ya betta check yo'self before ya wreck yo'self.

I met my first Negress sex toy around the time I graduated from college. She was a dark-skinned, big-booty sista from Allentown, Pennsylvania, who was so shy she used to undress underneath the sheets, but once you got her goin'...rrrrooWW! A real jungle cat. But come to think of it, I once had trouble getting it up with *her* after I'd blown off half my face snorting coke.

I have severe problems with the idea of paying for sex, but when someone offers you a free hooker, what do you expect me to do? Early last summer, a friend gave me and my entire travelin' crew a free pass at a Reno whorehouse. As I exited the blinding desert heat and entered the dark, icy-cold, high-tech bordello, the hookers lined up obediently in the front parlor. Wearing my gray Rebel soldier hat, I went straight for a 19-year-old dark-chocolate chick from Watts with a flat nose, big bubble butt, and greasy Jheri-curl ringlets. She said her name was "Bamboo."

She escorted me to a service desk and told the madame that I had chosen her for a private "party." We retired to her small room. She lit some incense, turned on the black light, and flicked on her boombox to some buttery soul music. As we lounged around her bed sipping soft drinks, she told me she only started hooking in Nevada two weeks ago in order to get money while her man languished in L.A. County Jail. I'm sort of surprised I didn't get a huge erection merely from listening to her hard-luck story. I wanted to reenact the Watts riots between her legs.

But I was thinking too much, and that's always a bad thing. I started feeling that dreadfully familiar stony/frozen apprehension. I explained to her that I felt weird because there's something... *artificial* about having sex with a hooker. My whole head trip revolves around knowing that the chick likes me and is willing to lose control with me, but a hooker...well, she's like a paid temp worker.

"Oh, but I'm *attracted* to you," she said, with no way of me knowing whether or not it was a lie. "I think I might even have an orgasm with you."

Nice try, honey, but I wasn't getting hard. She wiped off my pee-pee, still pathetically shriveled, with an antiseptic wet nap before trying to apply a condom. My pathetic wormy half-hard bone-bone nuzzled itself halfway up the condom before shooting a meager milky spurt *right as she was putting on the rubber*. Blop...blop...blop...a few quick, anxious squirts into the rubber, and I was down for the count.

I didn't even get a chance to stick it in her. It was an awfully weak orgasm, and I felt like an absolute idiot for blowing my load so quickly. When I told her I'd already cum, she laughed out loud. "I'm da bomb!" she shouted, thinking that her pulsating sexual heat was what forced me to shoot my gunk so quickly. No, she had almost nothing to do with it. It's all about me and my sick mind.

LATER THAT NIGHT, I was talking in the whorehouse parking lot with another black girl, a huge, stomping, Chaka Khan-styled hippo with a happy-happy, fun-fun personality. Wearing a swirly, leopard-patterned sarong thing, she said she was a fan of my writing. Then, out of nowhere, she offered to blow me for free in the front seat of her car, which was parked right in front of the cathouse entrance. Wow...*two* Negro girls in the *same night* in this almost-all-white state! Go, white boy, go! I became excited by the idea of getting caught and possibly lynched by an angry, torch-bearing mob of Nevadans. I unzipped my jeans and pulled it out.

I had no problem getting really hard. I was proud of my white-boy cock as her big bushy hair bobbed up and down on my lap. She stopped to compliment my dick and then kept sucking. She was good at it, too. I arched my back and shot a mighty load down her throat. Over a late-night breakfast at a greasy restaurant, she later told me she used to hook for a living and is now a madame at a whorehouse across town. A few days later she met up again with me in L.A. and we got a hotel room for the night. No problems at all. We both got off. The next day she drove me down the coast to San Diego, and white boy got a severe sunburn.

So why no performance anxiety in this case? Because this girl wasn't getting paid to do it...she *wanted* to do it. And that made all the difference to me. I enjoy being worshipped by women. If that makes me an asshole, well, just hope this asshole doesn't shit in your mouth.

MY ONE AND ONLY EXPERIENCE WITH A PROSTITUTE

154

WIENER DOG HEARTACHE

I am not proud to be telling you this, my friends. If there is any pride, any dignity here at all, it is that I'm mildly proud that I'm *not* so proud that I'd try to hide something this embarrassing from you. I'm sure some of you will be shocked by my story. Others will congratulate me for my candor. Others will call me a fool. Some will pat me on the back. Yet more will challenge me to a fistfight. These are the risks that one takes in life, risks that grow yet riskier when one reveals that as a teen, one tried to make one's brother's dachshund blow him.

How sad is it that I couldn't even get a *dog* to have sex with me?

And it was a *male* dachshund, which doesn't help things at all.

All I can say in my defense is that I was horny. My teen boner was a Fist of Life reaching toward the sun. From morn 'til midnight, I'd be walking around bumping into things with that vicious, snarling narwhal tusk, that divining-rod perpetual early teen soupbone, that never-say-die desperate sort of erection you never really seem to achieve again after those initial glory years.

'Twas an age when I feared that literal death would occur if I didn't masturbate at least once daily. Teen vagina still seemed unattainable, and at this point in the mid-'70s at a Catholic school, real live intercourse was rare. So I jerked off a lot. Jerked off to models in ads from *Philadelphia* magazine. I still remember one blonde with combed-back wet hair and a wet T-shirt...I came on her tits a few times....don't remember what the ad was for, though. Jerked off to the sound of Donna Summer's grunts on "Love to Love You, Baby" as it floated from the transistor radio in our bathroom. Within six months of discovering I was able to have an orgasm, I had yanked enough wads out of my dick to fill a gallon bucket of ice cream.

It was the fall of 1975, my freshman year in high school. Jethro Tull and Blue Öyster Cult ruled the airwaves. Sideburns and free sex and lava lamps and party vans and serial killers dotted the landscape. My favorite album was Queen's A *Night at the Opera*. The kids' favorite TV show at my school was *Welcome Back, Kotter*.

I was a lonely, socially crippled virgin, spilling cherry Coke all over myself at the mall during an excruciatingly awkward date with a real live girl, a girl I never even got to kiss, much less fuck with that eterna-boner of mine.

A social idiot, I lived almost exclusively within my own head. One lonely Friday night a few months prior to my sexual encounter with the dachshund, I'd gulped a half-dozen Vivarin diet tablets, danced my pale, jiggly ass off to The Sylvers' "Boogie Fever" blaring from my bedroom radio, then puked my guts out and swore to myself that I'd never do drugs again.

My brother lived in a sprawling, grimy apartment in a dead industrial patch near where south Philadelphia becomes Delaware. Oil refineries and bikers. Blueberry soda and swamplands. He had just finished with his first marriage and lived alone.

Well, not truly alone. Not if you count his dachshund.

For some reason which escapes me now as I'm older and fairly punch-drunk from life's indignities, my brother was gone that night and I was alone at his apartment at the edge of railroad tracks and biker bars and refinery towers.

Again...I was not *truly* alone. Not when one considers the dog. I forget his name. A stout little dachshund, the so-called "wiener dog." Before the evening was over, this particular dachshund would become a wiener dog in another, sicker sense of the word.

My brother kept a stack of porno magazines in his bathroom...1970s porn, the best there ever was, the best there ever will be...unabashed porn featuring women who had never been told that what they were doing wasn't dirty, who labored under the belief that they were doing something wrong and would someday be punished for it. Women revealing the sort of charms that men tend to forget when women are clothed. Lurid, garish bubble-gum twats hiding amid tall, thick bushes. Natural boobs hanging every which way. A girl who tied her flappy cuntlips into pretzel shapes. Ads for battery-powered devices ensured to save your marriage. Pornography seemed magical and golden back then rather than boring and clinical.

I can't remember which publication I settled on for inspiration that night...*Hustler* or *Oui* or *Gent* or *Swank* or *Cherry,* but something of that caliber and aroma. But it only took a few ganders at those curvaceous, Gerald Ford-era shrimp cocktails before I was veiny-hard and ready for action.

It was then that I looked down at the dog. The poor, innocent, unsuspecting dog.

After all, a warm, wet tongue is a warm, wet tongue whether it's on a dog or a human or a Martian, right? I mean, it's not like I was going to touch *his* dick, right? Are you with me? No?

My pants around my ankles, my cock hard as leather nunchucks, I waddled into my brother's bedroom, jumped on the bed, and summoned the dog to join me. He eagerly jumped up, unaware of the innocence-shattering abuse which would befall him. Somewhat firmly, I guided his head toward my rigid teencock.

I'm not really sure what I expected the poor beast to do. Did I really think he'd start sucking away like some seasoned sea hag?

Thankfully, the dachshund, unlike me, was born with the sort of instincts that told him this was *not* a good idea.

The dog sniffed my cock, took a few licks, and then jumped off the bed. He seemed bored, and perhaps disgusted, at the prospect of sex with me. I felt like a total asshole. I felt worthless. I didn't have a girlfriend...I didn't have *any* friends...and now I was forced to endure the unique shame that occurs when a presumedly inferior animal rejects your offer of some quickie bestial sex.

Nevertheless, I was still feeling randy. I pumped my still-hard wang until I shot my teen-goo all over my brother's bedroom. I don't even remember if I cleaned it up. If I didn't, well, I'm sorry, Johnny. And I'm sorry for the sexual abuse to which I subjected your pet dachshund, a creature that I'm sure has passed into another dimension by now...a pure, celestial dimension where things such as sexual abuse between different species don't exist...a safe, fluffy place where dachshunds aren't forced to suck cock and where lonely teenaged boys don't wind up feeling sexually rejected by canines.

MY EMBARRASSING TALE OF **SEXUAL REJECTION** AT THE HANDS OF A **MALE DACHSHUND**

PLEASURING MYSELF IN PRISON

Illustrations by The Pizz

An explanatory note to any correctional officials who may read this as it's sent from the facility: My story is pure fantasy. I have never touched my genitals while incarcerated, not even to wash them. I realize that masturbation is an obstacle to legitimate penological objectives. This essay is cautionary and speculative, a rumination of what might go through the sick mind of someone who practices sexual self-abuse in the slammer.

O lucky you, able to masturbate in the full privacy accorded you by the United States Constitution. I, however, have been stripped of such rights. I am currently serving a 36-month prison sentence for beating the fuck out of my ex-girlfriend. And yes, she deserved it. Pretty much everyone who knows her agrees. Yet, the absence of her mouth and vagina has created a void in my life... a void filled by my left hand. I spend much of my time—too much, perhaps—beating off behind bars. Pullin' my pud in the penitentiary.

This is a minimum-security facility with no cells. I inhabit a giant stuffy dormitory, sleeping on one of 110 army-barracks-styled bunks. The other 109 guys are semi-retarded reactionaries who, when they aren't rhapsodizing about slamming crank and robbing convenience stores, read the Bible and show me pictures of their kids. Everyone is doing short time and therefore doesn't wish to jeopardize their release date with trifles such as knife fights or anal rape. And they couldn't get away with it if they tried, for the open environment means there's an absolute lack of privacy. A huge window even runs along the shower room, making it possible for cons to see your sudsy freckled body from the recreation yard.

There isn't much pleasure here—sometimes you'll get a nice sunset, other times a slice of dinner cake with delightful coconut frosting. Masturbation picks up most of the slack. Yet the Department of Corrections frowns upon self-pleasure. I've been told that if a guard catches you wanking, you could forfeit part of your time off for good behavior. You might also be transferred to a bunk closer to the guard's office and kept under 24-hour surveillance to prevent unauthorized blanket motions. One inmate informed me that masturbation can result in a disciplinary infraction for "Sexual Indecency in the First Degree." I didn't want to ask a guard to confirm this, lest his suspicion be aroused that I've been getting suspiciously aroused.

IN THIS P.C. *REICHSTAG* KNOWN AS OREGON, the "Beaver State," pornography is forbidden. Under the rules of what constitutes prohibited mail is a subheading titled "Sexually Explicit Material," defined as printed matter *"which by its nature or content poses a threat or is detrimental to the security, good order, or discipline of the facility, inmate rehabilitation, or facilitates criminal activity, including...portrayal of actual or simulated acts or behaviors between human beings including, but not limited to, intercourse, sodomy, fellatio, cunnilingus or masturbation...bestiality...excretory functions...personal photographs...in which the subject is nude, displays male or female genitalia, pubic areas, buttocks, female breasts or any portion thereof below the top of the areola."*

Nary an areola. That's sad. Yet porn is so scarce here, I can almost get hard reading what's *verboten*. I've been down for ten months without pussy. I have only dim memories of what a vagina looks like. Counting my good-time credits, it's only, oh, somewhere in the general vicinity of another 577 days, 12 hours, six minutes, and 17 seconds until I'm released and can prowl for bona fide coochie again.

About three weeks after my arrest—long enough ago now for an adult couple to have conceived and given birth to a child— I was in a module of the county jail on the same floor as the dorm which held all the female detainees. At one point, deputies corralled about eight or ten of the ladies into a holding room directly outside our tank and clearly visible through the glass. What waste cases these girls were, far more dissolute than any of the guys. The black chicks on crack, fat and wobbly. The white chicks on meth, bouncing and pirouetting and running fingers through greasy, gravity-defying skank hair. The weighty African dumplin' who smiled and blew me a kiss. The pimply white girl with a big, dirty grin. Another mannish honky broad with sunken eyes who nodded at me and turned away shyly. None of them was remotely attractive even by the most generous standards, and yet I remember thinking that I'd fuck every one of them—or all ten of them in a massive, stinking, pigflesh orgy. All of them, that is, except the five-foot-tall, 300-pound Mexican lass with a bird nose, spiky-dykey hair, and her arm in a cast. Now I'm so desperate, I'd even ball her, too.

Spend enough time in the clink, and just about anything with a pair of bumps on its chest and a slit between its legs starts to look good.

Like the naked art-model hag on pages 141 and 146 in *The Big Book of Watercolor,* a volume which so far contains the only photographic representation of the raw female form I've been able to snag in the pokey. I mean, this girl has a face that looks like sheep intestines, but...yes, those are nipples, and...yeah, that's a bush—and yep, I get so throbbing and vein-laden over her, it's embarrassing.

I presume some inmates flog the dolphin while on the toilet, but that's a smidge too unsanitary for my tastes. I don't need being reminded of tuberculosis, hepatitis, and HIV while struggling to construct a workable fantasy. So my wondrous self-love sessions take place on my bunk while everyone's asleep, during the quiet darkness between "Lights Out!" at 11 p.m. and when they throw the lights on again at 5:30 a.m. Thank Christ for my sleep disorder, or I'd never get to wack off. There's nothing more frustrating than waiting in line for breakfast with a relentless morning hard-on and the knowledge that you have to wait another day to pop your load. So almost nightly, as if by unconscious design, I'll awake from a dead sleep and some sordid nightmare to the realization that now is the time to take matters into my own hand. This is when I digitally treat myself to a cornucopia of sex-positive delights. I'll remove my earplugs to better hear the warning sounds: the ghostly whine of an old coffee machine and a constant symphony of snores punctuated by lone bursts of flatulence in the night.

I'll then look to the left...and to the right...to ensure that the felons who occupy bunks within arm's reach on either side of me are asleep. An optimum situation is when both of them have their backs turned, but it isn't necessary. At times I don't even care if they see—I'll just close my eyes and get my nut. I hold up the blanket slightly with my right hand, creating an artificial plateau, a masturbatory mesa which probably appears as if a shoebox is resting on my crotch. But as ridiculous as that probably looks, at least interlopers are unable to observe the frantic tugging motions performed by my nimble, dextrous left hand.

Okay, the Mexican to this side is snoring. To the right, the blond country bumpkin has his back to me. Looks like it's safe. Yank, yank, yank—oh, fuck, the Mexican is stirring. Such interruptions mean I can go from hard to limp five or six times before I finally blow my stack. And I frequently have to keep switching fantasies.

My jerkoff imagery is treasonously Un-American: no movie stars, no California beaches with coconut lotion, nothing typically *Baywatch*—there has to be something dirty and flawed about the girl(s).

All right...I'm eating pepperoni pizza and talking on the phone with my mother while a bucktoothed Domino's delivery chick blows me.

Nah.

Three extremely fat broads laze about on beanbag chairs as I impregnate them one by one. After they fall asleep, I go through their purses and leave town with their money.

It ain't workin'.

I am a Mayan priest poised atop a terraced pyramid as jungle maidens stand in line to ceremonially worship my prong.

Too multicultural.

I playfully hide an amputee girl's prosthetic legs from her.

No, I've used that one too many times.

I am a State Trooper working a desolate stretch of Montana highway, and I chance upon an unconscious female car-crash victim pinned to the driver's seat.

I can't *believe* that one leaves me soft.

Well, the hillbilly triplets usually do the trick...

I dream of a shack in eastern Kentucky with a dirt floor and a wood-burning stove. And in that shack live triplet gals—Tammy Jo, Dolly Jo, and Reba Mae Dixie Jo—who are of legal age, of course, but not so old that you wouldn't ask them for I.D. at the liquor store. Each girl is missing the same front tooth, and they are only distinguishable from one another by the fact that each of them has dyed their bouffants a different color. Otherwise, even *they* would be unable to tell themselves apart. And since their parents were recently blown to bits in a tragic coal-mining accident, the girls need a man to chop wood and hunt possum. And I'm that man, arriving mysteriously by train one day at the little station over the hill and through the holler.

Great, my reverie's interrupted by the rubbery clacking of flip-flops on the cold linoleum as an overweight child molester shuffles to the bathroom for a middle-of-the-night piss.

Fine. All right, a slim redhead sits on a ratty sofa in a single-wide trailer, wearing nothing but panties and bunny-rabbit slippers. She's watching soap operas on a small black-and-white TV. She has braces on her teeth and is eating corn on the cob, stray pieces of which can't help but get stuck in those braces.

Oh, yeah—I love chicks with dental problems—*eat* that corn, baby—*let* that butter drip down onto your chin, you dysgenic mobile-home slut...

My toes curl in tension. I'm breathing rapidly, hoping not to shake the bunk too much. And then comes the release, the milky splatter. I shoot it all over my belly and let it dry there, a million criminally inclined tadpoles perishing on my stomach like microscopic beached whales.

The whole experience is often workmanlike and mundane, like taking a shit—just squeezing out the toxins. It's rarely what I'd call transcendent. But at least I forget about the razor wire for a while. I forget about all the ugly bodies I see in the shower. I forget about having to scrub and mop latrines. I forget about the IRS and the Victims' Restitution Fund. I forget about all the chances I had to leave this state before I got into trouble. I forget about the way men smell. Specifically, I forget about the smell of the fat farmboy's farts. More than anything, I temporarily forget that I'm in prison jerking off. If I truly pondered the fact that I'm a convicted felon with his dick in his hand, I'd probably never be able to achieve an erection again. What could be more pathetic than beating my meat in the Big House?

Reading about it.

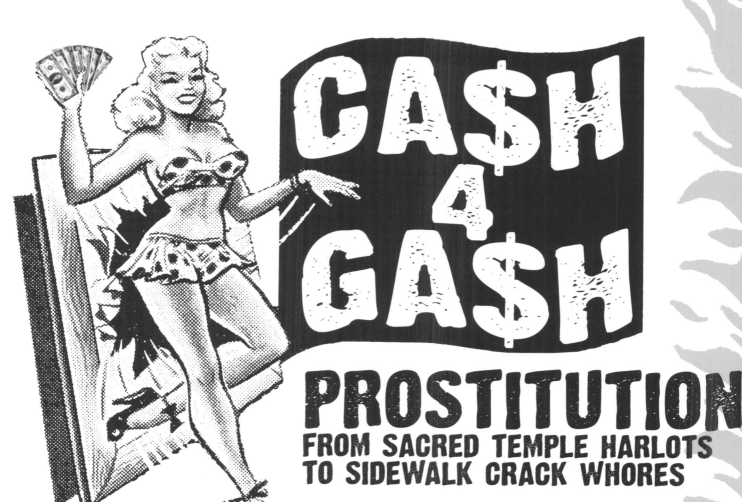

CA$H 4 GA$H

PROSTITUTION
FROM SACRED TEMPLE HARLOTS TO SIDEWALK CRACK WHORES

In our old, battered, ugly English language, the word "prostitute" signifies someone who sells both their body and their soul. To study the array of unsavory nuances we've slathered onto the word is to comprehend how our sick, impotent, double-standard-flaunting society views the lowly prostitute. The avid researcher also gleans a golden understanding about how our culture—yours and mine—views men, women, and sex. As always, it doesn't look good for the guys.

To *be* a prostitute means only to exchange sex for pay; but to *prostitute oneself* is a heavy bummer head trip involving spiritual suicide and a permanent fall from grace. To "prostitute" or "whore" oneself is to degrade, abuse, cheapen, and devalue oneself. It is to befoul, blaspheme, and contaminate thyself.

It matters not, my tastefully seasoned little butternut squash, whether you prefer to call her a harlot, strumpet, tart, trollop, concubine, courtesan, hooker, whore, or streetwalker. Each of these words, at least

Prostitutes are a necessity. Without them, men would attack respectable women in the streets.
—*Napoleon Bonaparte*

Whores...are dreadful, shabby, stinking, loathsome, and syphilitic, as daily experience unfortunately demonstrates....Women were made either to be wives or prostitutes.
—*Martin Luther*

Grown men should not be having sex with prostitutes unless they are married to them.
—*Jerry Falwell*

The profession of a prostitute is the only career in which the maximum income is paid to the newest apprentice.
—*William Booth*

For when she is sleepy, she cannot sleep; she must stay awake to caress some scurfy man, a huge, ugly buffalo, who has a mouth that smells like turds, and will bang away at all of her.
—*Pietro Aretino*

The prostitute is not, as feminists claim, the victim of men but

rather their conqueror, an outlaw who controls the sexual channel between nature and culture.
—*Camille Paglia*

Prostitutes are accused even by feminists of selling their bodies; but prostitutes don't sell their bodies, they rent their bodies. Housewives sell their bodies when they get married.
—*Florynce R. Kennedy*

QUOTES
ABOUT WHORES

when referring to the female members of our species who have historically comprised the majority of prostitutes, implies a woman who trades gash for cash. (Male prostitutes trade cock for cash...or ass for cash...or a cock-and-ass combo platter...but I'm not interested in male prostitutes here. I'm trying to make a point about prostitution and gender, and all those sweaty male jockers and hairless boy twinks just get in the way.)

Ancient Sanskrit is said to contain over 300 nouns synonymous with "prostitute," including *khumbhadasi*, which, roughly translated, means "sperm spittoon." To the Greeks, those wanton girls who would in more enlightened modern times be christened "sex workers" were known as "chopper-ups," "she-wolves," "kneading-troughs," "ground-thumpers," and "bedroom articles." The word "pornography" is derived from a Greek phrase meaning "the writings of a prostitute." The word "prostitute" itself has its roots in a Latin word meaning "to expose in public for sale." Among other colorful sobriquets such as "night moths" and "grave-watchers," the ancient Romans commonly referred to prostitutes as *meretrices*, meaning simply "girls who earn."

In many ancient societies, prostitution was inextricably tied to the sacred rather than the profane. It was an indelible feature of religious rituals worldwide, yet world religions ultimately turned against it and deemed it a bad, bad, naughty, evil, stinky thing.

It is my task to trace the historical trajectory of prostitution, from sacred to profane. Then, failing any substantial insight regarding the historical lesson, I will offer my personal opinions about why prostitution is forever doomed to be something less than kosher.

ALTHOUGH COMMONLY KNOWN AS "THE WORLD'S OLDEST PROFESSION," there is evidence that prostitution may be older than civilization itself. Throughout the zoological kingdom, girl animals consistently give up the pussy to the strongest male who controls the most turf. Biologists refer to this giving-up-of-the-pussy as "presenting behavior," in which the female

primate deliberately presents her genitalia to the male, signifying she's ready to GET IT ON. Animal behaviorists have observed female Bonobo chimpanzees exhibiting presenting behavior to males in exchange for food and protection. Male chimps will reportedly act much more tolerant of females stealing their food after having had sex with them. Similar behavior has been observed in female penguins—they're more likely to throw some pooty to whichever boy penguin can provide them with rocks for nest-building.

A LONG TIME AGO IN LANDS FAR AWAY, before the Christians and Jews and Muslims came on the scene to ruin everything, men would flock to the local temple and fuck the shit out of "sacred prostitutes." For a small honorarium, a man could simultaneously enter the harlot's vagina and the realm of the divine.

The Sumerians, who were around, like, a million years ago, employed "temple maidens" who accepted donations in exchange for a roll in the hay and a promise that she'd talk to God about providing abundant crops that year.

Sacred prostitution was likewise practiced in ancient Babylon, which required all Babylonian gals to turn a trick at the Temple of Mylitta (a.k.a. Ishtar) at least once in their lives. Women were not allowed to leave the temple until a male had tossed a coin (of any value) in her lap, uttered the phrase, "I summon you in the name of the goddess Mylitta," and took her hand as they proceeded to knock boots until he achieved the proper release.

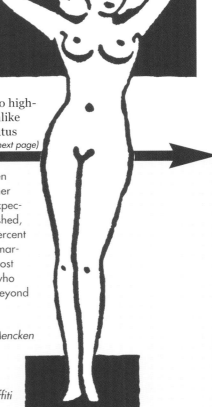

For thousands of years (until India finally outlawed the practice in 1988), Hindu *devadasis* (slaves of god) sucked and fucked their way onto higher karmic planes. Unlike the implicitly low status

(continued on next page)

Prostitution is not an idea. It is the mouth, the vagina, the rectum, penetrated usually by a penis, sometimes hands, sometimes objects, by one man and then another and then another and then another and then another. That's what it is.

—Andrea Dworkin

The simple fact that a girl can earn far more than in any other way, and earn it far more easily, by lying on her back and spreading her legs, is evident to every female.

—Hilary Evans

The truth is that prostitution is one of the most attractive of the occupations practically open to the sort of women who engage in it, and that the prostitute commonly likes her work, and would not exchange places with a shopgirl or a waitress for anything in the world....So long as the average prostitute is able to make a good living, she is quite content with her lot, and disposed to contrast it egotistically with the slavery of her virtuous sisters. If

she complains of it, then you may be sure that her success is below her expectations....It was established, indeed, that fully 80 percent [of former prostitutes] married, and that they almost always got husbands who would have been far beyond their reach had they remained virtuous.

—H. L. Mencken

Girls don't pay—guys pay!

—American Graffiti

Roman Emperor Tiberius liked his prostitutes so young that he was known to force *unweaned babies* to peform fellatio on him. In 84 A.D., such excesses eventually led Emperor Domitian to outlaw prostitution for any child under seven.

Ancient Tibetans believed that tobacco grew only if sprinkled with the blood of menstruating prostitutes.

Circa 100 A.D., Teutonic tribes punished Women of Ill

Repute by smothering them in feces.

The lawyer for an ancient Greek *hetaera* (high-class courtesan) named Phryne, sensing he was losing his client's trial for "impiety" charges, abruptly tore off Phryne's clothes, revealing her legendary breasts to an awestruck courtroom. The judges acquitted her.

In 1501, Pope Alexander VI allegedly threw an orgy featuring 50 nude prostitutes who

delighted onlookers by crawling between rows of lit candles while picking up chestnuts with their vaginas.

WEIRD
TALES OF WHOREDOM
THROUGH THE AGES

of modern-day stretched-out/dried-up crack whores, the *devadasis* were highly esteemed members of Hindu culture who occupied lofty tiers in a highly terraced class system. These temple prostitutes, and all their dirty positions which came in handy during fivesomes and sixsomes, are amply depicted in ancient Hindu sculpture and paintings.

Hebrew biblical prophets, those fucking killjoys, were among the first to publicly start hammering on the idea that low-cost sex with temple harlots was something less than holy. Then along came the Greeks and Romans to further secularize the prostitute and make her a strictly commercial being—a sex *worker* rather than a sex goddess. From then until now, in every culture under the sun, prostitution has been increasingly associated with the defiled rather than the divine. The fall from grace is now complete—civilization has plummeted all the way from bronzed temple goddesses to scabby, shit-stained crack whores who'll float you a beej for three bucks. We've sunk from royal courtesans of exquisite beauty and refinement to truck-stop lizards who'll let you stick fingers up their ass in exchange for a few hearty tugs on your meth pipe.

CONSERVATIVE CHRISTIANS AND RADICAL LEFT-WING FEMINISTS will tell you that prostitution is innately rotten—that it can't be rehabilitated or reformed and must be destroyed. They use different pathways to arrive at this dire conclusion—one side blames the Devil, while the other blames men, a.k.a. the Devil. But if prostitution is getting worse, they argue, it is only because bad things tend to get worse if left untreated.

Both groups will bark statistics at you about how the screaming bulk of prostitutes were forcibly diddled as children and shoved into the sex biz while barely in their teens. Some will claim that most prostitutes get raped at least once during their career...others allege they'll get raped multiple times a week on average...and some will claim that the very act of being prostituted is rooted in misogyny, rape fantasy, and smelly, beer-bellied, male domination.

Prostitution's opponents will enthusiastically trot out exhaustive and graphic tales of brutality for anyone willing to listen. They'll tell the stories about prostitutes being punished in olden days by having their noses cut off, cauterized with red-hot irons, dunked underwater while trapped in cages, and paraded through town on an animal cart while citizens jeered and threw doody at them. They'll talk of a global sex-slave market which pitilessly shleps around nearly one million starved, battered, bruised, and shrieking victims yearly, most of whom are ultimately burned with cigarettes while being forced to fellate a row of unwashed, HIV-positive guerrilla soldiers. They'll talk about herpes sores and pelvic dislocations and kicks to the face and forced hormone injections and multiple suicide attempts.

They'll dredge up Jack the Ripper's disemboweled strumpets and the dozens of soggy victims left strewn by the Green River Killer, who claimed he murdered whores because nobody cared enough about them to wonder who killed them. They'll talk about women stuffed into trunks and child prostitutes who drink detergent to kill gonorrhea and boy eunuchs in India who have priests create surgical vaginas for them in order to pimp them out for high-risk sex.

They'll tell you—and they wouldn't be lying—that there are as many hookers in the Philippines as there are factory workers and that Thailand has more whorehouses than schools. And they can't help but remind you that the Nazis were known to patronize sex workers of both genders.

PROSTITUTION'S DEFENDERS—basically a bunch of fat chicks in San Francisco—may concede that all

French whores in the 1700s could escape legal punishment by joining the opera.

In 1991, three men in Tennessee were arrested after soliciting a female police officer who was wearing a hat with the word POLICE on it.

Taiwanese police claimed in 2001 that they were attempting to aid an 82-year-old prostitute nicknamed "Grandma" in her journey to find a way out of the business.

Italian police arrested a 24-year-old prostitute in 2001 and charged her with "unfair competition" because her prices were too low.

In 2002, an Israeli man requested an escort for his hotel room and suffered a heart attack when his daughter arrived.

During 2005, a Richmond, VA, transsexual hooker named Monica Renee Champion had simultaneous arrest warrants as a male (south side of town) and a female (north side).

In March, 2006, after failing to receive payment from a john, a British prostitute bit his penis so hard that he required surgery.

such abuses exist, but they'd pin it on entirely different reasons than the ho-haters. To the whore apologists, prostitution truly is something sanctified, if not outright sanctimonious—it's just that a patriarchal pig society and its horrid suppression of Mystical Female Sex Juices has defamed and debauched and stigmatized this once-holy ritual. They argue that hooking should be legalized and that "sex workers" should receive governmental protection, support, and possibly even medals. They form

honest-to-God organizations such as The International Committee for Prostitutes' Rights and the Sex Workers Outreach Project. They hold events such as the Sex Worker Festival and the World Whores Conference. There's even a "Whore College" which holds seminars in "Boundary Roleplaying" and "Advanced Courses in Sexuality and Erotic Touch." These brassy wimmin teach workshops and build support groups and foster networking and offer alternative health resources. They strive for empowerment, dignity, respect, autonomy, and universal human rights, especially for sex workers. In short, they're possibly even more full of shit than their opponents. They're *prostitarded*.

NATURALLY, I DISAGREE WITH BOTH SIDES. I laugh at the sphincter-gripped censor-moralists because I don't view the flesh trade as a Bottomless Pit of Human Evil, nor is it worse than any other prohibited vice. I definitely don't see it as morally preferable to marriage, at least where the male is concerned. In marriage or any relationship, what incalculable fees does a man pay in terms of annoyance and grief? At times, marriage seems to differ from prostitution only in that it is far more complicated and miserable. But you wind up paying either way. This, sadly, is what it means to be a man.

I'll concede to the sex-positive sex workers, as well as all their proud sisters lurking in the mystical menstrual night, that hooking would probably be safer for all involved if it were legalized. But the idea of gash-for-cash ever being uplifting or noble or—gasp—sacred? Never in a million years.

It has nothing to do with misogyny or the idea that whoring degrades the whore.

Nope. It degrades the john. It degrades the overworked husband. It even degrades the male chimp who trades chimp food for chimp pussy. Underlying the whole stinking biz, there's an implication that when a male and female have sex, this somehow doesn't constitute an equal exchange of services. At the end of his orgasm, the man still owes. The female is expected to give sex; the man is expected to give sex plus something of *value*, because his sex is deemed worthless. The idea of men as lousy, inept, unsatisfying lovers is what underlies prostitution and taints the entire equation. It's unfair to men, and it hurts our feelings.

The same unjust principle applies from the temples out to the jungles. Females are expected to provide sex, and that's it. Males are expected to provide sex PLUS DURABLE GOODS. That's a fundamental inequality between the sexes. If you don't see that point, well, you must be a sexist. You don't find female chimps and penguins offering their boyfriends food or building materials or protection—nah, the girl-beasties just give up the gash and call it even.

What are you saying, Miss Ho? My sex isn't as good as your sex? Sex with me is worth less than sex with you? My pink ding-a-ling pales in comparison to your purple snapper? Fuck you—I'd rather jack off than give you a penny. Prostitution is a dirty business insulting to all males, from the dirty billionaire who buys a trophy wife all the way down to the dirty penguins and the dirty little chimps.

Rise up, boy monkeys, and revolt!

Linda Lovelace became the world's first porn star for her role in Deep Throat *(1972). She is not nearly as well-known for her earlier roles in circa-1969 film loops variously called* Dogarama, Dog Fucker, *and* Dog One. *Lovelace later claimed she was coerced, although in the footage I've seen, she seemed more amorous than the dog.*

In 1994, British wedding photographer Derek Jeffrey, 59, was found guilty of having sex with "Ronnie," a neighbor's bull terrier. Newlyweds and friends who'd gathered together to watch a wedding video Jeffrey filmed for them notified police after viewing hardcore dog-sex footage Jeffrey had forgotten to erase from the tape.

The infamous Led Zeppelin "Shark Episode" involved a red snapper rather than a shark. In July, 1969, at a Seattle hotel, band manager Richard Cole inserted the fish's head into a redheaded teen groupie's vagina while drummer John Bonham watched. Cole claimed "that girl must have cum 20 times." Zep groupies were also allegedly involved in separate incidents involving two octopi and a Great Dane.

If there's any act more flagrantly repellent to mainstream sensibilities than bestiality, I'd like to know what it is, 'cause I'll write an article about it. OK, maybe child sexual slavery or racially motivated crimes involving chains and pickup trucks, but that's about it. Aside from those banner-grabbing atrocities, bestiality pretty much takes the cake, eats it, and belches.

I will state for the record that I am an animal-lover to a degree which at its worst borders on a mental disorder and which at the very least is sort of gay and embarrassing. However, I am not sexually attracted to any beasts of the field, nor any domestic ones for that matter. I have never engaged in penetrative sex, whether aggressive or receptive, with any creature that could not at least vocalize the names of its parents. There was the incident when, at age 14 and comically horny, I unsuccessfully tried to get my brother's dachshund to blow me, but I've written about that elsewhere, so I think I've atoned for that. But apart from that regrettable blot on my otherwise spotless record of high ethics and clean living, I have never touched an animal's genitals nor had mine touched by one, unless it was accidentally.

So although I cannot empathize with the sort of person variously referred to as a **zoophile**, a **bestialist**, or a **zoosexual** in terms of carnal aesthetics and personal predilections, I will, like the bold, fact-digging, swashbuckling journalist that I am, attempt to understand the arguments both in support of and against the lifestyle, especially as it relates to me, because in the end, it all comes back to me.

MAN HAS BEEN FUCKING ANIMALS since before the dawning of history, and it seems that as soon as he was able to chisel two words onto stone, he started writing about fucking animals. A 10,000-year-old Italian cave painting clearly shows a man with a full-on raging bone-bone standing behind a doe. Swedish wood carvings from three millennia ago depict various tawdry acts between humans and other mammals. The ancients speak of "sacred goa[t] servicing Egyptian women while Egyptian men did the "Crocodile Rock"; of monkeys and baboons trained to show a good time to Middle Eastern clie[nt] and of beasties ranging from giraffes to cheetahs copulating with unwilling women and children in th[e] Roman circuses.

The Old Testament, however, mandates the death penalty to any man who "lies with a beast," and th[e] tradition continued into the Middle Ages, where mo[st] beast-fuckers, female "witches," and all of their hap[less] animal victims were burned at the stake for bumpin' uglies. In modern America, nearly all state[s] have laws which forbid human-animal sexual contact either outright or at least in cases involving cruelty.

Extending from ancient times into the present, the reasoning behind such prohibitions rested on the id[ea] that humans were inherently superior to animals an[d] thereby soiled themselves by engaging in sexual congress wi[th] lower life forms. It wasn't until v[ery] recently that anyone gave a fuck about the animals' feelings in all thi[s]. Pornographic depictions of bestia[lity] have come a long way from the cave paintings. With little effort, the enquiring mind is able to vie[w] "Hot Zoo Porn" where naked human nymphs suck off pachy-derms and dry-hump four-foot horse cocks. And my recent visit to p[orn] bestiality message board BeastForum.com (it was fo[r] research purposes only, although I shouldn't have to tell you that) revealed they'd hosted 598 unique vis[i]tors within the past 20 minutes.

BESTIALITY'S OPPONENTS will unfurl an impressively nauseating toilet-paper-roll-length list of man's sexual inhumanity to nonhumans: Nazi so[l]diers forcing Jewish women to hump dogs; chicken-fuckers who rip off the fowl's head at the moment o[f] orgasm because it enhances their climax when the bird's anus spasms; horse testicles ripped from their owners; and little baby monkeys who will never know the rewards of a meaningful, nurturing physic[al] relationship with a member of their own species.

Whenever they mention a case of human-animal

MAN'S BES[T]
FRIENDS

xual contact, it is within the implicit framework that e human *assaulted* the animal. They will tell you, d I quote, "Not all cases of animal sexual abuse ll involve physical injury to the animal, but all sexual olestation of an animal by a human is abuse." They ason that an animal can in no way *consent* to a xual act in the full, overwrought, dripping-with-aning manner in which humans typically proach it.

At every turn, they will compare zoophilia to dophilia. They will also eagerly exploit deep-rooted reotypes of zoophiles, depicting them as disturbed, ly, maladjusted sexual predators engaging in natural acts which threaten to crumble our civiliza-n to the point where there will be no more cell ones, convenience stores, or homespun spaghetti nners at the local firehouse. And above all else, ey will appeal to the innate distaste shared by an imated 95–99% of our population which declares at human-animal sex play is intensely *icky*.

HE DEFENDERS OF BESTIAL ELATIONS point out that the merican Psychiatric Association no nger classifies sheep-shtuppers as nerently disturbed. They'll guide u to recent studies suggesting at zoophilia is a legitimate sexual entation just like homosexuality. ey assert that not only aren't mans degraded by interactions any sort with animals, they might actually learn a ng or two from them about honor and nobility. They'll argue that consent is evident in the ihuahua who humps your leg...or the mare who esn't kick out your teeth when you vaginally pene-te her...or the German Shepherd who doesn't rip t your throat when you assay a handjob on him. d they'll remind you, even though you really uld prefer not to think about these things, that they ways make sure the animal has an orgasm, too. They'll argue that it's no worse to vaginally pene-te a cow than to corral her into a slaughterhouse, rder her, and eat her. In fact, they'd argue it's far tter, at least as far as the cow is concerned, to eat r *out* rather than to eat her.

"We seek to reach a state close to full equality with our animals," states one zoophile's manifesto. Starry-eyed sanctimony abounds in the literature of bestialist self-justification. Animal-human sex, despite its ran-cid odor, somehow conjures an Edenic wonderland that radiates spiritual purity to these folks.

Zoophiles are eager to distinguish themselves from abusive "zoosadists" who either actively torture ani-mals or show little interest in committing to long-term, mutually supportive relationships with them. They also caution against sex with smaller animals, since the heightened plug-to-socket ratio increases the possibility of pain for the creature. But if some lonely biochemist wants to go snorkeling and fuck a blue whale, will the animal really be any worse for wear and tear?

FOR KENNETH PINYAN, SIZE DEFINITELY MATTERED. He made worldwide headlines in 2005 after being horse-fucked to death at a farm in rural Enumclaw, WA. The act was videotaped, as were hundreds of hours of similar acts that transpired before police raided the farm in the wake of Pinyan's colon-popping ass-murder. But according to a brief snippet of videotape which I had the soul-scalding displeasure to witness, at least the horse, an Arabian stallion named "Bullseye," shot a hearty dollop of cum and presumably achieved some measure of physical satisfaction from the tragedy. Officials noted that the horse was not harmed during the incident. They were also befuddled about exactly how to proceed legally, because at the time Washington had no anti-bestiality laws.

Because I am a being who possesses a rare form of highly advanced morality, I cast no judgments on Kenneth Pinyan nor anyone who has non-coercive, non-abusive sex with other vertebrates. Although I personally deem such acts to be both highly repug-nant and extremely funny, I have ascended through enough tiers on the karmic plane that I withhold making juvenile condemnations of people I've never met and whose actions did not affect me. I will, however, say this: My 20-pound dog has an extremely tight pussy, but if anyone made the slightest sexual advance toward her, I would slay them as if they were a beast of the field.

In 1991, Englishman Alan Cooper, 38, was charged with "committing a lewd, obscene, and disgusting act on the 12-foot dolphin called Freddie as they frolicked for 20 minutes off the harbor mouth at Amble, Northumberland." Cooper allegedly jacked off the cetacean within plain view of a boat-load of horrified onlookers. He also heads a dolphin-rights organization called "Cetacean Defence UK."

In 1999, Maine resident Frank Buble, 71, attacked and severely beat his son Philip, 44, with a crowbar while the latter was showering. Philip had come "out" as a "zoophile" and depicted the attack as a "bias crime." Frank Buble was sentenced to eight years in prison. Philip unsuccessfully attempted to have his dog, named "Lady," attend the trial, even writing a letter boasting both his signature and Lady's paw print.

In 1991, a British tabloid called The Sunday Sport *reported that a married couple in Turkey divorced after the sexually dissatisfied wife discovered her husband having inti-mate relations with a mule on their farm named "Muffin." The husband, 55-year-old Husamettin Karacek, kept the mule and commented, "It's beautiful and does not nag."*

hE LEGAL, ETHICAL, AND PERSONAL ISSUES uRROUNDING BESTIALITY

Women Stink

the distinguished gentleman's guide to Vaginal Odor

When I'm not huffing spray paint from paper bags or negotiating peace in the Middle East, my thoughts often turn to women. And how they smell. And then I don't feel like eating dinner.

In my day I've smelled fishy cunts, skunky cunts, yeasty cunts, pissy cunts, sweaty cunts...too many cunts, probably. I've inhaled membrane-withering lungfuls of toxic twatfumes from vaginas that looked like rats dipped in Vaseline. I've borne witness to a stomach-pumping surfeit of swollen, bloody, scabby, mucus-spewing snatches. Too much oozing, malodorous cunt caviar, too many hairy hornet's nests of chickstink. And yet the self-appointed voices of reason assure me that "once you get past the smell, you've got it licked." How the fuck do you get past the smell?

Although the estrus-crazed arbiters of politeness would have us believe it's only a misogynistic myth, the existence of rank-smelling females seems to be a staple of all cultures' folklore. Most world religions—and rightly so—espouse some notion of women as "unclean." When angered, a foul-mouthed Chinaman is likely to yelp, "Tiu nia ma chow hai!" ("Fuck your mom's smelly cunt!") at anyone within earshot of his egg-roll stand. Reflecting the same sort of vaginal ageism, the French have observed, "Les conasses des femmes âgeé avez une odeur mauvaise." ("Old ladies' cunts stink.")

And though it's not considered polite conversation amid mixed company, most of us are aware of the distasteful folkloric scuttlebutt surrounding repugnant vaginal aromas. As a child, you most likely heard the cruel schoolyard jibes about "hot tuna." You've probably also groaned at the juvenile proverb which states that there are two things in this world that smell like fish, one of them being fish. You may have even encountered the puerile poem about the "seven wise men" who created the vagina: "Fifth was a fisherman, nasty as hell/He threw in a fish and gave it a smell." Even pudendal pseudonyms such as "the bearded oyster" hint at some level of olfactory displeasure.

From what I've been told, some men actually *like* the smell. Some men enjoy watching their corn-kerneled shit swirl down the toilet, too. Some men drink beer and get prostatitis. Some men like having their scrotal sacs nailed to sheetrock—what's your point?

Ooh, that smell. The first thing you're likely to sniff in this wretched life is a deep, sobbing lungful of your mother's afterbirth, yet that memory is usually too distant and traumatic to ever have a hope of salvaging. But after one passes the Age of Reason, you aren't likely to forget the full-frontal face-slap of a rancid pussy, even after extensive psychotherapy. And, if you're like me, your first indelible whiff of it came via an older friend's manual digit in the eternal tradition of "Hey, man, smell my finger."

The older friend's name was Mike. His girlfriend's name was Carol. We all wore denim pants and denim jackets. Under a cold nighttime sky set aglow by an aggressively white moon, I sat atop a small concrete wall, waiting for Mike to kiss Carol goodnight. It took a while. He must have rounded first base and headed for third, for after bidding Carol adieu, Mike proudly marched over to me and held his fuck-you finger an inch under my nostrils. Carol's after-stench was a heady, almost inebriating snoutful of urine and sea bass. It was there, on that concrete wall, where I concluded that a woman's vagina could be a place wherein considerable evil dwelt.

Not many years later, in a gesture of male nobility, I was able to proffer my own finger to a younger friend, encouraging him to nasally sample the mucosal femalia from a calamari-redolent Italian girl I'd diddled an hour or so earlier. I had indulged in "heavy petting" with the hairy-lipped wop lass outside her parents' house in West Philly, dropped her off, and drove deep out into the suburbs—and then took a quick dip in my friend's backyard pool—before I let him smell my finger. And yet it stank. Strongly.

But perhaps the worst pussy I ever had the displeasure of smelling was attached to an alarmingly overweight woman of Dutch extraction with whom I shacked up during a period when my self-esteem was dangerously low. Once you got past the rolls and rolls of stretch-marked hog fat, there sat her bedraggled pussy, crowned with a sparse reddish thorn bush. Her cunt looked like a fat slice of ham swimming in white gravy. Her crotch was a boiling fumarole of noxious emissions, a stinking puddle of snatch-slop. Her discharges were colored a sickly silver, with the gloppy consistency of herring sauce. The smells which emerged from between her bloated, floppy legs ranged from rotted onion to burnt crab to odors which were so fetid, I must force myself to stop thinking of them lest I scream.

But I don't want anyone to get the wrong idea.

It's not my intent to have you believe that ALL women stink.

As a cabdriver in Philadelphia, I was once flagged down by a hulking Negress, a dead ringer for Shirley *"What's Happening!!"* Hemphill, who instructed me to drive her to a nearby mental hospital. She then pulled a sopping-wet 20-dollar bill from her African vagina and handed it to me. Upon later inspection, I was relieved to discover that the soaking greenback offered absolutely no smell. It was as if the woman's vaginal flora had actually *laundered* the item of currency.

But, being the civic-minded feller I am, I started to worry about the other pussies—the less fortunate ones. What about them? Why do some gals stink, while others remain odor-free—free, indeed, to laugh, to love, to cuddle? Why do roses bloom in some fields, while manure festers in others? And finally, what in the name of the Homo Jesus Clown are the biological mechanisms behind vaginal malodor?

I'm a man who sees a problem with America—a man who wants to fix it.

My purpose isn't to offend the few clean-smelling women out there with the crude suggestion that EVERY vagina in the U.S.A. gushes with foul, gelatinous, swordfishlike discharges.

Only far too many of them.

I do feel, way down in my nose hairs, that this country faces a Cunt Crisis: Our streets are littered with good girls—honest girls—walking around smelling like sturgeon. Vaginal odor ruins romance and fosters much distrust between the sexes. Few things dampen an amorous male's affection more than the rank, odiferous stench of a woman who has degraded herself through poor hygienic practices. Many bright, well-meaning gals have seen their love lives dashed to pieces because their genitals' pungency suggested unhealthful habits and debauchery. Can these women be saved? Sure, but first they must be scrubbed. And disinfected. And schooled in methods of blunting their natural offensiveness.

To understand vaginal odor, you must first understand the vagina itself. The foul truth is that every woman carries a potential stink-bomb between her legs. There's a whole science-fair project going on in there, a wild kingdom of aquatic bacilli. Mucus oozes from her pussy walls like dirty water being squeezed from a floor mop. Her normal secretions serve to cleanse those sugar walls in the same way that saliva keeps one's mouth from becoming overrun with the slime of half-chewed pretzels. In a normal, happy vagina, certain "good guy" microorganisms such as the lactobacillus bacteria create an acidic pH balance which thwarts the growth of more sinister, odor-causing germs.

Candida albicans, more commonly known as vaginal yeast fungus, exists in small enclaves in every vagina. But once a pussy's pH balance is thrown off-kilter, yeast fungi may explode in number, causing thick, whitish, cottage-cheesy discharges to flow from its labia like thousands of miniature twat biscuits. An effulgent yeast infection, which is estimated to strike an estimated three of every four women at least once in their lifetimes, may smell vaguely like baking bread. When the yeast cells begin to die en masse, they release a molecular compound known as mercaptan, which has been targeted as the culprit behind the smells of dead flesh, poo-poo, and skunks. Mercaptan has also been described as smelling somewhat like burnt rubber. So if it looks like cottage cheese and smells like a car crash, yeast may be to blame.

The legendary fish odor may be a symptom of a syndrome known as bacterial vaginosis (BV), especially if the smell seems particularly tart directly following intercourse. As with yeast infections, BV is a sign that renegade germs have overthrown the vagina's normal bacterial balance. Microscopic critters such as *Gardnerella vaginalis*, thought to exist in a quarter to half of all human vaginas, come to prominence at the expense of more benign bacteria. These bad-boy microorganisms secrete waste materials which irritate the vaginal walls and yield discharges redolent of rotting trout heads. BV can be tamed through prescription topical gels.

Another root cause of feminine fishiness is a single-celled monster known as trichomonas (or "trich"), a highly contagious protozoan which infests upwards of 3,000,000 cunts yearly via toilet seats, towels, and sexual intercourse. One medical text describes trich as giving rise to a "yellow/green frothy discharge," accompanied by burning, itching, and the unmistakable air of seafood. As with BV, a little dab of the proper antimicrobial paste will slay the dreaded trich dragon and prevent one's pussy from being eaten alive.

Of course, foul-smelling vaginal discharges could be the symptom of something far worse. Chlamydia (or "the clam") is often accompanied by vulvular rankness, as is gonorrhea. In a worst-case scenario, your lover's malodorous muff may signal the immunodeficiency breakdown associated with AIDS. *Mangia!*

Then again, it could be something as simple as the fact that the slob doesn't wash very often. Some pasty amalgam of piss, feces, crotch sweat, fermented sperm, and menstrual waste could be causing the erection-killing fumes which destroy true intimacy. A little time spent Sudsing the Beaver couldn't hurt much.

Which brings us to the douche. Our society does not lack for douchebags. A woman can select from an array of vulva-scalding products—sprays, creams, pastes, potions, lotions, jellies, foams, and herbal extracts—all designed to blunt this, the cruelest of nature's jokes.

But as usual, nature has the last laugh. Not only does douching effect a genocide of undesirable bacteria, it also eliminates the good-guy germs which maintain a proper floral balance within the vagina, hastening yet more intra-pussy bacterial anarchy.

The pinnacle of douche ignorance is exemplified in a 1941 magazine ad for liquid Lysol. Over the course of four illustrated panels, the ad describes "how a young wife overcame the 'one neglect' that wrecks so many marriages." After another blowout argument with her hubby, the ad's feminine protagonist sobbingly visits her sister-in-law, who delicately explains, "You may be the guilty one, Sis. Often a husband's love grows cold just because a wife is careless—or ignorant—about feminine hygiene. It's one neglect few husbands can forgive." She then describes how her own doctor prescribed liquid Lysol "for intimate personal care." Taking her sister-in-law's earnest advice, the distraught heroine squirts an indeterminate amount of liquid Lysol up her gash and returns home, where her husband is waiting with flowers. The ad further states that "thousands of modern women rely on 'Lysol' for feminine hygiene." It is impossible to determine how many cunts were cauterized by such wrongheaded medical advice.

So tell her to put away the oven cleaners. Instead, gently suggest that she funnel a truckload of yogurt with live cultures into her gaping black hole. A fresh infusion of yogurt's acidophilus bacteria will replenish the healthful critters she'll need to fight the good fight against embarrassing odors. Vinegar or cranberry-juice douches are also recommended as sane ways to restore order between her legs. For yeast infections, a garlic clove wrapped in cheesecloth and rammed up the snatch may do the trick, as may a tampon dipped in a three-percent solution of potassium sorbate. And as mentioned earlier, doctor-prescribed topical creams can prevent the invisible fishies from ever swimming upstream again.

Do flies buzz around your paramour's pudenda? Does her quim make you queasy? If you're nauseated with all the flounder-flavored cunt-puke which flows from her hole like so much Girl Lava, it's your sacred obligation as a boyfriend to tell her about it. Should couples engage in frank discussions about pussy smell? Indeed. You can't blame a gal for smelling that way—only for not taking care of it. As her lover, you bear equal responsibility in assuring that she presents a clean, fresh-faced pussy to the world. It's your duty to offer gentle persuasion and softly muttered suggestions. And if the bitch doesn't clean up her act, you should abandon her like the mud-wallowing sow she is.

Perhaps Rome fell not because it threw so many orgies, but because it didn't clean up afterward. A woman's gash should be her highest treasure, but all too often it is her shame. A lady's cum-bucket can either be a gleaming tabernacle or a reeking Port-A-Potty. It all comes down to proper bacterial management. Sex should be something wonderful, not a test of one's endurance in germ warfare. The vaginas of America's women MUST be cleansed. If a nation cannot control the stink of its women, that nation is surely doomed to perish.

WHEN CUNTS TALK

Three cunts sit on the stage, talking about cunts, while 1,000 cunts—and about a dozen men—sit in the audience, listening.

It's OK if I use the word "cunt," because one of the cunts onstage—the black cunt, as opposed to the two white cunts sitting next to her—just led the audience in a rousing chant of "CUNT! CUNT! CUNT!"...We learned that the "C" stands for things such as "cute"...the "U" stands for "urge"...the "N" for "nice"...and the "T" for "tangy," so we've **reclaimed** the word "cunt," and now it's a nice word rather than a bad one.

As is "vagina," because the three vagina-bearing actresses onstage have helped us to reclaim that word, too. Sure, I used to think that "vagina" was a rather distasteful, malodorous, gamy, sticky, sweaty, pissy, moldy, bloody, slimy word myself, and the play *The Vagina Monologues* seems to imply that our culture finds the word repellent due to some sort of patriarchal conspiracy to make the ladies feel ashamed of their hoochie-noo-noos.

Much of the play's outrage...and be assured that it's a protected, suburban, abstract, *safe* sorta outrage...seems based in the idea that the sheer ugliness of the word "vagina" itself is part of a deliberate male plot to "rob women of our language," or some such nonsense, as if walking around with a "penis" and a "scrotum" is a real treat.

Vagina Monologues playwright Eve Ensler—may Goddess bless her *and* her vagina—has clocked phat bank by exploiting what is little more than a mildly clever Women's Studies project—she interviewed a coupla hundred women 'bout their vaginas, asking them

stock questions, many of them goofy: *Describe what it smells like....What would it wear if it got dressed?...What are its nicknames?...What would it say if it could talk?*...and she turned their answers into a manuscript. Some of the more compelling narratives became soliloquies with titles such as "Reclaiming Cunt," "My Short Skirt," and "My Angry Vagina."

According to a press release for the show, "the play brazenly explores the humor, power, pain, wisdom, outrage, mystery and excitement hidden in vaginas." Those must be some BIG vaginas to hide all that stuff in there!

"We live in a penis world," Ensler griped to a reviewer for *Metro Times Detroit.* "Everything about this world is phallic." The reviewer added, "Ensler wrote the play because she heard women talking about their vaginas and what they said surprised her. What she found out was that women were really 'hungry' to talk about them."

All those hungry vaginas have led to successful runs of the *Monologues* in London, Paris, Rome, L.A., New York, Chicago, and Beaverton (just kidding). The play was also transformed into a best-selling book and HBO special. It has become a cultural phenom in which women—from most appearances, wealthy white women—pay $30 for the privilege of chanting the word CUNT in a crowd of other women.

Since its premiere in 1996, the play has been performed by a rotating cast that has given solace to those who might have wondered whatever happened to Teri Garr...and Marla Gibbs...and Swoosie Kurtz...and Rue McLanahan...and Hayley Mills...and Marcia Wallace...and Loretta Swit...and Peggy Lipton...and Nell Carter...why, they're up there onstage in *The Vagina Monologues,* talkin' 'bout their furry little wet *verjingeys!*

Reading from cue cards, the actresses adopt the voices of a Bosnian rape-camp survivor; a 70-year-old woman who's never had an orgasm because of an embarrassing problem of over-lubrication; a Southern Negress who finds love and sex in the arms of another woman; and many other vaginal vignettes straight from the mouths of cunts.

MY BRAIN FELT LIKE A ROASTED CASHEW on this blazingly hot midsummer day, the sort of day I don't want to hear *anyone* yabbering, much less a cunt. My girlfriend and I slipped out of the sweltering downtown sidewalk sauna into the cushy, carpeted Newmark Theater to see the Portland leg (labia?) of a *Vagina Monologues* touring company. This particular cast's marquée name was Karen Black, a great actress whose eyes remained crossed throughout *Easy Rider* and *Five Easy Pieces* 30 years ago and who now must bear the relative ignomity of being a traveling vaginal monologist.

There were two other actresses: a dreadlocked black one and a blonde white one. The programs listed their names as Starla Benford and Kristen Lee Kelly. I'm guessing Starla is the black one, because I don't think I've ever seen a black Kristen. All three actresses were topnotch. They showed lotsa spunk 'n' sass, making for a spunky, sassy, spunkity-sassafrassy show. And they were all very good at doing different accents, although Karen Black's Bosnian rape victim sounded a bit like Bela Lugosi doing Dracula.

Although the tickets cost $30, we were treated to no real set design beyond the three chairs from which the actresses, all of them wearing red T-shirts, never budge. Thirty bucks a ticket apparently isn't enough to make the actresses memorize their lines, either—instead, they read from cards just to keep reminding you that these are the *real* words of *real* women, but to me it just seems like a lazy

REVIEW OF "THE VAGINA MONOLOGUES

ay to get out of learnin' yer lines.

Our tickets were for seats way in the back, and we found ourselves rrounded by giant mastodons and woolly mammoths. We were ndwiched between two women who must have weighed 300 pounds ch. Some lard-assed bitch behind me cackled at every joke in the ow, and believe me, there were a *lot* of jokes.

Men don't fare very well in the *Monologues*. One woman tells of w her meanie of a husband forced her to shave her bush and still eated on her anyway. Throughout the show's 90 minutes, from stimonial to testimonial, the only man who is apparently able to give y of these chicks an orgasm is some submissive doofus who insists staring worshipfully at her spread-eagled snatch and slobbering er it. We also learn that lesbian relationships are much more likely provide women with sexual and emotional fulfillment, existing as ey do apart from the evil clutches of MEN, who are so penis-sessed that they rarely know their way around a cunt.

HE PLAY MIXED COMICAL, LIGHTHEARTED, 'giney-related aterial with atrocity stories about clitoral mutilation and Bosnian rape mps. And it didn't mix well, either. Vagina jokes found themselves ashing headlong into rants against clit-snippin' (which, interestingly, ey claim is primarily an African phenomenon, and I wonder how at made the black actress feel). Truth be told, the only ones in the dience likely to have undergone systematic genital mutilation were e circumcised males…such as I, dear reader, such as I. Women don't suffer more…they just cry louder.

After a while, I had a Tourette's-like compulsion to start screaming t obscenities at the top of my lungs and possibly jumping toward the ge *à la* John Wilkes Booth. I wanted to shout out the most degrad-g racist, sexist, and homophobic remarks I could summon. I wanted to shout at these bitches to be grateful for what they have. *That* would've been *my* version of chanting the word "cunt."

And while you're reclaiming "cunt" and "vagina," ladies, here are some more terms for you to reclaim: twat, snatch, gash, slit, hole, slimepit, and cumbucket. Try *that* one on for size, all you grand-mas in Peoria who titter at *The Vagina Monologues*—reclaim the word "cumbucket" for me, will you? I wanna hear you chant the word "cumbucket," Granny!

I scanned the audience for the few male attendees, all of whom looked unhappy to be there, these poor, hunched-over cuckolds being dragged to this play. I wondered about their lives…I pondered the level of their pussy-whippification. I felt bad for them, but not bad enough to help.

THE STRANGEST THING ABOUT *THE VAGINA MONOLOGUES* for me, apart from its all-consuming silliness, is its constant equation of a woman's *vagina* with a woman's *self*. I'm not sure what they're getting at there, but it ultimately sounds sort of…objectifying. I was under the impression that for years, feminists have fought against the idea of equating a woman's body with her self. And *I* fight against that idea, too.

I *love* the vagina. It's the *monologues* I have a problem with. It's not the cunt…it's the

talking. The self-absorption. The automatic presumption of innocence and victimiza-tion. The inability to confront your own potential for malice and hurtful behavior. And the eternal double standards, which you never seem to oppose so long as they benefit you.

I can separate the vagina from the per-son, and it's usually the person I wind up hating.

> I tell ya, us twats don't get no respect! I want respect, and I won't shut up until I gets me some!

EVE ENSLER HAS USED SOME OF THE MUCHO DINERO she's earned from *The Vagina Monologues* to launch an organization called "V-Day," which is described as "a movement to end violence towards [*sic*] women." One website boldly claims that *The Vagina Monologues* "gave birth to a global movement to stop violence against women and girls."

What about violence toward men and boys? Is that somehow better? Is that somehow less prevalent? Is that more acceptable? Are your vaginas more precious than our penises? Saying we should end violence against women and girls reminds me of a conversation I once had with a rock star…the only rock star I've ever known…where he noted that the movement to "stop black-on-black violence" somehow implied that it was preferable to be violent against white people.

Not once, through all my 'net-surfing about V-Day, did I get an inkling of what they were actually DOING to end violence against women, apart from raising money. And what evidence did they provide to support the idea that they know *why* violence against women hap-pens and what can be done to stop it?

Maybe it has something to do with the fact that mothers hit their little boys more often than daddy does, and that mommy hits those boys more frequently than she hits her little girls. That's what the statistics say, anyway.

Oh, sorry—didn't want to complicate the story.

If you want to stop vio-lence against women, why don't you buy us all earplugs so we don't have to listen to you complain?

FOR $30, I WANNA SEE a chick shooting ping-pong balls out of her pussy. I want to see her mop a floor with the mop handle shoved up her twat. I want to see her blow out candles with the force of her vaginal muscles. I want to see her play the flute with that cunt. I want to see her make disturbingly loud duck sounds with her vagina. In fact, I want to see **Honeysuckle Divine** rather than *The Vagina Monologues*. Honeysuckle did all those things in a poorly reproduced video that was originally filmed at a San Francisco grindhouse in the early '70s. I still have the video somewhere in stor-age. Honeysuckle Divine—now *there's* a talking cunt I can get behind. The other twats are just blowing hot air.

> I just flew in from Vegas, and boy, are my fallopian tubes tired! So…how many vaginas es it take to screw in a light bulb? Only one, but it has to do it VERY CAREFULLY…No, seriously, t's good to see so many vaginas out there in the audience tonight! I love all you cunts! Let's all chant the word "CUNT" together…

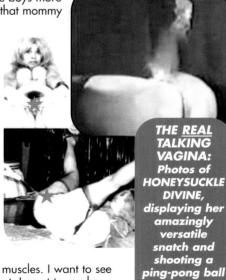

THE REAL TALKING VAGINA: Photos of HONEYSUCKLE DIVINE, displaying her amazingly versatile snatch and shooting a ping-pong ball from her twat.

167

what's with all the lesbians?

Used to be you could walk a country mile and not see a lesbian. These days, you can't sneeze without spraying a dyke. Used to be you were able to see the mountains from downtown Portland, but now all the lesbians are blocking the view.

Was I asleep the day the whole world became a dyke bar?

I swear, you can't turn around without bumping into a lesbian these days.

Shopping malls. Airport waiting lounges. Ski lodges. There you'll see the lesbians, walking hand-in-hand.

There are far, far too many of them.

Portland's soggy, mossy ground fairly trembles under the feet of so many stampeding bulldykes.

Weekend spree lezzies and the lifetime clam-gobblers.

Shopping for incense and battering each other.

Eatin' buckets and buckets o' pussy.

Dykin' out.

Munchin' carpet.

Hatin' men.

Wearing each others' underwear.

Checking each others' breasts for lumps.

Drinking chamomile tea and buying organic reusable tampons.

They read books about lesbian nutrition and smear their lesbian toothbrushes with gobs of lesbian toothpaste.

They take lesbian vacations and use lesbian cell phones.

They cry lesbian tears and pass lesbian bowel movements.

They wear lesbian ponchos and decorate their lesbian apartments with lesbian dream-catchers and ancient lesbian pottery from ancient lesbian tribes.

They drive lesbian cars and shop at lesbian supermarkets.

They swallow lesbian laxatives made from lesbian grains grown on lesbian farming collectives.

They watch lesbian TV channels with lesbian sitcoms and lesbian nature specials.

They use lesbian fishing rods to haul in lesbian trout hooked to lesbian worms.

They enjoy lesbian sporting events such as lesbian rugby and lesbian cage matches.

They clasp lesbian hands together and admire lesbian skylines dotted with lesbian clouds.

They sip lesbian drinking water from lesbian cups.

Their lesbian ovens yield lesbian pot pies stuffed with lesbian chicken chunks.

The lesbian nightly news shows lesbian helicopters rescuing lesbian war victims.

> "Can we, as a country, all agree to tone down the lesbianism just a little bit?"

Ooohh...that's a whole lotta lesbians.

WHAT'S WITH ALL THE LESBIANS?

They're everywhere.

They sprouted everywhere like a sudden case of the hives.

Portland is the Lesbian San Francisco, no doubt. At this juncture, I'd reckon that dykes outnumber fags in P-Town by ten to one.

It's like the Hundredth Monkey. We've reached critical mass. We've reached the Hundredth Lesbian.

Can we, as a country, all agree to tone down the lesbianism just a little bit? We've reached our lesbian quota, I'm sure. I think we already have enough lesbians, and any more would be overkill.

AT A LESBIAN COFFEEHOUSE near 28th and E. Burnside, a lesbian magazine talks about high colonics and nutritional empowerment and bedwetting support groups and candle-making seminars and dry lesbian oatmeal scones. You know—lesbian stuff.

Nearby, a group (officially, it's called a "bevy") of four lesbians huddles together near a bus stop in the cold, rainy, patriarchal mist. Three chunker dogs and one cornstalk girl. They bear all the visual trappings of latter-day alterna-lesbos: short, sloppy "bed-head" haircuts dyed platinum blonde or flaming pink, facial piercings, dirty sneakers, and tribally tattooed bellies and ass cracks exposed.

When I heard the phrase "lesbian identity" float from one of their mouths into the air, I decided to seize it.

I boldly approach the bevy of lesbians.

"What's with all the lesbians? I mean, you guys are *everywhere!* What's going on with that?"

The lesbian standing closest to me seems shocked by my apparent bigotry. "I don't like putting labels on myself," she says with a look of animal wariness.

"But you just used the phrase 'lesbian identity'!" I say. "Isn't that a label?"

The lesbians seem flabbergasted by my rudeness.

"What you're doing is very uncool," says the four's spokeslesbian.

A bus pulls up and the lesbians embark upon it. They say nothing to me as they leave. I asked an actual group of lesbians what was with all the lesbians, and they wouldn't tell me. They didn't want me to know. Or perhaps they don't know, either.

TWENTY YEARS AGO in a suburban Philly garage, an all-girl punk-rock band pounds out snotty covers of Ramones and Blondie songs. Emily and Vicki are pretty bottle-blondes who play guitar and bass, respectively. Their drummer, Becky, is a lesbian. Becky wears a spiky brown mullet and is always trying to get in Emily and Vicki's pants. But these girls are natural-born heterosexuals and are repulsed by Becky's advances. We all have a cruel, jolly laugh at Becky's expense regarding her compulsive sexual perversion. Men id not find Becky attractive, so she became what's known as a sbian-by-necessity. Rumor spreads that Becky is that rarest of reatures—a girl who is sexually attracted to other girls.

Twenty years later, all the girls are like Becky. Rare is the girl who asn't licked another girl's snapper.

Twenty years ago, male homosexuals were all over pop culture, vhile lesbians were the Silent Homos. Flamboyant butt-jockeys such s the Village People, Boy George, and Disco Tex were shaking their airy tushies all over the place, but rare was the mainstream lesbo.

But amid AIDS wreckage and a general cultural devaluation of naleness, the gay male has been buried like an anal gopher. You on't even see male fags anymore. Well, maybe once in a blue moon. blue, faggy moon.

Except for the not-having-vaginas-and-breasts part, male fags vere able to capture everything that made being a woman interest-ng. They possessed all the skittish drama which is one of the few edeeming qualities of being a female.

That has all been replaced by the dry moralism of cardboard ykes, who hate everything that's male but are as boring as the ullest males.

Back in those fag-friendly days, lesbianism seemed ugly—vomanhood stripped of everything that made womanhood attractive r alluring.

Chick-on-chick pussy-eating was the sole reserve of women who ooked like men who couldn't get women. It was a lesbianism of the onely hearts' club and the nuns' convent. A lesbianism of ugly, oyish women whose vaginas were not deemed desirable enough in vhich to spill seed.

O WHAT CHANGED? It was quite simple, really.

It followed roughly this pattern:
1) Women said they wanted sensitive men.
2) Men became sensitive.
3) Women turned lesbian.

When the men turned into women, the women turned to other vomen. That's the history of Lesbianism's New Wave in a tiny esbian nutshell.

But it isn't entirely the ladies' fault. Not entirely. The fact that he American male is terrifyingly inept in the ol' sack played a part s well. American men have no finesse. No game. They're dumb, lrooling, easily excitable hairy apemen who'd turn me into a dyke f I were a chick.

Dykes are made, not born. A woman's physiology is constructed to enjoy a thorough ramming by a hard, warm, REAL tool rather than a cold rubber instrument or a girl's wet tongue.

When men become men again, lesbianism will evaporate like so many wet spots in the morning sun.

I think that Dyke Chic will peter out, and a lot of women are going to be embarrassed. They'll have a lot of explaining to do to their grandchildren.

I've made it a policy not to be with any more chicks who've had lesbian experiences.

C'mon, fellas, let's wield the powerful force of SHAME. Let's make them feel ashamed about being lezzies. Let them feel as if there's something lacking in their reproductive desirability. Let them feel as if their DNA is misfiring. Treat them like freaks of nature and evolutionary mistakes. Act like the daddy you were born to be and scold your little girl. The day will come when they wish they'd kept their panties on and their tongues in their mouths.

HOW DO WE PUNISH the lesbians in a way that seems equitable? And how do we prevent future lesbianism from occurring? How do we get rid of the lesbians once and for all? How do we dispose of the lesbians in a safe, legal manner? How do we stop it? How do we stop it NOW?

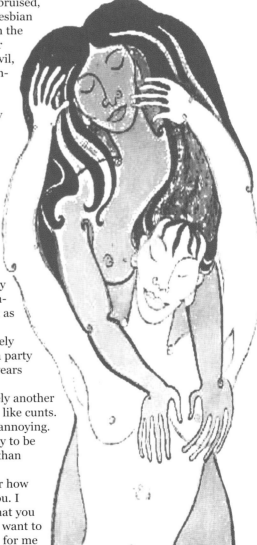

Take pity on the eternal, boring, self-righteous, easily bruised, stridently annoying, lesbian crusader, snuggling in the fetal position with her sisters, far from the evil, brutal clutches of men-folk, free from the heartache that MEN bring, with their hairy backs and repellent hanging genitals.

I don't mind the pussy aspect of it. Pussy's great. Yay, pussy! It's not the vagina, it's everything sur-rounding it. The holiness that sur-rounds their holes.

There's an insincerity about all the new fash-ion lesbians. They act as if they're blazing new trails, yet they're merely little girls at a pajama party playing "Doctor" 20 years too late.

Lesbianism is merely another way for women to act like cunts.

Another way to be annoying.

They've found a way to be even more annoying than heterosexual women.

I don't want to hear how your father abused you. I don't want to hear what you did with other girls. I want to hear what you can do for me right here, right now, on your knees with your mouth open.

REQUIEM FOR A HEAVY BREATHER

This used to be a hell of a good country, a place where you could leave your door unlocked at night, where you could stroll down Main Street and everyone knew your name, and where lonely pervs with their cocks in one hand and a telephone in the other could scare the shit out of unsuspecting females.

But just as video killed the radio star, technology has rendered the obscene phone call an emblem of a bygone era during which sexual predators could roam the fiber-optic prairie free from the fear of Star 69.

Like streaking and flashing, the obscene phone call has become a lost art, conjuring daydreams of a simpler time's golden perversions. Before the emergence of gizmos such as answering machines, digital voicemail, and Caller ID, a mildly imaginative deviant was able to satisfy himself merely by dropping a thin dime into the big slot. But our precious Global Village has shrunk to the size of a cramped studio apartment, and privacy has gone the way of the wood-burning stove and the home-baked loaf of bread.

Granted, technology makes us safer, but it also enslaves us. We now have safety because there's no place left to hide. Sure, some menopausal librarian with her hair in curlers and a Noxzema-smeared face will never again be forced to pick up the phone and endure some faceless meatball describing the veins on his dingy, but at what price to our cherished freedoms?

THE OBSCENE PHONE CALLER plumbs the shallow end of the deep, dark ocean that is Sex Offenderdom. Too timid to go buck-wild and forcibly seize what he wants, he cowers behind the receiver and commits Rape Lite™. He is more an annoyance than a threat, more a jerk than a menace. Too uncomely to attract a mate, too timid to rape someone, he is a small soul who takes small risks. He is alone. This is implicit. He has been unable to secure himself a suitable mate. We all understand this.

And so does he. He knows this all too well. So he goes for what he knows. He drools and snorts, pumps and chortles, tugging, twisting and pinching his greasy, inflamed Love Antler, huffing and puffing his way to a blown wad and a dial tone's despondent hum.

The obscene phone caller is typically a loser in the Sweepstakes of Love. He can garner no female attention other than through being feared and rejected. The schmo has no other way to wield power over the women who intimidate him. His victim is everything he wants, everything he'll never get, everything he'd never be able to procure if he were to step into the harsh spotlight and reveal his monumental homeliness and insurmountable inadequacies. So he

pleasures himself by causing displeasure in someone who has denied him pleasure.

Pity the poor victim. Perhaps she was fixing herself a cozy mug of hot cocoa, the kind with the friendly miniature marshmallows floating carefree on the top. Then came the phone call, and with it an unwanted sexual encounter that will tatter her frilly emotional fabric for life. Although there was no sexual contact, it was sex nonetheless, a disembodied bodily function. And though he leaves no physical evidence, he squirts an invisible cum shot onto her brain. He and his unwanted penis enter her consciousness, leaving an indelible gravy stain on the once-virginal apron of her mind. His grimy boots mercilessly trample upon her sexuality's delicate flower garden. Even in her own home, after all the showers and scrubbing, she'll never feel clean again. One hopes she'll be able to get over it, but given her typically feminine emotional brittleness, such hope is doomed from the get-go.

TECHNOLOGY KILLS THE OBSCENE PHONE CALLER

"HANK" (NOT HIS REAL NAME) is a former obscene caller who was convicted of misdemeanor harassment stemming from a nasty habit of cold-calling women and talking dirty to them. (A minister's wife whom Hank had repeatedly badgered finally nailed him using Star 69.) As part of a plea agreement, Hank served six months in county jail and is now midway through a three-year probation. Hank spoke on condition of anonymity through an arrangement with his Seattle-based probation officer. Predictably, Hank insisted that he contact me via phone rather than the inverse.

Though Hank is nearing 50, he has never been married. He displays a near-palpable bitterness about his romantic failures. He lives in a basement room in (surprise!) his mother's house. Beyond that, he is reticent to reveal much about his personal background.

Hank admits that in his heyday, he was making up to a dozen obscene calls daily, yet he's evasive regarding the calls' juicier details. When I ask whether he thinks any of his victims enjoyed his overtures, he's silent, as if their capability for pleasure never occurred to him.

Hank swears that he'll never lapse into his old ways, not because he feels what he did was wrong, but because the risk is too high. "You just can't get away with it anymore. They've got it rigged so it's impossible to be—what's the word?—anonymous these days."

Hank downplays the idea that his actions caused anyone harm. "Really, what did it cost THEM?" he asks, some emotion finally seeping through his voice. "Maybe they got a little upset for ten minutes after I called. But I spent six months in JAIL! I went through a lot more than THEY did! Where's MY justice?"

Life grows hard for the anonymous pervert. Where can the cowardly phone predator go these days? The Internet comprises a thick new pipeline for covert sexual harassment, but as yet, a keyboard and monitor lack the obscene phone call's luscious immediacy. And yet there remains hope that the dedicated sociopaths among us will manage to keep pace with technology. If there's a match for the vast scope of human technological ingenuity, it is surely the bottomless depths of human sexual perversity. When the going gets tough for perverts, there is no choice for the perverts but to get tough. And so they soldier on, searching for a techno-loophole through which to slip their lonely dicks.

THE COCKS OF ROCK

We're all made of meat, even the not-so-meaty among us. We like to pretend we are something more than meat, yet when we die, only the meat remains.

Women, because they are congenitally insane, are the most fervid propagandists of the idea that we possess something beyond mere flesh, blood, bone, and the occasional waste product. Women, especially when they get older and their meat starts to sag, invariably lose their minds and indulge psychotic delusions such as the notion that we all have a "soul." And since they clutch their aging chicken claws onto this notion with bloody desperation, they are the first to shriek when someone alleges that they are, in the end, meat. In spite of the fact that there is zero evidence of the soul's existence, these cackling cunts demand that we squint and lie about the Empress's New Clothes.

The fundamental aspect of female psychology is an eternal hypocrisy and the concomitant inability to ever acknowledge it. Therefore, the same bloated hens who picket outside clubs where females with desirable bodies flash some tits 'n' snatch are also the same hens who manically stuff five-spots in the speedos of Chippendale's dancers when hubby's out of town.

Despite what the feminist thought police would have you believe, it's a fact that women objectify men. If anything, they are more brutal and cynical in their estimations than men could ever be.

Case in point: a website (www.metal-sludge.com/LongShort.htm) in which rock stars' cocks are reviewed in the manner that a restaurant critic reviews meals. Groupie-for-life Donna Anderson pools her own experiences along with the gossip of her groupie friends, concocting an often-hilarious list of 180 rockers and their cocks. With ball-shriveling candor, Anderson 'n' pals present a staggering array of rock-cock, from toothpick-sized to the length and girth of a mud shark.

Firmly ensconced within the Stud Stable are bitch-slapping ex-Crüe drummer Tommy Lee (of course), Phil Anselmo from Pantera and his "MONSTER power tool," Evan Seinfeld from Biohazard, Tracii Guns from LA Guns, Yogi from Buckcherry, and (surprisingly) little blond fem-doll singer Robin Zander from Cheap Trick, whose girlish features and gooberish voice would ordinarily indicate a peanut-sized penis. Each of these gents is rumored to possess a hog measuring ten inches or more.

Much more fun to read are the catty descriptions of petite-penised prima donnas such as Twiggy Ramirez from Marilyn Manson ("he has a small dick and it's frequently limp due to excessive cocaine use"); James Lorenzo from Pride & Glory ("about the size of a pinkie finger"); Stefan Adika from Dad's Porno Mag ("hung like a baby and is a quick shooter"); Slik Toxik's Rob Bruce ("small cock, plus he only has ONE BALL! He lost his other ball in an accident"); Dokken's Mick Brown ("maybe 3 inches if you pull on it"); one-time Van Halen singer Gary Cherone ("so small if somebody saw you sucking his dick it would look like you were smoking a joint!"); Jack Russell from Great White ("Mushroom CAP & that's it, ONCE BITTEN and it never grew back!"); Tommy Thayer from Black-n-Blue ("so small crabs could use it as a flagpole"); Marq Torien from BulletBoys ("so small he probably pisses on his balls"); Glenn Danzig ("his cock is just like him, short"); and Quiet Riot's Carlos Cavazo. ("Not only a very sloppy and boring lay, but he is very, very, very small. There is no riot going on in his pants.")

These girls don't hesitate to let us know about the guy in Papa Roach who has bad breath; the chap in House of Lords whose back is so hairy, it "looks like he's wearing a sweater!"; the singer from Everclear whose crotch "smells very dirty"; the member of Medicine Wheel who has "hair growing out the side of his shaft"; the Marilyn Manson underling who digs licking asses, tasting his own cum, and "is into the whole 'pour wax on my dick' thing"; the allegation that David Lee Roth employs his lady friends to give him enemas; and which members of Slaughter, Saigon Kick, and Flotsam & Jetsam enjoy having items rammed up their asses.

And not only does size matter, it's ALL that matters to these broads. To these starfucking, cock-hungry mucus pits, the measure of a man LITERALLY becomes the measure of his manhood. There is a comical equation of penis size with human worth. When a rocker is revealed to have a large schlong, these girls tend to forgive any shortcomings of character. But when his pathetic underendowment is brought to light, no measure of his good deeds or community-service hours can atone for the fact that everyone laughs disdainfully at his biological misfortune. All in all, this is very refreshing.

I wonder how I'd rate on this chart? I've noticed that my paramours' estimation of my love-hog's length varies wildly depending on how well we're getting along. When a girl is in love with me, my penis hovers somewhere around eight inches. When I dump her, it shrinks to a paltry four inches.

I don't mind being objectified. The fact that I have a body is far less dangerous than the idea that I have a soul.

THE VANISHING HANDJOB

MOURNING THE DEATH OF "HEAVY PETTING"

> If the boy has a car, they usually go for a ride and park in one of the half-dozen popular petting spots—the Buggy Wash, the Three Pines, near the Boy Scout Camp, in the park, near the graveyard. Heavy petting followed by sexual relations often occurs in the parked car, except in the very coldest weather.
>
> —*Marriage and the American Ideal*, by Floyd M. Martinson, 1960

> Petting…is now not only permissible but an almost universal practice to a greater or less degree….[T]he desire thus aroused can carry over when they sit down together on the sofa or out in the car parked in the shadows outside. This is the danger in petting….Everybody is as full of unexpected characteristics, good and bad, as a plum pudding is of nuts and candies. Youth is a time for learning in many ways. Boys and girls need to talk and talk and talk, about anything from outer space to inner beliefs. They should play games, from tennis to crossword puzzles…. They should…eat with the crowd at Pete's Pizza Heaven, alone on sandwiches they brought in their pockets on a hike, or with each other's families in their own homes.
>
> —*Sex and the Adolescent*, by Maxine Davis, 1960

A long, long time ago, teen pregnancy was a matter of deep shame rather than an easy way to get out of high school and onto *Maury*. These days, your typical mongrelized TV-addled hamsterfucker knows what a "DP" and a "Dirty Sanchez" are by age six, and chances are they've tried one or both.

But back in the 1950s and early 1960s, open talk about sex was still taboo, which made it more exciting in the same way that severe hunger makes a hamburger taste better. The female orgasm was still only hinted at, like the Lost Continent of Atlantis. Males and only males were thought to have uncontrollable sex drives, and the only way to give them "relief" while still retaining one's hymen and reputation was through the act of "heavy petting"—what today is crassly referred to as a "handjob." Petting was sometimes mutual, and the

occasional female received a sloppy finger-banging, but its chief purpose was to contain the Male Genital Tyrannosaurus until which time it could be used for the pro-social purpose of marital intercourse and its implicit baby-making.

The euphemism "petting" dates back at least to the flapper era of the 1920s, when renegade youth would throw "petting parties," but it didn't fully blossom until the post-nuclear, whole-milk Eisenhower days of the 1950s. "Petting" was distinguished from "necking" in that it covered all areas below the neck, with "heavy" entering the fray once one wandered south of the beltline. On the "baseball" continuum of sexual slang, it hovered around third without heading for home.

But that was ages ago, before everyone and their aunt was doing anal, and today a handjob seems quaintly unnecessary unless you're jacking yourself. Heavy petting has gone the way of the hickey and the non-penetrative first date. One must not forget its functional impracticality: A chick's hand on your cock is always more inept than your own, and I would assume the same applies for finger-banging her. They'll jack and knead and tug and yank, but it's all cow-milking ineptitude, an impediment to copping one's sacred nut.

Properly speaking, I've only heavily pet with one girl. She was an Italian maiden with a faint mustache, hair around her nipples, and a monster muff surrounding her implausibly stanky snatch. This was back in the 1970s, and her technique was straight up-and-down with no hint of flashier methods such as The Double Whammy, The Anvil Stroke, The Shuttle Cock, The Bookends, The Flame, The Base Clutch, The Love Tug, The Two-Timer, or the Thigh-Swatter. Sitting in her parents' living room listening to an Electric Light Orchestra album, we fumbled under a quilted comforter, poking and grasping for hours without ever approaching orgasm.

These days, though, I think it would make me cum, because we've reached a point where even felching is no longer dirty, so reaching third base and getting a hickey suddenly are.

> "Back in the 1950s and early 1960s, open talk about sex was still taboo, which made it more exciting in the same way that severe hunger makes a hamburger taste better."

As a young boy, an unlaid boy, a bottle-fed ex-baby boy, I'd often find scraps of '60s and '70s porno mags strewn through the mossy woods near our tract home. Having led a tit-free youth in a titless world where tits were even more oppressed than black people, these soggy paper boobshots were religious documents to me. Tits fascinated me. The bigger, the better. Down to her knees—the best!

I knew that a woman had something between her legs where you stuck your pee-pee and then a baby came out, but I never equated that area or process with pleasure—hers or mine. (I STILL don't equate it with hers.)

But then my testicles descended and my groin sprouted hair like a Chia Pet. My voice got deeper and I was able to shoot applesauce from my wiener. Like they say in the Jewish religion, I became a man. I got myself some pussy and realized that tits were for kids. It's not that I dislike them; it's that they're about as sexually useful as kneecaps.

"There's always titty-fucking," you limply suggest. Yes—titty-fucking. No, nothing awkward or stupid about THAT, so let's just move right along.

You ever see some stank-ass hippie bitch flop out her saggy jug at a restaurant just to quiet her mewling infant? THAT'S what tits are for, and it ain't pretty. Think of them as two baby bottles, THEN tell me you still get aroused. Have you ever seen one of those lactation fetish sites? It's enough to put you off the teat forever.

It's not as if I'm repelled by a nice pair of casabas—I just don't focus or fixate or obsess on them. I grew OUT of that phase. And I really think you should, too.

Yes, I can enjoy looking at tits, just as I can enjoy looking at a woman's calf, wrist, or eyelashes. But those tits are merely accessories. A woman can find a man's biceps sexy, but if she doesn't move on (and downward), she's a little bit W-A-C-K-Y. That's because biceps, like tits, serve no real sexual purpose. Yeah, maybe SHE gets some sexual pleasure from having them touched, but when did we start worrying about HER pleasure?

It's very unbecoming for a grown man to seek out women for emotional nurturing. You were supposed to have settled that deal a long, long time ago. It was called "weaning." And I have a secret—women don't like men with mommy complexes. They want a daddy, not a son.

What fucking AGE are you that you still need to be nurtured by a woman? I'm sorry that your weaning was incomplete, but it's a little too late, fair soldier. I was not breast-fed, and I have no desire to make up for lost time.

> "Any adult male with a breast fixation OBVIOUSLY still wants to suckle milk from his mother's teats. You have a problem with that? Take it up with your mammy—TITBOY."

Tit-obsessed men generally have far less real-world sexual experience than other men, and I can state this as a fact, because it is I who just made it up. Sigmund Freud would tell you the same thing, except he's dead.

You can be an ass man or a leg man. You can even be a bush man and a vulva man like me. But you CANNOT be a tit man. You can only be a tit BOY.

Does your mommy wipe your bottom with a warm, wet washcloth, Titboy? Does she tuck you in at night and call you her Widdle Wubbly Woo? Do you like to play with the big bouncy balloons, Titboy? Do you like those red-nosed clowns bobbling in your face...Titboy?

Any adult male with a breast fixation OBVIOUSLY still wants to suckle milk from his mother's teats. You have a problem with that? Take it up with your mammy—TITBOY.

That's right, Baby Huey, nuzzle up to them mams. Then put your knickers on and kiss Mumsy goodbye as you tweedle-dee your way to Nursery School.

Grow the fuck UP, man. PUSSY is where it's at. THAT'S where you commit all the felonies. Tits are just misdemeanors.

In my adulthood, pockmarked as it's been by scandal and infidelity, I've often had gals—with their boobs jutting toward me in the post-coital motel-room haze—ask me why I don't pay more attention to their breasts.

Don't you like them? Are they misshapen? Should I get a boob job? Should I get another boob job? Should I get a breast reduction and then get yet another boob job?

No. Shut the fuck up. I don't want to suck on your boobs just like I don't want to wear a diaper. I bang you like a jackhammer and go down on you better than a dyke—you don't need me to slap your tits around.

Funny how they're never so hung-up on their *vaginas*, which is where most of the aesthetic atrocities occur.

I guess the pussy is ultimately for making babies, too, so I really don't have much of a point. Ignore everything I just said.

tits are for kids

The Catholic Schoolgirl Fetish...

THE SINS OF THE CATHOLIC CHURCH are without peer in the wretched annals of Western Civilization. Although the papacy is thankfully in decline, it once wielded a cold steel boner over the world, channeling its terrified followers' sexual energies into global Sadism Pageants. The church subsumed the faithful's carnal appetites and gave them back bloody Crusades, brutal Inquisitions, and public witch-burnings. It systematically extorted poor, hardworking souls in exchange for the cynical promise of a heaven that doesn't exist. It ostracized and punished and often killed those who dared challenge its divine authority. Its insane oligarchy's warped libidinal misery forbids abortion so that the fetuses can grow into little children ripe for physical and sexual abuse at the wrinkled hands of a depraved clergy. Chastity belts and mohair shirts and self-flagellation. The dead-flesh smell of incense, the rote torture of Mass and the rosary, the constant screaming threats of hell, hell, hell...

The Catholic Church has been a naughty, naughty boy.

Catholicism is an S&M cult masquerading as a religion. It is the largest, longest-running Fetish Ball in history. There are heavy sexual undertones in its aesthetic of darkness, in its mandatory confession of sins, in its clerical vows of celibacy, in its nutty doctrine that priests can *literally* turn bread and wine into Christ's flesh and blood, in its teaching that the son of God popped out of a virgin's vagina, and in its insistence on showing the crucified Jesus in all his gore-splattered pain. (Note that Protestants display empty *crosses* rather than crucifixes.) It's no coincidence that sadomasochistic role-playing borrows heavily from Catholic iconography: undefiled virgins, stern confession-booth priests hearing your most embarrassing secrets, and evil nuns, who were history's template for the modern dominatrix.

The Holy Roman Church has been in power for nearly 2,000 years, and it is therefore responsible for more human suffering and sexual repression than modern-day pestilences such as fascism and communism.

Despite all that, it has also given us the Catholic schoolgirl uniform, so I hereby declare all its sins forgiven.

Hi, my name is Sandra and I used to attend a nice Catholic Girls School in the Philippines. I am now 21 years old and have kept my uniform but only just realized that men like me to wear it when we have sex. I personally like to wear it without any underwear on underneath then sit on a man's face while he licks my bald pussy.

—Ad for a Hong Kong porn site

The young Catholic schoolgirl was being overpowered by her own budding sexuality. Almost by reflex, she slid her already-short skirt farther up her thigh. She took her pen and pushed it up the rest of the way under her skirt, rubbing the bottom of the pen against her pink panties.

—From a fiction piece posted on alt.sex.stories

THERE IS NO CLOTHING FETISH MORE COMMON than that for the "naughty schoolgirl" outfit. It is so universal—so catholic, in the lower-case sense of the term—that it hardly seems like a fetish at all. It is a mandatory item in every stripper's wardrobe. In virtually all pornographic magazines and videos, you'll find some pigtailed maiden in a short plaid skirt acting young and innocent. Countless websites cater to the obsession, boasting come-ons such as "Who wants some tight Catholic schoolgirl pussy?" and "Catholic School Girls in uniform...and out....oops!"

The schoolgirl fetish is by no means limited to Catholic girls. In England, where they killed all the Catholics, the "naughty art-school girl" is a star player in erotic fantasies. In Japan, sexualized schoolgirls are a national obsession on a par with rape-themed comic books and penis enlargement.

The libidinous fixation on schoolgirl outfits belongs to a broader fetish for all uniforms, such as those for nurses, waitresses, and cheerleaders. Uniforms are sexy because they harness the individual. They depersonalize you and make you interchangeable with others in uniform. They imply tight, repressed, vacuum-sealed, anti-individualistic discipline...until the wearer can stand it no longer, at which time the buttons pop off and the zippers unzip. Uniforms bear something S&M about them that becomes more troubling when the uniform in question is common among underaged girls. Nurses and waitresses are presumed to be adults; cheerleaders and schoolgirls aren't.

ASK THE AVERAGE MAN: "Do you like Catholic schoolgirl outfits?" and his answer will be, "Yes."

Then ask him: "Are you a pedophile?" and the answer will be, "No."

Yet since Catholic girls only wear uniforms until the end of high school...and since most high-schoolers only reach age 18

it's not just for pedophiles!

during their senior year...any adult male who's aroused at a girl wearing such finery is essentially fantasizing about sex with someone the law defines as a child. It's not as clearly pedophilic as "big daddy/little girl" psychodrama, but it's still dicey.

AS PART OF MY LABORIOUS RESEARCH for this noble essay, I asked about a dozen guys—none of whom seem like baby-rapers or cradle-robbers—whether they thought Catholic schoolgirl outfits were sexy, and they all said yes without hesitation.

So I can either conclude that they're all chomos, or that the main appeal of Catholic schoolgirl outfits lies outside the sickly realm of child molestation.

I should confess that I speak as one who shares the fetish. I believe that if a woman insists on wearing clothes, at least let it be a Catholic schoolgirl uniform. I find them so hot, my testes swell like boiled eggs whenever I see one. My cock is drawn to a plaid skirt like a big pink moth to a flame. I can't describe it because it is beyond words...it is spiritual. 'Tis something more mystical than the divine mysteries of the Eucharist. It is the power of the Holy Ghost moving between a girl's thighs.

Her plaid skirt is the matador's red cape, and my cock is the bull. I see that red tartan pattern, and I need to get at the little furry monkey beneath it. The girl could have the face of an algae-eater, and yet in that uniform, I want to make more little Catholics with her. Like someone liberating the German camps, I want to set free all that repression in her vagina.

Raise that Cunt Kilt and fuck her. Pull her pigtails and fuck her HARD. Spread her legs

like the Red Sea and savagely defile the wench. Stick your pope-thang up her. Fuck all the guilt out of her. Fuck all the Hail Marys and Our Fathers clean out of her. Nail her as if the bed is a wooden cross, she's Jesus, and you're a Roman centurion. Grab that hot Catholic ass and get busy.

I WAS RAISED CATHOLIC, so don't start squawking that I'm prejudiced. I was given a 12-year sentence in their school system, so I know of what I speak. Twelve years of near-daily exposure to those uniforms. My testicles descended, my voice changed, and I sprouted pubes while surrounded by a forest of 2,000 Catholic schoolgirls in uniform. My high school eschewed plaid kilts in favor of one-piece blue polyester zip-up things with a light-blue shirt underneath, blue knee socks, and a little patch on the left breast. The ample boobs of the girl who sat behind me in sophomore year's homeroom class yearned to break free from their blue-polyester prison...or at least that's what I hoped.

I lost my virginity at age 12 with a Catholic girl, and I can attest that the "Sluts for Christ" rumors are mostly true. There is more sweat and desperation in their love-making than the public school girls with their "sexually healthy" attitudes. For a faith so allegedly sex-hating, Catholicism produces females who swallow cum like it's holy water. They're the sort of girls who'd raise Jesus from the dead just so they could blow him. They are wanton cesspools of carnality, sticking themselves with dicks like a junkie uses needles, taking in cocks like a chain-smoker lights cigarettes, one after the other, more, more, MORE....

It makes sense that a religion which strove to destroy the sex drive would wind up producing oversexed progeny. It's as simple as a law of physics: You push it down hard, it comes back up harder. Tell her she can't do it, she'll do it twice.

Poor girl. The church acted as if it owned her vagina, forbidding her from having an abortion, denying her the choice of having a baby or dumping it in the clinic wastebasket. But all the attempts to neuter her have ultimately backfired. The church placed a psychological cork in her vagina that couldn't help but pop. She could only "hold it in" for so long. How many thousands of times during her schooling has she been forced down onto her knees, eyes closed and mouth wide open, awaiting the bland Christ wafer? So the first time she takes it upon herself to get down on her knees, be sure she'll put something more substantial in her mouth.

So I'd speculate that the fetish for Catholic schoolgirl outfits has little to do with an attraction for underage chicks and much more to do with the allure of sexual repression finally unleashed. When it comes to Catholic schoolgirl uniforms, the word "school-girls" is far less essential than the words "Catholic" and "uniforms." It's not pre-pube innocence which drives men wild—it's the LIE of innocence.

Whatever papal flunkey thought these outfits would be a good way to harness female sexuality was a Class-A Retard.

Or maybe not.

Perhaps there's something more devious at work. Drowning in scandal and dwindling membership, maybe Rome is using the Catholic schoolgirl outfit as a last-ditch recruiting tactic. I see similarities to the Children of God cult from the 1970s, where female missionary-prostitutes won converts by having sex with them.

It doesn't bother me, so long as you keep making those uniforms.

CATFIGHT!

Among all forms of human violence, the catfight is unique because everyone enjoys it.

"At its most basic level, a catfight consists of two girls battling over one cock—a woman fighting another woman for the sake of a man."

Is there a more delightful, arousing, and hilarious natural spectacle than the sight of two fiery temptresses clawing at one another's eyes? The catfight appeals to us in ways simultaneously sexual and comical. It bears an unhinged quality so extreme, people laugh in disbelief. There's something hilarious about the utter loss of decorum, the absolute regression to feral animality. It still surprises and amuses us to see women acting violently.

We live, my poor savage jockstraps, in a culture where women are encouraged to "kick ass" because nearly everyone finds it funny, arousing, or both.

All across the nation, girls claw at one another's eyeballs and tear clumps of hair from one another's scalps and make insensitive comments about one another's appearance. These pussycats are shorn of inhibitions, ripping at one another's flesh. They are bitches in heat, tearing at one another's souls. Their clawing and hissing and arching of backs approximate the feline war dance, hence the term "catfight."

For better or worse, catfights give credence to the sexist archetype of the Hysterical Female. Prison guards and bar bouncers will tell you that the only sort of tussle they dread stepping in between is one involving two women. There is a ferocity to girl-on-girl violence that the boys could never match. Men merely try to *win* a fight; women seek to maim, blind, and disfigure. They claw at one another's cheeks like weasels in heat.

And sometimes it goes too far. A recent fracas between two Portland strippers ended up with one girl suffering brain damage and the other one headed to prison.

Although such fights are rarely so extreme, both women will always, of course, need new vaccinations after each catfight.

IN THE CATFIGHT, SEX AND VIOLENCE GO TOGETHER LIKE SONNY AND CHER. LIKE THE CAPTAIN AND TENNILLE. LIKE K.C. AND THE SUNSHINE BAND.

At its most basic level, a catfight consists of two girls battling over one cock—a woman fighting another woman for the sake of a man. Women will step on each other's necks in order to get to a big cock, a handsome face, or a fat wallet. The catfight is an ancient evolutionary dance, one vagina leaping over another as it ascends the Pussy Pecking Order…one vagina knocking the other vagina out of the way as it seeks its place in the sun. It is the female analogue to when males "cock-block" one another—one might call it "cunt-blocking" if they were prone to such vulgarities.

While a catfight's participants may be stripped of a certain feminine daintiness, they retain—nay, they *enhance*—everything else that it means to be a woman. Even though a catfight may be *unladylike,* it is nevertheless very, very female.

Nature pits one vagina against another in a brutal struggle for dominance. Nestled between every healthy woman's legs is a microscopic cluster of eggs yearning to be fertilized. Although women fight with their hands and teeth, it is their *genitals* that truly are at war. They clash in the grand Darwinian battle for survival, two female mastodons fighting for the right to have their woolly wombs impregnated.

Do not be offended by these shockingly refreshing comments, my friends—my statements are sexist only if nature itself is sexist, and we know that's impossible.

THE INTERNET IS RIFE WITH WEBSITES THAT INDULGE THE CATFIGHT FETISH. SADLY, MOST OF THESE VIDEOTAPED "CATFIGHTS" ARE STAGED EVENTS BETWEEN ACTRESSES WHO HAVE NO REAL BEEF WITH ONE ANOTHER. THE DIALOGUE USUALLY GOES SOME-THING LIKE THIS...

Yes, you did!
"No, I didn't!"
Bitch, yes you did!
"Tramp, no I didn't!"

...whereupon the women flash their finger-nails and engage in bloodless combat, followed immediately by hours of hot lesbian sex.

For many men—the ugly, unoriginal ones—it matters not whether the fight is staged. For them, the catfight's appeal is purely ani-malistic. It's all about the meat. They want to see what is unavailable to them in real life. To them, catfights represent the possibility that clothes will be ripped from bodies and they'll catch a peep at what they've only imagined, oh, so many times on those cold, lonely nights.

For the more complicated and attractive souls among us, the catfight appeals on deeper levels. We derive pleasure from the idea of women hating women—it sorta takes the heat off us male misogynists. And if we have any sexual experience, we acknowledge the scientific fact that hot-tempered women are better in bed.

My personal definition of a "catfight" is: *Women attacking women to the delight of male observers."* Although a strict definition would omit the "male observers" clause, for my purposes it is crucial. It's like the old Zen riddle: If two women engage in a catfight and no male observers are around to be delighted by it, can we be sure it really happened? Behind 95% of all catfights stands some studly male, stroking his pole and laughing at these dizzy broads.

In my romantic sojourns, my staunchly muscular charms have inspired the occa-sional catfight. One extreme case even featured a blunt instrument and a hospital visit.

It always thrilled me that my body was the item up for grabs. How hot is it to have not one, but TWO women who crave exclu-sive bragging rights over your cock so badly, they'll resort to vio-lence? It made me feel as if I had market value as a potential mating partner. My balls felt potent, warm, and loamy to see these girls clashing over me. I savored the attention and the implications it had about my desir-ability. It made me feel sexy. It made me want to run around my apartment naked, my wiener flapping about freely. So long as they're fighting over me, nothin' gets my tail a-waggin' like a good catfight. *Woo-haw! Gooba gooba goo!* It's great to be alive and to be a man, watching women fight.

Keep fighting, girls! You're clawing and scratching and shrieking your way into our hearts as you tickle our funnybones and tug at our crotches.

Let us now praise the catfight and acknowledge its glorious role in the evolutionary process. Let the women fight. Let the women scratch. Let the women rip. Let the women scream.

One girl wins and one girl loses, yet both of them suffer. And the men, those sick creatures, all stand around jerking off.

MY FAVORITE MOMENTS IN POP-CULTURE CATFIGHTING

FIST CITY by Loretta Lynn, 1968. The greatest catfight song ever recorded, sung in impeccably quavering PMS fashion by the Queen of Country Music. You can *hear* the sharp nails in her voice: "If you don't wanna go to Fist City/You better detour around my town/'cause I'll grab you by the hair of the head/and I'll lift you off of the ground."

The 1997 episode of **SEINFELD** where Elaine was being stalked by an ultra-violent Molly Shannon. Instead of taking her threats to Elaine seriously, everyone responded with condescending hisses and meows. After Shannon destroys her office and Elaine shows the wreckage to her boss, he grinningly exclaims, "I am smack-dab in the middle of a good old-fashioned catfight!"

THE WILD WORLD OF HASIL ADKINS documentary (1993) features a catfight scene filmed as it happened in a Boone County, WV bar during a concert by the psychobilly pioneer. A fight erupts between two ladies vying for the right to sit next to one-man-band Hasil while he performs. After watching a knock-down, drag-out battle during which one girl eventually betters the other and tosses her out of the bar, Hasil merely says, "Hi-de-ho!" and continues playing.

why
WOMEN
love to
FIGHT...

...and why
MEN
love to
WATCH

Muslim Girls
TURN ME ON!

Men are in charge of women, because Allah has preferred men over women....As to those women on whose part ye fear disloyalty and ill-conduct, admonish them; banish them to their couches and beat them.
—Holy Quran (4:34)

If a man and a woman are alone in one place, the third person present is the Devil.
—The Prophet Muhammad

These are days of moral decline and spiritual malaise for the West, what with compulsory lesbianism among grade-school girls, not to mention lotsa slobbering, sourpussed, clit-stapled, hairy-pitted female bulldoggies who never resolved their daddy issues hanging around all the places where I like to buy coffee.

There are no dykes in Afghanistan, and that's reason enough to move there.

Chicks are ruining the West. Over here in this neck of the world, a sloppy Goddess Goulash stinks up the skies...while the Middle East, with its well-endowed macho God, starts to smell like paradise.

Wherefore art thou going, O wayward Western woman?

The Western woman has become defiled.

The Western woman has lost her soul amid the godless quest for mammon.

The Western woman has gotten all uppity and stuff, always ordering the most expensive desserts when you take her out to dinner.

The Western woman does not realize that there is no higher satisfaction for a woman than to please Allah.

Here in the land of the Great Satan, we extol feminine character traits, and yet we still expect to win a war against our unflinchingly butch enemy.

The man who falls prey to feminine wiles is no man at all. Those Muslims know that once you surrender your mighty natural-born male-warrior spirit to female charms, you become a pathetic, undignified cuckold. You become an unmanly lad.

What's worse, you incur the wrath of Allah, who's *really* hard to deal with when he's pissed.

Women have desires that have to be fully suppressed lest they lure the righteous believer into the pits of hell. Whorish immorality is the natural female state. Observe how the four-year-old girl rubs her crotch up against the coffee table while you have guests over, and you'll agree with my premise here. Once a woman realizes she is capable of sexual pleasure, she becomes vexatious and troublesome to the righteous man. You get her started, and a few weeks later she's gobblin' chubby strangers' cocks in piss-encrusted truck-stop bathrooms, and that's not cool. That's not cool *at all*.

Unlike the vaguely faggy virgin Jesus, the Prophet Muhammad was a stud-muffin. Hung like Allah, too, I'll bet. Here was a religious leader with a robust enjoyment of carnal delights. He liked 'em young and tight. He liked 'em old and loose. He liked 'em, period. But he didn't like 'em if they *had* their period, 'coz that's disgusting. While the homo Christ chose to laze around with 12 other males, Muhammad plowed through at least a dozen wives, plus scads of hot, horny slave chicks. He married a six-year-old girl when he was 51. He died at 62 on the lap of a 17-year-old bride. A true pimp daddy, Muhammad was. The Original Gangsta.

And his followers were nearly as burly as the Prophet himself. His cousin Ali wisely stated that "The entire woman is evil.... Men, never ever obey your women....They complain of being oppressed when in fact it is they who oppress." Omar, Islam's second caliph, counseled Muslim guys to "Adopt positions opposite those of women. There is great merit in such opposition." Indeed, these were men of great wisdom and holiness. Righteous bro's. Ain't no fun if the homies can't have none!

And I want some. I want some sultry Saudi sirens. Some cock-hungry Kuwaiti cuties. A classy Pakistani lassie with a sassy chassis.

The Muslim girl oozes mystery. She teases, tempts, and tantalizes. She keeps her mouth shut, too, or they'll cut off her tongue. All that repression is simply irresistible to me. Her delicious subservience. The way she does what she's told.

The way she understands that all these rules are for her own good. Think of all the repression which has been crammed into her swarthy body. Think of all that coiled libidinal energy, 100 times more pent-up than in the most guilt-stricken Catholic girl. Think of how fun it would be to fuck all that repression out of her.

Suddenly I'm transported to a harem tent stuffed with big fluffy pillows, hash-filled hookahs, and totally hot chicks in silk costumes who wanna blow me. A summery breeze floats in from the oil fields. The smell of cocoa butter and fig newtons intoxicates my nostrils. A big, sopping, matted, goat-herd shrub waits nestled between her legs.

She's wrapped up like a mummy, peeking out from the slit in her *burqa*. I watch lustfully as it takes her four hours to get all those clothes off. I sniff her Islamic vagina. Tweak her Quranic nipples. Poke my finger inside her Middle Eastern anus. Go on a Crusade 'tween her legs. Invade the Holy Land. A hummus-like paste forms between her thighs. When I finally insert my falafel, she shrieks with delight.

Happy Arabian boners pop across the Middle East. Millions of brown, hairy nutsacs tighten in unison. Proud Muslim girls hoist their lovers' cocks like AK-47s. Muslim women...YES! Muslim women...NOW! Muslim women... GROOVY! Muslim women...FUNKY FRESH!

I want to take her home and tell her to do things. Vacuum that carpet, Muslim girl! Fetch me a hoagie and some cold lemonade, thou handmaiden of the One True Prophet! Keep your olive-colored bazooms tightly under wraps, Muslim girl. Stay in the house, Muslim girl. Stay ignorant. Stay preggers. Stay down. Down, girl, down!

The word "Islam" translates literally as "submission." God wants us to keep the wimmens down with head scarves and clitoridectomies and ceaseless beatings. Shred and sew up their genitals in order to contain their relentless, meandering lust. Righteous men nod approvingly as Revolutionary Guardsmen disfigure the faces of women who've worn makeup. Wives suspected of immorality are doused with gasoline and torched to a crisp. Thousands of randy Muslim bucks cheer and laugh as sin-stained women are herded into stadiums for public floggings.

Islam offers several advantages for the believing man's enjoyment, almost all of them sexual. On Earth, a Muslim man can marry up to four wives at once. In heaven, he is greeted with a minimum of 72 submissive virgins poised to please him eternally...72 Muslim broads who never break a sweat, never age, never get their periods, and never tell you to take out the trash. In paradise, a man is given the sex drive of 100 men. It's like Islamic Viagra! Lo! My Penis is ever High, Exalted, Great.

The Holy Quran advises us: "Men, your wives are your tillage. Go into your tillage any way you want." I think that means the Hershey Highway is OK with God. If you were so inclined, you could probably get away with the Dirty Sanchez and the Dutch Oven, too.

The more I hear about Islam, the more I like it. Islam is such a cool, violent, sexy religion! Islam rocks! Those Islams is good people. Those Muslims know how to keep their bitches in line!

And I ask the nonbelievers...what's so *wrong* with all of that? And I wonder...are we really on the right side in this war? It is a war of gender philosophies that we're fighting, and we may be on the wrong side, dudes. The Western man would be wise to take a second look at Islam, if only for the chicks.

Would you be willing to trade some of our cherished freedoms for the right to enslave and abuse women? When one ponders all the sexy perks offered to Muslim men, it becomes obvious why they're willing to die for their faith.

The attack on the Twin Towers was intrinsically phallic in its symbolism. Woe unto the emasculated Western Man, mocked by his women as he drools and begs for sex. Woe unto the West, where women dominate and the culture falls apart. The West will fall because it is pussy-whipped. We may have the money and the technology, but we just don't have the starch in our shorts anymore.

However the winds blow, the war on terrorism will be a good thing for the American male. If we win the war, we get their women. If we lose the war, we get to treat *our* women like they treat *their* women. Who's to complain?

OPINION

Pornography exists everywhere, of course, but when it comes into societies in which it's difficult for young men and women to get together and do what young men and women often like doing, it satisfies a more general need....While doing so, it sometimes becomes a kind of standard-bearer for freedom, even civilisation.

—Salman Rushdie, "The East is Blue," 2004

Inside Arab Teens you will get access to brand-new Arab girls straight out of Iraq...ready to show you what goes on when you're not allowed to fuck in public for decades and suddenly you can because Saddam is gone.

—Arab Teens website

HOT MUSLIM TWAT!
PORNOGRAPHY INVADES THE ISLAMIC WORLD

PERHAPS THE MOST SIGNIFICANT CULTURAL FALLOUT of September 11, 2001, was the dawning realization that we can no longer ignore the Muslim world and must somehow find it in our hearts to jerk off to their women.

There is no more sexually repressed pooty-tang on earth than Islamic pooty-tang, and thus there is no pooty-tang that's sexier. Almost everywhere that the Star 'n' Crescent hold sway, you'll find Muslim vaginas squashed under a hairy Quranic thumb. From Malaysia to Bahrain, the hapless babes of Islam get blamed for any sexual savagery that befalls them. Rape victims are routinely slaughtered by relatives seeking to reclaim the family's dignity through an "honor killing." Under the Taliban, an Afghan woman was once beaten to death by a mob for accidentally exposing part of her arm. Every year, roughly 2,000 Bangladeshi ladies accused of "indecency" are permanently disfigured after acid is tossed in their faces. Egyptian gals suffer routine clit-clippings. In Saudi Arabia, you're allowed to kill your bitch merely for talking to another man.

And if you star in a porno in Iran, honey, they'll stone you to death.

Not an angry mob. The *government* will do it.

To Western reporters such as I, her name remains hidden beneath an invisible metaphoric *burqa* of secrecy. But in May of 2001, a 35-year-old Iranian woman was ritually washed by guards at Tehran's Evin prison, swaddled in a white shroud, and buried alive up to her armpits. She was then pelted to death with rocks which, according to the Iranian Penal Code, "should not be too large so that the person dies on being hit by one or two of them [but not] so small either that they could not be defined as stones." Her gruesome demise was the culmination of eight years' imprisonment after being convicted of starring in a 1993 underground hardcore porno video. The film, described as having a grainy, home-movie quality, was thought to be the first specimen of pornographic cinema filmed in the Islamic Republic of Iran since 1979's bloody revolution. Although the film makers blacked out the actors' faces, investigators traced a serial number on a water meter filmed in the background. The hot Iranian twat was arrested, found guilty of "corruption on earth," and murdered by rocks carefully selected according to government guidelines. No word on what happened to any of the film's male actors. They were probably among the rock-throwers. Like I said, it sucks being a Muslim woman.

"I didn't want to insult Islam," pleaded Amal Kashua as she recovered in a hospital bed after being violently mobbed by Muslims in her Israeli hometown of Tira. A 38-year-old mother of eight and self-described drug addict, Kashua was the female star of 2002's *Yussuf and Fatima,* touted by its producers as "the first Israeli-Arab porno." *Yussuf and Fatima*'s video box featured the couple posed erotically in front of a minaret. Kashua's costar and reputed husband, a Palestinian male known only as "Amir," was also beaten in the attack. "The whole town is satisfied and dissatisfied at once," said a Tira resident after the mobbing. "Satisfied at what happened, because we tried to protect our honor, but on the other hand dissatisfied because she didn't die, nor her husband." Kashua's family posted a death decree against their daughter in the town square. "If I could, I would eat them both raw and spit them out," her brother told Israeli television.

The film's producer remained upbeat. "Since this whole story over *Yussuf and Fatima* broke out, we have sold hundreds of copies, most of them in the Arab sector," he told a reporter. "We may make another Arabic film. It pays."

ANYWHERE THAT YOU HAVE BOYS AND CAMERAS, you will have pornography. Muslim countries are no exception to this eternal principle, but the punishments are so over-the-top that very little porn is actually produced there. Most of it oozes in from the Evil Infidel West.

The Holy Quran explicitly condemns nearly all public displays of female flesh: "Al-rijal qawwamun 'ala al-nisa' bi ma faddala Allahu ba'duhum 'ala ba'din wa bi ma anfaqu min amwalihim."

Oh, wait—duh! You guys speak English! Sorry: "Good women are obedient. They guard their unseen parts because Allah has guarded them."

These "unseen parts" wield a strong erotic undertow among: 1) Muslim males who've never seen pictures of an unseen part; and 2) Western males who've never seen Muslim unseen parts. Under this cultural exchange, Arabs get to finally see vaginas, and non-Arabs finally get to see Arab vaginas. Everybody wins!

The Middle East has the lowest per-capita Internet representation on earth. Even frickin' Africa has a higher percentage of people logging on. Still, a recent study concluded that 80% of all Internet traffic in Arab countries heads straight for the porn sites. And the mullahs are scrambling to stop it.

Responding to allegations that Asian female attendants were rendering sexual favors to clients at private Internet cubicles, Kuwaiti officials recently shut down 50 Internet cafés. Kuwait also recently outlawed Bluetooth software, alleging that men were using it to trade indecent photos on their camera phones.

In Yemen, all computer screens at Internet cafés must be turned so that the public can view them. If you try to access porn from any computer in the United Arab Emirates, a popup will announce that the site is on the "Emirates Internet Control List" and prohibited from public viewing. All Net traffic in Saudi Arabia passes through anti-porn filters at the King Abdul Aziz City for Science and Technology. In 2000, Saudi officials blocked access to all Yahoo! clubs, responding to reports that frisky Saudi citizens were using the clubs to swap nude snapshots.

Porn is so antithetical to the Islamic consciousness that Western invaders have repeatedly used it as part of their psy-ops programs. For no other apparent purpose than to outrage Muslims, the CIA reputedly hosts several "Islamic porn" sites depicting alleged Muslim women huffing cock and riding the baloney pony. In 2001, the website for militant Muslim group Hamas was hacked so that surfers were led to "Hot Motel Horny Sex Sluts." In 2002, an Islamic News Network TV program in the scaldingly fundamentalist Iranian province of Hamedan was interrupted with three minutes of hardcore sex. When Israeli troops occupied the West Bank town of Ramallah in 2002, they seized three of the city's four television stations and broadcast nonstop pornography. And after their pillaging of Fallujah in May of 2004, U.S. troops reportedly littered the deeply religious Iraqi city with thousands of hardcore porno pictures.

In the same month, two pro-Muslim websites as well as the venerable *Boston Globe* were hoaxed with pictures purportedly depicting American soldiers sexually brutalizing anguished Iraqi maidens. In reality, the pictures were from staged pornographic shoots featured on "Iraq Babes," a site hosted in Pennsylvania, and "Sex in War," which originates in Hungary. (Apparently, the *faux* raping of Muslim chicks has become a cottage online porno industry since the war started.) A Tunisian website mistakenly declared that the photos were part of the Abu Ghraib prison scandal, where, if you'll recall, American soldiers made *actual* S&M pornography using Muslim prisoners.

Yet I am not one to condemn our fine boys and girls over there doing a good job civilizin' the sand nigras. As Salman Rushdie said, pornography is a sign of civilization. A pox upon those who call us savage imperialists. We have liberated the Evil Bearded Caveman Middle East. We have brought them freedom and pornography, and more importantly, the freedom to *view* pornography. Triple-X videos are said to be doing brisk business in Baghdad's streets. And in once-prehistoric Afghanistan, satellite dishes are sprouting all over rooftops, tuned into hot naked action beamed from the wonderful, wonderful West. Phone sex is said to be all the rage in Saudi Arabia, and those crazy Turks have gone bonkers for gay porn.

Lift that *burqa*, baby. I wanna see what you got under there.

HILLBILLY PUSSY ONLINE!

On the fringes of the masturbation ocean called the Internet, far beyond where brave men dare to surf, there exist niche markets serving the needs of men whose tastes run counter to the mainstream boob-job hordes. Out there, things which might repel the average red-blooded male...things, such as, oh, missing limbs, morbid obesity, or poop-munching parties... become sexually charged fetish items, sharpened arrows which strike deep at the pleasure center.

By accident—I promise—I recently stumbled across the phenomenon of porno sites designed to appeal to persons who become sexually aroused at seeing naked pictorials of the sort of mangy, dentally handicapped, histrionic, low-class, inbred-and-continuing-to-inbreed white skanks paraded daily across the tube by the likes of Jerry Springer.

Hard as it might be for us, uh, normal people to believe, there's a cottage industry providing jack fodder for men who fancy themselves having sex with white women of meager means.

I know...it's almost too terrible to ponder. One clue to these sites' possible appeal is the social archetype of the insatiable hillbilly gal willing to fuck ANYONE ANYWHERE ANYTIME. These girls flaunt the presumed alley-cat sexuality of the underclass. Their all-consuming rageful lust impels them to have sex with anyone...even the malformed horndogs who have to pay for coochie on the Internet. They are cum-chugging Cunts on a Hot Tin Roof who are constantly yowling and yammering for cock. One website barks that "Trashy White Girls in the trailer parks are the easiest pussy in the world." Another avers that "Trailer park girls are TOTAL sluts!" OnlyWantSex.net, which claims to feature "more than 35,000 White Trash Girls," states as indisputable fact that "WHITE TRASH GIRLS ARE THE EASIEST TO FUCK OF ALL THE AMERICAN WOMEN." This unique sales pitch inverts the typical porno strategy of precious unavailability...these girls are always available. They want to fuck you—even YOU.

The standard porn advertising strategy is further inverted by the fact that these sites often go out of their way to admit that these girls "ain't runway models" or "aren't all that good-looking."

Many of these sites feature black-on-white gang bangs, and it's hard to gauge whether that's a racist or a non-racist gesture—are these girls "white trash" because they gobble black cock, because these photo shoots portray their cum-splattered blonde heads like white croquet balls being batted around by huge black mallets? Are they relegated to the trash bin merely because of their race-mixin' ways? Who can tell? But when one woman naughtily exclaims, "My husband would kill me if he knew I kissed him right after sucking a big black man's salty balls," you know she's trash whatever way you slice it.

Currently, I'm unaware of any websites that cater to a fetish for, say, "nigga project hos" or "wetback hotties" or "subjugated Injun squaws." There are other ethnic niche markets for "Chocolate Cuties" and "Lovely Latinas," but only low-class white gals get subjected to such outright disdain. Under any other skin tone, this would be unacceptable stereotyping. Someone should write a book about such double standards, I swear.

And considering the availability of stock photos and porno's hallowed tendency to "create" erotic situations, it's also difficult to gauge how "authentic" many of these sites are. Rather than being uploaded from a shack in the Tennessee hills, many of these sites seem as if they were slapped together by some geeky Cali technerd trying to guess what someone with a white-trash fetish wants to see.

But the more disturbing question is: Who patronizes these sort of sites? You can rule out "real" white trash. They don't want to see their downtrodden lifestyle so savagely lampooned, their hard-luck women depicted as circus beasts. Real white trash seeks "class" in its pornography, so who buys this shit? Inhibited white rich men? Vengeance-minded horny black men?

I wanted to e-mail one of the webmasters and ask them, but once you make contact with a person like that, you get put on their list. And once you get on their list, you get put on other lists. And when you finally are able to remove yourself from the first few lists, you've already been put on two dozen new lists. It's not worth the trouble.

So instead of investigating further, I've provided capsule analyses of a half-dozen "trashy white girl" sites, some of which are now defunct. There are many more than these half-dozen. Some would say too many....

SITE NAME: DIXIE TRAILER TRASH

URL: www.dixietrailertrash.com

THEIR DESCRIPTION: "The Souths [sic] Nastiest Sluts And Horney [sic] House Wives [sic]....You will see thousands of photos of the girls from my trailer park taking it up the ass, in the mouth and getting their pussy fucked over and over!!...You will see white trailer trash women performing acts you won't believe; like only White Southern Trailer Trash can do. Keep a close watch because you might see your cousins fucking each other!...You will see these trashy sluts both barefoot, in stockings, heels, sandals and even sometimes with filthy feet from having to feed their barnyard animals!!"

MY DESCRIPTION: An online photo journal depicting the carnal adventures of fat, horrid, stretch-marked, desperate, menopausal, tore-up-from-the-floor-up, sub-Mason-Dixon cocksocks on a frantic quest to stuff every hole in their body to the gills lest those empty holes remind them—even for a second—of their station in life. The site is run by "Felicia," a 47-year-old grandma and PTA member who doesn't look a day over 90. Sections include SLUT PICS OF THE DAY!, INTERRACIAL GANG BANGS!, RED NECK [sic] LESBIAN LUST!, and SEX STARVED TRAILER TRASH! Adventurous minds will wonder the coercive measures needed to enforce the steadfast proclamation that "every nasty slut on this site is REQUIRED to swallow cum!" Points get subtracted due to the annoying popups and ever-replicating "consoles" and non-related porno links which keep exploding on the screen like daisy-cutter bombs, forcing you to quit your browser. I've never seen this happen outside of porno sites, and it really should be illegal.

MOST DISGUSTING PASSAGE ON SITE: "Most of the gals that come to Dixie are 'Anal Virgins', but when they leave our parties they are shitting sperm."

SITE NAME: CUM DUMP MAMAS

URL: cumdumpmamas.com

THEIR DESCRIPTION: "Thousands of candid fuck shots of the nastiest girls in the South!...We are southern sluts....We are a group of seven girls who have moved in together under one roof. We live and play in a cabin in the North Georgia mountains and we do some of the nastiest things you have EVER seen!...About 15 girls party here every Saturday night and they are ALL cock whores!...We do go on road trips to the local truck stop, pool hall and a few clubs around here and we fuck the shit out of some of the guys at these locations but other than that, it's ALL from the cabin and from houses in the neighborhood!"

MY DESCRIPTION: The site's logo is rendered in a typeface that looks like wooden slats nailed to the side of a ramshackle cabin. The letters drip with huge white gobs of what is presumed to represent male ejaculate. The mamas include a cracker ho whose "fantasy is to be gang fucked by a biker club" and a black woman who claims to have "sucked off more redneck truck drivers than anyone I can think of and my little asshole has been fucked so much that I think I need a ring job." I must admit that I found myself highly attracted to the site's big-boobed, bee-sting-lipped, vaguely swarthy proprietress "Sindy," allowing me to forgive, even temporarily, the endless shots of jizz-gargling, ass-fisting, and turkey-baster-inserting.

MOST DISGUSTING PASSAGE ON SITE: The name.

SITE NAME: TRAILER TRASH GIRLS

URL: www.trailertrashgirls.net

THEIR DESCRIPTION: "Trailer trash. White trash. You know the type. Tattooed, Camel smoking, Jack Daniels drinking sluts...who like to sleep til noon in their doublewide with three refridgerators [sic] out front, an engineless 1964 Dodge Dart in the back home to racoons [sic] and rats....We've got tons of nasty, skanky trailer trash girls, strutting their stuff and proud to do it. These white trash strip for you, have lesbian sex for you, play with their favorite dildos for you. Hell, even the pregnant ones get it on for you."

MY DESCRIPTION: Subtitled "Doublewide Sex and Porn," the site's home page features a shot of a nasty redhead skank holding a purple vibrator in one hand and clutching a miniaturized dilapidated trailer home between her legs. The Trailer Trash Girls logo is rendered in a Confederate flag pattern. The site also boasts a section devoted to "Trailer Trash Lesbians" engaged in explicit, fluid-laden activities. But since that's all they show you before you have to pay, that's all I know.

SITE NAME: AMATEUR TRASH

URL: www.amateurtrash.com/preview2.htm

THEIR DESCRIPTION: "I meet most of [the models] in the trailer park I used to live in....Amateur trash is more fun than getting drunk and playing with firearms!...Amateur trash is better than your pet pig winning the blue ribbon at county fair....You will love Amateur trash as much as your three legged dog."

MY DESCRIPTION: A small, amusing site sleazily rendered in that cheesy Comic Sans typeface favored among low-rent web pornographers. Thematic consistency isn't important, as one of the girls is black and another is a decidedly un-trashy 18-year-old Korean. One shot shows the webmaster's alleged ex-wife doing dishes, placed alongside a shot of her looking menaced by a faceless hard-on behind her. The site has a jokey feel which leads me to believe it really isn't hosted by an actual guy who used to live in a trailer park—it seems more like some tech geek basking in the blue glow of a computer screen somewhere deep in the SFV.

MOST DISGUSTING PASSAGE ON SITE: "Here is a good white trash whore for y'all. She has been dancing at the local strip club to support her boyfriends [sic] drinking habit. Now he talked her in to doing a scene for us so he can buy some more beer and pretzels."

SITE NAME: WHITE TRASH AMATEURS

URL: kinky-amateur-girls.com/trash

THEIR DESCRIPTION: "Guns, Tattoos, Pickup Trucks....Pics of real amateur white trash trailer trash redneck nasty girls naked....These girls have nothing better to do than hang out at the Burger Barn and flash their titties at people while they wait for some guy to offer his cock to her. They sure know what to do when they get their mouth on one too!"

MY DESCRIPTION: Very little to see on the "free tour." The main model looks too Mediterranean to qualify as proper white trash—sort of a muddier Valerie Bertinelli. Plus, she's posing naked except for high heels and a BASEBALL CAP, which is never sexy under any circumstances. There is, however, one redeeming shot of a peroxided, sunken-eyed, faded-cutoff-wearing skankasaurus whose very being conjures images of meth-pipe burns and children given up for adoption—in other words, HOT stuff!

SITE NAME: THE FARMER'S DAUGHTER

URL: www.sexontap.net/farm_girls/farm_girl.htm

THEIR DESCRIPTION: "The Farmer's Daughter is about beautiful, erotic young teen women and animals, in the fields, on horses, and on farm equipment....Young firm bodies playing with each other and barnyard animals... no bestiality, beastiality, [sic] or animal sex—just hot young farm girls playing with each other, animal [sic], and tractors."

MY DESCRIPTION: I'm not sure what to say. I mean, they get a bunch of hot young farm girls together, place them next to some hot young farm animals, and yet no bestiality? No "beastiality," either? You'd think that they'd at least give you one. Or the other. Or, in a righteous world, both.

MOST DISGUSTING PASSAGE ON SITE: "Girls who breed animals (animal husbandry) are not sqeamish [sic]. They know how to have fun. After all, animal sex is normal (that is how you get a baby animal). So seeing animal sex (not bestiality) makes a teen girl horny and ready....And every girl loves horses. Feeling their strong, powerful bodies between their legs, (yes, rubbing against their pussy—still not bestiality or sex, but animal sensual massage) makes them hot and wet for erotic pornography."

a short, stinking review of websites that cater to a fetish for "trailer-park sluts"

HAND-HELD SHOWER NOZZLES...

We're in trouble, guys. For thousands of years we've had the upper hand. And soon our power will slip through our fingers like...like...like a pulsating jet stream of hot, steamy water.

The danger is real. It's the greatest threat currently facing men and manhood and maleness and manliness and machismo and masculinity...and Guy Stuff in general.

What is this threat, you ask, growing somewhat impatient and ready to flip the page to ogle more tacky pix of naked erotic models?

It isn't feminism, because, well, feminism's ridiculous. No one takes that shit seriously anymore. It isn't lesbianism, because it's common knowledge that women can't get along with one another for very long. It's not even male brutishness, because that has flourished for eons, and the patriarchy has chugged along unhampered.

No, the threat is simpler. More pervasive. More seemingly innocent, and thus all the more sinister.

The threat to every American male lurks quietly in bathrooms from coast to coast. And that threat, my brothers, is the hand-held shower nozzle. That cocky, arrogant plumbing appliance. That evil, steely, praying mantis. That simple bathroom appliance, available at any K-Mart or Home Depot, will topple 10,000 years of male rule. That inanimate shower device symbolizes feminine liberation. It betokens a rising gynocratic dictatorship. The ultimate, irrevocable downfall of male supremacy.

Good for her. Bad for you. Bad for all men.

Scared, fella? You should be. There is reason to be afraid.

Mention the topic of shower nozzles to a woman...*any* woman...and her lips will curl into a smile. Her eyes will assume a far-away look of forbidden love and giggly secrets.

She's a little more distant these days, isn't she? A little less eager to please, right? And still you wonder why it takes her that long to take a simple shower, you silly little fool.

She loudly slams the bathroom door shut. She rudely clicks the lock, shutting you out of her private aquatic self-pleasuring session. She defiantly strips naked and slinks into the shower. And there she stands, nozzle in hand, coldly mocking the patriarchy. She cranks up the faucets, spritzing herself 'tween the legs. The relentless downpour assaults her crotch like a mini Muff Monsoon. The nozzle gushes at full force, crop-dusting her nether regions. Battering her swee'pea like a boxer clobbers a punching bag. Plastering her clit like an astronaut's rubbery cheeks in a G-force test. Pummeling her shiny li'l pencil eraser into pink liquid ecstasy.

Banished and abandoned, you sit outside the bathroom, jealously enduring the yelps and groans and grunts and war-whoops of insane pleasure, the sort of pleasure you never give her. The sort of pleasure you CAN'T give her.

You can't compete. There's no way.

DEMON ENEMY OF THE PATRIARCHY

You're flat-out fucked. You don't understand her body like the shower nozzle does. No matter the size of your canoe, it's no match for Niagara Falls. Your organ may be able to thrust...on occasion, it might even throb...but alas, it cannot PULSATE, *mon ami*. Your tongue may be able to flick like a hummingbird's wings, but it cannot match the thousands of spurts-per-minute clocked by a high-tech nozzle. You say you can please your lady all night? The shower nozzle can please her until the city reservoir runs dry.

You have been replaced by a household item. With a mere 20 or 30 dollars, she buys herself lifelong satisfaction. She may need you to install it, but after that you're history.

The penis is obsolete. Shower nozzles do not grow fat and bald. Shower nozzles never fail to achieve an erection. The hand-held shower nozzle is the horseless carriage of human sexual relations. And you, kind sir, are the sickly old horse, put out to pasture.

There is one small chink, however, in the shower nozzle's shining armor: A woman is unable to nag and torture a shower nozzle like she can a real live man, so one of her primary yearnings will go unfulfilled.

Keep hope alive!

I may be the only person alive who understands The Slut. She needs to be tackled in three ways—first, as ignorant males misunderstand her...then, as she misunderstands herself...and finally, as is my wont, I will crack open my skull and beam a supernova of light upon her.

Most of what is "commonly understood" is instead a widespread *mis*understanding, and the slut is no exception to this rule. As commonly understood by the typical rude, fat, wet-farting, hogfucker hairy male, a "slut" is a girl who can wantonly have sloppy sex with multiple partners without ever attaching meaning to it. Sluts are thought to be like males in this respect, and this is exactly what threatens such males and why they feel compelled to demean her. If a woman acts like a man in any way—but especially as it pertains to sex—such males feel like homos and inevitably go on killing sprees.

Many men, God forgive them, suffer a near-total compartmentalization of the Madonna/Whore Complex. They want one woman they can take advantage of and another they can take home to mom. They want one woman to take a money shot in the face and another to bake cookies for the kids. At the end of the day, they'll discard the slut like a dried-up Kleenex and scurry home in favor of a normal, "well-adjusted" woman who's lousy at sex but is willing to squirt out his babies, marry him, and trap him into wage slavery for life. These sort of men almost act as if sex and love are opposites.

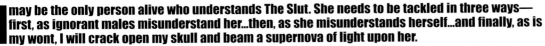

THE SLUT, ON THE OTHER HAND, can't tell the difference between love and sex. Except for the fucking-everything-that-breathes part, all the sluts I've known—and it'd take a calculator to tally them—embody the near-opposite of the stereotype. They attach MORE nonsexual importance to sex than the most romantic-minded "nice" girl could ever conjure. Sluts don't merely *attach* meaning to sex—they inject, infuse, and *saturate* sex with meaning. They INFECT sex with meaning. Sluts are not only better in bed than "normal" girls—they're usually much more *romantic*, too. The second you touch her, she's making wedding plans. The slut is more clingy, intense, weepy, and emotionally involved than any "normal" girl.

I've known a few nice girls who can have sex simply for pleasure, but the sluts never seem to have sex for sex's sake alone. Sex is incidental, merely the worm on a hook. Because the slut can't discriminate between body and mind, she'll let you enjoy *one* hoping it'll automatically force you into esteeming the *other*. That's like handing someone a cupcake and hoping it'll make you appreciate their penmanship. It's like walking around in a scuba-diving outfit, complaining that nobody sees your skin. You're expected to walk straight up into her vagina and find her personality there. She believes that if a guy enjoys having sex with her, he must love her. She's truly that stupid.

Every time a slut sticks a dick in her mouth, it's as if she's screaming PLEASE LOVE ME! into a big pink microphone. Whatever it was that warped her—daddy's cock, mommy's backhand, or just the usual, everyday, run-of-the-mill, soul-choking cloud of lovelessness and abandonment—it left her with a bottomless hole in her heart and the unshakable notion that all she can offer to others is a pair of spread legs. She seeks to fill the hole in her heart by constantly cramming things between the other hole. And over time, both holes get bigger.

SO ON ONE END OF THE SPECTRUM you have the average male, a punch-drunk Sperm Taxi who can almost never love someone and have sex with them at the same time. And on the other end you have the slut, a cum-drunk Ovum Rickshaw who can almost never have sex without falling in love with someone.

And in the middle, hovering high above the others—yet not so high that I deign to leave the writhing masses to their own devices—you have me, an intensely well-adjusted prophet and soothsayer endowed with the wisdom to realize that although love and sex frequently overlap, they are NEVER the same thing. After all, I love my dog, but I'll never fuck her again.

"Discrimination" didn't used to be such a naughty word. It used to mean you could tell the difference between things. I discriminate whenever I get the chance, and I can tell the difference between sex and love.

My problem with sluts isn't that they're hypersexual or oversexed or even nonorgasmically nymphomaniacal—the problem is that they think it all *means* something. My advice to all you sluts is to be like me—enjoy sex as much as you can, and forget about the other thing. Love hurts. Sex, at least after the first time, usually doesn't.

Take comfort, All Ye Sluts—I will never judge you for your promiscuity. I'm much more repelled by your crippled, tragic, dangerous quest for love than by your prolific sexual exploits.

...reconsidered   Feel better? Good. That's my good girl. Now get over here and blow me.

REPUBLIC
THE HOTTEST BITCHE

I'm here to rain on y'all's parade. I declare without equivocation that 99% of the armchair political analysts who bitch and piss and moan about corrupt, stupid politicians are themselves WAYYYY too fucked-up to EVER acquire, much less maintain, anything resembling political power. So, really, for cunt's sake, all you career alcoholics and junkies and sex addicts and welfare cheats who get on a soapbox and cry about your leaders, I'm here to tell you that no matter how moronic those leaders may be, they do a better job at it than you could ever hope to do, and deep down in your dysfunctional aortas, you KNOW I'm right. That's the TRUTH, bitches. That's why they're in power and you're not. Sorry to break it to you, but somebody had to do it.

When big-eared idiot George W. Bush wins again—this time by a landslide—it still gives you no excuse for your shambles of a personal life. [Note: This was written in October of 2004.]

OK? Now I feel better.

This article was initially intended to be a contemplative rumination regarding a study released a decade or so ago concluding that Republicans have sex more frequently than Democrats.

I'm not making this up. I distinctly remember reading newspaper accounts and seeing TV-news broadcasts about the study. It shocked many people at the time, because Democrats, the insufferably self-righteous pustules that they are, have convinced themselves that *they* are the free-lovin', liberated, loosey-goosey party and that everyone in the G.O.P. is a sexually repressed psychopath who ejaculates at the sight of innocent blood being spilled and who walks around with a large black dildo secretly stuffed up their ass.

I don't identify with either major U.S. political party, and I'm always bemused to see people who should have more discernment fall prey to the divide-and-conquer scheme which underlies the two-party system. No matter whom you vot for, Republican or Democrat, it's going to be an insanely privileged millionaire who is paid even MORE money to decide in what manner they're going to STEAL 40 percent of your wages. Republicans and Democrats are merely two fist-puppets on the same predatory monster.

I'm not a Republican or a Democrat. I'm a felon who isn't allowed to vote, and I wouldn't vote even if they let me. I just enjoy fucking with people's heads and proving, more often than not, that the world is upside-down.

You don't think the world is upside-down? Consider these facts:

• More Germans died in World War II than Jews.
• Blacks commit racially motivated hate crimes more frequently than whites.
• Women commit acts of domestic assault more frequently than men.

These are all FACTS, bitches, and I can back them up with the relevant studies, while none of you will be able to prove me wrong, so don't even try. I savor these facts only because they prove that the truth is often the opposite of public perception. And it is for this reason—not because I like Republicans—that I'm inclined to believe that Republicans have sex more frequently than Democrats.

However, no amount of earnest Googling was able to track down this study. So instead of the sober, frank, political analysis for which I am widely renowned, I instead offer you a rundown o the hottest twats, past and present, who people the party of Honest Abe Lincoln.

Elephants have bigger dicks than donkeys. Case closed.

NAME: Condoleezza Rice
RELEVANCE: National Security Advisor under soon-to-be-reelected President George W. Bush.
WHY SHE'S SEXY: She's the world's most powerful black woman this side of Oprah. She has a gap between her teeth. She has a cute button nose. She advises the president to kill people.
WHAT I'D DO TO HER: Disprove most of the stereotypes about white men except perhaps the fact that we smell like wet dogs.

NAME: Laura Bush
RELEVANCE: Faithful, loving wife of soon-to-be-reelected President George W. Bush.
WHY SHE'S SEXY: Her eyes are full of fun 'n' mischief. She seems like she'd keep her cooch relatively clean. And according to a recently published book, she allegedly sold weed while in college.
WHAT I'D DO TO HER: The Dirty Sanchez while taking bong hits.

AN GASH
F THE G.O.P.

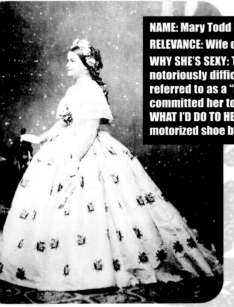

NAME: Mary Todd Lincoln
RELEVANCE: Wife of slain President Abraham Lincoln.
WHY SHE'S SEXY: This feisty daughter of Kentucky slaveholders was a notoriously difficult and flighty personality whom Lincoln's aides referred to as a "hell-cat." She was so nuts, one of her sons eventually committed her to an asylum.
WHAT I'D DO TO HER: Sneak under her petticoat and massage her clit with a motorized shoe buffer.

NAME: Elizabeth Dole
RELEVANCE: Former U.S. Transportation Secretary and one-time presidential contender. Wife of crotchety Viagra spokesman and former Prez-candidate Bob Dole.
WHY SHE'S SEXY: Beautiful teeth. Nice eyebrows. Smart, assured, and powerful. Remains pretty even though she's now, like, 80 years old. I can instinctually tell that her vagina would have a pleasant aroma.
WHAT I'D DO TO HER: Ask her for career advice while she blows me, insisting that she keep my cock in her mouth while she talks.

AME: Betty Ford
ELEVANCE: Wife of klutzy ex-Prez Gerald Ford. aging alcoholic who sobered up and started a linic where stars go to sober up.
HY SHE'S SEXY: I'm a sucker for the bouffant. lus, I recently viewed a previously unaired arbara Walters interview conducted while etty was First Lady. The bitch was so snock-red, she could hardly stand up.
HAT I'D DO TO HER: Get her drunk again and let ature have its way.

NAME: Marilyn Quayle
RELEVANCE: Wife of semi-retarded ex-Vice Prez Dan Quayle.
WHY SHE'S SEXY: Looks like Loretta Lynn with an overbite.
WHAT I'D DO TO HER: Let her nibble on my dick like it's corn on the cob.

NAME: Debbie Brannigan
RELEVANCE: Curator of conservative website CapitalistChicks.com.
WHY SHE'S SEXY: Will ya look at the pair of barkin' McGuffeys on her?
WHAT I'D DO TO HER: Have her ride me on top while she wears a party hat, plays the kazoo, and wears pasties on her ta-tas.

NAME: Lauren Bush
RELEVANCE: 16-year-old niece of soon-to-be-reelected President George W. Bush.
WHY SHE'S SEXY: Nice eyes. You can just tell she ain't had no real dick yet.
WHAT I'D DO TO HER: Dry-fuck her ass the day she turns 18.

leTURNED-OUT

AS SCHOOL BELLS RING throughout Multnomah County and thousands of Portland students return to school this year, several questions nag me:

How do we prevent their teachers from having sex with them?

Failing that, how do we ensure that their sexual relationships are healthy, safe, and satisfying?

And even if they're none of these things, even if the teacher winds up in prison and the student comes down with an array of eating disorders, why do so many of us find the subject of teacher-student sex so arousing?

These are serious questions and ones that bear more sober scrutiny than perhaps your average strip-club habitué is capable of mustering. God forbid we should try to UNDERSTAND why our dicks lead us around like dogs on chains.

WASHINGTON STATE EX-TEACHER MARY KAY LETOURNEAU,

42, was recently released from a seven-year prison bid that resulted from her ongoing sexual relationship with Vili Fualaau, a former student who is 21 years her junior.

The case has slalomed in and out of the news for nearly eight years, yielding a TV movie (*All-American Girl*), a cable documentary (*Forbidden Desire*), and a book (*If Loving You is Wrong*). Note the naughtiness in each of these titles, their steamy-sexy-*oh!-la-la* tone.

The truth is that Americans are TURNED ON by the Letourneau case, and that's why it's received such huge attention. The major media don't dangle anything before us which, despite how twisted or sublimated or non-sexual it might seem, doesn't stroke our deepest libidinal impulses.

"He dominated me in the most masculine way that any man, any leader, could do," Letourneau would say of the cockroachy-looking Samoan-American student who was

Mary Kay Letourneau: In French, her last name means "fucks her students."

only 13 when, as his 34-year-old teacher, she first bedded him. Letourneau, who at the time was married with four children, eventually popped out two more saplings conceived from what Fualaau estimates were 300-400 rounds of unprotected rutting.

Fualaau first became Letourneau's student in 1989 as a second-grader. In the sixth grade, he again found himself Letourneau's pupil. Letourneau, by that time weary of a loveless, sexless marriage, formed a romantic attachment to her gangsta-stylee student. Even during summer break, she'd constantly have him as a houseguest, allowing him to smoke cigarettes indoors and endlessly complimenting him to her husband. This gradually grated on hubby Steve Letourneau's nerves. After one family blowup in the summer of 1996, Vili ran out of the house to avoid a confrontation with Steve. Mary Kay hopped in her van and searched for Vili, tracking him down at a local marina. He got in the van. She started crying. They kissed. They kissed harder. Harder.

Police flashlights halted their passion. Cops initially believed that Letourneau had kidnapped the youngster, but she lied and said he was 18.

Only days later, they fucked for the first time.

HOT HOT HOT. Middle-aged white cuckold husband shamed by 13-year-old Samoan boy. Teacher's out fucking her student while castrated hubby sits home and takes care of the kids. Fucking in her car and in her husband's bed and in school closets. Thick brown Samoan boycock pounding fertile teachercunt. She's getting her first good dick in years—maybe ever. He's gorging on her like she's a smorgasbord. Little teacher's pet...petting her pussy. She's teaching him, all right. Teaching him all anyone ever really needs to know.

THEY FUCKED ALL SUMMER and well into the winter. In late February 1997, with Mary Kay visibly pregnant, Steve Letourneau discovered that not only wasn't the baby his, it had been fathered by his wife's little pet, who'd been hammering her for months. A day after Steve's discovery, his cousin ratted out Mary Kay to a school-district administrator. The next day, Mary Kay was arrested and charged with statutory rape. A law that only applies to male offenders in other states such as California, statch-rape is gender-neutral in Washington.

analyzing the **Mary Kay Letourneau** case: was it rape, love, or just **really good sex?**

Three months after her arrest, Mary Kay bore her first child from Vili. In August of 1997, she pleaded guilty to two counts of second-degree child rape. She was forced to spend 80 days in jail and forbidden from further contact with Fualaau under threat of imprisonment for up to eight years. Less than a month after her release, police again found her inside her van's steamed-up windows, caught *in flagrante delicto* with Vili.

She couldn't stay away from that cock.

The vehicle contained extra clothing and $6,200 in cash, leading authorities to believe the pair intended to vamoose without a trace. Letourneau appeared in court three days later, looking disoriented and well-fucked. Her probation was revoked, and she began a prison sentence that only ended in August, 2004. In 1998, while imprisoned, she bore her second child from Vili, who cared for their two children while living with his mother.

Letourneau's husband divorced her and moved with their kids to Alaska. Mary Kay, the daughter of a right-wing California congressman who'd been forced out of public life when his extramarital affair became publicized, found that most of her own family members abandoned her.

She was left with only a prison cell and her memories of Vili.

And the world continued to argue whether it was love or rape.

Remember when the magic started, but it still seemed only safe to send our feelings through music and movie themes? Do you remember when I knew we needed each other each day, constantly, when "I love you" was disguised so we could say it all day in front of everyone? All the love songs seem to have been written for us.
—love letter from Letourneau to Fualaau

MARY KAY INSISTED IT WAS LOVE.
She noted that even Vili's mother pleaded with the judge for lenience, believing that her son and Letourneau were possibly in love. For the length of her sentence, Mary Kay professed undying affection for Vili. Even when he said he'd lost feelings for her, even when almost everyone in the world was certain that he was out there fucking teenaged girls while she sat in a cell, Mary Kay never wavered in her conviction that theirs had been a deep, mature, undying love that would blossom again upon her release.

"I would never regret my relationship with Vili Fualaau," she told a reporter while in prison. "I wish for everybody in life that they would be blessed with such a mutually loving and respectful relationship."

Sad, really.

DID SHE RAPE HIM? Some would argue that she operated like a classic predator, abusing her power to ensnare a gullible victim through sex.

There's an undeniable double standard regarding gender and adult-child relationships. If Letourneau had been a man and Fualaau a young girl, there'd be no gray area here, no question of whether it was love, and certainly not the merest murmur of whether the sex might have been good.

But is it POSSIBLE for most 13-year-old boys, with their constant erections and 24-hour obsession with getting laid, to be raped? When I was 13, my DREAM would have been to be "raped" by a teacher…or even a goddamned nun. In other cultures and at other times, 13-year-olds are considered adults. And since most "children" that age are able to repro-

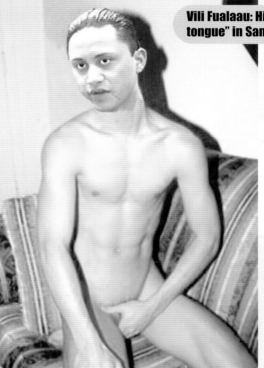

Vili Fualaau: His name means "big dick, long tongue" in Samoan.

duce—young Vili knocked up Mary Kay *twice*—nature apparently considers them adults, too. Our culture also suffers from a delusion that 13-year-olds are unable of willful acts, of being smart, wise, or manipulative. And one doesn't dare MENTION the fact that they're highly sexual, maybe more so than any adult.

From all accounts, Vili initiated sex between the two of them. He'd even bet a fellow student $20 that he'd be able to seduce Letourneau. Much later, he pocketed thousands by telling his story to a tabloid. And he unsuccessfully tried suing the school district for his "victimization."

AT FUALAAU'S REQUEST, a judge lifted a no-contact order between the two shortly after Letourneau's release. Since Vili is legally an adult, it's impossible that Mary Kay can commit statutory rape against him again. It's possible they'll fall deeply in love again and silence those who've cried rape all these years. Or, most likely, they'll have some good sex and drift apart.

I predict that Fualaau will dump her, leaving her emotionally shattered. Vili will be fine; Mary Kay will be a wreck. And after a seven-year prison stretch, the loss of her family, and public humiliation, it will become clear who the victim was in this case all along. That student turned his teacher into a ruined whore. That li'l boy with the hot brown cock left her le-turned-out.

did JESUS have WET DREAMS?

Wet dreams are a natural bodily function that we have no control over. This included our Lord Jesus Christ. Given the fact that he was fully human as well as fully divine gives us the place to say that it is conceivable that He had wet dreams, and since He was a man without sin, wet dreams cannot be a sin.

—Post on soc.religion.christian, 3/1/1994

When you are encamped against your enemies, keep away from everything impure. If one of your men is unclean because of a nocturnal emission, he is to go outside the camp and stay there. But as evening approaches he is to wash himself, and at sunset he may return to the camp.

—Deuteronomy 23:9-11

the dubious role of NOCTURNAL EMISSIONS in HUMAN SPIRITUALITY

JESUS:
Exactly how human WAS he?

Most major world religions, from Buddha in the East to Muhammad in the West, in areas reaching from the majestic polar bears at the North Pole to the humble penguins down in Antarctica, preach that the physical plane is implicitly defiled and corrupt. They regard our fleshly state as a fall from grace, a tainted existence, a dirty pigpen filled with pee-pee and ca-ca. If we lived in a state of innate purity and innocence, and if all is natural and nothing is forbidden, there'd be no need for religion or God or redemption. If we lived in the Garden of Eden right now, who the fuck would need God?

At least that's how the ancients saw it. Accordingly, world religions tend to equate the human condition—and the sexuality which perpetuates it—with dirt and sin and separation from God. But more modern-minded people see nothing wrong with being human. They believe we're born perfect. They believe we live in heaven right now, which, if it's true, is a BIG FUCKING disappointment.

But some people try to have it both ways. They vainly attempt to reconcile modern sexuality with ancient sex-hating spirituality. Such latter-day menses-crazed mulligatawny-soup-scented hippie attempts to cram square pegs into round holes are doomed from the get-go.

Therefore, sex-positive Christianity is a contradiction in terms. There's nothing Christians hate more than some sex. Put on that fig leaf and forget about it. So if Jesus was a sexual being, as the New Age Earth Mommas insist he was, he couldn't have possibly been the son of God as 99% of Christians define it. And if he was the son of God, ambassador of a spiritual realm forever elevated above carnal stickiness, it would have been a mite undignified if he was runnin' around waxin' ass and jackin' off.

"But Jesus was human," they'll remind us. Well, not exactly. Regardless of denomination, Christians agree that Jesus never sinned. But they'll also claim that being a sinner is a crucial part

of being human. It's an inherent contradiction of the messiah myth. Christians can never fully explain exactly HOW human Jesus really was. And while we're at it, why would God need to BECOME human in order to understand what it's like? He CREATED humans, so we assume the old senile bastard wrote the Owner's Manual. It gets complicated. After a while, it's like asking questions about Santa Claus—none of it makes sense.

I'm not a Christian. I don't *expect* any of it to make sense. I believe that one should only feel guilty about sex when it's done poorly. Personally, I don't believe Jesus was divine. I don't think he had God's cell-phone number handy or anything like that. I think he was probably a bravely masochistic human being with all sorts of twisted sexual proclivities. C'mon—running around with 12 other guys at age 33?

But for the sake of fun, let's pretend that Jesus was indeed whom he said he was. Since he had a body, we can assume that he pooped and peed and farted and slept and ate. These are all things that humans do. But world religions never equate spiritual guilt with any of these functions—only with sex. So sexual energy must be something a little different. Sex is forever entwined with the idea of creation—several ancient religions portray the Big Bang as some sort of divine ejaculation. But interestingly, they depict the event as an act of *will,* with God either masturbating or intentionally impregnating someone. It's never accidental.

Are wet dreams accidental? Is there a difference between a "nocturnal emission," which sounds like an involuntary physical act, and a "wet dream," which implies that one's consciousness actively creates a pornographic scenario?

Assuming that Jesus was God...and that willfully having sex is part of the sinful human condition...wet dreams would HAVE to be accidental in order for Jesus to have had them. Ya dig?

If Jesus ever ejaculated, one cannot help but wonder about the sperm. Was it, too, divine? When it dried up, were millions of tiny deities killed? Did Jesus shoot an average-sized load or a gargantuan Divinity Wad? And dare one wonder about the size, texture...and *taste*...of his genitals?

The Gospels never allude to Christ as a sexual being. But God DID send a son, not a daughter, so we assume that at the very least, Jesus had a penis. Jesus had a beard, so it must be assumed that he had pubic hair and probably even frequent morning erections. We know that he could suffer...but could he feel pleasure? *Sexual* pleasure? What sort of chicks might Jesus go for? After a sweaty day of carpentry and eyeballing Israeli maidens, was he tortured by dreams of their carnal allure?

Given that the Old Testament clearly forbids the wasting of one's seed (in Genesis 38, God slew Onan for spilling his jizz on the ground), we can rule out that Jesus masturbated.

So it all hinges on whether or not Jesus had wet dreams. I'm sure the apostles were having them. They were having wet dreams left and right. The apostles were a buncha squirt monkeys.

The quote from Deuteronomy gives us the answer, my brothers and sisters. Israeli soldiers who had nocturnal emissions were regarded as "unclean" and thus tainted by sin. And sin is always a choice, never an involuntary spasm. So the God of the Bible regards a nocturnal emission as the willful act of a sinner.

So, at least within a biblical framework, there's no possible way that Jesus had wet dreams.

IN JEWISH MYTHOLOGY, Lilith was Adam's first wife, but she was a little too butch for him and split for the Red Sea when Adam insisted on the missionary position. She whiled away the hours having group sex with demons, whom she claimed were better in the sack than Adam. By the Middle Ages, her legend as a semi-divine nympho was such that

LILITH:
Said to induce wet dreams in medieval men

Hebrew men began blaming her for causing their nocturnal emissions. They believed that Lilith or her daughters would visit at night and squat atop their unsuspecting cocks. It was also said that if a male infant laughed in his sleep, Lilith was trying to fondle him. Christians altered the Lilith story into the legend of the succubi, ethereal sex kittens who drained believers' balls as they slept. To ward off their charms, monks would sleep with their hands over their crotch, clutching a crucifix. Christian females could blame their sexual dreams on an incubus, the male counterpart to a succubus; in a pinch, they could also blame the incubus for an unwanted pregnancy.

Of course, nobody blamed *themselves* for these erotic dreams, nor for the fluids left in their wake.

THE WIZARDS OF MODERN MEDICINE aren't sure what causes wet dreams. As soon as one theory gains credence, some new study will come along to knock everything askew again. Pragmatic explanations for wet dreams have focused on the purely physiological, pointing a finger at everything from full bladders to excess testosterone. Others blame an accumulation of sexual tension which has found no release through ordinary outlets. It has been speculated that nocturnal emissions are the body's way of flushing out sperm that has aged well past its vintage, but this doesn't account for the fact that some sexually inactive men *never* have wet dreams, while some sleeping studs squirt all over the duck-down comforter two nights in a row even when enjoying lots of pooty-tang in their waking hours.

What *is* known is that both men and women are capable of reaching orgasm while asleep, although it's much harder to spot the evidence with females. But the fact that women can also cum while sleeping would cast doubt on the idea that nocturnal emissions are caused primarily by friction—an involuntary rubbing of the penis on bedsheets, a mattress, or one's pajamas. It's difficult for a woman to *accidentally* rub her clit against something.

Sleepy-time orgasms occur during the REM phase of sleep, during which most healthy men achieve at least a partial erection and most women lubricate vaginally. But what remains blurry is the role of dreaming...i.e., the role of human consciousness and willfulness...in taking physiological arousal to the level of orgasmic release. If there's a required element of fantasy, then wet dreams are no accident. They are the physical result of human beings creating pornography in their minds while sleeping.

If one can choose to have a wet dream, it would stand to reason that you could will to *not* have one, too. For me, the proof is in the pudding... or, rather, the lack thereof.

Kind readers, I was a hardcore Christian for nearly two years from the age of 14 to 16. Those mid-teen years are supposedly the prime of one's nocturnal emitting. Before becoming Christian, I'd spurt out a cream-container's worth of early teen REM-jism. Rarely a day went by that I didn't wake up with Alfredo sauce all over my drawers. But after giving my heart to the imaginary Jesus hologram in my head, I didn't have a single wet dream. Not once for two years did my body feel the need to involuntarily flush aging sperm from my sanctified nuts. So I must conclude that willfulness is a part of all sexual thought, whether waking or asleep. If you dream that you're sucking your dad's cock, it isn't "just a dream"—you *really* wanna huff papa's bone.

So if you wake up one morning with applesauce all over your boxer briefs, don't listen to the pop psychologists who say you shouldn't feel guilty. It wasn't an accident—your dirty mind caused it.

"Wet dreams are no accident. They are the physical result of human beings creating pornography in their minds while sleeping."

The JACK SHACK
Manly Porno Reviews from a Man Who Hates Porno

My pet pug, an ultra-hyper sloppy little girl named Cookie, awakes me every morning, climbing her little buff body onto my chest, standing on my throat, digging her claws into my larynx, and licking my face until it's impossible to sleep. It's cute, but it's also annoying. Recently she received her first menstrual period, and my tiny apartment looked like a slaughterhouse, especially the bed-sheets. She has this mystifying little protrusion which normally juts out of her snapper, a tiny jellybean-styled fleshy nub; when she was greeted with Eve's Curse, said nub swelled up to the size and color of a strawberry. It was caked in dried blood and gave off a foul, metallic, fishy smell. Did I mention that she barks a lot, too? Cookie manages to be cute, annoying, and repellent all at the same time.

Kinda like Bridget the Midget.

All three feet, ten inches of her.

During *Strap On Midget*'s opening montage, a shot of an eager, manic Bridget in bed, flailing around atop a full-sized girl's chest, instantly reminded me of what my pug does to me every morning. Bridget is tiny like my pug. She is rough and graceless like my pug. And she has a DISGUSTING VAGINA, just like my cuddly widdle pug.

Nine or so months ago, there was talk around the office about flying me down to the Moonlite Bunnyranch in Nevada to fuck Bridget the Midget and then write about it. Since Bridget has a sexy gap in her teeth and would be able to blow me while we both were standing, I was more than willing to oblige. But at the time I had a rather jealous girlfriend, and my Midget Rendezvous never materialized. But I've finally managed to extricate myself from tiresome, constricting, boyfriend-and-girlfriend scenarios, and recently my thoughts turned once again to Bridget, that pint-sized fleshy lump o' fun. I thought of resur-recting my Midget Fuck story. I seriously pondered flying to Reno and plopping my penis straight into a midget's vagina.

This all came crashing down the moment I first laid eyes on that HORRIFYING SNAIL TWAT of hers. *Strap On Midget* offers no soothing soundtrack music, no muted camera focus, to blunt the gut-walloping pain that greets the viewer during those first awful frames which spotlight Bridget's splayed-open groin area. I am not stating this for effect, only to share a dreadful, dreadful truth with the reader, to hopefully try and exorcise—or at least *dim* some-what—a ghastly image which is burned into my brain: the sight of Bridget's wee, miscolored vulva, with its two-tone lips and generally slimy appearance, caused me to scream, physically tremble, and even dry-heave during the entire sequence where a goofy, faggy tall guy per-formed the act of oral love upon her horribly uncomely genital region. A loose string dangling from her pull-up stockings onto her general, er, groinal area didn't help the visuals, either. Neither did a black-widow spider tattooed right above her bristly muff—it merely looked like it was walking into a spider's den where hundreds of other arachnids creepy-crawled around. Nor did the brown nimbus surrounding her butthole. I've seen a lot of disgusting things in my life—on many occasions, I've sought them out—but Bridget's disturbing midget cunt is right up there near the tippity-top.

There isn't even the pretense of a plot here—the title says it all. You get a midget with a strap-on, and very little in the way of a stunning narrative or emotional complexity. There is no foreplay, no annoying dialogue leading up to the sex. It's nice, actually.

Here's a sample of the verbal interaction:

Bridget: [with Faggy Guy's cock in her mouth]: "Mm-hmm?"... *Faggy Guy: Oh, yeah* ..."Ha!"... *Ha!* ..."Mm-hmm?"... *Mm-HMM* ..."Mm-hmm?"... *Aww, yeah* ..."Mm-hmm?"...*Whew!*

Bridget suddenly appears with a pink rubber strap-on dildo that is almost as large as Bridget. Faggy Guy sort of half-heartedly protests, but soon he's sticking

his legs back behind his ears bunny-rabbit-style and taking it in his faggy, acne-ravaged butt. The dildo makes a cringeworthy splatting sound when it enters his rectum. Bridget taunts him about his tight asshole. Her thrusts are disturbingly rough and eager, her little dinosaur arms flapping in syncopation with her munchkin pelvis. At one point, the camera zooms in on a what appears to be a smear of shit or blood near the dildo's tip. Faggy Guy grunts and groans in pain: "Stop! Stop!" but you know he loves it.

Bridget then wields the strap-on with a middle-aged woman who has a bird face and saggy tits and a hilariously outdated Rolling Stones "lick" tattoo on her flabby belly. Bird Woman has a foul Yonkers

STRAP ON MIDGET
Filmco / 2000 / Director: Morgan Load
Stars: Bridget "The Midget" Powers, Kathy Jones, Candy Cooze, Angi Wilson, Dick Nasty, Mr. Sexy

accent and wears rings, gold chains, and the always stylish Italian Gold Disco Horn Necklace. She looks as if she smells like sour boiled cabbage. Her moans of ecstasy sound somewhat like puking: "BLAHHH! BLAHHH! BLECHHH!"

"What a big dick you have here, lady!" she barks at Bridget before proceeding to perform fellatio upon the inanimate phallus. She pretends it's a real dick, and Bridget pretends that having Bird Woman suck on the rubber implement feels good for her, too. Bird Woman makes exaggerated, surreal expressions as she bobs her head ostrich-style up and down on the huge phony tool. She laps at Bridget's plastic balls, too, feigning pleasure all the while.

Her rolls of fat are stacked like white tires, and her saggy jugs swing around with far too much ease and slackness. When Bridget goes down on her, it looks as if her face is buried in a vast white snowdrift.

And then, just like Bridget's twat had previously bum-rushed my eyeballs, there it is—a *hemorrhoid* on Bird Woman's ass, a pumpkin-seed-sized rectal inflammation in all its itchy splendor.

I realize I want to die.

Bridget's next strap-on victim is a blonde woman who appears to be approximately 800 years old. Her hair is peroxided an eye-burning blonde, and her wrinkled lids are thickly smeared with butane-flame-blue eyeliner. Picture an old reptile with blue eyeliner and a Vince Neil wig, and you're getting close. Her visage bespeaks a lifetime of abuse, bad breaks, heartache, and blown chances. Her veiny hands grab desperately at Bridget's rubber tool. So old, so much waste, so many battle scars and tire tracks. A foul human being all around. Her burnt-toast vagina finally requires artificial lube in order to receive all of Bridget's strap-on rubberiness.

The film ends with a straight hetero scene featuring a bald guy and a blonde woman with hard-shell coconut sur-gical tits. No Bridgets, no midgets, and no strap-on devices. He shoots it all over her face...THE END.

If your weary soul has been searching hi and lo for a video in which a female Little Person joyously fucks a guy's pimply ass with a strap-on dildo, look no further than *Strap On Midget*, another blockbuster of questionable taste from our friends over at Filmco. I don't know what they charge for these videos— we get them for free at the office. All I *know* is that I don't want any of these people to have orgasms EVER again. And all I *learned* is that Mother Nature sometimes makes mistakes.

The brother gets a new crib. He invites these fine sistas over to party. What do they do? Piss all over the damn place. He don't mind, they fuck and suck him and his bro's til'll [sic] they dry!

—*Video box to* **Sista's Gotta Piss**

I piss so frequently, it's a wonder I find the time to do anything else. There's a recent aimed-at-geriatrics TV commercial that claims you may have a problem if you urinate more than eight times within 24 hours. Fuck, there are times I urinate more than eight times an *hour*. What's wrong with me? Is it diabetes? Frickin' prostate cancer? Too much coffee? I really should see a doctor about this, but I'm scared.

Let's say I'm having sex, and let's just say the girl's on top and doesn't realize her thigh is pounding down on my bladder, and why don't we just say that I have to excuse myself, run to the bathroom with my hard cock boinging around, and beat that erection into submission so I can drain my bloated, itchy bladder? Are you with me?

Sex and urination have become hopelessly intertwined for me, so it was with great interest that I approached Filmco's *Sista's Gotta Piss* series. American race relations are also a personal obsession, if only for the comic potential. So you have me, a hyper-urinating race-obsessed porno reviewer, paired with a video series depicting fudge-colored L.A. hood-rat nubiles pissin' all over the damn place. Hey—you got sistas on my piss! No—you got piss on my sistas! It's two great tastes that taste great together!

The first *Sista's Gotta Piss* boasts a beautiful pair of twin slim Negresses with wild green eyes

SISTA'S GOTTA PISS
Filmco / 2001 / Director: MC Piss Hammer
Stars: The Twins (Chocolate & Mocha), Lola Lane, Skyy, Tony Eveready, Devlin Weed, Byron

SISTA'S GOTTA PISS 2
Filmco / 2001 / Director: MC Piss Hammer
Stars: Black Cat, Sierra, Diamond, Destiny, Dominico, Julian St. Jox, Tony Eveready

named Chocolate and Mocha. In the opening segment, one of them (they aren't identified in the film) is shown pissing on the poolside cement of some lavish, my-man-sells-lotsa-crack, SoCal mansion. She

DO NOT
ENTER

says her little piss puddle is her "autograph." She then leads her amiable male companion into a bedroom where, under very bright, very clinical lighting, they proceed to have sex while wacky, bongo-driven canary music chirps in the background.

Her partner is a heavy-lidded dreadlocked homeboy with a massive Scud-missile dong. His cock is so big, it scares you when you first see it. A mighty hammerhead shark. A giganto-choco-cock. A real rhinoceros. Much bigger than, say, the average human bowel movement. Naturally, he can't fit it all in her. He doesn't even get the lower part of the shaft wet. Lucky bastard.

Crouching on the bed, she gives him a looooooooong blowjob while he stands at the bedside, as motionless as a bank teller. Later, as things heat up, a whitish paste forms on his armpits. Is that what blacks refer to as "duck butter"? Or is it more properly "pit butter"? And as the couple is flailing about athletically during intercourse, weird gummy white morsels start forming on his cock and her ass cheeks. Is *that* possibly "duck butter"? Or maybe it's a combination of "nut butter" and "twat butter." Whatever it's called, I say "hats off!" to the blacks for their bodies' natural-born self-lathering capabilities.

The green-eyed twin suddenly interrupts their coupling to run outside and piss. They finally resume fucking, his pachydermal nutsac tightens, and he dumps a huge load of tapioca pudding on her brown cheeks.

It is around this time when I realize I have to pee.

The next segment begins with a chubby black girl at the same poolside, looking off-camera and squirting a bold, high-arced yellow stream from her snatch. It's unsettling how the piss comes out in a solid projectile as with males. It looks like it's coming out of a dick, only there's no dick there. I sort of thought that with chicks, piss sort of sprayed outwardly, or maybe it just dribbled down their legs or something.

A shaven-skulled hi-yella brudda with convict-style tattoos approaches the errant urinatress and reprimands her about piddling on his property. He then whips out his dingy and begins pissing, too, just to show her how wrong it is. This excites her. She explains that she pissed outside because it was such a beautiful day, which seems fair enough to me. She even offers to clean it up. They repair into the house. The wide-eyed strawberry then gives him a blowjob while sensuous guitars strum on the soundtrack. She then blurts out a piss stream *Exorcist*-style on his hardwood floor while blowing him. "Why'd you do that shit?!?" he asks, and she just keeps sucking his knob without answering. *"Sista's jus' gots ta piss, dat's why,"* is what her silence seems to convey.

I pause the tape and run into the bathroom to drain my main vein. Roughly a quart of foamy yellow pee-pee gushes from my Love Faucet.

More scenes, more urinating Negresses, more black blowjobs and black intercourse. Another chubby black girl with vulva-enshrouding lingerie pisses in the kitchen sink. She sports hanging tits with nipples the size of chocolate donuts. There's a possible cesarean scar. Like prior segments, this one's extraordinarily sparse on dialogue. Black dude walks up. Braids and sagging jeans, big belly. He strips down to sneakers and socks. She blows him. Together they engage in Negroidal coitus, her balloonish boobs bobbling in syncopation with their thrusting. He shoots a very tiny load on her face.

The first *Sista's* was apparently such a raging success, its sequel was released less than two months later. The pattern is the same as with the first film: A black woman pisses, is scolded, then becomes suddenly aroused and engages in 45 minutes of sucky-fucky. The sequel features a scene of a black man eating a black woman's pussy, a phenomenon so apparently rare that some had relegated it to the realm of urban legend. But mostly it's lots of blowjobs and very little cunnilingus, which is the way I suspect it is with most couples.

I must take this opportunity to complain about the general level of poor spelling within the black porn industry. I mean, sometimes I realize it's for effect...to be "cool," to be "ghetto," to be "hippity-hop" or whatever...but other times I have to conclude that some of these dumb fudgesicles simply can't spell, especially when they spell the SAME THING different ways. For example, while the film is called *Sista's Gotta Piss* on the box, it's *Sista's Gotta Piz* on the actual film's credits. Likewise, it's *Sista's Gotta Piss 2* on the box and *Sista's Gotta Pee Too!* on the credits. And performers identified as Devlin and Chocolate on the screen credits are called Delvin and Chocalate on the box. And what's up with the apostrophe in "Sista's?" Do they *know* it's wrong? Do they care? It's a disgrace, and such lackadaisical attitudes only tend to drag their people down, especially after everything they've been through. The black porn industry would be wise to spell-check their creations.

I should note that I was unable to make it through either film without having to pause the videotape and go piss.

Sistas gotta piss...and so's do I!

As *Airtight Granny* begins, a written disclaimer states that all actors are 18 years of age or older.

NO SHIT!!!

"Gerontophilia" is a clinical term describing a sexual fetish for the elderly, and judging from the near-constant flaccid state of this video's male participants, none of them are afflicted with it. Almost all of this film's drama hinges around the visible struggle of nearly a dozen fat, balding, sallow studs vainly trying to maintain their erections. One guy never takes off his underwear; he just lets his cock poke through the cotton and looks very uncomfortable being there. Another is naked except for his wristwatch and eyeglasses—classy! The men keep lazily massaging their bread loaves throughout the video, rubbing sweat off their faces and looking bored. Their intensely glum disinterest is so strong, it's nearly edible.

The *Granny* of the title is one "Jenette," a shrieking harpy whose naked body looks like it belongs to a plucked, anemic bird. Her saggy flesh hangs like gray elephant skin. Jenette claims to be 72 years old. I'm sure she was a hottie sometime long, long ago, back when Mickey Rooney was a big film star. But time is kind to no one, and Granny stands as Exhibit A. Wearing tasteful pearl earrings, a pearl necklace, and sheer white leggin's, Granny is spunky, sassy, eager to please, possibly drunk, and so old that nothing short of Carbon-14 dating would be able to determine her exact age.

I'm unsure what the "Airtight" in the title refers to, but it surely can't be any of Granny's orifices. Her sloppy twat and saggy ass don't seem particularly snare-drum tight as they slosh around on one dry, brownish cock after the next. In fact, big veiny rigs slide in and out of her

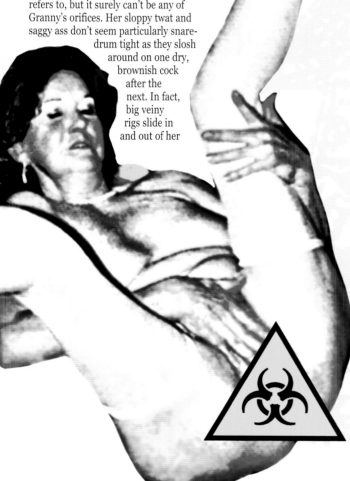

A-hole with the ease of a paper towel wiping the insides of a large drinking tumbler. You could hide a beer can in her ass and one in her snatch, and no one would suspect anything.

All the action, however measly, is filmed under harsh, unforgiving video lights in a small, couch-equipped space that might as well be the back room of the *Exotic* office. A sky-blue backdrop lazily hugs the rear wall. A potted plant sits in the corner. A rainbow-colored blanket adorns the couch.

Hilariously plastic electronic "Peach Pit"-style rubbery fake '50s music, replete with farting saxophones and lotsa deep "ooma-ooma-oomas" and falsetto "ya-ya-ya-yis," bubbles in the background while these disinterested cocks put Granny through the motions. One guy bends his pimply ass over for Granny to eat as burly male voices sing "bop-shoo-waddy-waddy-bop" on the soundtrack. The producers apparently didn't budget enough for the music, because several tunes get repeated near the flick's end.

Granny shares her life with us through these revealing comments:
• "People are too serious. Life is too short. You must smile all the time."
• "I don't go to church, because I don't believe in church. My church and my spirit is in my heart."
• "The monster is in my ass!"
• "You guys enjoyin' yourselves?"
• "Anybody like their butt eat out? Oooh, I love it! It's a very sensual thing for a man, having that done....It's a very sensuous spot."
• "Get down to the bottom of the pit!" [while being ass-fucked]

AIRTIGHT GRANNY
Filmco / 2001 / Directed by Morgan Load
Stars: Jenette "The Promiscous [*sic*] Granny", Will Savage, Paco Pasque John Janiero, Arnold Schwarzenpecker, Talesin, Dick Nasty, Titus, Blake Palmer, Claudio, Hunk Hollywood

• "God Bless America!" [before shoving a fat dick in her mouth]
• "What a sweetheart!" [after someone spooges on her face]
• "Where there's a will, there's a way." [taking one in the mouth and one in the ass simultaneously]
• "Oh, boy, he's sweaty!" [after burying her face in a guy's ass]
• "We got the German helmet at attention!"
• "Fuck my ass, you asshole! Fuck it good, you asshole!"
• "I wear [size] seven-and-a-half gloves—for a woman, that's large."
• "All women should have my attitude. It's a shame."
• "I'll never get old, you guys. I'll always be young!"

WRONG, Granny. You'll NEVER be young again. You'll always be old...or dead.

At one point, the director's voice is heard joking about one of the actors having a sesame seed on his dick, and it's that sort of cheap lowbrow moment which summarizes the festivities. When one guy starts smacking Granny on the head with his *schvanz*, it's appropriately degrading. While sucking cock, Granny makes several disturbing "mm-mm" and "nummy-nummy" sounds. She explains that she loves when men splat their money shots all over her body, because cum serves as an anti-wrinkle cream. My only advice is MORE CUM, Granny, because it ain't workin'! Closeups repeatedly feature Granny's terrifyingly old face smooching at the camera and wagging her tongue. Half-hard cocks comically try squashing inside her holes like slimy ferrets seeking a burrowing den.

The director apparently realizes that the film would be about three months long if it were left up to Granny to satisfy everyone, because the last few minutes consist of a series of fully hard cocks, apparently stimulated by something other than Granny, running up to her and dumping their goop on her face. The final shots of a dazed, cum-splattered Granny staring into the camera bear the queasy unease of a snuff film. And then, as Granny's talking—I LOVE THIS!—she's cut off in MID-SENTENCE, and the phrase "THE END" bounces onto the screen. It's a fittingly disrespectful gesture toward an old tart who deserves nothing less.

It's hard to be sex-positive about this film. Some people shouldn't have sex. Some people should stay clothed. Sex and death are exciting. Sex and old age are merely disgusting. Everyone gets old and dies, but most of us don't do it on camera. With the Graying of America, we all face an important choice: to grow old gracefully, or to thrash about under hot video lights, squawking dockyard-hooker obscenities while our ancient, melted-candle-wax bodies try without much success to keep nearly a dozen bored donkeys fully erect.

There can't be a God, because He wouldn't allow things such as this septuagenarian gang-bang to exist. Same goes double for Goddess. When you are exposed to something such as this, you are permanently tainted. You can never really wash it all off. If Granny's grandkids have any sense, they'd have her committed immediately.

The JACK SHACK

In past installments of *The Jack Shack*, I've written about mutant hardcore porn—urinatin' Negresses, cock-gobblin' grandmas, and strap-on midgets. Before I progress to amputee gang-bangs and colostomy-bag splash-fests, I figure it's time to take a break and go to the other extreme—this month, we're gonna dim the lights and bring you some softcore. Some fluffcore, if you will.

"Nudie-cutie" is a term describing what were typically short, silent films from the 1940s through the 1960s in which women gradually removed their undergarments while fluttering their eyelashes, acting coy, and looking off-camera for further instructions. These films betoken a simpler, more wholesome time in our cultural history, back when it was a culturally significant event to see an onscreen nipple in all its nipply naughtiness, back before all the important First Amendment battles were fought, back before creeps like me came along to jeopardize *all* our freedoms. But times change like the wind blows, and when the floodgates opened for clinical hardcore porn in the late 1960s, the nudie-cuties were rendered extinct.

Something Weird Video claims to have released 50 two-hour tapes—100 FUCKING HOURS—of nudie-cutie reels onto VHS, and if the 18 girls in this tape can be considered an average haul, that means this series features about 900 garter-wearing, red-lipped, crazy-bouffanted, high-heeled, big-bushed chickie-o's grinding and pouting to dangerous lowlife jazzy cocktail music and hair-burning psychedelic shag-outs.

It's nice that these gals lived back in an era when things were FILMED, because video makes everyone look as if they're undergoing chemotherapy. Film brings out a lushness which video only bleaches away. It also probably makes a lot of these girls' bruises, scars, birthmarks, moles, and cellulite look less scary.

Judging from the bulletproof beehives, I'd place the girls from Volume 50 somewhere firmly in the mid-1960s. A lot of these girls have no natural grace, rhythm, or screen presence. They all have lumpy asses and bellies of varying sizes.

tight brown beehive, and shiny red pumps. She wriggles around on a beautiful pearly-white wedding-cake-ornate bed, playing with a surreally large giant green hat.

• Two black-stockinged topless girls teasing one another with feather dusters. One of them is a dead ringer for my brother's first wife: short peroxided hair teased upward, large nose and tits, and beautiful dark circles under her eyes. Her play-partner is a chunky, apple-faced redhead. They seem highly embarrassed to have been placed in this *faux*-lesbo scenario, and I find their embarrassment highly arousing.

• A monkey-faced white girl with razor-sharp Bettie Page black bangs, diamond-patterned black fishnets, and gigantic psychotic black eyes. Her tits are proud and forceful as they hover over a skinny rib cage, and she just about slams those tits into the camera. She grinds around on a plaid sleeping bag looking like she knows how to squirm around on a dick right proper an' all. And just when I'm thinking that she looks like she shot up a spoonful of smack about ten seconds before filming, there they are—TRACK MARKS on her arm! Maybe this IS hardcore porno!

• Another stoned-looking prom girl wearing a silver-lamé party dress. She has a shiny forehead framed by straight, long, greasy, parted-in-the-middle hair. She yanks off the party dress quickly to reveal feisty little Reese's Cup tits and proceeds to writhe around on a bed, her eyes rolled up in the back of her head as if she's having a bum trip. When she finally removes her sheer-red panties,

NUDIE-CUTIE SHORTS, LOOPS, AND PEEPS, VOL. 50

Something Weird Video / 1995 / Stars: 18 hot 1960s mamas with beehive hairdos, black stockings, high-pump heels, false eyelashes, natural tits, and big bushes

Some have mottled skin and huge noses. And since this is the '60s, those that go crotchless reveal one Gigantor muff after the next. It's an assembly line of super muffs. *Ain't nuttin' wrong wit' dat!*

A lot of the scenes look like they were filmed in the same hotel room, and the idea of fly-by-nite '60s cutie-porn is oddly exciting to me. Eighteen sexually repressed girls trapped under the patriarchy's evil dirty thumb. Eighteen girls with teased-up hair, licorice-thick false eyelashes, and sinful black lingerie jigglin' their lumpy tushes in anonymous motel rooms. There isn't one girl among the 18 that I wouldn't do, but I'm notorious for not having any standards.

Among my favorites:

• An Italian-looking pickled olive with giant black-snowflake eyelashes, dangling gold earrings,

she reveals the best bush of the bunch—a thick perfect V. It is the sight of this bush which finally sends me to the bathroom to relieve some tension. After four *Jack Shacks*, finally I stumble across something which impels me to pleasure myself. Nice goin', '60s girls!

These girls are probably all dead or unfuckable now, but I dig their crazy style. This is back before girls wore T-shirts and sweatpants, back when they put a lot of attention into girl stuff—hair, makeup, undergarments, and high heels. I realize I'm weird, but I think these broads are so much hotter than the alien mannequins who pass for porn stars these days. They're a step closer to the animals, and I can almost smell their jungle funk wafting off the screen. If you're like me, and you like girls who look more like monkeys than androids, this film is for you. There are no tattoos, piercings, fake boobs, or shaved beavers here. The word "empowerment" hadn't even been coined yet. The phrase "sex-positive" didn't exist. This was back before women realized they were able to have orgasms and all the trouble that erupted after THAT fateful event.

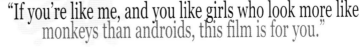

"If you're like me, and you like girls who look more like monkeys than androids, this film is for you."

RELIGION, SEX, & TABOO

Religions are retarded for many reasons, not least of which is the fact that so many people believe in them. The surest way to prove a belief system is false is to offer evidence that a lot of people accept it as true. Most people wouldn't know truth if they were beaten to death by it, and few would know how to be an individual if you stranded them on an island all by themselves. Groups are, by nature, superstitious and stupid. All human social factions worship around the dual thrones of patently obvious falsehoods (the "sacred") and obviously illogical prohibitions (the "taboo").

The taboo is the glue that holds societies together. All groups, no matter how *outré* or "edgy" they consider themselves, are hopelessly infected with the Taboo Germ. This holds true whether the group defines itself as a "religion" or an enlightened alternative to religion. With every taboo that gets killed at the roots, a fresh taboo grows in its place. Boner-wilting new folk religions masquerading as "social movements" are no better than the caveman religions: The Divine Temple of the Anti-Racist Lynch Mob and The Pap-Smeared Church of the PMSing Sex-Positive Goddess are as punch-drunk with dumb rules and bloodthirsty group idiocy as the granddaddies of the Judeo-Christian-Islamic tradition.

But let's give props where they're due. The ancient Hebrews are thought to be the first religious culture to equate sex with sin. The first thing Adam and Eve decided to do upon being ejected from Eden was to blush at their nakedness. Of the 36 crimes for which Mosaic law mandated the death penalty, 18 of them pertained to sexual transgressions.

To this day, Orthodox Jews make a big hoo-hah about the alleged spiritual impurity of menstrual blood. The tiniest droplet of Vaginal V-8 is enough to taint anything upon which it alights. At the end of a Jewish woman's cycle, she must undertake a ritual "cleansing" immersion, and everything she touched during her period is to be burned. In one tradition originating in Eastern Europe, a Jewish girl's mother slaps her daughter in the face upon hearing of the girl's first menses, undoubtedly harshing the teen's mellow. But the Jews are not alone in demonizing Aunt Flo: Followers of everyone from Muhammad to Zoroaster feel much the same way. In fact, even the word "taboo" is thought to be derived from the Polynesian *tupua*, meaning "menstruation."

The Hebrews hated homos, too: Leviticus 20:13 prescribes the death penalty for the "abomination" of hot, steamy, guy-on-guy sex. The Christians eagerly picked up the homo-hating baton: Romans 1:26-27 alleges that God condemned "men...[who] burned in their lust one toward another."

But a big "hats off!" to the Muslim world for taking homophobia to lofty absurdist extremes. According to one Muslim cleric's proclamation, "When a man mounts another man, the throne of God shakes....Kill the one that is doing it and also kill the one that it is being done to." According to another, "You should know that being murdered by a man is better than having homosexual intercourse with him." To this day, homo behavior is illegal throughout the Islamic realm. At least a half-dozen Muslim nations, including U.S.-occupied Iraq, warrant the death penalty for faggin' off. In Iran alone, an estimated 4,000-plus men have been put to death since the 1979 revolution for, as the kids like to say, "mixing the smells of anus and hummus."

One must not forget those zany Christians, whose literary giants are repressed ballsacs such as St. Paul and St. Augustine. Christ's sheep are no slouches when it comes to sex-hatred. For nearly 2,000 years now, celibate psychopaths have pushed their noses WAY up the asses of sexually functional, relatively well-adjusted peasants, resulting in hatred, violence, stake-burnings, and Catholic girls who French-kiss better than anyone on earth. Perhaps no other religion describes "immorality" in such purely sexual terms.

You were born free of taboos. It takes a society to smack them into your head. Taboos are social-engineering scams designed by unscrupulous, shifty characters who intend to rob you of your vital energies and cram you into a steel pigpen with other mindless swine. Religion exists to siphon away your sexual mojo in exchange for the promise of a Divine Orgasm that never comes. There's always been only One Way to heaven, and it's right between your legs. Your body, as disgusting as it might be (to me, at least), is the only temple you'll ever have, the only cosmos you'll ever know. This is as good as it gets. You get nothing more. That stinking, slimy, rutting act—however you enjoy it, you sick fucks—is nature's best and only gift to you. With that in mind, squires and maidens, I urge thee to obey the One True Law: Do what thou wilt, but try not to get caught.

Fuck religion. Fuck taboo. Fuck society. Fuck you, too, while you're at it. All you'll have left is to fuck, and there ain't a fucking thing wrong with that.

THE INDUSTRY

I was editor at Portland's *Exotic* magazine for 13 months until my all-consuming distaste for the town's "sex industry" and my specific choice to publish an article brutally disdainful of strippers led to my resignation. *(For further details, see "Biting the Whore That Fed Me," p. 220.)*

"The Industry" was my monthly column for *Exotic*, and it reveals me as an editor pecking away at my keyboard like a computer virus, a man in a shockingly adversarial relationship with both my job and the subject matter I was supposedly hired to champion. Looking back, I find it startling (and amusing) to be reminded of what a *dick* I was, not only toward the general concept of reverence for "the industry," but also toward many of the specific players in our retarded, whore-laden soap opera. My favorite passages here are my shamelessly public firings of the insufferably pious "sex writers" whom I inherited when I took over the reins. In my defense, I am forced to point out that if they didn't suck both as writers and as people, they never would have invited such scorn.

★★★★★★★★★★★★★★★★★★★★★★
THE INDUSTRY
#1 ★ DECEMBER 2001
★★★★★★★★★★★★★★★★★★★★★★

I'M THE NEW EDITOR here at *Exotic*. Some of you will celebrate. Some will mutter curses under their garlic-scented breath. Many of you, the vast cluster of functional illiterates snuggled within this marvelously nurturing, mentally stable community known as the SEX INDUSTRY, will emit a mild burp of indifference. But the important point is that I, as editor of a sex-industry-themed magazine, am now also a member of the sex industry. In short, I am a sex worker, too. We're all in this together, people, and I think we'd all agree that selling sex for profit is a noble, proactive, *human* thing to do. My only advice is that you all get used to my presence. Think of me the same way you might have once thought of anal sex. It hurts at first, but you might actually grow to like it.

***EXOTIC* EMPLOYEE* OF THE MONTH** I was all set to inaugurate a breezy new column whereby each month we'd profile a different staffer here at The World's Most Fun Place to Work. The idea seemed harmless enough—poke a little fun at one another, but also share with our dedicated readers a taste of the sweetness 'n' light that is this office, especially around deadline. My first choice was a man whom we'll call "Butts." I bestowed upon him the rare honor of FIRST EVER *Exotic* Employee* of the Month because he is by far the most psychologically fascinating member of our Wild Bunch here. Butts is a thoroughly Machiavellian character, with perhaps a twist of Wilhelm Reich's "Little Man" thrown in to give it that bitter, vengeful intensity. He was involved in some sort of dealings with the Russians during the Cold War. His father was said to have been the man who first appeared on the scene after the crash at Roswell in 1947. We have nicknames for Butts...things such as "Porno Turtle" and "Li'l Smutty." Sometimes in the office, he'll wear his "Funky Monkey"

T-shirt and sneeze so loudly, you'd think a gob of his lung was gonna fly out through his nose. His adolescently high-pitched voice will shriek things such as "Neener, neener, neener!" and "I wanna Nutty Buddy!" He uses decidedly unarousing terminology for sexual organs and practices...words such as "pooper" for "ass" and "tallywhacker" for "cock." He always makes sex sound soulless, disgusting, and obscene. I could say more...MUCH MORE... but then I think of Butts in his Scooby Doo boxer shorts, eating a Nutty Buddy all alone on a rainy winter's day, cruising eBay to see if anyone's buying his Osama bin Laden Styrofoam Toilet Targets, and a heady Roman Catholic sense of guilt sets in. Despite what he may think, I love the guy. And no matter how he squirms, I think he enjoys it when I hug him.

Perhaps with good reason, Butts was immediately suspicious of my intentions regarding this so-called "profile." In front of an office full of employees* who'd shown up for the Monday Afternoon Free Lunch, Butts's normally dough-colored skin turned an even more sickly ashen tone as his chubby little body popped up and down, insisting that he not be profiled or identified AT ALL in this magazine. I laughed and wondered what the hell he was hiding. I was amazed and depressed—but not surprised—that someone who'd spent his life with a magnifying lens up the ass cracks of others would run like a titmouse when the lens turned toward him. It's also ironic that he's so freaked about one of us getting him in trouble for something; fuck, everyone *knows* that he's the office stool pigeon! Woe unto the hypocrites, saith the Lord Jehovah.

*The publisher would like to clarify that for tax purposes, there are no Exotic "employees" per se; we're actually "independent contractors."

TITS, ASS, AND HALLELUJAHS
Speaking of apparent hypocrites—and I guess the very act of calling someone else a hypocrite is kind of hypocritical—I was a mite befuddled this week to receive two copies of *The Hallelujah Times (Formerly the T&A Times)*, a pair of one-sheet *mea culpas* from currently incarcerated pornographer Phil Yoder. Yoder was jailed back in February and charged with a stack of heavy Rape and Assault charges after a rendezvous with a lady friend went suddenly sour. In the first "issue," written by Yoder in jail and released by his friends in August, he claims that his six months behind bars had at that time "opened my eyes and heart to a whole new world, which now includes a belief and faith in GOD through Jesus Christ." He also claimed that his accuser was lying and had a history of lying about other men. In the second issue, dated October/November 2001, Yoder claims he was intimidated by the weight of his charges into accepting a plea bargain which should release him back into our world sometime late in 2002. "With the recent Terrorist Tragedies," Yoder writes, "I'm reminded of the fact that we don't know about tomorrow (please read Matthew 6:34). If you don't know if you're Saved, or whether you'll have Eternal Life in God's Kingdom," etc., etc., blah, blah, blah, give me a fucking break.

Now...I don't know Phil Yoder. And I really don't care what he did or didn't do to this girl or who was lying. Chicks lie all the time about this sort of shit. But as far as I can tell, they're both still able to walk around, so whatever happened must not have been *too* bad. And, yes, the justice system is fucked-up. Amen, my brother.

But what bugs the FUCK out of me about this

Hallelujah Times goobiness is the ultra-cheesy, ultra-predictable CHRISTIAN CONVERSION. When I was in prison, the surest sign of a sex offender was the Bible tucked under his arm. All the rapos would gather together and pray to Jesus, the only person who'd forgive them. I don't care about the Yode-man's guilt or innocence only to comment that his newfound faith makes him look guilty to *me*. And I worry about Jesus's safety once all those rapos and chomos get up to heaven and pin Jesus in a corner. "Hey, no, guys, really—STOP!..."

I WAS THE DOORMAN throughout October's fantabulous Ink-N-Pink 2001 competition, a traveling tattoos-and-vaginas circus which blazed through six local strip clubs and one weird hippie-style loft place with a bad draft. I cherish many warm, meaningful memories from Ink-N-Pink, but perhaps my favorite is the sight of *Exotic*'s own beloved Spooky cavorting around in a *Seinfeld*-styled "puffy shirt" and wearing a *Phantom of the Opera* mask. Or maybe it was Reed McClintock's balloon trick, which just got better with each repeated viewing. Or maybe it was the packed house on Halloween night when Miss Ink-N-Pink 2000 winner Sage commented that the entire competition had been "very emotional." I've done many things in my life of which I'm not proud, but being involved with a group of folks who actually *care* about the plight of tattooed stripper chicks is not one of them....

WHAT WERE "SEX WORKERS" CALLED 20 YEARS AGO?
Whores.

★★★★★★★★★★★★★★★★★★★★★★★

THE INDUSTRY
#2 ★ JANUARY 2002
★★★★★★★★★★★★★★★★★★★★★★★

PROSPERO AÑO NUEVO, all you lonely, creepy masturbators of the greater Portland area! Just holding a copy of *Exotic* in your hands makes you sexier, doesn't it? There's enough jack material in this issue to keep your bony li'l paws busy for a month. And lest you grow uneasy, I'm here to assure you that there is nothing shameful about masturbating to *Exotic*. All right, there's *plenty* that's shameful about it, but we butter our bread by peddling the illusion that being a pathetic, inadequate, sex-starved spud is somehow redemptive, so go wild, you crazy jerkoffs!

As your editor and personal guide, I've made it my mission to usher in a new era of sex-negative literature. In each issue, I plan to print at least one thing that'll kill that hard-on of yours. In fact, that's my New Year's Resolution: to render a dozen of your erections noodle-limp.

It's right before Christmas as we go to press, and I get a warm, crinkly feeling seeing all the naked sex workers mincing through the *Exotic* office for last-minute photo shoots. Our humble compound is stuffed with so many freaks, desperadoes, and drama queens, one could write the whole magazine without ever having to leave the office.

EXOTIC EMPLOYEE OF THE MONTH
Henry, a.k.a. The *Exotic* Distributor Formerly Known as The Real John Henry, has been working in the sex industry since before most of you whippersnapper strippers were able to shave your pubes.

I fondly recall prior encounters with Henry...the

THE INDUSTRY

time he showed up in the middle of the night when I was sleeping on the couch in the back room, scaring the shit out of me...the time he confided that I was one of the few staffers whose face he didn't want to FUCKING SMASH IN every time he saw me...the manic, hilarious, utterly frightening phone message where he harangued our beleaguered publisher with desperate exclamations such as, "I'm not your nigger, Frank!"...and the time he and a lady friend burst into our office, sweaty and panting, claiming that a rival publication's distributor had threatened their lives.

Henry is psychotic. He'll tell you that himself. He's been diagnosed and everything. Henry has two moods: He's either exceedingly polite or he's threatening to crush your skull. If it hasn't happened already, Henry will probably kill someone someday... and then feel bad about it...and then justify it...and then feel bad about it again. "In this life, I've lived many lives," he tells me, and I believe him.

In contrast to some difficulties we've encountered with the award in the past, I'm glad to report that our lucky winner this month is also an eager participant in the proceedings who pledges to fulfill his Employee of the Month duties to the utmost of his capabilities. Not only did Henry graciously endure a grueling photo session, he also supplied me with endless cartoons, poems, and background information about himself.

Henry also left me a microcassette player containing a tape on which he breathlessly recites a ghetto-themed "The Night Before Christmas"—"The Crips were selling crack on the corner/And the Bloods were hidin' under their beds/With visions of drive-by shootings dancing in their heads." Henry also generously bequeathed to me a stack of old Christmas-themed 45s, including "Yingle Bells" and "I Yust Go Nuts at Christmas" by Yogi Yorgesson, "I'll Be Home for Christmas" by child-batterer Bing Crosby, and "Santa and the Kids" by country superstar Charley "The Only Negro in C&W" Pride.

There are no formalities with Henry. He exudes the refreshing, cut-through-the-bullshit candor of the truly insane. He's a sparking, sputtering live wire of restless psychic energy, a whirling dervish who tends to become so wrapped-up in whatever he's talking about that he doesn't realize he's being VERY, VERY LOUD. Looking into Henry's eyes is like beholding the face of madness. He has the battle-scarred bearing of a man who's stared into the face of Pure Evil without flinching. I'm quite fond of the guy.

BYE-BYE, VIVID BLUE

We bemoan the loss of yet another *Exotic* contributor: VIVID BLUE, authoress of the much-loved and to-be-sorely-missed "Sex Around the World" column, recently called our office all huffed-up about the rude treatment she'd received at the hands of an unidentified staffer who'd answered her previous call. According to Vivid, when she asked the staffer, "Who is this?," she was greeted with a lecherous, "Well, who do you *want* it to be?" Upon resigning, Vivid let it be known that she's written for such prestigious publications as *Swank* and *Genesis* without ever having to deal with such rude, dastardly, and unprofessional behavior.

My only previous run-in with Vivid was a few months ago when she left a series of frantic

(sexists might say "hysterical") calls to our office, claiming that she was being stalked and demanding that her real name be removed from her column. (Er, if your stalker already knows your real name, what's the sense of trying to hide it now?)

We wish Vivid Blue the very best and hope she continues having sex all over the world.

RACIAL INJUSTICE JUST AIN'T COOL, DUDE The female owner of a local lingerie boutique recently visited the *Exotic* office and made it a point to loudly assure **Bobby Baldwin**, our production anchor and widely thought to be The Only Sane *Exotic* Employee, that she had always opposed prejudice in all its forms, even before it was considered cool to do so. (Bobby is black.)

★ ★ ★ ★ ★ ★ ★ ★ ★ ★ ★ ★ ★ ★ ★ ★ ★ ★ ★

THE INDUSTRY
#3 ★ FEBRUARY 2002

★ ★ ★ ★ ★ ★ ★ ★ ★ ★ ★ ★ ★ ★ ★ ★ ★ ★ ★

SO I'M DOWNSTAIRS AT DANTE'S DURING DEADLINE doing my "Dice" Clay fake-doorman routine as one of those events peculiar to THE INDUSTRY transpires before my cynical, world-weary eyes. Some emaciated male with a hot-pink mohawk is swinging around onstage, suspended by meat hooks plunged into his shoulder muscles as an appreciative crowd whoops, hollers, and enjoys whatever sense of "community" such a spectacle engenders. An ocean of "modified" people mills about with sewing thimbles plunged through their earlobes and "tribal" tattoo work denoting tribes to which they have absolutely no ancestral connection. An arrow through the head—now, THAT's hardcore. But a bottlecap in your earlobe? Why don't they just go the whole nine yards and put dinner plates in their lips? If they were to set foot on soil where this sort of "self-expression" originated, they'd be instantly cannibalized.

Supposedly, this is a fundraiser for some "troupe" of body-modification rapscallions. I was unaware they were strapped for cash. I was under the impression that, no matter how they try to emulate their oppressed brethren in Zaire, this was a "scene" populated by ultra-rich, ultra-bored, ultra-uninspired trendy snotrags. Don't they already, like, charge *millions* of dollars to punch holes in other people's bodies? Are staple guns getting *that* expensive?

***EXOTIC* EMPLOYEE OF THE MONTH** Let's face it—*Exotic* is now the only interesting publication in Portland, and perhaps the country. For years, if I may be so bold to state this, the five or so percent of the magazine devoted to editorial content flailed about like a dying fish on a wooden deck, choking to death on a dreadful, sour-tasting "sex-positivity" which postured itself as intellectual but was actually the rankest sort of infantile self-absorption.

I will state my case for the record—there is NO NEED to be positive about sex, just as there's no need to be positive about defecation or nose-picking. People are hard-wired to enjoy sex, and writing about how a base animal function is spiritually empowering merely RUINS the experience for those of us who have sex in the flesh rather than in front of a keyboard. It took one man's bold efforts to remedy the mag's editorial crisis. Because of this man's tireless dedication, people now realize that *Exotic* actually contains *articles* you can *read*.

There's a buzz about town regarding the "new" *Exotic,* a buzz engendered and nursed to fruition by one man with a messiah complex and an indomitable drive to prevail.

That man is me. My name is Jimbles Lee Deuteronomy Goad. And it's high time I selected myself Employee of the Month. No matter how much my predecessors may moan about me being a talentless schlockmeister, the truth is that I've got them all—*combined*—beat in terms of both underground cred and mainstream success. And I could whup all their asses in a Spelling Bee. Fuck *all* o' y'all. Seriously. I *hate* other writers.

EXOTIC EX-EMPLOYEE OF THE MONTH

Speaking of despicable writers, it has come to my attention that my immediate predecessor, regarding whom I've tried to be quietly gracious for lo, these many months, recently made an appearance at Dante's to pick up an installment check of the blood money he so undeservedly drained from our esteemed publisher as severance pay. No matter that while in our publisher's employ, said predecessor made it a habit to talk shit about our publisher to whomever willingly endured his whiny milk-cow voice, or that the consensus opinion among other employees is that said publisher just may be the Coolest Boss in World History. No matter that my immediate predecessor was still receiving blood money AFTER he LIED to our esteemed publisher about not trying to snitch him out to governmental authorities about (falsely) alleged illegal employment practices.

The bitter little, unsung, hunched-over, fingerless-glove-wearing, hand-rolled-cigarette-smoking, too-late-to-be-a-beatnik made it a point during a conversation with an *Exotic* staffer that he couldn't even bring himself to read the new *Exotic,* so horribly juvenile and anti-literary was the mag's new direction. He's threatening to take his bad self and his stable of newly unemployed, scarily talented, world-renowned ex-*Exotic* writers and start his OWN magazine, an announcement which understandably had me trembling.

It's notable that when I started working here over a year ago, I had never heard of our former editor, although he knew who I was. And this disparity, I fear, is what caused all of his animosity toward me. For months, he'd systematically shoot down my article ideas in favor of TERRIBLE, themeless, ill-conceived, rock-band Q&As and aimless cuntly navel-gazing by female scribes on whom he apparently had crushes. On the odd occasion I actually had something published, he'd bury it in the back and make sure it wasn't printed in color. The suggestions he gave for "improving" my articles were always dreadfully misguided, especially since he let verbal atrocities fly from other writers which never should have seen ink set to paper. I'm sure it irked him that the only articles in the magazine people were talking about were those I'd written.

His own writing smelled like bad feet. This is a man who could pen things such as "my zipper whispered of things to come" and "I was never the hunter, always the hunted" without a hint of the comical irony such phrases beg.

He was curt and graceless in all his dealings with me, despite the fact that I covered his ass by finding *hundreds* of typos—both in articles and ads—which he was being paid to catch.

He was the sort of person who sucks all the charm out of a room when he enters it. He was a rude little dismissive cunt to friends and girlfriends who'd call or stop by the office looking for me. His repellent personality would have possibly been warranted had the man possessed the merest shred of talent, yet it quickly became apparent that his behavior was engineered precisely to

compensate for a *lack* of talent. No one I know ever had a positive thing to say about him.

The guy was paid a living wage for coming in three hours a month, handing over e-mailed text articles to me from his stable of crappy, unknown writers, then going home. That was his job as "editor," and he should have been grateful that he was getting away with it. Instead, he bleated like an old goat about how horrible it was to work here and what a dick Frank supposedly is. He once told me, with a straight face, that he was the only *Exotic* staffer who had any vision or integrity, and it was an effort to keep from laughing heartily and spraying saliva all over his shaggy goatee.

I truly felt bad for him because he's old, bitter, and headed for nothing. I appreciated this fact. But I kept my feelings about him to myself.

This all changed back in August when he commanded me to shut my "fucking dog" up because it was barking and apparently interrupting his concentration on a canon of work that he probably feels will one day—not in our lifetime, of course—be appreciated for the genius that it is. I then, somewhat angrily but certainly not threateningly, told him I'd bitten my lip for months and endured his pissiness, but that he'd better be respectful regarding that slobbering little pug I love so much.

"You lay one hand on me," Mr. Bohemian Radical stated, "and I'll send you back to the jail where you came from." I sort of half-laughed and said, "You really *are* an old Jewish woman, aren't you?" Fucking little snitch faggot. Yeah, fuck authority, dude, until you get a little scared, and then you go dropping a dime and begging for police protection. I'm a better writer than you are. I'm more well-known than you are. I'm fucking far better-LOOKING than you are. I'm a better dancer than you are. And I could beat you at arm-wrestling. So just shut up, go away, and try to repair your mess of a life.

You tried to sabotage me as best you could while you were editor, but my kung fu is too strong. What are you gonna do now? You CAN'T beat me with words—we both know who'll win every verbal altercation.

You can at least take comfort in the fact that you never sold out. Not that anyone ever offered you the opportunity.

He should at least be grateful I'm giving him the attention no one else in the publishing industry seems willing to give him. But since he says he doesn't read the magazine anymore, he shouldn't be bothered by any of this, right?

★★★★★★★★★★★★★★★★★★★★★★★

THE INDUSTRY

#4 ★ MARCH 2002

★★★★★★★★★★★★★★★★★★★★★★★

I AM NOT A CONSUMER OF PORNOGRAPHY. I've never bought a porn magazine, and except when I'm reviewing them, I never watch porn movies. I've never paid for sex. On the few occasions when I find myself in strip clubs, I'm unable to ogle the girls—it all seems so artificial and silly. If I ain't gonna *get* the pussy that night, I don't want to stand around *looking* at the pussy. I believe that the sex industry, despite what the activists would have you believe, is far more degrading to men than to women. It is far more damaging to the human soul to *shell out* cash in exchange for physical intimacy than it is to *receive* cash for it.

I'm sure you'll be happy to hear that I've been masturbating a lot lately, and my mental imagery never involves the airbrushed porn confections you find in *Exotic*'s pages. It's always some broad I've either nailed in the past or have a likely chance of nailing now. The scenarios are realistic, raw, and human. Bodies are never as important as psychological situations, and her tits are never as important as the way her hair smells.

Sometimes, I just don't know about you guys and your porno.

EXOTIC EMPLOYEE OF THE MONTH

He started life as a small, greasy peasant child somewhere in the Italian Alps, and through a series of machinations, some of them questionably legal, he was able to climb his way to the top of P-Town's porn industry and become entrenched as *Exotic*'s ruthless, much-feared general manager. I speak of **Bryan** "Don't Call Me 'Rico'" **Bybee**, who, along with **Bobby Baldwin**, has the most alliterative name in all the *Exotic* family. Bryan Bybee. Bryan Bybee bought his bouncin' black baby a burnt biscuit in a big brown box.

The most fascinating component of Bybee's psychology, judging by his modes of dress and vocal inflections, is his apparent conviction that he is a black American male. This is especially pronounced when an *actual* black American wanders into the office. Bybee, whose speech might be somewhat comprehensible ordinarily, is suddenly all *hizzit in the shiznay* and *bang-bang boogie said up-jump da boogie to the rhythm of the boogie-da-beat*. It's quite a startling transformation. He greases his hair with something called African Pride, a typically gooey, coconutty, tree-bark-spackled urban hair-care product. His CD collection is composed almost entirely of urban mating songs and tropical canary music. He's always "dissing," as they say in the "hood," everything white—white people, white skin, and everything else non-Negroidal, seemingly unaware of his own obviously Caucasoid ancestry.

And just like the stereotype of his would-be African brethren, Bybee has recently taken to acting all uppity. Whereas we once had come to know (and mildly care for) a genial and cooperative (though still-greasy) general manager, we have lately been confronted with a power-hungry, porno-peddling, two-legged shark who has lost all semblance of his former humanity. Whereas he'd once tolerate rampant drug abuse, chronic absences, refusal to fulfill one's duties, spendthrift behavior, and defiant displays of verbal and physical aggression among the *Exotic* staff, Bybee has switched to more oppressive managerial tactics in a self-aggrandizing effort to whip our motley crew into obedient, efficient servility. Whereas our staff once enjoyed lavish restaurant meals and an open drink tab during our weekly Monday-afternoon meetings, we now—if we're lucky—face two lukewarm pizzas and maybe a cold beverage. This is simply intolerable, and if conditions continue, it won't be too long before the staff explodes. For now, Bybee has earned an unsavory nickname among the underlings he seeks to squash—to us, he is **The Man Who Took Our Meals Away.**

EXOTIC EX-EMPLOYEE OF THE MONTH

After a celebrated stint of something like 30 years writing for *Exotic*, **Darklady**, the world-renowned, internationally published Queen of the Sex-Positive Literary Netherworld has been given her walking papers by yours truly. I'd say a recent contributor summarized my decision with the statement that "the two of you don't seem like you should exist in the same universe, much less the same publication."

Having heard horror stories that the girl had an ego to match her girth, I initially dreaded giving her the axe. At first she responded to the news with a terse e-mail inquiring what had brought me to such a "monumental decision," and for a moment I thought she was being sarcastic... but then, mulling over whatever thought processes are laid bare in her writing, I realized that she might actually consider her dismissal from *Exotic* to be an event of monumental importance, not only for her and her alleged legions of sex-positive naked mole rats, but for perhaps Western Civilization itself. I wrote back stating that it was a matter of simple aesthetics, and when you're trying to form a punk-rock band that plays well together, a classical musician is out of place. I was trying to be diplomatic. She fired back a hostile, I-was-never-asked-to-the-Prom-flavored, well-I-guess-you're-just-too-cool-for-your-britches-Mr.-Goad e-mailing. Although the anticipated flood of outraged letters from irate Darklady fans (read: friends) never came, there's always next month.

We hope that Darklady continues writing about her life, her loves, her self...um, her *self*, and whatever else it is she writes about.

PORTLAND-AREA DAUGHTERS OF SAPPHO

were outraged by last month's "What's With All the Lesbians?" feature. One woman identifying herself as a sex-industry worker left a vituperative voicemail message at the *Exotic* office stating that the article was "fucked-up, dude," that we needed to fire the editor, that half of Portland's strippers are bisexual, and that she wasn't going to buy [?!?!] the magazine anymore. And the funny thing is, she didn't *really* sound like a subliterate walking garbage bag who's snorted so much crank over the years that it rotted her teeth out straight from the roots, slurring her speech but making her blowjobs that much better. Another woman identifying herself as bisexual e-mailed *Exotic* with a stern, "I had no idea that lesbian-bashing was the in thing to do at your so-called publication....What does it say about your publication when you allow Mr. Shrimpstien [*sic*] to write anti-lesbian statements such as this, encouraging straight men everywhere to make lesbians feel ashamed of themselves and to get down on their knees in front of him with their mouths open, as he put it. After reading this article, my husband (who is supportive of my bisexuality) and I will not be buying [?!?!?!] your publication anymore." At least one advertiser, allegedly a lesbian-owned store, dropped us. And over at dyke paradise **The Egyptian Room**, word is that the gals were none too happy. [I would *love* to do a spoken-word thing over there.] A representative for the Egyptian stated that the article would encourage people to bash lesbians and commit hate crimes against them, but this is untrue. That topic will be addressed in our upcoming article, "I Think It'd Be Really Cool if We Bashed Lesbians and Committed Lots of Hate Crimes Against Them."

★ ★

THE INDUSTRY

#5 ★ APRIL 2002

★ ★

THESE DAYS IT BOILS DOWN to a choice between writing and fucking, and sometimes I ain't too crazy about the writing. Deadline's breathing down my neck, and I was

THE INDUSTRY

supposed to finish this column last night. But the **Grim Reaper**'s also breathing down my neck, and I chose to have my face buried in a nice silky pussy instead of staring half-retarded at a computer screen. I'd rather hear a girl say, "Oh, my God!" when I shove myself inside her than sit here pecking away for the fleeting amusement of the 1% of you who exhibit the vaguest comprehension of what I'm trying to get at with all these words, month after month.

Total real-life drama last night, too, the kind that words can never quite capture. At a dark, crowded club, I bump into a girl whom I've wanted to fuck ever since I met her a few months ago. I thought she hated me, though, so I never pushed the matter. She pulls me aside and says she can't stand her boyfriend. He's stupid and doesn't understand her. She says I'm the only smart guy in the club, the only one that could possibly hold a conversation with her. She's crying. She's *nuts*, too, but I tend to go for that type. I ask her if she wants to go somewhere and talk. We whisk past her boyfriend and out of the club.

We find a quiet place. She says that she's drawn to me. I confess that I've had a crush on her. A light kiss. And then the chemicals start flowing.

I tell her I feel bad about her boyfriend.

And then I tell her I don't feel bad enough to stop.

You know when it feels right and when it doesn't.

This felt right.

I sent her off in a cab this morning and came down to work, but now I wish we had just rolled over and kept sleeping. Instead of watching her walk around in my bathrobe, now I have to deal with morons who sell *crotch* for a living but somehow are righteously offended by my words.

Words aren't dangerous. What's dangerous is how stupid people react to them. Smart people never freak out over mere words. If you need someone to take you by the hand and tell you what's right and wrong, I ain't the guy. And if you're that simpleminded, why would I want to breathe the same air as you?

EXOTIC EMPLOYEE OF THE MONTH

There is only one man in the *Exotic* office who has the lanky frame, cheetah-like grace, two-tone hair, leopard-patterned shoes, and tumultuous personal life that spell "rock 'n' roll SUPERSTAR in the making." There is only one man who has been rockin' since the early '80s and who absolutely flat-out *refuses* to quit rockin'. Wherever this man is, there, too, is rock 'n' roll.

This man is **John "Spooky" Voge,** *Exotic* ad representative, photographer, and gracefully rockin' *bon vivant*. He is so thoroughly rockin', such a torch-carrier of the never-say-die rocker spirit, that I have rechristened him **Jon Bon Voji.** When I first saw him, I thought, "Gee, now *there's* a man who rocks." If you were to, say, look up the term "rockin' Portland sex-industry dude" in the dictionary, I'd bet dollars to donuts that there'd be a devilishly mischievous picture of ol' Spooky, his eyes saying, "Let's Rock!"

Speaking of pictures, John threw a snit-fit last month after I accidentally stumbled across a naked photo of him while skimming through a computer folder in search of a new mug shot for *Erotic City*. There, amidst a comical portfolio of late-'80s Howard Stern-style shots of Voge looking rockin'-but-sensitive, was a self-portrait of an apparently stoned Spooky, naked as the day he was born,

his rockin' penis dangled teasingly in the frame's bottom. He looked lazily off-camera as if unaware that it was he who was taking the photograph of himself. I gasped, laughed, and then closed the picture. When Voge found out, he seemed genuinely hurt. In response, we tracked down a photo of Voge's penis tethered to a stripper's vagina with some *Modern Primitives*-style steel wires, and we placed the incriminating pic on his computer desktop.

We haven't had an Employee of the Month more apprehensive about his profile since the infamous freakout by "Butts" when this award was first tendered. All month long, Voge would groan whenever he passed me, almost cowering like a dog who's been abused. It got me wondering about what skeletons might be hanging in Spooky's closet. I mean, doesn't everyone already know about the substance abuse, the domestic stuff, and the fact that the Korean Mafia has placed a hit on him? That's *old news!*

The most embarrassing thing I was able to find on him—and it's mild, really—was a cyber-dating profile he'd posted of himself a few months ago, never suspecting that my informants are many. In the profile, he describes himself as an "Exotic Bad Boy with Good Heart" and describes his style as "kind of Mötley Crüeish, before they all shaved their heads." He claims to enjoy wine-tasting and snowboarding and describes both his hair and his occupation as "Other," which seems about right. His dream mate would be "Wild, Sexxy [*sic*], Exhausting, Affectionate (PDA's okay by me), Loyal, Honest, Beautiful inside and out, trusting and confident."

DARKLADY'S SO BIG, IT TOOK TWO ISSUES TO FIRE HER

Big-boned temptress **Darklady** is up to her ol' Internet-spammin' ways in the wake of my rude, unfeeling dismissal of her last month. She is apparently wired up to a bunch of those eternally FUN sex-positive online discussion groups and recently tried to rally her minions to bombard the *Exotic* offices with outraged e-mailings decrying the fact that we no longer squeeze the Big Lady into that Small Column.

A whopping SIX people responded. Amusingly, three of them defended Darklady, while three of them were relieved to see her flushed down the editorial commode. Even on her own turf, *half* of the people hate her. Delicious!

Comments from her detractors include:

I think I might like to shake your hand for firing her. She's horrible.

The darklady author is gone. No tears here. She's on several lists that I enjoy participating in and it never fails....I unwantingly know more about her goings-on than my own dog's perusings.

I would like to personally thank Jim Goad for having the chutzpah to pull the plug on *Tales of the Darklady*....I have been irritated by Darklady's insipid, sexist, unsexy drivel for months. Now I might reconsider picking up a copy of *Exotic* magazine once again.

Her supporters claimed that *Exotic* was becoming a bastion of "pure vile hatred." One of her acolytes, a person who claims to be affiliated with something called Senior Unlimited Nudes, warned that we were sending a message to current and future employees, freelancers, advertisers, news sources, and other associates: After

Jim Goad has finished using you, he may try to humiliate you.

Fair enough.

Another exasperated sex-positive-but-probably-sexually-unattractive Darklady fan gasped,

Jim Goad's a convicted felon with an unsavory nationwide reputation, who has written vast volumes of painfully misanthropic material. And you put him in charge of a magazine?

Yet another easily freaked-out "transgressive" type wrote that

people would be *happy* to run from Mr. Goad as fast as their feet can carry them, and I must agree my image of Darklady would only suffer from any association with him....

The Big Gal herself, the one who is presumably called "Darklady" because she casts a huge shadow wherever she waddles, moaned that *Exotic* was becoming "anti-sex" and that she had meant to leave anyway—but somehow musta forgot—before I shit-canned her:

I consider it to be a matter of pride to have been fired by this guy....I figure it's only a matter of time before Goad's found beating the hell out of a stripper somewhere...

Well, you know how it is with us compulsive woman-beaters. We just can't help ourselves. Since Darklady so graciously brought it up, I'd like to share with you what a typical Jim Goad day is like:

9 a.m. ... Wake Up
9:15 a.m. ... Continental Breakfast
9:30 a.m. ... Start Beating Women
Noon ... Lunch Break
1 p.m. ... Resume Beating Women
6 p.m. ... Dinner Break
6:30 p.m. ... Write About Beating Women
10 p.m. ... Sleep

You know, Mama Darklady, I could beat the hell out of a *thousand* strippers, and your writing would *still* suck. Your name would *still* be a punchline. Oh, how primitively Catholic is your priggish moral tut-tutting of whatever demons you think I represent. Clean thine own nest, thou filthy, bitter bird. Hey, did you ever consider that maybe the "new" *Exotic* is not sex-negative at all...just opposed to the idea of sex with people such as Darklady?

THOSE WACKY ACTIVIST GIRLS over at **Danzine** and **Miss Mona's Rack**

would like it announced that they are hosting a "Bad Date Line" whereby female sex workers, as well as normal gals who *don't* charge for the pooty tang, can tattle on physically or sexually abusive males with the hope that other women stay away from them in the future. They have compiled a list of Bad Dates and are willing to share it with interested parties. I have several misgivings about the idea of a Bad Date list, chief among them the fact that the name **Jim Goad** was not included.

I ATE BOBBY BALDWIN'S MANDARIN DUCK out of the *Exotic*

office refrigerator during a sleepwalking episode at about 4 a.m. during the last deadline. I woke up dazed, wandered over to the fridge, and gobbled it up. I would like to publicly apologize. Bobby, let's go out to the Candlelight sometime soon. I'll buy the drinks, and we'll both mack on big-booty white chicks.

REED McCLINTOCK ROCKED THE HOUSE along

with brothers **Porter, Boyd,** and **Groin** as barbershop quartet **The B.M.s** (Brothers McClintock) crooned their way into the hearts of an initially skeptical **Dante's** audience in late March. Reed,

who is known to Portland crowds as One of the World's Top 20 Coin Magicians (which would seem to imply that he didn't make the Top 10), exhibited some rare emotion at the sight of all those McClintocks reunited in one place. "I haven't seen **Grandmama Bundt McClintock** in what seems like ages," Reed said, a tear swelling in his eye. Reed's father **Rind** chipped in: "It's good to see the kids and the old people together again. And, ooooh, can those boys sing! *Hot tamale!*" For this writer, the evening's highlight was when Reed's little sister **Blintz** came onstage to play dulcimer as her brothers belted out a spellbinding "Sweet Adeline." If you haven't yet seen the B.M.s live, I'd suggest you catch the wave before it rolls over you, because this shit's gonna blow up MAJOR!

AM I A NEO-NAZI? No. I'm an *old-fashioned* Nazi. But thanks for asking!

★★★★★★★★★★★★★★★★★★★★★★★★★★★★

THE INDUSTRY
#6 ★ MAY 2002

★★★★★★★★★★★★★★★★★★★★★★★★★★★★

THE STEAM SKIMS OFF THE TOP OF MOLTEN-HOT BATH

WATER as I float like a bloated Caucasian matzoh ball, washing the sex off me. My slobbery scrunchy dog is scratching on the outside of the bathroom door, trying to get in. **The Jew** is sleeping in the bedroom with a smile on her face.

I'm sneezing from all the pollen churning through the air, all those spores that recently exploded from the cold winter ground in a spermlike rush to fertilize things. **Springtime**, when my brains turn to mush. All I can think about is goin' up inside that girl. Like this hot bath squeezes the toxins out of my body, the warmer weather pushes the hormones straight out through my pores, and all I think about is sex.

Whoever designed the **pussy** knew what they were doing. More and more, just about every second lately, I find myself either rammed up her tight little sugarcave or thinking about doing it. I see her walking next to me on these warm spring days, and my instincts just flutter down to her kangaroo pouch. It's only natural.

They say I hate women. Well, yeah, if you remove their bodies from the equation.

Here at *Exotic*, where **The Industry** pays our rent, buys our toilet paper, and puts cream in our coffee, we paddle our boat through a pinkish ocean of pussy and sometimes aren't as grateful as maybe we should be. We sit here all day, Photoshopping pimples and bruises off chicks' bodies, wondering what it all means. Dipping your head inside a huge boiling cauldron of sex-for-cash, day after day and month after month, can't be nearly as injurious to the human soul as the critics allege, could it? Sure, there's a seamy side to this industry, but this industry also shows people at their best—naked and enjoying themselves, their genitals flapping all over the place.

Our industry actually *benefits* society by...by...by, um...by giving *us* cash and by giving *them* sex. We fulfill each other's needs. It's very nurturing! It's a *good* thing.

And the people who try to suppress, regulate, or abolish our industry—*they're* the bad ones. *We're* the good ones and *they're* the bad ones.

I've heard that there are more **titty bars** in Portland per capita than anywhere in the WORLD. I'm too lazy to research whether that's true, but I just wanted to pass it along. It wouldn't surprise me. Everywhere you turn, someone's doing a pole dance.

When I moved up to Portland eight years ago, I couldn't believe how huge the sex industry was. While one was forced to drive miles and miles through P-town to find a gas station, there was a strip club on every corner serving up shaved pussy, cheap beer, and Chicken 'n' Jo-Jo's Blue Plate Specials. Every other girl I met was either a stripper or she sold dildos and bongs along 82nd. I was intrigued by the idea that Portland seemed so sex-crazed. It might be a gloomy place where everyone was fat and pasty, but all the rain and drugs apparently drove everyone indoors and into the bedroom. Even while I was married and living in L.A., I fantasized about moving up to Portland and gettin' myself one of those **stripper girlfriends**.

I made my fantasies come true and embarked upon a romantic relationship with a girl who used to dance at Magic Gardens and J.D.'s. It didn't work out too well, but at least I'm **off parole** now.

But I wouldn't be so petty as to blame the industry for my misfortune. That would be immature. This is a fine industry, and it's already received enough undeserved blame. The industry does not abuse women. It does not churn their bodies through a meat grinder, spitting them out as old and unwanted by the time they turn 23. Nothing shady goes on within our industry. No one gets hurt or exploited. No one suffers psychological damage from all this.

One shouldn't bite the twat that feeds them, and I fear that this is exactly what I've been doing for the past six months...but I promise to do it no more. I am here to state, on the record, that this is an absolutely COOL industry, and I can't think of another industry in which I'd rather toil!

I have resolved to chide the industry no more. If I even *try* to chide, you should tan my hide. I will not engage in my trademarked, intermittently amusing character assassinations of the sundry personages who wade through our industry like so much toxic bilge oozing through a sewer pipe. From this point on, I will refrain from making smug, catty comments about their appearance and character, no matter how homely or despicable they may be in real life.

As the daffodils sprout outside and the skies turn from grey to golden and the children wave their bubble blowers through the air, I consider it my moral duty as editor of this fine publication to say **I'M SORRY** for all the hurt feelings, misunderstandings, recriminations, and litigation that have erupted since I manned the wheel of the Good Ship *Exotic*. As a man grows older and his days dwindle, he ponders life's finer points with a cold glint in his bloodshot eyes, and my conscience has lately been pricked (ouch!) by the troublesome notion that my endlessly self-absorbed public wrestling matches with my psychological demons—wrestling matches which should be kept private, with only me and my demons in attendance—have been unnecessarily hurtful to the fine folks who used to people our pages with their poignant, pithy pontifications.

Henceforth, I will no longer make sport of the writers, no matter how dreadful, who used to splatter

their black ink on our white pages. In fact, I would like to take this opportunity as is my duty in this sacred editorial role which you guys used to play, to **SALUTE** all you *Exotic* writers and editors who are no longer a part of our warm, womblike family and who may, yes, unwittingly suffer at the expense of our merciless, never-ending, oft-creative, in-office jibes. I sincerely wish you a **LOT OF LUCK** in your burgeoning writing careers. We should all get together for a nosh sometime soon.

So, again, peoples—I'M SORRY if I caused you any undue stress, and I DIDN'T REALLY MEAN IT when I said your writing sucked.

In the same spirit of remorseful, self-hating, shit-eating reconciliation, I salute **all you lesbians!** I've thought it over, and I've changed my mind...now I think it's REALLY COOL that you lick each other's pussies. That's *rad!* And what's better, it's *brave!* It's also awesome when one of you straps on a fake cock and pretends you're a guy. **I was ABSOLUTELY WRONG** to make sport of your precious lifestyle! What the hell was I thinking? I'm sorry I hurt your feelings! Maybe I had given you more credit than to think you'd react so bitterly and humorlessly...just like the Christians who persecute you. But I'M SORRY that I gave you so much credit. You obviously need reassurance. You need to be patronized, and I'm just the guy to do it. You chicks are cool! *Slurp on, sistas!*

I salute the girls...ahh, **the *girls*...** the ones who whisk through our lives like a warm, lilting summer wind...the ones who leave voicemail threats to our publisher from in and out of mental wards...the one who stole a $1,000 video camera from an *Exotic* staffer...the one who rushed into our office after being attacked by a coworker upstairs...the ones who run escort ads to help feed their three kids...the escort girl whose cell phone rings with clients the entire time she's here placing her new ads...the one who shoved brightly colored dildos up her Eskimo snatch in the back room when we were doing Internet porn...the ones who struggle valiantly with chemical-dependency issues...the ones who strain with every fiber of their being to try and forget what their fathers did to them...the ones who find a new Mr. Right just about every three weeks or so...the ones who stay in the industry long after they should have left...the ones who couldn't buy enough makeup to cover it up... the ones who place themselves in situations where they'll find plenty of good reasons to keep hating men...the ones who won't recover from it, who never developed the skills to get past it...the ones who give you that look, as if you'd possibly have any answers for them...the ones to whom you could explain it very clearly, and they still wouldn't understand...all I can say is that I'M SORRY if I ever suggested that any of you are unstable. You girls—YOU are the ones to whom I pay special tribute as I celebrate this wondrous industry that pays for the honey which I lovingly ladle atop my steamin' morning oatmeal.

I will no longer question the motives nor intelligence of the innumerable young ladies who pass through our office and walk through our hearts. That's a promise. That's right, I *salute* the estimated 2,000-3,000 Portland girls who swap their female charms for cash—why, you're the tops! I love you dames!

We all know that the stereotype of the unstable, formerly abused, histrionic erotic dancer is merely that—a stereotype—and is hardly typical of the fine gals who populate our noble profession. For every

THE INDUSTRY

borderline-personality-disorder harpy who leaves death threats and is always attempting suicide, there are a dozen other female sex workers who are clean, well-adjusted, and eager to please. There's a big basket fulla female sex workers out there in P-Town—don't let a few bad apples spoil the bunch for you, guys!

I salute the **strip clubs** where men, couples, and the occasional lesbian gather in order to sate their primal need to see naked people with whom they have no chance of having sex. The strip club, truly, is the Temple of the New Goddess, a church where seekers congregate to worship the life-giving pelvic nexus variously referred to as the vagina, the cunt, the snatch, the snapper, and the stinky woodchuck. Plus, the drink prices are reasonable, and sometimes the food isn't that bad.

I salute (and apologize to) the ***Exotic* readers,** whom we have unfairly depicted in the past as lonely, inadequate schmuckjobs who are unable to procure sex partners without waving $100 bills in front of them. This was an unfair, cruel accusation, and if I was able to apologize to every one of you personally, I'd surely do it. I have reconsidered my beliefs, and now I'm of the staunch opinion that you guys pay for sex because, well, you must *like* paying for sex.

But even beyond all that rigmarole and poppycock, we, the employees of *Exotic,* gather together to defer, pay homage, and submit in a quasi-sexual manner to this shapeless mass that no one has ever seen but everyone calls **THE INDUSTRY.** Let it be declared that there will be no *Exotic* Employee of the Month this month. No, not this month. Next month, but not this month. If someone asks you whom the *Exotic* Employee of the Month is this month, you'll have to tell them, "No, no, there isn't one this month." Instead, we have selected **THE INDUSTRY** as...

EXOTIC EMPLOY**ER** OF THE MONTH.

And what a damn fine employer it is!

Hoist your mugs, ye mateys, and let's drink to another 100 years of sex-for-cash in Portland!

★ ★

THE INDUSTRY
#7 ★ JUNE 2002
★ ★

I JUST FLEW BACK FROM NEW YORK, and boy, are my arms tired!

That's what happens when you beat the fuck out of a chick and strangle her to death.

And jack off to pictures of her being beaten.

And get beaten senseless and hung over a ledge by some Mafia thugs.

And get thrown out of a Brooklyn bar onto the sidewalk by a fat Elvis impersonator who then hocked a gob on my cheek.

And hire a prostitute who was so blasted on heroin that she, too, loogied on my face while riding me on top.

And drink bottles and bottles of whiskey.

And what's best, it was all good, clean, LEGAL fun!

I committed all of the above acts in my role as Detective Jim McCormick, a vile, washed-up, alcohol-swilling private dick who spends 15 minutes thrashing and killing the title character of *The Suzy Evans Story*. The feature-length film was scripted by **Dave "Doomsdave" Taylor** and *Exotic* columnist

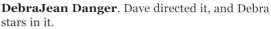

DebraJean Danger. Dave directed it, and Debra stars in it.

Acting's so much easier than writing. Acting has been a lifelong deferred dream for me. I wanted to be an actor throughout my teens. I even got accepted to study theater at NYU in 1979, but I never went. But more than 20 years later, these spoony-eyed kids offered me a golden chance: not only the chance to act, but the opportunity to beat a woman legally and in front of a camera.

During the totally improvised murder scene, I got all Stanislavski on everyone's ass and went buck-wild. Breaking glass. Screaming. Threatening. Slapping. Dragging. Strangling. Talking all psycho. Then smoking a cigarette, looking defeated, and walking out of the room. Since it all happened at 3 a.m. in a midtown apartment building, it's a miracle no one called the cops.

After the scene was shot, Dave was crying and said it was one of the most powerful things he'd ever witnessed. DebraJean was shaking: She thought her arm was broken and says she actually lost consciousness during the filming.

Fun times. Good places. Summer nights.

I LIVE IN THE WEE CITY OF PORTLAND, but I was Philly-born and raised. Grew up amid soft pretzels and white knuckles and brick buildings. Then I spent a couple of years in the NYC area. Then I lived seven years off Hollywood Boulevard. And then it's been Oregon since 1994. But my mannerisms are still more East Coast than West, more jerky douchebag than surfer dude.

This recent trip was only the second time I'd been back East in the past 15 years. I flew back with **The Dancing Jew**, who's from Portland but sounds more New York than everyone in New York and is more East Coast than the very soil which comprises the East Coast. We spent a fun week together in her Upper Manhattan pad, then the little cartoon character flew on to London while I kept filming in N.Y.C.

I had brought a thick deadly chest cold with me from Portland, hacking up rubbery green sea creatures, the cold-spring N.Y. mist making it worse. Hacking and straining like the old man I nearly am, I vainly searched for an antibiotic to suck the disgusting green pudding out of my lungs. And since drugs are bad for the immune system, I didn't do any Ecstasy, Viagra, heroin, acid, cocaine, magic mushrooms, Xanax, or weed. (New York is about ten times bigger than Portland, which means that by the time you get the drugs, they're ten times weaker.) Bored, I shaved my balls one morning, chewed on some raw garlic cloves to try and chase away my chest cold, and then worked out to The Jew's sister's Lynyrd Skynyrd CD.

Ashen-colored, depressed-looking huddled crowds. Shitty exhaust-pipe air. Gunmetal raindrops and the purring wheezing air conditioner in the back of the late-night First Avenue bus, liquid filth churning into the sewers from a sudden spring rainstorm. The rude, invasive, bug-swarm humidity. 4 a.m. subway rides where everyone on the train is stoned or crazy or both.

I didn't go to Ground Zero and I didn't see a Broadway Show and I didn't go skating at Rockefeller Center. I ate a cheese cannoli and slurped a root-beer water ice in Hoboken, gobbled a potato knish at LaGuardia Airport, and walked around The Bronx by myself, feeling like John Wayne among the Injuns, munching bravely on one of those Puerto Rican Meat-Filled Pop Tart things. There are fewer places on earth I love more than the blown-out, psychotic, don't-ever-go-there

Bronx, a million crumbling tenement buildings like jagged teeth in the Devil's mouth. I got kicked out of a South Bronx *botanica* because I was sniffing too many of the essential oils. *No es bueno, no es bueno,* admonished the little brown voodoo man, shooing me out the door. The Bronx is still the *real* New York, but, sad to say, even The Bronx has seen worse days.

New York sports a lower Lesbian Quotient than Portland, or at least fewer openly lesbian gals. Whether this is good or bad depends on where you stand on the whole Lesbian Question. And there are clearly more fags in N.Y.C....and every one of them skips faggily through the Village leading a fruity French Bulldog around on a gay little leash.

EVERYTHING IN NEW YORK SEEMS
HAPPIER and gayer and safer these days. One never expects a city to *heal* once it starts going bad, especially one that used to be as sick as New York. To my dismay, I kept finding that places such as Williamsburg and Alphabet City, bullet-ridden wastelands when I left New York back in 1987, are now yuppified hipster finance zones. These days, apart from 9/11 and anxiety about another terrorist sucker punch, New York seems almost uncomfortably tame, like a huge tumor in permanent remission.

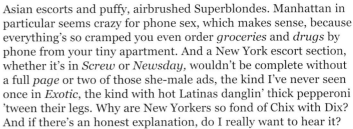

I almost felt sorry for this pitiful giant of a town which used to fascinate my Philly-boy mind. New York used to scare the hell out of me, and that's why I idealized it. But against my better wishes, I learned a long time ago that the average New Yorker wasn't a serial killer or a jaded sophisticate, but rather a female Mets fan from Queens with a slight mustache riding the subway with her four kids. The girls aren't any prettier there and the people don't dress better. I moved away from there almost 15 years ago, and I don't regret it.

New York seemed more fascinating in the 1960s and '70s, back before I was ever there, back in the Dark Ages of Son of Sam and garbage strikes and The Great Northeast Blackout. New York, psycho heroin murder mecca, babies thrown out of project windows, Kitty Genovese murdered while her neighbors watched and did nothing. That was the New York I never got to see.

Back in those days, New York and San Francisco were *inventing* what we now call the sex industry which thrives with such viruslike hardiness in Portland. **Al Goldstein** and **Ralph Ginzburg** were getting busted for obscenity left and right back in the day, planting all those seeds of destruction which would render something such as *Exotic* publishable almost 40 years later, making room in the world for such a beacon of all things good as Yours Truly.

Times Square used to be Sex Industry Central. It was to sex what the Lower East Side still is for drugs...you could get anything you want, so long as you had the cash and the imagination. XXX movies and peep booths and sales on dildos and real hookers and fake heroin for the stupid white boys from Queens. It was cheesy and microbial and dark and shame-ridden. It was nice.

But then came along Nazi Mickey Mouse Mayor Rudolph Giuliani, who wiped away the Times Square sex industry as if it were a glob of snot on his Mercedes windshield. Times Square is now a Disney/McDonald's glistening Tokyo-style Jumbotron monument to All Things Family.

There's still a New York sex industry, boldly sputtering within the police-cordoned yellow-tape zone where the authorities have quarantined it; you see it in most N.Y. dailies and weekly-freebies, whose back pages are stuffed with full-color ads for bony, scared-looking

Asian escorts and puffy, airbrushed Superblondes. Manhattan in particular seems crazy for phone sex, which makes sense, because everything's so cramped you even order *groceries* and *drugs* by phone from your tiny apartment. And a New York escort section, whether it's in *Screw* or *Newsday,* wouldn't be complete without a full *page* or two of those she-male ads, the kind I've never seen once in *Exotic,* the kind with hot Latinas danglin' thick pepperoni 'tween their legs. Why are New Yorkers so fond of Chix with Dix? And if there's an honest explanation, do I really want to hear it?

The New York sex industry is still there, if shamefully and fatally neutered by Giuliani's morality police. But there's no OBVIOUS sex industry like there used to be in New York and like there still is in Portland, where there seem to be as many strip clubs as Plaid Pantries and certainly more jack shacks than gas stations.

PORTLAND LOOKED SO PITIFULLY SMALL as
I headed toward downtown on the Max from the airport, such a feeble excuse for urbanity that I wanted to nestle it under my armpit and protect it as if it were a malnourished baby canary.

If porn's your thing...and judging that you probably picked up this magazine at a strip club, porn is, sadly, your thing...there's no real need to go back East anymore. The sex industry, pound for pound, is much healthier here than the bleeding East Coast sex beast which the authorities have almost fatally gored. The cops and the laws, for the time being, are cooler here about everything industry-related than they are back East. Just pray that no psychopathic sadist such as Kevin Mannix becomes governor and does to Oregon what Giuliani did to New York. The Banana Joe-ification of Burnside has already started, and I think I feel sick.

But we still have Bigfoot and Buzz Martin and STRONG coffee and whitecapped mountains. We have Lars Larson and Tom Peterson and Scott Thomason and Pete Scottersen and all the rest of those dudes. Fuck, this town is so backward that everyone still gets excited when a movie is filmed here.

We have the perfect cultural collision of loggers and lesbians, of rural and urban. The omelettes are better out here. The air is fresher. The jails are nicer. You know, Portland, I've faced one high-scale personal disaster after the next since moving here almost eight years ago, but I still love you, baby. You're almost the Perfect American City.

Just like in sex, bigger and dirtier doesn't always mean better. Not always.

Cities are like hookers. The most expensive ones aren't always the best. And these days, Portland's looking mighty cheap and nice.

★★★★★★★★★★★★★★★★★★★★★★
THE INDUSTRY
#8 ★ JULY 2002
★★★★★★★★★★★★★★★★★★★★★★

AREN'T NINE-YEAR-OLDS FORBIDDEN TO VIEW PORN?
Exotic is nine years old! That's...spectacular! Happy spectacular nine-year anniversary, *Exotic*!!! To celebrate the spectacularity of our nine years, I bring you this, our **9th Anniversary Spectacular!** Actually, this issue offers very little in the way of comments, photos, or retrospectives regarding our nine years...and to be honest, there isn't much that could rightly be termed "spectacular" in this issue...but force of habit and an innately vain sense of entitlement impel us to note every year's passing with a

THE INDUSTRY

giant, irrelevant cover headline.

Have I really been working here nine years? Fuck, no! I haven't even been in *Portland* nine years. Frank gave me a job here when I got out of prison nearly two years ago because he knew that gainful employment was one of my parole conditions. And all things considered, it's been really, really gainful here. Spectacularly gainful.

Though I'm an industry neophyte...an upstart...a mere sapling...someone who, to be fair, doesn't know very much about the industry and isn't making any effort to educate himself...my uncrushable sense of destiny, of my congenitally programmed superiority, gives me the sort of arrogance to declare with utmost authority that the following sentence is The Greatest Line Ever Uttered About Portland's Sex Industry:

I know more Jasmines than I know Daves.
—**Kook Dogg**, an *Exotic* graphic artist who insists he will resign if I select him as **Employee of the Month**

What a shimmeringly concise summation of life in Rip City's sex industry—"I know more Jasmines than I know Daves." That says it all. Down here in the Valley of the Sex Workers, stage names outnumber real ones like fake boobs outnumber homegrown taters, and a fella indeed runs across fewer Daves than Jasmines. Kook Dogg, you are not alone—I, too, know more Jasmines—not to mention Jazzmens, Yazmins, Jaszmeens, and Ys'm'n's—than I know Daves.

Speaking of fake names—"Kook Dogg" is a euphemism I've affectionately bestowed upon our newest *Exotic* staffer, a man who, as he's told me several times, made a deal with Frank when he joined our mutually nurturing porn-publishing family that he would up 'n' quit if his name or likeness were *ever* featured 'tween our covers.

Good sport that I am, I will not tell you Kook Dogg's real name. Neither will I offer any physical descriptions of him so that any of our fine readers who might be disposed to, say, murder him...or not hire him...if he were unflatteringly spotlighted in *Exotic's* pages will have to do a HELL of a lot of research to track him down. Not that it's impossible to find him if you really wanted to. Where there's a will there's a way, I guess. And money always helps, if you know what I mean.

A clinical diagnosis might reveal that Kook Dogg suffers from afflictions both neurological and cognitive. He displays a disturbing, unsettling, oft-annoying energy. When confronted with my assessment that he is possibly unstable, he graciously agreed. For his first couple of months here, his sputtery nerves proved nearly unbearable for the other staffers. I've never seen him relaxed. He's either talking too much or he's quietly moping because everyone told him he's talking too much. Many times when he thinks I'm making fun of him, I'm not. And other times, when I'm stone-cold goofin' on K-Diggity's ass, he takes me seriously. He's fun that way.

I will not write much about Kook Dogg beyond speculating on his paranoiac reluctance to be written about. When I broke the good news to K. D. that even though it was only his third month here, I had jockeyed him up to the head of the pack and had designated him Employee of the Month, he became visibly sweaty. When I told him that for his celebration photo, I wanted him to pose topless and oiled-up while eating a banana, he refused.

And like a few other spineless she-men who shall remain nameless (at least for now), Kook was also afraid to participate in this month's whimsical **café BEEF-CAKE** photo shoot. He told me that it might possibly jeopardize the other job at which he toils when he's not sitting five feet away from me, staring at a computer and wondering whether or not I really like him. He also explained that once the economy improves, he hopes to get a "real" job at an advertising agency, and any association with a free strip-club rag would irreparably damage his chances at snagging said job, much more so than, say, his own questionable social skills.

When I told him that I was going to write about him anyway, his body began emitting radiation waves of panic.

"What are you gonna write about me?" he asked, not even attempting to conceal his anxiety.

Whatever I want to write, I deadpanned like a grizzled old newsman along the lines of Jimmy Breslin or, say, Lou Grant.

And then he muttered some ominous Chinese parable that ended with everyone waking up in the morning with their balls chopped off.

Even now...*right this second*...as I'm writing this, he's asking me if I have this article done yet so he can see what I've written about him. I'm fairly assaulted by the waves of fear that roll from his body less than two yards away from me.

Kook, my friend, I'm writing about you because you're currently the most interesting—and thus inkworthy—character in the *Exotic* office. We're all well aware that you've done some unspeakably weird things when you thought no one was looking, and this is the part I like about you—the insecure, neurotic weirdling rather than the boring, oversocialized, wannabe citizen. I prefer the "Kook Dogg" within you over the "real" guy with the regular name and the overblown sensitivity.

I like you, Kook Dogg. I think you have a good heart. But you want so desperately to be liked, you end up fucking it up every time. You don't have to try so hard—in fact, it's the trying-so-hard part that's irritating. It's the *freaky* part of you that I like, not the part that struggles to hide it. "Weird" is not a pejorative in my book. To me, "weird" means "complex...colorful...interesting." To be abnormal is good when one considers the norm.

Sadly, Kook Dogg presses onward in an ultimately doomed attempt to shield the world's eyes from the Weirdness Within Him.

OBEYING THE MUSE™ One of this industry's main perks is the ceaseless pipeline it provides to fun new experimental BONER DRUGS such as Viagra. Our office was recently mailed a product called **MUSE**, manufactured by Vivus, Inc., who hunger for a slice of the Pharmaceutically Enhanced Erection Pie which is now almost entirely gobbled up by Pfizer's Viagra. MUSE contains **alprostadil**, a blood-vessel dilator that occurs naturally in semen. A booklet called *Restore the Feeling,* published by the manufacturers, claims that MUSE is at least as effective as Viagra, and possibly more so, when it comes to givin' ya a woody. The main difference between Viagra and MUSE is in its administration:

1) Viagra is a pill that is comfortably swallowed...

2) Muse is a plastic "urethral suppository" which you jam down your dickhole in order to inject a tiny pellet.

At first, MUSE seems more like the stuff of political torture than bedroom hijinks. When the MUSE suppository and instructional booklet arrived in our office, the male

THE INDUSTRY

staffers stood around the package cringing, reluctant to even touch it. I know of few males who are enthusiastic about the idea of ramming ANYTHING down their fragile pink urethral tunnel.

But I'm a self-starter. I'm all for improving my attitude and improving my erections. I become the volunteer Astronaut Chimp for this sexual pharmaceutical. Everyone else in the office was too timid to try it, so, as usual, I had to step up to the plate and hit a home run.

My unwitting female guinea pig is, of course, **My Jewish Companion**. One early summer night, as she lies in the bed of my plush East Burnside penthouse awaiting another round of our interfaith sexual frolicking, I excuse myself to the bathroom and rip open the tinfoil which holds the foreboding Plasticine Dick Injector.

The booklet instructs me to piss first in order to lubricate my urethra. Then I pinch and pull at my pud in order to ensure pliability. Then I jam the cold two-inch clear-plastic proboscis inside my dickhole. At first it doesn't go in more than a half-inch, and it pops out almost as if my cock had spit it out. I finally manage to plunge it in deep, ever fearful of the booklet's admonition that it's possible to tear my urethral lining and cause bleeding. The drug is contained within a tiny pellet encased in the plastic tube, and I press down on a button that releases the pellet. Then comes the most uncomfortable part—I have to *jiggle* the device inside my urethra for five seconds to make sure the pellet is dislodged. Then I slip out the tube and massage my cock between my hands as if I was rolling dough.

Initially, the drug afflicts my penis with an uncomfortably hot sensation as if someone's burning a Zippo lighter inside my dick, but that soon fades. In ten minutes, I'm in bed and my cock is hard enough to knock someone unconscious with it.

The Jew says things such as:

"Jesus Christ, you're hard like steel!"

and then...

"Oh, my God—you're in so deep!"

and finally...

"OK, OK, you're gonna have to stop, or I'm gonna pass out."

She tells me she lost count after eight orgasms. I shoot a grateful load after about a half-hour of fuel-injected eight-cylinder pumping. I won't tell her I've used the penis pellet until the next morning. At one point during the night she reaches over, gasps, and says, "Sweet Baby Jesus, you're hard *again!*" But I'm not really hard "again"—I'm STILL hard. My dick is a mallet. I could play a round of croquet with it. I was a slab of pink granite for nearly two hours after I came. At one juncture, mesmerized by my tool's firmness, she squeezes it in her hand with such force that I thought my cock would pop off my body in a bloody explosion. I yelp with pain. She apologizes.

Despite the fact that MUSE made me harder than Viagra did—almost frighteningly hard—I'm sad to report that it boasts none of Viagra's druglike effects, none of its Garden-of-Edenlike euphoria. Arousal and hardness aren't always the same thing. The penis pellet affected my cock but not my mind.

Restore the Feeling claimed that MUSE would give me "a natural-feeling erection," which is false. Rather, my boner felt uncomfortably swollen, as if 100,000 Kurds had fled Iraqi persecution and were seeking asylum within my cock. The booklet also cautioned that one shouldn't use MUSE if you have "an abnormally formed penis." In my case, not to worry. My penis is so beautifully formed, they should hang it in an art museum, I swear.

See? Unlike Kook Dogg, I'll tell you everything about myself, ESPECIALLY the things you don't want to know. I'm the Master of Giving Too Much Information.

I AM NOT GOING TO GLOAT about the news I recently heard regarding the editor who immediately preceded me, except to note that I may think of patronizing him the next time I need a taxi.

SOME OF MY FAVORITE THINGS:

• When a chick calls another chick "man"...
• When people emphasize the wrong syllable or word...
• When the cure is worse than the disease...
• When the innocent get blamed...
• People who can't speak a word of English...
• People who can't speak a word of anything *but* English...
• Butte, Montana...
• All of West Virginia...
• The words "Negro," "nougat," and "treat." [I've even combined them into a sentence: *The group of inner-city youths sat lazily on the picnic blanket, nibbling on their **nougaty Negro treats**.*]

★★★★★★★★★★★★★★★★★★★★★★★

THE INDUSTRY
#9 ★ AUGUST 2002

★★★★★★★★★★★★★★★★★★★★★★★

"WOULD YOU SUCK A COCK FOR TEN MILLION DOLLARS? How about takin' it in the ass? Would you take it all the way up the ass for ten million?"

There we stood, three *Exotic* staffers—all of us men—standing in the soft summer sunlight on the rooftop of our downtown building, discussing which supposedly degrading homosexual act we'd do and how much money it'd take for us to do it.

One of them, the Ganja Gandhi, a.k.a. **Ganji**, said that sucking cock was more degrading than getting it in the ass, and I was afraid to ask him why.

But everyone agreed that it would be worth ten million bucks to either suck a cock or get it in the ass. "Ten million bucks is a LOT of money," Ganji said, and we all nodded in agreement.

What does that say about us as men? As Americans?

Beyond that, how much is one's hetero-male dignity damaged after admitting you'd do it even if you know that no one's *really* going to give you $10 million to do it?

Against our better judgment, we found ourselves falling into the Whore Pit.

I SAW A WOMAN WITH A FULL BEARD the other day as I was ordering my hipster coffee at a politically, um, *aware* hipster coffee joint on East Burnside. The Bearded Lady turned to me and my friend as we were talking, smiled, and then muttered some pleasantries, but all I could focus on was that BEARD. I smiled like George Costanza did in *Seinfeld* when his date removed her hat to reveal a bald head—a polite smile, but one which has no hope of masking its bleeding discomfort. And this beard wasn't the scraggly, wispy, pubic kind you sometimes see on chins in P-Town's dykier enclaves, either—I'm talking a full-on *Jerry Garcia* beard, and it was on a woman with a woman's voice and a woman's tits and a woman's annoying mannerisms.

What am I supposed to do about this? How am I supposed to feel about it? Am I supposed to approve of it, to say it's politically OK...*desirable*, even...when every fiber within me is repulsed by it? Am I required to have sex with her just to prove I'm a nice guy? Is this what the Sexual Revolution has wrought? I was almost as afraid of this Bearded Lady as I was terrified...and I mean full-blown psychotic nightmares...by all the freaky animals in Dr. Seuss books when I was a lad.

It's called shaving cream, honey. It's called electrolysis. I don't think the Goddess looks like Allen Ginsberg, and I don't think you should, either.

INK-N-PINK TO SINK? *Exotic* staffer **Jon Bon Voji**'s fabled, mocked, oft-despised, world-renowned, unintentionally hilarious **Ink-N-Pink** competition will inaugurate its third—and final—trip 'round the mulberry bush this fall. If you like tattoos and vaginas—together—then you'd probably like Ink-N-Pink. But sad to say, the once-proud, once-profitable, once-vibrant "event" is but a wheezing semblance of its former self. Whereas the first two years saw a *series* of runoffs and qualifying rounds throughout some of Portland's greater adult establishments (meaning anyone who'd take it), this year's Ink-N-Pink competition has withered down to a *single* night of undoubtedly yawn-inducing festivities at a club yet to be determined. After that, Bon Voji will call it quits on Ink-N-Pink. The buzz within the industry is that my proposed **Twats wit' Tats** competition has Voge and his ilk runnin' scared, and rightly so. *My* competition will feature the hottest twats with the raddest tats! If you're a twat with tats...and you covet the title of Miss Twats wit' Tats...contact the *Exotic* office.

HOW MANY LOADS OF JIZZ are shot daily, on average, in Portland? How many female orgasms are there? How many chicks fake it every day? How many guys try to get it up and can't? How many different DNA samples would forensics technicians be able to scrape off that couch in the back of the *Exotic* office? How many wads have been blown back there? How many in the bathroom?

And more importantly, young laddie: How many dirty pictures will it be 'til you've had enough? How many tweaker strippers hanging from scuffed brass poles as some sludgy shit-rock blares from the speakers will it take before you've had your fill and push away from the buffet table? Have you ever thought about that? Have you ever thought about *anything*? Or are the pictures enough for you? I need to know.

ONCE YOU'RE IN THE INDUSTRY, can you ever really get out? Earlier today around the water cooler, the fellas were talking about the brawlin' bitches in the Beaverton bar and some whacked-out stripper chick who's addicted to Ecstasy and is a great fuck but is totally insane and the lingerie model who does so much tweak, her eyes get crossed. And then I look at **Kook Dogg** hunched over there at his desk, slapping naked pix of Portland chix onto the scanner's cold glass and

feeding their bodies into our computer system, and I wonder if the poor hapless youngster will ever really have a chance to make it in the "real" world after being exposed to something as degrading and soul-crushing as *this*. I hope he doesn't read this, because I predict a future of heartache, alcoholism, and nonstop porno for him.

Earlier tonight, the girls from the jack shack upstairs were standing outside the front door of our building on Burnside, all tarted-up and handing out flyers advertising their shows. It was almost like being in Amsterdam's Red Light District, and suddenly I felt myself whisked away to a land of herring sandwiches, windmills, festive clog dances, and hash brownies. It was a sweet moment, and I wish I could have captured it on one of those disposable cameras. I can't complain. It's not entirely unpleasant to be stuck here in the fuzzy belly button of downtown Portland on deadline...deadline, when I feel as if 50% of my body is composed of Dante's pizza, while the rest is coffee and Altoids. By the way—wouldn't "Altoid" be a great name for a black guy?

SO WHAT'S NEW IN GOADVILLE? If I told you what really happened this month, you wouldn't believe me, and I'm unsure whether you've behaved well enough to deserve hearing it, anyway, so I'm not going to tell you just so you have some time to sit around and think about your mistakes.

The *real* news is that I'm going to tinker with my image somewhat. The country truck-driver thing is getting played-out. My plan is a simple one: I'm going to *dress* more like a Nazi, but *listen* to nothing but wigged-out Afro-licious black soul music from the late '60s and early '70s. I'll be stomping around in motorcycle-cop leather boots and a starched black work shirt buttoned up to the throat, groovin' out to Sly and the Family Stone and Curtis Mayfield on my Walkman. That should make everyone happy, I think. It's best to cover all bases, you know?

That's the thing about me. You could talk to me for 12 hours straight and still wind up confused. The Redneck Express is a hard train to stop, my niggas. I'm more of a freak than y'alls could ever be, but I'm also more solid than you could ever manage. I'm smarter and stronger than you. You're nobody, and I'm somebody. I could kick your ass on paper and in the streets. And I never throw the first punch. But the second through the last are all mine...ain't that right? I keep hitting back. Harder than you do. And you know it, bitch.

All I'm saying is: I'm not going to let any of you retarded-jackass, inverted-jackboot, inconsequential gnatty cloneboys think you can fuck with me. Nuh-uh. Flavor Flav ain't goin' *out* like dat.

I DIDN'T WATCH ANY PORN videos this month, didn't see any live strip shows. Didn't read any porn mags, didn't go to any jack shacks. Didn't hire any escorts, didn't pick up any hookers. I haven't even done any erotic dancing ever since the Health Department shut down café **BEEF-CAKE.**

So what qualifies me for this job?

I don't know. I just think they're afraid to fire me.

THE INDUSTRY

AN IMPENDING WAR WITH IRAQ, as well as strict new laws designed to cripple the local sex industry, recently forced *Exotic*'s general manager, **Bryan** "I Really Should Go Back to the Old Haircut" **Bybee**, to lay down a series of tough new restrictions governing the behavior of *Exotic* staff members.

In between bites of a roasted-chicken sandwich at a downtown P-town bar 'n' grill during one of our legendary Monday-afternoon pizza feeds, Bybee complained about a new law forbidding erotic dancers and lingerie models to touch themselves in "intimate" places during their performances. Pausing to softly burp, he then railed against an even newer statute that prohibits all girls under age 21 from performing in strip clubs and lingerie shops.

Wasting no time in transferring his personal anxieties regarding these new laws onto his dutiful workers, he then assumed a stern tone, enumerating our new guidelines as an incredulous staff gasped and made tasteless, inappropriate noises:

• The *Exotic* staff is no longer permitted to consume illegal drugs on the roof of our building.
• We are no longer allowed to bring firearms with us to the Monday-afternoon meetings.
• We are no longer permitted to threaten other employees' lives.

• The free bowl of Viagra pills at the front receptionist's desk is being discontinued.
• We now have to bring our own toilet paper to all *Exotic* events.
• There will be no more free nonalcoholic beer for me at Dante's.
• We have to unchain and set free all the girls we were keeping in the "secret room."
• If we have sex in the back room of the *Exotic* office, we are now required to throw our used condoms in the garbage can.
• **Kook Dogg**, after a two-month sanction of enforced silence, will once again be permitted to speak.

After laying down these new laws, Bybee sipped some water, smiled to himself, placed some papers in his briefcase, checked his watch, sprinted out of the restaurant, and disappeared down the road on his futuristic motorcycle.

We all looked at one another, dumbstruck and flabbergasted. We knew it was the end of an era...a lazier era, perhaps, and certainly one which was less cost-effective, but an era that MEANT something to us all here. The old regime meant FREEDOM, man. It meant doin' your OWN thing. But here comes our general manager with his number-crunching and sales projections and pocket calculators and plastic slide rules and efficiency experts flown in from the Dakotas, all of it designed to bum our high and take away our happiness, dude. *Exotic*'s on a one-way bus ride to Squaresville, baby.

WHILE ON THE TOPIC OF ONE-WAY TICKETS, I have finally decided to issue a nonrefundable one-way pass on the next train out of *Exotic*land for the last columnist remaining from the old regime (if you don't count **Flagstone Walker**). The editorial cleansing that began so many months ago is now complete. Ahh, relief....

I will try to take the high road here. I mean, I guess I could get nasty if I wanted. A lot of people have offered personal testimonials regarding our newest ex-columnist, and there's some pretty juicy stuff amidst it all.

But instead of *personally* attacking her, I will now list many of the *business*-related reasons why this particular "writer," who goes by the ridiculous moniker "Goddess Severina," is being given the heave-ho:

1) She always hands her column in late...always later than everyone else, as if she is somehow more entitled than the rest;

2) Unlike all the other columnists, she can't seem to figure out how to e-mail her column directly to me, forcing me to rush over to another computer in order to fetch her substandard prose and forward it to mine;

3) She is grossly overcompensated and currently receives goods and services worth more than FOUR TIMES what other columnists receive;

4) She's supposed to be a dominatrix, but in a column she wrote intending to attack me, she didn't hit *one* of my weak points. Everyone was amazed at how tepid that column was. I mean, isn't a dom's job to sniff out someone's weak spots and nestle inside them? I'm sure there's some 200-IQ psycho dominatrix out

there who might write an interesting column about sadism, but this dom isn't the one.

5) She can't write. That's the biggest problem. So...dom-diddy-dom-dom...she's fired.

What *is* it with you industry workers? Just because someone pays for the privilege of licking your feet doesn't make you an artist. Just because you do a sorry retread of naughty bondage movies doesn't mean you can write. OK? I never claimed to be a stripper, but it's amazing how many of you assume you are writers. And for years, this very magazine was staffed with editors who nurtured the delusion that you're all much more than people who take your clothes off for cash.

So after I made sport of Dommy O'Domina in print yet again last month, her boyfriend, who seems much more levelheaded than her, politely asked me for constructive criticism about how she might be able to write a better column, and I tried to offer some, but it was ultimately hopeless. You can lead a horse to water...

The last straw came the other night when she began talking shit about me to my girlfriend, **The World-Famous Jewish Cowgirl**. She went so far as to call The Man Who Makes Her Text Legible an "asshole." Well, I understand physiology somewhat, and it seems that an asshole's job is to take a dump, and that's what I've just done.

Our newest dumpee is telling people that the negative attention I've given her is somehow evidence of a personal obsession on my part.

Funny—a former female *Exotic* editor who's now trying to jump-start her nonexistent career by running for the state legislature (and who, in an apparent fit of non-libertarian spite, recently tried to SUE *Exotic* for printing a photo of her jowly self), has inferred the same thing. THERE'S some solid ol' jilted-female logic fer ya—I got RID of them because I can't stand living WITHOUT them.

I ADMIT I'VE SMOKED CRACK,

even though it was a long time ago. Never had a habit—I smoked it maybe a half-dozen times. It gave me the same weather-balloon-sized head rush as nitrous oxide or amyl nitrite. But I am the only one in the office who admits I've smoked crack. They say that crack's an East Coast thing. Many of them freely admit to having smoked PCP, but crack? *No, no,* they shrug dismissively, as if I'm uncultured merely for suggesting it.

This all comes as a HUGE surprise to me. I thought *everyone* smoked crack. You look at some of those dancers at some of the slimier places, and you'd swear that half of their bodies were *made* of crack. I thought this industry's economy *revolved* around big yellow golf-ball-sized crack rocks, huge white clouds of crack smoke spewing from the lungs of strippers and wealthy businessmen scraping melon balls out of each other's brains in a doomed quest to find that last unmet need that hides deep within their skulls.

But I was wrong. I stand corrected. Crack cocaine does not rule the sex industry, at least not in Portland. That honor belongs to **crank.**

GOD, THE ETERNAL SADIST, has cast us back into the Dark Months. Summer flew by too fast, as it always does up here. Now it's scant daylight and heavy rains. The clouds marched in and will stick to the sky until next June.

The clouds are also dark and heavy within the collective soul of the *Exotic* staff, this bold brigade of harlequins and troubadours who comprise what very well may be The Finest Staff of a Free Sex-Club Magazine the Northwest Has Ever Seen. A once-happy, carefree office crew has lately assumed the morbid demeanor of pale, creepy characters in some cheesy Edgar Allan Poe story. An uneasy sense of impending trouble pervades the office. The drama and intrigue seem to be reaching a crescendo, with a new sex-and-violence scandal popping up every week:

• One of our staff recently spit on a bar bouncer who's 100 pounds heavier and a foot taller than him. He's also plunging deeper into a Hatfield & McCoy-style feud with an ex.

• Another staffer beat the fuck out of somebody who hit him first....I really can't say much more than that right now, other than it looks like his hand's broken. That, and I really didn't think he had it in him...you go, boy! He was also alleged to have thrown a ceramic gargoyle at a chick recently, but I'm sure he'd deny it.

• Another was jumped by a gang of seven jocks outside Dante's and valiantly fought back, kicking one of them in the head.

• Another is fearful that he was infected with one or more Sexually Transmitted Diseases after a few encounters with a local girl who's rumored to get around. Our worried staffer also complained numerous times about foul odors wafting from this girl's vagina, as have others.

• Another staffer recently twisted his ankle in a skateboarding accident. He has also developed gout in his ankles. [Chicks *love* gout!]

• Another one revealed to me, during a tender smoke break in the office bathroom, that they compulsively masturbate and sometimes miss important appointments because they have to finish themselves off.

So what's going on here? Why all the drama? Why do we seek to slake our restless souls' thirst with cheap violence and cheaper sex? Why do we seek fulfillment in the pleasures of the flesh rather than the glories of the spirit? Why do we make bad decisions, then *continue* to make bad decisions after our decisions are revealed to be bad? Why do we find ourselves committing acts we thought we'd never sink low enough to commit?

The answer is easy:

It's all **Karla**'s fault.

ONE OF THE REASONS WE'RE SUPERIOR

to the Islamic countries...maybe the *primary* reason we should bomb them into a flat sheet of glass and get it over with...is the whole **beard** thing. Apart from the fact that no one looks better in a beard except guys with third-degree burns all over their face, I personally just can't manage that much facial hair.

I'd make a scraggly-chinned Muslim, no doubt. And their God is really too pissed-off, even for me. I tried reading the Koran while I was in jail, and that there Allah's got some serious anger-management issues. One verse he's saying he's merciful, the next he's threatening to scorch your ass into the desert sand. Doesn't sound too merciful to *me*, jackass. Although, I will admit, the 72-virgins-in-paradise promise really was a stroke of marketing genius worthy of the craftiest sex-industry promoters.

THE HANGING RUBBERY NIPPLE of

Cookie, my pet female pug, recently slipped into the mouth of **The Salty Jewish Ballerina**, my pet female girlfriend, one morning as we all lolled about in bed. As my gal was talking, my hyperactive 20-pound dog walked over her face, inadvertently forcing one of her long, pliable dog-teats into my ladylove's oral cavity. She stopped talking. After the initial shock wore off, she described the nipple as having felt warm and oddly comforting.

FUNNIEST VOICEMAIL MESSAGE WE GOT THIS MONTH: *Yeah, this message is in reference to your* [In Search of the] Prostate Gland: a.k.a. "The Male G-Spot." *I just had some hooker come over and try that for me, and it was the most horrifying experience of my goddamned fucking life. You guys must be a bunch of ass-packers, because I don't know what the hell that was all about. We followed your instructions. I think maybe you need better instructions, because this chick could just not figure it out, and now I'm scarred for life. Thanks a lot.*

THERE HAVE ALWAYS BEEN TOO MANY UGLY PEOPLE,

but lately the problem has gotten out of hand. Just as disgusting little cockroaches reproduce and survive with greater ease than the beautiful swan, the ugly people out there are replicating themselves with such ferocity that we beautiful ones are threatened with extinction. Human sexuality is a warm, wonderful thing when left in the capable hands of physically attractive people. But when practiced by the ugly and deformed, human sexuality becomes something closer to a crime. Ugliness leads to rejection, which leads to heartache, which leads to anger, which leads to desperate criminal behavior. As editor of this, the finest, um, free sex-industry publication in the entire Northwest, I've tried to refrain from clubbing you all upside the head with politics. But the problem of ugliness needs to be addressed before the entire human race gets swallowed up in the Sea of Ugly. In my opinion, we need the government to do two things:

1) sterilize the ugly;
2) offer tax breaks and monetary stipends to enable physically attractive couples to reproduce.

Over one or two generations, human ugliness would be eradicated. How could anyone who isn't ugly be offended by this plan?

A FOND FAREWELL, YE MIGHTY KOOK DOGG It is with equal
measures of sadness and relief that I announce the abrupt departure of **Kook Dogg**, the incurably neurotic pullout-section graphic designer who wormed his way into the staff's consciousness, and into the pages of this magazine, over the past three or four months. Why, it was only last month that the big man with size 16 sneakers finally loosened up, donned a grass skirt, and posed topless for several playful pictures in the office, a few of which made it into the magazine and apparently led to a new career for Kook as a professional belly model.

We used to make fun of Kook. But these days, he won't even return our phone calls. Things are blowin' up for Kook Dogg. Now he has a Hollywood agent and TV contracts and percentages of the merchandising. We launched his belly into superstardom, and now he doesn't need us anymore. Back in the day, back when we thought we had Kook under our thumb, when our barbs and insults became too frequent and vicious, Kook would vow that he'd show us all and move on to a better, more legitimate job.

And now it appears that he was right. *We* were wrong, Kook, and *you* were right. You showed us. You used our cruelty and turned it back against us. You had the last laugh. You're a world-famous belly model, with your comically hairy gut popping up in TV and magazine ads all over the world, while we labor in obscurity amid the shadowy, borderline-legal industries of this glorified cowtown.

Kook has been replaced by **Peter**, who has only been here a few days and is so quiet that he's difficult to gauge at present. He looks like he might be a member of some Mexican gang or something.

YOU'RE ALONE LATE AT NIGHT and you leaf through this
magazine and decide tonight's the night you're finally going to call one of those girls in the pullout section. And so you pick the one who has the hair and the tits and the facial expression that inflame your loins so much, you don't consider it undignified to throw a couple hundred bucks at her.

So when she shows up, what do you say to her? Do you lie about how much money you make and how important you are? Do you tell her about all your problems and how you've never met a woman... before her...who understands you? Do you convince yourself that she really likes you? Do you have a true appreciation of how closely your money is linked to the fact that she's taking her clothes off for you? Do you feel the least bit *weird* about the situational dynamics? Or are you too drunk and/or dumb to feel self-conscious?

I really don't want to hear the details of what the two of you did or didn't do. Believe me, I don't. The idea that you *have* a sex drive is offensive enough—I don't need to hear the specifics. But I *am* curious about whether the experience was *satisfying* for you. I'm not asking whether you shot your load, because I'm sure you did, but that's not all there is to satisfaction.

I suppose it's rude of me to ask such questions, and I'm sure that any measure of sober self-analysis would ruin the thrill of your little call-girl escapades for you, but this whole sex-for-cash thing still baffles me. And the fact that I don't understand it is probably the chief reason why I find myself unable to treat this industry with anything properly resembling respect.

THE INDUSTRY

THE INDUSTRY

★★★★★★★★★★★★★★★★★★★★★★

#12 ★ NOVEMBER 2002

★★★★★★★★★★★★★★★★★★★★★★

I'M FLAT ON MY BACK ONSTAGE, and three strippers are writhing around me, wagging their twats in my face as the cheesy sex-disco beat plods on like a retarded dinosaur. After about a minute of this fake dance of seduction, at a point when the girls start to take my shirt off, I feel someone tugging at my feet, dragging me down off the stage. It's my girlfriend, **The Strikingly Attractive Jewish Drum Majorette**, and she's witnessed just about all she can take. As I stand up and try to compose myself, she reaches down and cups my package with her hand to check whether or not I'm aroused.

Are you *kidding* me?!?

I'm shriveled-up like a jellybean!

It isn't the girls' fault...they looked fine and were only doing what the DJ was telling them to do.

It's the *situation*. So silly and cheap and stupid. So flat and soulless and phony. Such an embarrassment. A loud, wet, smelly fart on a crowded elevator.

Rather than getting a hard-on, I had wished that the stage would open up and swallow me in a single bite. At one point during the Phony Lesbo Love Dance, I looked up at the blonde topless stripper hovering over me and said, "I hope they're paying you a lot for this, because they aren't paying *me* anything!"

I had agreed to appear live at a local tattooed-stripper competition at the behest of the DJ, who for the last two years has been my coworker—one whom, it will soon be revealed, no longer works for us. He was the one who thought it would be cute if I staged an open debate with some local lesbians. But because the ad copy he'd hurriedly scribbled made it seem as if this was a private party, no real lesbians showed up, and, well, he really didn't have much other entertainment planned. So he makes everyone sit around in an unforgivably smoky bar for THREE HOURS before he finally tells me to go up. So after I sing a karaoke version of Scott McKenzie's "San Francisco" (but with new lyrics about Southeast Portland bulldykes), I'm left standing there onstage with the mic as the DJ keeps spinning loud, gurgly-burgly, industrial shit-rock. I vamp as well as I can, but it unravels quickly. The DJ and current *Exotic* Ex-Employee of the Month—did I mention that he's a fine, fine fellow?—then springs a highly theatrical "surprise" on me—namely, that I should lay on my back and have three strippers wriggle around me.

Apparently, within the industry, this is what is known as a "creative idea."

To me, it just looks like a loose pile of shit.

Later that night, as me and some other studs of *Exotic* were driving back downtown, I said, "It's going to take a long time to wash all the shame off me."

INKY-PINKY EPIPHANY The next night, as the brilliantly conceived and highly tasteful tattooed-stripper festival moved to another club, I sat at my merchandise table, gazing disconsolately at the Porno Cattle wading around, these lost nobodies looking ACTUALLY EXCITED that there were nude twats wit' tats almost within

arm's reach...I sat slumped, profoundly depressed at the spectacle of these pathetic, potato-normal schmendricks shelling out their dehumanizingly hard-earned Benjamins to get a closer look.

Empty. Couldn't be emptier. You couldn't fit any more emptiness inside them.

And you know they're burning those real-live naked images onto their minds so they can weave down the road toward home all half-tanked, then rush indoors and pull all their rage and rejection out through their little pink dicks in angry hot spurts.

I'll give you $40 if you say you want me. Fifty if you wink and say you really mean it.

Funniest moment of the night:

Little bottle-blonde bim nuzzles down to her only customer at the rack, then stands back up and says, "A DOLLAR? That's all you got—A DOLLAR?"

Contestants come up to my table and ask me to vote for them. I tell them that I'm a felon and my voting rights have been stripped. That's usually enough to get rid of them.

At one point, the tattooist who had apparently been promised our table comes up and tells us that the event's organizer...the DJ from the prior night...the guy who up until only days ago had been with *Exotic*...the man who milked our publisher's kindness for all it was worth and then betrayed him severely...the guy toward whom I'd never done anything remotely underhanded or malicious...told the tattoo guy that he could have the table anyway because he was going to kick us out.

What a bitch.

You don't have to kick me out. I'm leaving.

I don't belong here. You do.

IT WAS ONE OF THOSE COLORLESS, crisp, early autumn afternoons where you almost brace yourself because your bones can tell that summer has finally given up for good and you're being rushed headlong into something darker and deader.

On gray, blustery Burnside Street that afternoon, he matter-of-factly told me about his betrayal. He said they came to him, offered him a lot of money, and it was time to move on, anyway, and he really loved Frank and didn't intend to hurt him, but, you know, it was a lot of money, so, really, anybody else would do the same thing in his position, so he really doesn't know why everyone thinks he's the Devil.

It didn't seem worth mentioning that no one had called him the Devil.

Nor the fact that there are some people who won't do some things for money.

I ALWAYS HATE TO SAY that there's anything redeeming about humanity, but sometimes people will come along and fuck up my program by consistently acting noble and generous for no apparent reason. This rare strain of human is so good, so decent and fair in all their dealings with others, that I call them "asshole barometers"—anyone who'd dare say negative things about them would have to be an asshole.

Our publisher is one of the finest asshole barometers I've ever met, and I've met some world-class ones in my time. A stunning testament to his highly evolved character and eminently likeable personality is the fact that in the two years I've known him, he's never done *anything* that came close to annoying me. That's nearly a miracle. And the few people I've met who've spoken ill of him or wished him harm have, invariably, been assholes.

THE INDUSTRY

I'm not getting paid to say this—I mean, I *am* getting paid to say this in the sense that I get paid to fill this space by saying things, but he's never told me what to say or what not to say.

There was no pressing need for him to hire me at this magazine other than the fact that I was ten days out of prison and needed a job as a condition of my parole. Basically, he created a job for me because he knew I needed one. And throughout the all-too-frequent personal crises in which I've found myself during the two years since he gave me a job, he's always been levelheaded and helpful. I've probably had 100 jobs in my life, and I've never worked for a better person, nor someone more tolerant of his workers' limitless personal and professional defects.

Look, if you know anything about me, you know that I'm pained to say good things about *anyone,* so my persistence here should give you some inkling of what a solid, stand-up cat this **Mr. Franklin J. "Flatch No More" Faillace** is.

He'd shrug and say he's really not that good, but so does everyone else who really is that good. Trust me—he is. He's *that* good.

But one of life's cruelest truths is that goodness isn't always rewarded. It often seems to get punished instead. I've seen it happen to Frank again and again...whiny, tantrum-throwing, underperforming, talent-deprived ex-editors who blamed him for the fact that they weren't getting anywhere with their writing...and whose pissy, infantile behavior Frank stoically endured like the world-class gent he is...and who wound up trying to sue Frank, anyway. And, of course, there's that one worker at Dante's who everyone in the city knows should have been fired a long, long time ago...but who is still there because Frank is so tolerant, scientists should use his blood to make a vaccine to fight intolerance.

And I've never seen his tolerance muscles tested so thoroughly as they were by an *Exotic* staffer named John over the past year or so. John had been selling most of our ads and shooting most of our photos during most of my nearly two-year stint here, but the past 12 months had seen a serious erosion in his duties, job performance, and personal behavior.

Most of his downward spiral...and I'm merely speculating... seemed linked to an unhealthy ongoing relationship with a girlfriend who, as luck would have it, was also a member of the industry. At least that's what John told me, oh, a month or so ago. He blamed it all on her. She got blamed for all his office fuckups and how he tested our nerves every month on deadline. She got blamed for all the property damage he caused in our office building. She got blamed for all his self-destructive episodes, and believe me, there were a lot of them.

For a year, it seemed as if I was watching John slowly disintegrate. Concerned about his well-being, I counseled him to be careful about the dangerous direction his relationship seemed to be taking. When I chose him as Employee of the Month, I went really, really easy on him because I could sense he was mired in some deep ongoing crisis, and I didn't want to make his condition any more fragile.

Month after month, I was amazed he was still alive. It seemed only a matter of time before the inevitable crash into the wall.

Through it all, Frank was good to John. When John had a heartbreak-related mini-nervous breakdown and was curled in the fetal position on the sidewalk near Powell Blvd., Frank rushed to the scene, rescued him, and put him to bed. He took care of him, even though John's business performance and personal behavior really didn't warrant it.

And then John turned around and stabbed Frank in the back.

AS LOW AS THAT BITCH MOVE WAS, consider that John pulled it while he was living under the roof of our business manager **Bryan Bybee**, who, like Frank, was being perhaps a little more kind to John than might have been wise. As much of a jackhole as everyone in the office knows Bybee can be at times, he also has a soft side, and he can do the occasional nice thing from time to time, despite how he's constantly reminding you about it. And since John is paying rent, Bryan can't legally evict him, even though John's recent shenanigans directly threaten the livelihood of Bybee and everyone in the office. So Bryan tells me that he came home at 3 a.m. in the morning this week to find a drunk John standing in his underwear in Bryan's kitchen, laughing about how he's going to bury us all. And Karla says John called her and said her worst nightmare is coming true. And last night he apparently threatened to call the cops on pretty much the whole *Exotic* office, quite a bold move considering his own vulnerabilities on the criminal-behavior tip.

But his character...really, his lack thereof...fits the mold of a snitch. They're always the guiltiest ones.

John is apparently under the impression that I was going to wag around a bunch of embarrassing personal secrets about him, but he's apparently missing the point. There's a lot of dirt I could have written about, but dirt mostly clings to the surface. He's quite a tacky fellow, and I mean that in a way that runs much deeper than his silly fashion proclivities or weird sex practices.

I just wanted to write about what he did, and to note for the record that despite all the trash he's talking about us in his quest to sell ads, he's a lower form of life than everyone who still works in this office. John is Industry Standard, really. Straight off the assembly line. Rocker boy speak with forked tongue.

At its core, there's something stilted about the idea of paying for sex. It would follow, then, that there'd be a lot of bullshit surrounding an industry rooted in phoniness, and John is one of the industry's Bullshit People...cheap, replaceable, airbrushed figurines who think money or attention somehow make them less of a cartoon and enable them to squeeze into some identity a bit less grotesque than what they are.

★ ★

THE INDUSTRY
#13 ★ DECEMBER 2002

★ ★

OUR NEW PRO-ISLAMIC EDITORIAL SLANT Even though nobody on earth besides our president and his father consider **Saddam Hussein** an immediate threat, it appears likely that "we'll" be sending "our boys" into combat and tuning into CNN to watch live-action feeds from videocams attached to all the cool new bombs and missiles we've been waiting to try out. While I certainly hope this doesn't happen...well, no, not really, bombs could be droppin' all the way from here to Japip, and unless they blow up the place where I get my morning coffee, it differs not a whit to me...I *do* worry about the possible outcome. What—eek— if we were to *lose?* What if the new Islamic occupational regime forced everyone in the office...even Karla...to grow beards? How would you feel if all the strippers and escorts you see depicted in *Exotic*'s pages, these deceptively beautiful girls, were all forced to cover their

THE INDUSTRY

odies head-to-toe in raditional Islamic women's garb? What if you had to pay $100 at a ack shack merely for a hick to show you the nside of her wrist? To all it "culture shock" would be putting it mild-y. So, operating in the est interests of myself nd my readership like I lways do, I've decided o beat our possible Muslim conquerors to he punch and steer our ditorial content toward more pro-Islamic space...just in case things go bad, you know? Next month will herald the inauguration of a new column, l-Exotiq. It is designed to address the hypothetical problems f being an Islamic sex worker...you know, things such as how o give a good pole dance even after the town elders amputated our limbs as punishment for accidentally removing your urqa in public. We are actively seeking a female Muslim sex orker willing to write al-Exotiq. Interested applicants should rite a 750-word essay centered around the theme "Why I Want o Be Exotic's New Muslim Chick Columnist" and e-mail it to he magazine.

ET ANOTHER BONER PILL Exotic headquarters recently got its ands on a new pill whose manufacturers seek to slice a few inches ff Viagra's near-monopoly of the boner-pill market. The newest ockpill on the block should soon be released in the U.S. by Eli illy under the trade name **Cialis.** Whereas Viagra's dick-nhancing properties are caused by a compound called sildenafil itrate, the newer Cialis draws its erection-conjuring mojo from a ompound called **tadalafil.** If you repeat it fast enough, it starts ounding like "the daffodil." Manufacturers claim it works more uickly and lasts MUCH LONGER than Viagra—usually for 4 HOURS.

Hard cock for 24 hours straight? Please correct me if I heard ou wrong, but do you mean to say that from the moment I wake p...until the NEXT DAY when I wake up...I'll be aimed and ready o fire? I'll be walking around the apartment poking my shit in he fucking TOASTER. I'll be playing sandlot baseball using only ny dick and a rolled-up ball of tinfoil. Mr. Publisher Man, reach nto that magical satchel of yours and kick me down one of them here daffodils!

Another staffer had tried Cialis a few days prior and said it nade Viagra look like aspirin. He said that unlike Viagra, it not nly made him hard—it made him almost unbearably HORNY. Vhen I asked about the 24-hour thing, he just laughed, looked way, and nodded his head.

The pill itself, a beautiful solid-blue gel cap, was quickly down ny throat. I figured that within 20 minutes I'd be home, hand-in-and with **The Big-Boobed Jewish Pelican.** A few months go, that sassy, spicy, saucy lass had unknowingly allowed her agina to serve as a snug little airplane hangar for the Jumbo et-sized erection induced after I self-administered the errifyingly effective MUSE urethral suppository. onight, without her knowledge, her yoo-hoo would gain be used as a Test Cunt for yet another new Dick Drug.

We get home. I fix myself some hot cocoa. We

watch some TV. She takes out her contact lenses and brushes her teeth. One hour. Two hours. Still no riot down in Crotchville. We slip into bed and start performing the ritual. I'm hard, but still no harder than usual...which, I'm pleased to announce even though you didn't *ask* me, is impressively hard for someone who's zeroing in on senior citizenhood like I am, much harder than it was when I was half this old...but still, this is just another one of my nice, everyday, Jew-ticklin' hard-ons. Nothing that seems chemically enhanced. My thick cock-veins aren't bulging as proudly as they do on Viagra. And it's nowhere near the pink plumbing pipe wrought by MUSE.

In the morning, my wakeup hard-on was no heartier than usual. Throughout the day, the cycle of *goadus erectus* proceeded no differently than normal. The only mild change I noted was perhaps an increased feeling of being sexy. Not horny—I just felt kind of sexy, like even more of a sexy guy than I usually feel I am. But after 24 hours, I had noticed no significant *penile* effects induced by Cialis...or tadalafil...or the daffodil...or the dud pill. Maybe it was an off day for me, and I'd surely be willing to pop another one just to see if nothing happens again.

Next month, I'll review a new pill that promises an average 24% temporary increase in PENIS SIZE. We've ordered a case for the office! And it's a tax deduction to boot!

SO WHO'S THE FAG? A precious morsel of in-house gossip has recently crossed the *Exotic* news desk. Reliable sources tell us that our general manager, a man who can't let a day go by without calling us all "fags" at least five dozen times, sports a BELLY RING. Ahhh-*HA!* This must be why, although he toils in an industry that greases its gears with nudity, he has never ONCE appeared topless around the office. I should admit some bias and reveal that body piercings annoy me pretty much top-to-bottom. I believe that if the Lord wanted us to staple our bodies, He would've made us all into pieces of paper rather than human beings—can I get an "amen"? I can't recall ever seeing human flesh rendered more beautiful as a result of being PUNCTURED BY BIG UGLY PIECES OF METAL. But some-how, the idea of a belly-ring-wearing *homophobe* takes it to a whole 'nother level. An *earring* I could see. Maybe even one of those dumbass mini-bar-bells people cram through their nipples. But a BELLY RING? Who are you—Gwen Stefani? What's next—hip-hugger jeans that accent the soft curves of your child-breeding pelvis? Permanent eyeliner? Collagen injections? Sometimes you baffle me, Bybee. And by the way, I need another advance on next week's paycheck...

THE ONLY MENTION I'll make of **John Vogina** this month will be to note his new nickname, which I've just done.

THE INDUSTRY

THAT SINGLE-MINDED ORGANISM CALLED THE PORN INDUSTRY,
whether it likes to admit it or not, harbors a deep loathing for its consumers and tends to view most of them as sex-offending psychopaths-in-training.

Enter one Bryan Sullivan, a black tumor on the X-ray of porn, a wild-eyed bogeyman haunting the caverns of porners' deepest fears.

He describes himself as "the Antichrist," "King of the Mind Games," and "the greatest human being on the face of the planet."

Porners describe him as "evil," an "asshole," and "the porn biz's favorite Internet terrorist."

He is known for carpet-bombing the e-mail inboxes of nearly the entire industry, sending out spooky, violent, racist frothings under such screen names as "pornhater2002" and "zodiac_killer."

"I love f-cking with people," Sullivan has written, "it makes my dick hard." He has depicted female porners as "shiftless, nonproductive sperm receptacles, who can't do any better than porno." He scoffs at the notion that they are different than street whores, saying that the only difference is in their pay scale. "These are whores NOT Suzy Homemakers," he has written, "therefore they must be punished!"

In August, 2001, Sullivan made an online admission to hacking porn star Samantha Sterlyng's site, causing it to crash. He also threatened to destroy her career by publishing alleged photos of Sterlyng engaged in bestiality. Although, as Sterlyng put it, Sullivan "basically admitted to a felony" by admitting he hacked her site, he was never charged with a crime for it.

Sullivan seems to bear a particular animus for Jenna Jameson, whom he recently described as an "overrated, tranny-looking, IR-dodging, sneaker-endorsing, crack-smoking, pussy-sucking, man-hating, dick-dodging, trout-smelling, virus-sending...cum-guzzling, white trash lesbian video hooker."

He was banned from SimplyJimmyD.com's forum for a post which included the line "I WANNA RAPE JENNA IN THE ASS SO BADLY" and a description of how he fantasized about Jameson puking in his bathtub. In August, 2002, Jameson posted on Gene Ross Extreme that Sullivan sent her "about a hundred hateful e-mails" which disturbed her to the point where she "forwarded them to FBI. So many of his e-mails are threatening and just flat out scary," Jameson wrote. "He is the type a [sic] guy who slips a gear and ends up killing people!"

As with Sterlyng, Jameson's efforts to put Sullivan behind bars were for naught. He was never charged with a crime for harassing her.

AS IF THE WHORE-BAITING WASN'T ENOUGH,
Sullivan has given porners ample reason to believe he's a violent psychopath. He has likened himself to Jack the Ripper, Ted Bundy, John Wayne Gacy, and Jeffrey Dahmer. An April, 2002, message regarding Tera Patrick stated, "f-cking butt-ugly gook; shoot one dead today!" Two months later, a message Sullivan CC'd to virtually every porner with an e-mail account stated that "Rob Black's a piss-drinkin', sh-t-eatin' rodent. I'll stab 'til dead 3 times over both him and the sewage called his wife, Dizzy Whorden. Martin Brimmer a hush puppie-shoe-wearin'-crumbcake. I'll lay your f-ckin' wig wide open, boy, with a fireman's axe." Another message from June, 2002, CC'd to 38 porno bigwigs, stated, "I'll blow every f-ckin' head off who recieved this e-mail." A message sent to Dave "I'm

Old, That's My Shtick" Cummings said, "I can forsee your fate... Your ugly white face grinding into the pavement...blood pumping into your lungs...."

Cummings, a Vietnam veteran, was so sketched-out by a Sullivan e-mail from May of 2002 titled "Nam Was The Best Time Of My Life" that he forwarded all Sullivan's e-mails to the FBI's San Diego branch. The message read, in part:

I remember when I was first at Nam, I was ordered to kill about 20 tied up filthy smelly f-cking gooks....I would find a gook whore, put a knife or gun to her head, and rape her. Normally up the anus. It felt so f-cking good that tight gook asshole, making it bleed from excessive force. If they f-cked with me or tried to fight back or escape, they would be instantly slit across the throat....The best thing I ever did though was, found some beautiful [for a limey] useless whore, knocked her out with my rifle, and f-cking f-cked her ass, cunt, mouth, ears and eyes like there was no tomorrow. When I started f-cking her eyeballs she woke up. So I slit ITS throat, and f-cked her eyeballs as hard as possible. That was the hardest and longest I have ever laughed in my life.

"I was particularly concerned about the ones he sent out bragging about him killing innocent women and children in Vietnam," the amiable Cummings tells me via e-mail. "Ethically and morally, I just couldn't assume he was lying or mentally unstable, so I felt it best to forward the matter to the experts."

But although the Feds visited Sullivan's Kansas City home in October 2002—they had previously in April of 2002, before Cummings became involved—a "media liaison" for the FBI's San Diego branch informed me that their investigation of Sullivan has been discontinued due to "lack of prosecutorial merit."

In an e-mail to porn screenwriter Rodger Jacobs, Sullivan said the F "went through my hard drive and looked at all my e-mails and one them said, 'This is more comical than threatening.'" Even though one federal agent said that Sullivan's online antics undoubtedl constituted crimes, Sullivan's only punishment was a stern

PORN
is BRYAN SULLIVAN danger

warning to cease harassing porn stars, especially females.

A wired.com feature from October 2002 stated that Sullivan was 37 years old and an electrical engineer for Kansas City Power & Light. But a call to the Employment Information department at Kansas City Power & Light yielded a brief conversation with a bored-sounding woman who said they have no record of a "Bryan Sullivan" working for them.

Dave Cummings says that after the FBI visited Sullivan, one agent told him that Sullivan is a black man in his mid-50s, who, due to a leg injury from the Vietnam War, walks with a cane and is often confined to a wheelchair.

On the former Mr. Marcus online forum, Sullivan claimed that the FBI supplied Cummings with misinformation "JUST TO GET HIM TO STOP BUGGING 'EM...I AIN'T NOWHERE NEAR 50...FOR SOMEBODY WHO'S HOOKED TO A RESPIRATOR, WALKS WITH A CANE AND IS WHEELCHAIR BOUND, I SURE AM NOT HOME A LOT." Sullivan, who calls Cummings an "UGLY OLD SCARECROW UNCLE FESTER" and a turtle who "can't shed his skin anymore," wrote on one porn forum that Dave had "been played like a fiddle. Once by me and the other by the FBI."

The now-dead Gene Ross Extreme website reported that the Feds had slappe Sullivan with a 21-count indictment related to Internet harassment and forced him to post a $100,000 bond to remain free. The FBI reportedly also visited the Extreme Associates office asking questions about Sullivan. Not long thereafter, almost all of the piss-drinkin' and borderline legal content allegedly vanished from Extreme's site.

In a December 2002 phone interview with Jimmy DiGiorgio of SimplyJimmyD.com, Sullivan said that the 21-count indictment story was a complete fabrication concocted by Gene Ross. He challenged anyone to find a public reco of said indictment. Sullivan claimed that Ross encouraged his online fulminatio and seemed to imply that Ross provided some of the e-mail addresses that Sullivan later used to harass porn stars.

"Within a few moments of speaking to him," DiGiorgio writes of Sullivan, "m

porter's instincts seriously doubted
at he's a freaking wacko, that he has
warped or deranged mind, or that he
ses any threat to anyone in this busi-
ss or any other....The only thing he might be guilty of is being Gene Ross's
wn." Sullivan told DiGiorgio that the FBI reported back to their San Diego
fice that they didn't feel he was much of a threat, either.

A post on the former Mr. Marcus message board implied that Gene Ross
pplied Sullivan with porn stars' e-mail addresses and was fired from
xtreme due to his coddling of Sullivan.

S DEADLINE FOR THIS ARTICLE APPROACHED, I e-mailed Ross, who
d ignored a prior inquiry of mine regarding Sullivan, requesting his side of
e story. I simply asked him whether he was fired due to providing a forum
r the ravings of someone that many industry members consider a danger-
s madman. It was an innocent question with a subtext that implied Ross
t a raw deal. Ross fired back a dismissive, "Any suggestion that my deal-
gs with Sullivan had a falling out with Extreme [sic] is fairy tale nonsense."
e then quickly shot off an e-mail comparing himself to Jimmy Breslin
!?!), acting as if he had proprietary rights to the Sullivan story, alleging that
tgo.com's writers were "smoking crack," and whimpering that "there's
ever been an ounce of truth written about me on that site of yours." I then
sulted his advancing age, he sort of challenged me to a fight, and I demurred,
ting the possibility of encountering his legendary halitosis. After the
xtreme/Gene Ross meltdown, the former Mr. Marcus message board is the
ly place where I've seen Bryan Sullivan allowed to graze around uncen-
red. Perhaps in response to the FBI's warnings, he has curtailed
e whore-bashing in favor of straight-ahead Negro bigotry.
eclaring that "STRAIGHT HOMOPHOBIC BLACK RACISTS
ULE!," he calls interracial sex "THE DEATH CERTIFI-
ATE OF THE RACES." He refers to rapper Eminem as

HATER
ust a huge pain in the ass?

"HE MODERN DAY AL JOLSON" and compares the
ovie *8 Mile* to Steve Martin's *The Jerk,* with Eminem cast
the "I was born a poor black child" role. "WHEN'S THE
AST TIME DIGITAL PLAYGROUND HIRED A NIGGER WHO
ASN'T THE JANITOR?" Sullivan asks, and I can't answer him.

Almost without a doubt, Sullivan has two alter egos on the former Mr.
arcus board—their style is nearly identical to his.

Alter ego #1, JONNIBOY, specializes in humiliating white men due to their
irported underendowment...

HE WHITE MAN NEEDS A TIGHTER FIT NOW CUZ ALL HIS WOMEN
UCKOLD HIM WITH HUGE NIGRA DICKS. WHITE WOMEN ARE NOW
AYLOR MADE FOR BLACK DICK, AND THEY SASS HONKEY MEN THE
AME WAY THE NIGRA WOMEN DO....YOUR DAUGHTERS ARE TAKING
LACK POLE IN EVERY HOLE ALL OVER THIS COUNTRY AND THERE AIN'T
 GOATFACED, PIGSKINNED, PALE MUD-FLAP ASSED, WET DOG
MELLIN, NEEDLE-DICK SPORTING, SUNKIN CHEST, DWEEB, NERD, DORK
OOBER, REDNECK, CASPER, HAIR-LIPPED, FAKE-TANNED, BAD PERM,
RINKLED SKINNED, REDFACED, SPINDLY DEVIL, MUTHAf-ckING THING
OUR PATHETIC SONS CAN DO ABOUT IT!!!!!!.....

lter ego #2, DANNIBOY, chides blacks for being civilization-destroying savages:

LEASE KEEP TALKING ABOUT PYRAMIDS AND WE WERE KINGS ONCE...
ND ILL TURN ON CNN AND WATCH SOME LITTLE ZIMBABWE NIGGER
ATING RICE WITH FLIES ALL OVER HIS BLACK ASS....LOOK AT AFRICA,
EED I SAY ANOTHER WORD....ADMIT IT THE WORST NIGGER GHETTO
N THE USA IS BETTER THAN THE NICEST PLACE TO LIVE IN THAT FILTHY
OTTEN CONTINENT AFRICA.....

ullivan surfaced on setgo.com in May of this year. Calling himself "The
ullivan Klan" and "The White Devil Assassins Alliance," he continued in the
igra-racist vein he honed on the former Mr. Marcus board. In one post, he

inverts a long-suppressed Abe Lincoln speech condemning
"Negro equality" and turns it into a screed against "Caucasian
superiority." In another, he takes an old screed by Israel Cohen
about manipulating white guilt to achieve a communist victory
in America and converts it to a blueprint for blacks taking over
the U.S.A.

But his setgo posts also showed a return to the sort of murderous
hooker-hatred the FBI had warned him about. "I GET OFF ON BRUTAL SEX
WITH WHORES," read a message from May 3:

*Having brutal sex with a whore makes me cum buckets every time. I like tak-
ing a whore by the throat and slamming her into the wall till she's [in] the
state of unconsciousness. Once there, she's had her slutty panties torn
off, her dirty face punched repeatedly, her smelly twat penetrated vigorously, and her rotten ass pumped like a Texas oil well. I like to make it
bleed, then blow it all over her dead body....*

IT WAS SUCH FOAMINGS-AT-THE-MOUTH that caused setgo.com to
ban him from its forum. The site subsequently asked me to write a story about
Sullivan. Setgo's owner and webmaster both appear to think that Bryan Sullivan
is a dangerous sociopath who deserves imprisonment or worse.

Me, I'm not so sure.

If he's a potential serial killer, he's the funniest one ever. "I'm looking
for a woman who will pretend to be my wife for the sake of
my parents," reads one post-FBI-visit Sullivan post.
"They don't know I'm a serial killer. I'll pay you
$37.50 a week."

And though much of his verbal spooge is
undeniably creepy, he's also capable of
intensely witty passages such as these:

*Is it just me or do porn and stupidity
deserve one another?*

*I was walking around today and, in one
of those split seconds of abject fear that
tend to stay with you for a while, I realized
that my dick was caught in my zipper.*

*MARLIN BRANDO...HIS SECOND GOOK
WIFE WAS SERVING HIM EGGROLLS AND HE
MISTOOK HER FOR ONE AND ATE HER....*

Beyond his humor, I found a strange poignancy...and maybe a
clue to the "real" Bryan Sullivan...in this post about Vietnam:

*I DIDN'T COME HOME TO NO FANCY PARADE OR HAND-
SHAKE FROM UNCLE SAM. JUST A BUSTED LEG AND A HEAD
FULL OF NIGHTMARES WAS HANDED TO ME BY THE G-MEN FROM
THE BUREAU, COURTESY OF THESE UNITED STATES OF A STATE.*

MY INSTINCTS MAY BE WRONG, but I suspect that Bryan Sullivan is a
highly intelligent Vietnam veteran who has been physically and emotionally
crippled by his war experience. Just as Vietnam disproportionately brutal-
ized American blacks, the porn industry has historically excluded them.
So Sullivan takes out his post-Nam frustrations on porn.

Sullivan did not respond to inquiries I sent to several of his published
e-mail addresses, nor to a voicemail message I left at a phone number he
listed online as his own, nor even to an open plea for an interview I posted
on the former Mr. Marcus forum. He just ignored my post and kept on posting.

I am left to wade through an ocean of misinformation and loose ends.
Sullivan remains a riddle wrapped inside a mystery hooked up to a respirator.

But, comedian or not, a mind that can conjure those sort of fantasies doesn't
seem too far removed from a person who can enact them.

Somewhere between thought and action, there sits Bryan Sullivan in
his wheelchair.

BRASS-POLE BABYLON

Over the past generation, feminism has made tremendous headway in excusing the most inexcusable female behavior. Whether a woman is killing her husband or drowning her children, there's always someone else to blame, almost without exception a man.

But it hasn't been until very recently that feminist scribes have assayed to redeem that perennially maligned female archetype—the whore. And whether that whore be the literal type who spreads her legs and gives up the pootie for cash, or the more subtle type who merely displays her pootie for cash in a strip club, fem-power apologists find ingenious ways to blame everything that's wrong with whores on someone else.

Much of the literature which seeks to justify the existence of "erotic dancers"—i.e., whores who strip—bends over backwards and does a triple somersault trying to discount the negative stereotypes attendant to the profession. And when the ugly facts are too stark, too unavoidable to dismiss them as myths, they'll take the easy path and blame it on a piggish patriarchal society. For all the blibbity-blah about "empowerment," the last thing that feminists want women to do is take responsibility for their own actions.

Portland, OR, is said to host more strip clubs per capita than anywhere else on the planet. Portland is also perhaps the most politically correct burg in the galaxy. In a collision of these two ugly realities, the literature that justifies the sex industry is wont to describe strippers as sassy, empowered, capable, functional "sex workers"…even "Goddesses."

"It's not unusual for people involved in the adult industry, particularly women, to be condemned," writes Theresa "Darklady" Reed, who, to my knowledge, has never been a stripper and yet for some reason feels qualified to speak for them. "For instance, drug or alcohol addicted women who use their work to maintain their addictions are depicted as the standard….It doesn't take a great deal of effort, however, to disprove these people…" writes Reed before I tire of her delusional cant and abruptly cut her off.

"I wanna talk about how great you are," writes Teresa Dulce, editor of *Danzine*, a now-defunct Portland publication targeted to sex workers and based on the assumption that they can read. "About how you're making things happen for yourself….About how you're providing for your kids….About you going back to school, quitting school, learning a skill, switching careers," etc., etc., etc., about how you're anything but a victim of childhood sexual abuse who's doing table dances to work out your psychodrama.

"Sex-positive" stripper apologists such as Reed and Dulce would have you believe that the negative stereotypes are inaccurate, that most strippers are actually the well-educated, empowered, spoiled, pretentious, don't-really-represent-more-than-two-percent-of-all-sex-workers harridans that these girls are.

Is it really true that the average stripper is a nonviolent, sober, motivated woman who takes care of her family's needs before all else?

Suspicious that what these girls write might actually be

a wheelbarrow full of happy horse shit, I decided to ask some people who are actually CURRENTLY WORKING in Portland's sex industry…rather than wistfully writing about it…to see whether these sex-positive ogres are right.

What I uncovered shocked even me, and I quickly realized that my worst suspicions about Portland strippers were far too tame.

DAVE, 32, works for Big Dog Entertainment, an agency which books strippers for clubs throughout Portland. He's been toiling in the sex industry for much of his adult life. He says that over the years, he's had to pick up a "plethora of disembodied fingernails" from strip-club floors after stripper-on-stripper catfights. He relates another story where a stripper left in the middle of her shift due to a "family emergency." When he found her drinking at another club later that night and confronted her about it, she threw a pint glass at him, hitting him "square in the face." He tells of one stripper mom whose daughter came into the club to audition while mom was dancing, and both women finished the shift together.

One of Dave's particularly harrowing tales doesn't do much to dispel the "myth" of drug-addled strippers. "About three years ago," he tells me, "I came in one night to a club I was managing and found one of the girls DEAD from an overdose in the main part of the bar. Her friends just thought she was asleep, and they were trying to wake her up, but I could tell that she was more than just unconscious. When I said she was dead, her friends started going through her pockets, stealing all her stuff, and then they took off.

"I took her to the hospital in a taxicab. I mean, she was just dead weight, just flopping around, but at one point during the cab ride I attempted CPR, and she took like three breaths, then just went limp again.

"When we got to the hospital…this tiny little female doctor who weighed about 100 pounds finally came out. The stripper girl was about 140 pounds, so when the doctor tried to pull her out of the taxi, the dead stripper fell right on top of her.

"They were able to revive the stripper with those electrical zappers….The next day, the girl showed up in the bar in overalls. From the side, you could see the patches under her tits that they used to apply the zappers. It was the next day, and she hadn't even removed the patches! Unbelievable! She came back to see if she had left any of her drugs in the club."

BRENDAN, 28, books girls to dance at eight or nine local strip joints. He has been working in Portland's sex industry since he was 22.

Like Dave, Brendan doesn't do much to buttress the notion of

drug-free, pro-family strippers. "I had a girl whose dancer name was 'Stormy' working for me," he says. "She had done some really bad meth in the back room. It came time for her to go up onstage. Normally, the girls wipe the pole down. She was really sweaty from the meth, and while she was wiping the pole down, the towel found itself up her butt cheeks. Somehow, she left a turd nugget on the towel big enough to smear about two feet down the pole—she didn't do this on purpose, but she was so high that she was oblivious.

"That was the most fucked-up stripper story I experienced.

"Number two was at the same place a couple of weeks later. We were really hurting for girls. This girl came in who was butt-ass ugly, but it was a Tuesday, so I decided to give her a shot. She wasn't up there for five minutes when I started to get complaints. It turns out she has Band-Aids all over her body—I'm talking like 25 or 30 of them—on her stomach, arms, everything.

"I go up to the rack and ask her what's up with all the Band-Aids. 'Oh,' she says, 'my two kids have ringworms and they gave it to me.' Ringworm is communicable, you know, so if she so much as sits on the stage, all the other strippers are going to get it. So I told her to go home, too."

CLEO, 30, sells ads for a
Portland strip-club guide and used to book dancers for local clubs. She tells of a stripper who was at home and locked out her live-in boyfriend, who was nursing a leg injury at the time.

"He was on crutches and he tried to crawl in through her back window because she wouldn't let him in," Cleo says. "So he gets one crutch in through the window, and she grabs it and starts beating him about the head with it. The cops were called, and she went to jail for it."

When I ask Cleo if she believes that strippers enter the business more for attention than money, she says, "Absolutely. I think if you're a stripper, you've been sexually, physically, and emotionally abused some time in the past. There was probably some sort of mental anguish inflicted on you, and they are driven by a need to fill a sort of void. I don't think they'd cut it at a regular job. They've been made to feel they're worthless outside of their sexuality. It's like a needle in a haystack to find one with the ability to grow and do things constructively. But when it comes right down to it, it's all about them. Because they know that they're nothing anywhere outside of the club.

"If I had to sum up strippers in one word: succubus. They use what a person finds pleasurable against them to deplete them.

And once they've been sucked dry, they'll drop 'em and go on to the next one."

I ask Cleo whether, among the estimated 2,000 strippers in Portland, she knows of any sober ones. "Yeah, I do," she replies—"one."

LADY LUX, 22, has
worked as a stripper since she was 18. She's a petite girl with a baby face and a tattoo of intertwined serpents running from her chest down to her vagina.

She refers to sex-positive, pro-stripper writers as "trendy hipsters. I think they're try-hards. The way they carry themselves, how they preach—it's all wrong. It's really unbecoming."

Lux tells me of one "fat girl with huge, veiny tits" who'd give blowjobs to customers outside the strip club and would brag that her husband and kid didn't know about it. She mentions another stripper who "would brag about how she would do crystal meth right in front of her kids. She'd just offer up all this degrading information about herself." And she tells of more than one dancer who had a habit of pissing on other people's belongings when she was angry. Along with throwing glass objects, that's a theme that runs through most of my interviews—when Portland strippers are angry, they tend to piss on things.

Lux strikes another blow to the notion that most strippers aren't substance abusers. "I've met only one completely sober girl in four years of dancing," she says. "There was one girl who used to shoot cocaine and heroin in the crevices of her fingers, which were all bloated and ballooned-up and she had these bulbous wounds, these raunchy scabs, and she would touch everything, of course, with her scabbed hands—the pole, the rail, everything in the club. She used to leave blood trails on the bathroom door, the bathroom wall, and the toilet seat….I would beg the owner and the manager to fire her because she would shoot up in front of me in the bathroom on numerous occasions, and she told me she was Hep-C-positive."

Although Lux admits to getting violent with customers on more than one occasion, she says, "I think ALL strippers are fucked-up, except for me. [laughs] They're all pathological exhibitionists that are desperate for approval. And they're quick to judge, but they don't want to be judged. They get into it because of desperation. Or they're attention whores. Or they need the money. But mostly because they're lazy, probably.

"I don't think most of them hate men. I think they hate themselves. [laughs] It's true! [laughs again]…They use these sob stories of sexual abuse to gain sympathy from people and to gain attention. Getting attention, without a doubt, has more to do with them becoming

strippers than the money….I think most strippers will dance until they're in their 40s. They'll keep doing it until they can't. They'll accomplish nothing, they'll become nothing, they are all total wastes of flesh. If I had a license to kill, I'd shoot 'em all point-blank."

JOHN, 37, is an ex-Californian who has
labored in Portland's sex industry for seven years. In the past he has sold ads and photographed strippers for the city's major strip-club magazine. He is currently a DJ at a popular Portland strip club. We sit in a patio outside the club and discuss his years in the business.

He says the only Portland stripper he's ever known to be sober is his current girlfriend—"until about a year ago," he adds, when she, too, started drinking.

John describes a previous stripper girlfriend as having been "severely alcoholic. She'd have weekly blackouts. She was arrested for DUIs three times. She'd wake up in unfamiliar places, sometimes naked. One time she woke up laying in a pile of her own feces, surrounded by empty bottles of Black Butte Porter."

He recalls one girl who was "violently dysfunctional. She attacked a bartender with a curling iron, a bouncer with a shoe, an agent with a beer bottle, and finally a DJ—me—with a glass fishbowl, splitting my head open and resulting in four stitches. She did it because I had scolded her for fighting with her equally doped-up stage partner. They were fighting because her partner had thrown up on her during the third song in their set.

"Sometimes the fucked-up behavior isn't only fueled by drugs and alcohol—sometimes it's money. One dancer had drained a repeat customer—make that a repeat trick—down to the point of bankruptcy. Eventually, the trick started to unravel. He began stealing from his boss, lost his job as an auto executive, lost his wife, and on a Christmas morning two years ago, he drove his car through the stripper's parents' house, then put a shotgun to his head and blew his brains out.

"There's a lot of them that aren't dysfunctional," he adds, trying to be fair. "They stick out like a sore thumb, though." For evidence, John points at a serene-looking stripper with long, curly hair. As she listens to our conversation, I search the woman's face for a trace of the craziness endemic to her cohorts but find nothing damning.

"John's right," she says to me with a kind smile. "Being functional makes you dysfunctional within the world of strippers. Like he said—it makes you the weird one."

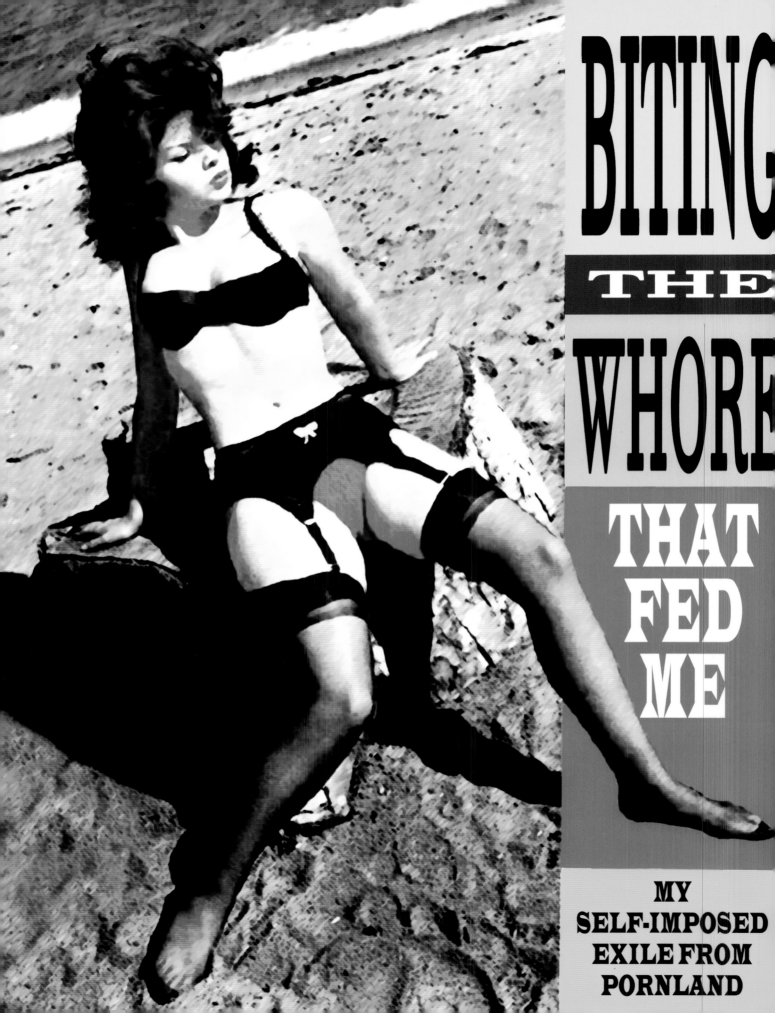

BITING THE WHORE
THAT FED ME

MY
SELF-IMPOSED
EXILE FROM
PORNLAND

Portland, Oregon. An emerald paradise tucked 'tween snow-capped mountains and roaring ocean. Icy rain and steamin' coffee. The world's fattest junkies, hairiest dykes, and most passive-aggressive liberals. Plus more strippers, call girls, and self-described "sex workers" than any place should rightfully have.

Everything you need to know about the city is distilled in the fact that it has only one daily paper, two free weeklies, and three free strip-club magazines.

Those who make their living in the city's sex industry—an estimated 2,000 strippers alone—call the town "Pornland." When I first moved to P-Town nearly ten years ago, it seemed as if there was a strip bar on each corner. It's almost as if Rudy Giuliani had used a giant broom to sweep all the sex shops out of 42nd Street, and they all landed way out here in Bigfoot Country.

Nowhere on earth, with the possible exception of Annie Sprinkle's dungeon, does pornography struggle so boldly to paint itself in redemptive, artistic, community-building, empowering, "sex-positive" (gak) strokes.

Pornland's porn apologists go one step further than trying to make it respectable. They make it cutting-edge…empowering, even. No other city on earth more aggressively nurtures the idea that taking off one's clothes in a dark smoky bar filled with swollen prostates automatically qualifies one as an artist, or at least a "sex worker," rather than a stripper, or, Goddess forbid, a whore.

Obviously, taking off your clothes doesn't make you an artist any more than taking a shit. Sure, I realize that even a sanitation worker is capable of performing his job with some measure of grace and nobility…but he's still a trash man. One can scratch their balls with a certain degree of finesse, too…but they're still scratching their balls.

If there's one thing more retarded than pornography, it's the attempted *intellectualization* of pornography. Porn is theorized to death up here. Most of the "literature" that attends Portland's sex industry is glutted with fatuous, transparent, misguided screeds about our "rights" and "free speech" and "pro-sex attitudes," and "educating society," as if leaving a trail of Twat Slime up and down a brass pole was not only the ultimate act of artistic expression, but also of political commentary. Whores magically become goddesses, proving that the only thing more ridiculous than arguing that pornography objectifies women is trying to argue that it doesn't.

Not to mention the starkly ironic fact that pornography and "sex-positivity" are natural enemies. Pornography actually DEPENDS on the partial suppression of sexuality, or nude chicks wouldn't be so special that people would pay to see them. The most farcical thing about this whole "sex-positive" crusade among sex workers is that if people were TRULY sex-positive, meaning sexually healthy and functional, the industry would DISAPPEAR. Fat flaccid old men with cockeyed toupees wouldn't be throwing dollars at 18-year-old meth-addicted runaways with snare-drum-tight skin and shaved-bald beavers.

Still, to fend off the fundamentalists and the local D.A., this amorphous mass of pimps, hos, and johns that calls itself "the industry" has to justify itself. To survive, it must struggle to appear "classy" in the same way the habitual sinner strains to appear righteous. Therefore, it must pretend it's something that it isn't. Flipping through these free strip-club magazines, it's astonishing how often the word "classy" pops up in the ads for strip clubs, lingerie-modeling emporia (known affectionately as "jack shacks"), and call girls. One escort service calls itself "Classy Ass," and if ever a pair of words didn't belong together, it is those two. But that epitomizes the industry—it sells ass, but with a thick, phony lacquer of "class."

The industry floats atop a fluffy pillow of fantasy. Chief among these fantasies:

The strippers have to pretend they like the johns.

The johns have to pretend the strippers like them, too.

Sorry, but I just can't pretend. Strippers don't create anything that lasts. There is no message in their performances besides, "Guys like to look at my crotch." And I'm supposed to respect them? To view them as goddesses? As artists? How many of them could draw a stick figure or write a sentence? How many of their brains could burp up one…just ONE…original idea? Their entire job is to prey upon men's lonely vulnerability and suck money from their pockets.

You can paint a turd all you want, but you're still selling gash for cash.

I'M A MAN OF STRANGE TASTES. I generally find that there's nothing less funny than a comedian and nothing less arousing than pornography.

Porn held a fascination for me when I was 12 and had never seen a live, breathing vagina, but once I actually started HAVING sex, pornography seemed degrading. And not to the girls…to ME. Why should I pay for something I can get for free? I've never paid a dollar for sex in my life. I've never even bought a porno mag.

To me, sex is instantly corrupted when money enters the equation. I'm not sex-negative, but it might be fair to call me cash-negative. As I see it, sex is cheapened and distorted and, most importantly, rendered dishonest by money. That's what money does to everything.

I don't object to porn for prudish reasons, nor would I argue that sex without cash is necessarily uplifting. I hate pornography for overwhelmingly aesthetic reasons. I'm not saying it's immoral. But it IS artificial, and that's much, much worse. It isn't BAD and EVIL. It's SILLY and TACKY. Strippers and the men who ogle them shouldn't feel GUILTY; they should feel FOOLISH.

By and large, porn is stupid. Bad shit-rock and bad haircuts and bad childhoods and bad, bad, BAD taste. It's all a joke, told at its own expense. Pornography is little more than reality TV without clothes.

SO I WAS ONLY TEN DAYS FREE after a two-and-a-half-year prison stretch for domestic violence against a Portland girl who was more violent than me.

She was a stripper when I met her.

Before I got out, a friend had told me that ex-cons, no matter how much time they had spent locked down, almost immediately sense upon their release that their prison experience happened a thousand years ago and a million miles away.

He was right. The prison world, so alien to me when I entered it, became instantly foreign again upon my exit.

A writer friend had directed me to a local publisher of a free sex-industry magazine distributed in the billions of nude bars, jack shacks, and dildo huts which blemish Portland's visage like so many Kaposi's sarcoma dots.

There are at least one of these sort of rags in every major city. Their ads-to-editorial ratio is typically, oh, about 90 to one, and what meager editorial content exists is pure industry-promoting Kool Whip designed to make you patronize the advertisers.

The free Portland sex mag in question was a notch above the competition mainly because the publisher is a gracious and noble man, and his essential decency somehow leached into the magazine's pages. He was also a fan of my writing and created a job for me because he knew full-time employment was a condition of my parole.

Unfortunately, the editorial situation I inherited was awash with insufferably righteous "sex-positive" folderol cranked out by scribes who, if their homeliness was any indication, spent a lot more time *writing* about sex than actually *having* it.

THE MAGAZINE'S OFFICE was located on Burnside Street downtown near the river in the sleaziest part of Portland, a three-or-four-square-block chunk that is the city's only remotely urban sector. Homeless alcoholics with snot and blood encrusted in their gray beards. Black whores in stretch pants picking at scabs on their exposed bellies. A jack shack was located on the floor above us, and a nightclub that sometimes featured topless dancers was right below us.

A constant flow of drugs and thong-wearing 18-year-old call girls coursed through the office. Tattooed strippers would excuse themselves in the middle of photo shoots to go hit the meth pipe in the bathroom. And there was so much dried DNA on the back-room couch, you could start a new civilization with it.

Despite the steady stream of naked cunt that swirled around me at this job, I had no desire to fuck any of these girls, nor, saints preserve us, to shovel down under their makeup and silicone to see if anything human lied beneath it all.

The only interesting thing about most of them was that they were fucked-up enough to get naked for cash…beyond that, they were as subnormally unexceptional as your average prison convict.

Most of them displayed a hatred for men that can only come from constant exposure to how low and desperate and sweaty most men can be when nature has left them no other option but to pay for sex.

Almost all female "sex workers" seemed to HATE the men for whom they were paid to preen and smile…and this was never considered "biting the hand that feeds them." The more these miserable putzes worshipped and idealized the strippers, the more the strippers mocked them.

One busy lady who worked as a stripper, jack-shack model, AND call girl told me in confidence that she enjoys the POWER she feels over these poor tricks. She enjoyed humiliating them and made no mention that her job might be degrading to her. She thought, like I do, that it's much more degrading for the tricks.

Who came up with the insane idea that it's more degrading to be PAID for sex than to PAY for it?

For all the fuzzy postmodern cunt-positive rhetoric about how hazardous this business is for women, none of these girls ever seemed to face remotely the same sort of legal hassles and prison time that their employers did. Oregon's legal system tends to overprotect females, even predatory ones. In the two years I worked there, I never saw one girl get busted for prostitution, but their bosses kept getting slapped with one sex-crime charge after the next.

I witnessed one case where a willful, oversexed, violent 16-year-old who wanted to be a "sex worker" so badly that she provided false ID to a jack-shack owner wound up being considered the victim, and the owner, even though he was acting in good faith, went to jail for promoting child prostitution.

So I developed a hearty contempt for all these goddess-artists. I despised the johns, too, but my loathing was tempered with some bemused pity. I didn't pity the girls. I didn't see how sex workers were any more exploited than any other worker. And I sure as fuck couldn't feel sorry for girls who earned in a five-hour shift what I made in a week.

SO I'LL BE THE FIRST TO ADMIT that I was inappropriate for the job. The magazine became a Trojan Horse inside which I crouched, ready to pillage the industry. I was paid a living wage to bite the whore that fed me. I was allowed an almost unconscionable amount of editorial leeway, and I stretched it every time. It was as if a monkey had taken over the controls and was pushing all the red buttons. Like a tomcat playing with cockroaches, I systematically fired one sex-positive columnist after the next, then made a public mockery of them in that month's issue.

I replaced them with writers whose abilities I admired, but I still wound up writing more than half of every issue myself. I called my monthly column "The Industry" and designed a logo for it that featured a toxin-belching smokestack. I ended my first column with a joke:

Q: What were "sex workers" called 20 years ago?
A: Whores.

I'm not sure how Webster's defines it, but for me, the word "whore" has two meanings:

1) Someone who trades their sexuality for cash.
2) Someone who does something they don't want to do for cash.

I WAS WRITING EXACTLY WHAT I WANTED TO WRITE, so I didn't consider myself a whore. I couldn't write about the sex industry with any degree of honest respect, so I relentlessly lampooned it. The writers I hired weren't much kinder to the industry. "I Hate Sex" and "The Cum-Hungry Genius" were columns written by females who routinely took potshots at pimps, johns, and hos. The author of the latter column called one of her monthly installments "Female Castration is Where it's At."

The magazine created an understandable buzz. People were reading it, but their demographic barely overlapped with those who patronized our sponsors. The readership and the target advertising audience were not the same group and may even have been at odds with one another.

People in the industry didn't know what to make of it all, and most of them, dumb bricks that they are, took it at face value. We received countless phone calls requesting directions to "Stinky's" nightclub, where the women are so ugly, people pay them to get dressed.

Our competitors tried to use the editorial content against us, wooing advertisers with the notion that these articles, rather than all the jack-shack ads that surrounded them, were unforgivably sleazy.

About six months ago, I hired someone whose pen name was "Office Partridge" to write a column called "Hard Justice." He's the son of a fairly well-known feminist author, and maybe he's still rebelling against mom a little bit.

It was less than a month ago that he handed me a column whose lede was, "Strippers are garbage." He continued:

"I'm a man of strange tastes. I generally find that there's nothing less funny than a comedian and nothing less arousing than pornography."

Uh, excuse me, ma'am? Could you get your fucking life out of my way? I'm trying to look up your asshole. Thanks. I can look at the place on your body that shit comes out of. Anytime I want. For a dollar. And you have feelings? I can see your pooper! Is this a joke?

Youch. Truer words were never spoken in the magazine, but the context couldn't have been less appropriate. "It's as if we did a magazine with ads for coffee machines," said one of our designers, "and every article was about how much coffee machines suck."

I grimaced, knowing the article would cause trouble. Then I ran it.

It caused more trouble than I anticipated. I was unaware that many of these strippers were able to read, but apparently they can. All the whores responded with the sort of outrage peculiar to those who've been hurt by the truth, the oddly familiar shock that comes when the obvious is articulated clearly for the first time. If you aren't REALLY whores…if we didn't REALLY hit a nerve…if you weren't REALLY ashamed deep down of what you were doing…then why are you freaking the fuck out?

Fanning the fire, our competitors trotted the article around to our advertisers, who began threatening to pull their ads. Without consulting me, our publisher yanked the offending article from the magazine's online version, replacing it with a bent-over-backwards apology. He wrote that we'd convened an emergency editorial meeting in which the staff expressed shock and dismay that this article, which was supposedly handed in at the last minute, flew in under our radar and somehow got published. He wrote that Officer Partridge would never write for us again. He wrote that we'd never publish anything like it again. He wrote that the next issue would be chock-full of apologies and sundry expressions of our bottomless remorse for ever suggesting that women who trade sex for cash are whores.

There were several problems with what the publisher wrote. First among them was the fact that this "meeting" had never occurred. Another was that the article was handed in way before deadline. By foisting all the blame onto Officer Partridge, the publisher was offering me an easy way out. If I, too, pretended to be shocked and outraged, my job was secure.

But I couldn't do it. The problem, by and large, was that I agreed with the article. I wouldn't apologize for all the money in the world.

That's because I'm not a whore.

SO I QUIT.

As I was clearing out my desk, two whores from the jack shack upstairs came down to "confront" me, only to be further outraged when they realized I wouldn't apologize. *No, honey, you aren't a whore. You stand in a cubicle sticking dildos up your ass for cash while some schmuck watches you and beats off, but you're not a whore.*

The magazine's staff is still scrambling to repair the damage. They've hand-delivered written apologies to all the clubs and jack shacks and have hired three Mexicans armed with box cutters to remove the offending article from all remaining copies.

They hired a sex-positive stripper to replace me.

Funny—no one said we were "biting the hand that feeds us" when we repeatedly made sport of johns, whose money greases the entire industry. One female columnist routinely wrote fantasies about murdering men whom she felt had inappropriately drooled over her. In the same issue as the offending "Hard Justice" column, she gleefully and remorselessly wrote about a real incident where she'd punched some guy so hard, she had pieces of his flesh stuck to her hands. And no one was offended by that. Nor did anyone object to the same issue's "I Hate Sex" column, which was an extended murder fantasy regarding a man who had committed the murder-worthy crime of stealing the author's panties. Without a hint of irony, both of these articles openly advocated violence toward johns, while "Hard Justice" merely made unflattering comments about strippers.

Such are the dangers of Goddess Culture—the girls get away with murder, while brimstone rains down upon males who do nothing worse than imply that girls…EVEN THE WHORES…are less than sacred.

IT'S ALL FURTHER PROOF that one can never tell the truth in a medium driven by advertising. I spent almost as much time in the porn industry as I did in the Big House.

It's been less than a week since I left, but it already feels like a thousand years ago.

Just like prison.